Classical Liberalism
and the Austrian School

Classical Liberalism
and the Austrian School

Ralph Raico

Foreword by
Jörg Guido Hülsmann

Preface by
David Gordon

The cover design by Chad Parish shows the Neptune Fountain, at the Schönbrunn Palace, in Vienna.

Copyright © 2012 by the Ludwig von Mises Institute. Permission to reprint in whole or in part is gladly granted, provided full credit is given.

Ludwig von Mises Institute
518 West Magnolia Avenue
Auburn, Alabama 36832
mises.org

ISBN: 978-1-61016-003-2

*Dedicated to the memory of the great
Ludwig von Mises*

Table of Contents

Foreword by Jörg Guido Hülsmann ix

Preface by David Gordon xiii

1. Classical Liberalism and the Austrian School 1
2. Liberalism: True and False 67
3. Intellectuals and the Marketplace 111
4. Was Keynes a Liberal? 149
5. The Conflict of Classes: Liberal vs. Marxist Theories 183
6. The Centrality of French Liberalism 219
7. Ludwig von Mises's *Liberalism* on Fascism, Democracy, and Imperialism 255
8. Eugen Richter and the End of German Liberalism 301
9. Arthur Ekirch on American Militarism 331

Index 339

Foreword

> *"History looks backward into the past, but the lesson it teaches concerns things to come. It does not teach indolent quietism; it rouses man to emulate the deeds of earlier generations."*
>
> *Ludwig von Mises*[1]

The present book contains a collection of essays written throughout the past twenty years. I read virtually all of them when they were first published. They have been a central part of my education in the history of liberalism and of the Austrian School of economics, and I consider myself privileged indeed to have encountered Professor Raico and his work early on in my intellectual development.

Raico's profound and extensive knowledge of intellectual, political, and economic history are evident in each of the following essays and, in fact, virtually on each page of this book. His readers will also appreciate the warm passion he brings to the study of his subject, as well as his dry wit. Drawing from original sources in German, French, and Italian, as well as English, Professor Raico provides us with original scholarship on the history of liberalism from a decidedly liberal, though not exclusively Anglo-Saxon perspective. What is more, he definitely has the talent to rouse his readers to emulate the deeds of earlier generations. It was through Raico's book *Die Partei der Freiheit* (The

---

1 Ludwig von Mises, *Theory and History* (New Haven: Yale University Press, 1957), p. 294.

Party of Freedom)[2] that I and many other Germans first heard of Eugen Richter, the champion of true liberalism in *fin de siècle* Germany. Forgotten by virtually everyone except for his social-democratic detractors, Richter has made a comeback in the past ten years and some of his major writings are again in print. Today his words and deeds inspire a new generation of intellectuals and politicians. Thank you for that lesson, Professor Raico! If Germany returns to the tradition of true liberalism, we shall have in Berlin a Raico Straße leading to the Richter Platz.

Ralph Raico's scholarship did not just appear out of the blue sky. It is the fruit of hard work, and it is also based on the work of predecessors and contemporaries. Ralph Raico adds to the legacy of his mentor, Ludwig von Mises, who was himself a distinguished historian and to whose memory the present volume is dedicated. They first met when Raico was still a high-school student in the early 1950s and when despite his young age he was admitted to Mises NYU seminar. There he met Murray Rothbard and many other young intellectuals who in the decades to come would turn into pillars of true liberalism. In the Mises seminar these young men would receive a lesson on the meaning of scholarship. A scholar is not a living inventory of a great number of loosely connected facts, or the crafty technician of some sophisticated method of research, or a member of "the order of discourse" (Foucault) whose main ability is to handle the abstract language of an intellectual sect. A scholar definitely is a master of the nuts and bolts. He is perfectly familiar with all the relevant facts and methods, and he is conversant even with the latest fads of terminology. But, more than that, he truly penetrates his subject. He can explain his facts in terms of cause and consequence rather than merely juxtaposing them. He sees through terminological fads and writes in an unpretentious style, because he does not seek to impress, but to transmit. And he is able to transcend the necessarily narrow realm of any scientific investigation. He is able to put the concrete subjects of his field, and the field itself, into proper context and perspective. He is able to open horizons.

---

2 R. Raico, *Die Partei der Freiheit* (Stuttgart : Lucius & Lucius, 1999). The book is available online at http://docs.mises.de/Raico/die_partei_der_freiheit_raico.pdf

These are the marks of scholarship that we find in the works of Ludwig von Mises and of Murray Rothbard. These are also the marks that we find on the following pages. Professor Raico covers all aspects of his field: deeds, persons, and ideas. But he is not just a historian, but a great educator within a great tradition.

Jörg Guido Hülsmann
Angers, France
November 2011

Preface

Ralph Raico in this brilliant book calls to our attention the dictum of Augustin Thierry: "The great precept that must be given to historians is to distinguish instead of confounding" (p. 136). Thierry, as Raico shows, did not always follow his own advice; but the remark perfectly describes the historical writing of Raico himself. He is master of the fine discriminations that F.R. Leavis thought essential to the task of the critic. His profound scholarship and keen intelligence make him a great historian. Indeed, he is our foremost historian of classical liberalism.

Raico begins his work of conceptual clarification by asking, what is classical liberalism; or, better, what is liberalism, since only the classical variety qualifies as liberalism properly so called. "[T]here was no 'classical' liberalism, only a single liberalism, based on private property and the free market, that developed organically, from first to last." (p. 1)

Raico answers his definitional question in the book's initial chapter, "Classical Liberalism and the Austrian School." Liberals believe that the main institutions of society can function in entire independence of the state: "Liberalism . . . is based on the conception of civil society as by and large self-regulating when its members are free to act within the very wide bounds of their individual rights. Among these, the right to private property, including freedom of contract and exchange and the free disposition of one's own labor, is given a high priority. Historically, liberalism has manifested a hostility to state action, which, it insists, should be reduced to a minimum." (p. 2)

Liberalism, so defined, seems to have an obvious affinity with Austrian economics. But here a problem arises: is not Austrian economics a value-free science? Adherence to liberalism, obviously, entails value judgments. The relation between them, then, cannot be that the economic theory logically implies the political doctrine. Indeed, enemies of classical liberalism have at times embraced tenets of the Austrians. The Fabian Socialist George Bernard Shaw, influenced by Philip Wicksteed, accepted the subjective theory of value; and, Raico notes, the analytical Marxist Jon Elster finds Marxism compatible with methodological individualism. Nevertheless, Raico claims: "On the level of policy, Austrianism's individualist and subjectivist methodology tends, indirectly at least, to sway decisions in a liberal direction." (p. 8)

Here Raico confronts a challenge. Austrian economics, as developed by its greatest twentieth century exponent, Ludwig von Mises, relies on *a priori* reasoning. Does not this style of thinking lead to dogmatism and intolerance, inimical to the spirit of classical liberalism? Milton Friedman, himself a noted classical liberal, has pressed exactly this accusation. Raico easily disposes of it: "How such an argument could emanate from such a distinguished source is simply baffling. Among other problems with it: Friedman's theory would predict the occurrence of incessant bloody brawling among mathematicians and logicians, the non-occurrence which falsifies that theory in Friedman's own positivist terms" (p. 11)

Those who condemn *a priori* reasoning often champion instead the fallibilism of Karl Popper. Whether they are right to do is eminently questionable, and Popper's many advocates err grievously when they enroll him in the liberal tradition. As Raico points out, "Most damaging to any claim that Popper represents authentic liberalism is the fact that he accepted the traditional mythology of industrial capitalism as a system of oppression of the working class, only gradually made tolerable by social reforms effected in part through socialist agitation. In *The*

Open Society and Its Enemies, Popper wrote that Marx's protests against capitalist oppression "will secure him forever a place among the liberators of mankind." (p. 12)

Judged by Raico's criterion of liberalism, even his mentor Friedrich Hayek falls short. Though an undoubted classical liberal, unlike his friend Popper, he conceded too much to the welfare state. "The state, Hayek insisted, is not solely 'a coercive apparatus,' but also 'a service agency,' and as such 'it may assist without harm in the achievement of desirable aims which perhaps could not be achieved otherwise.' . . . Predictably, Hayek's endorsement of state activism in the 'social' sphere has provided knowledgeable opponents of the laissez-faire position with a rhetorical argument of the form, 'even F.A Hayek conceded . . .'" (p. 29)

In "Liberalism: True and False," Raico advances further in his quest for conceptual clarity about liberalism. Nowadays, supporters of the welfare state usually call themselves liberals, but Raico maintains they are not entitled to the name. To accede to their takeover of the term from its nineteenth-century usage promotes confusion.

Instead, we should, learning from Max Weber, construct an ideal type for liberalism. If we do so, we will discover that "modern" liberals differ too far from the standard to be included. "The ideal type of liberalism should express a coherent concept, based on what is most characteristic and distinctive in the liberal doctrine—what Weber refers to as the 'essential tendencies.' . . . Historically, where monarchical absolutism had insisted that the state was the engine of society and the necessary overseer of the religious, cultural, and, not least, economic life of its subjects, liberalism posited a starkly contrasting view: that the most desirable regime was one in which *civil society—that is, the whole of the social order based on private property and voluntary exchange—by and large runs itself.*" (p.65, emphasis in original)

How did the current confusion over liberalism develop? Raico ascribes a good deal of the blame to the "saint of rationalism," John Stuart Mill, of whom he is decidedly no admirer. Following the Mill revisionists Maurice Cowling, Joseph Hamburger, and Linda Raeder,

Raico contends that Mill was very far from bring a friend of liberty. Despite his frequent paeans to individual autonomy, he had an ultimately conformist ideology. He aimed to demolish religious faith, especially Christianity, and received mores, on the way to erecting a social order based on "the religion of humanity." (p. 53)

Mill's disdain for tradition, expressed especially in *On Liberty* [which Raico calls "presumptuously titled" (p. 166)] led naturally to the new liberalism, with its reliance on the state and displacement of property rights from their formerly central position. "It [Mill's view of tradition] also forges an offensive alliance between liberalism and the state, even if perhaps contrary to Mill's intentions, since it is difficult to imagine the uprooting of traditional norms except through the massive use of political power." (p. 53)

Raico has constructed an ideal type of liberalism, but of course the historical phenomenon that this ideal type encapsulates did not arise fully grown but developed through a long process. And this process occurred in a particular place, namely Western Europe, though the principles of liberalism claim universal validity. Why did liberalism first arise there?

Raico's response emphasizes the Christian roots of liberalism. John Neville Figgis famously claimed that "Political liberty is the residuary legatee of ecclesiastical animosities"; but, unlike Figgis, Raico does not look to the Reformation and its quarrels for the source of freedom. Rather, he focuses on the universal Church as an alternative source of loyalty to the state in medieval Europe. "That culture was the West—the Europe that arose in communion with the Bishop of Rome. . . . The essence of the European experience is that a civilization developed that felt itself to be a unity and yet was politically decentralized. The continent devolved into a mosaic of separate and competing jurisdictions and polities whose internal divisions themselves resisted central control." (p. 59)

Classical liberalism, one suspects most readers of this book will agree, is a very appealing system. Unfortunately, most intellectuals dissent: they spurn capitalism and its brand of freedom. More than a few intellectuals lacked the sense to resist the blandishments of Stalin and

Mao. In the third chapter, "Intellectuals and the Marketplace," Raico carefully surveys the main contending theories that endeavor to account for the intellectuals' opposition to the free market. Naturally enough, he devotes careful attention to the views of Mises (to whom the book is dedicated). In *The Anti-Capitalistic Mentality*, Mises stressed the resentment and envy felt by failed intellectuals. Raico does not dismiss this, but he prefers an analysis that Mises advanced in an earlier article. "Citing Cicero's *De officiis* as an exemplary text, he [Mises] identifies the contempt for moneymaking deeply ingrained in western culture as the source of the hostility towards capitalists, trade, and speculation 'which today dominates our whole public life, politics, and the written word.'" (p. 85)

If Raico is attracted to Mises's earlier account, Hayek fares less well at his hands. In *The Counter-Revolution of Science*, Hayek described an engineering frame of mind that to a large extent, in his opinion, attracted intellectuals to socialism. Scientific experiments and engineering projects require conscious planning: why not extend such planning to society as a whole? With characteristic acuity, Raico raises a strong objection: "from the fact that many particular engineering projects have succeeded it does not follow that a single vast engineering project, one subsuming all particular projects, is likely to succeed; nor does it seem likely that most people will find such a claim plausible." (p. 79)

As we have already seen, Raico places great emphasis on the distinction between true liberalism and its modern counterfeits. It should not then be difficult to surmise his answer to the question posed in his next chapter, "Was Keynes a Liberal?" According to Robert Skidelsky, among many others, Keynes fully adhered to liberal values. True enough, he rejected laissez-faire; but his interventionist measures aimed to cure a defect of capitalism, not to replace that system with socialism or some other revolutionary alternative.

It at once follows from Raico's characterization of liberalism that Skidelsky *et hoc genus omne* are radically mistaken. Regardless of his supposed love of the English liberal tradition, someone who relied on the state to the extent that Keynes did could hardly have believed that civil society has no great need for the state. But Raico does not leave it at that. Keynes, far from being a wholehearted lover of freedom, viewed with some sympathy the fascist and Communist 'experiments' of the 1930s. In a notorious article, "National Self-Sufficiency," which appeared in *The Yale Review* for 1933, Keynes wrote: "But I bring my criticisms to bear, as one whose heart is friendly and sympathetic to the desperate experiments of the contemporary world, who wishes them well and would like them to succeed, who has his own experiments in view, and who in the last resort prefers anything on earth to what the financial reports are wont to call 'the best opinion in Wall Street'." (p. 109). This passage, Raico notes, has been omitted from the version of the article in *The Collected Writings*.

Nor was this the only occasion on which Keynes had good things to say about totalitarians. In a broadcast for the BBC in June 1936, he praised highly the notorious *apologia* for Soviet tyranny written by Sidney and Beatrice Webb, *Soviet Communism: A New Civilization?*

What lay at the basis of Keynes' hostility to capitalism? As he did in the previous chapter, Raico finds the answer in disdain for money. Keynes went so far as to appeal to Freudian psychology to account for the supposed "irrational" desire for money. Raico amusingly comments, "This psychoanalytical 'finding'—by the man Vladimir Nabokov correctly identified as the Viennese Fraud—permitted Keynes to assert that love of money was condemned not only by religion but by 'science' as well." (p. 113)

Marxists would respond to the analysis Raico has so far pursued with an objection. Raico has spoken of ideas as if they possessed an independent existence; but in fact, are not ideas really reflections of class interest? Does not classical liberalism embody the interests of the bourgeoisie of a certain period, rather than enshrine some universal truth? In "The Conflict of Classes; Liberal vs. Marxist Theories," Raico directly confronts this challenge. Ideas do not, as Marxists imagine, reflect the interests of conflicting economic classes. The free market rests, not on irreparable class conflict, but on a fundamental harmony of interests of people who benefit from social cooperation.

It remain true, nevertheless, that class conflict is a fundamental motor of history. Marx and Engels were not altogether wrong when in the *Manifesto* they said, "The history of all hitherto existing society is the history of class struggles." But the conflict lies not among conflicting groups in the free market but rather between producers and those who seize their wealth, principally through statist predation.

We owe the correct account of class struggle to a group of early nineteenth-century French liberals. "Liberal class conflict theory emerged in a polished form in France, in the period of the Bourbon Restoration, following the defeat and final exile of Napoleon. From 1817 to 1819, two young liberals, Charles Comte and Charles Dunoyer, edited the journal *Le Censeur Européen*; beginning with the second volume (issue), another young liberal, Augustin Thierry, collaborated closely with them." (p. 124)

As the members of this group saw matters, "In any given society, a sharp distinction can be drawn between those who live by plunder and those who live by production. The first are characterized in various ways by Comte and Dunoyer, including 'the idle,' 'the devouring,' and 'the hornets'; the second, are termed, among other things, 'the industrious' and 'the bees.' (p. 127).

This view of class conflict led Dunoyer and his associates and followers, who were called the Industrialists, to a new theory of the French Revolution. The revolutionaries aimed to secure government positions for themselves: "With the emphasis on state functionaries, a new and surprising interpretation of the Great Revolution is presented by the Industrialist writers. The Declaration of the Rights of Man and of the Citizen of 1791 proclaimed admission to government jobs as a natural and civil right." (p. 130)

Raico is naturally dismayed that well-known scholars have lavished attention on the inferior Marxist theory of classes, while ignoring the contribution of the classical liberals. Here he excoriates a famous authority for this scholarly lapse: "Needless to say, Professor [Albert O.] Hirschman is equally blithely ignorant that the use of the concept of "spoliation" was as common among the Italian as among the French laissez-faire liberals." (p. 124)

Raico greatly admires Hayek, especially as an economist; but he differs greatly from Hayek in his understanding of the history of liberalism. In "The Centrality of French Liberalism," he challenges Hayek's attempt to "distinguish two traditions of individualism (or liberalism). The first, basically a British and empirical line of thought, represents genuine liberalism; the second, French (and Continental), is a no true liberal tradition, but rather a rationalistic deviation that leads 'inevitably' to collectivism." (p. 143)

Already in his dissertation, written under Hayek's direction, Raico had pointed to problems with Hayek's dichotomy. Thus, he noted that Lord Acton, one of Hayek's chief exemplars of tradition and common sense, evolved to a more rationalistic position: "By the time he delivered his two lectures on the history of freedom, Acton had revised his view of the supreme role of reason in this area: the achievement of religious freedom in England is ascribed not to fidelity to received ways, but to a deliberate rejection of them." (*The Place of Religion in the Liberal Philosophy of Constant, Tocqueville, and Acton*, Mises Institute, 2010, p. 111).

Hayek was no doubt aware that two of the most eminent French liberals, Constant and Tocqueville, were the opposite of constructivist rationalists, in his pejorative sense; and, in fact, Hayek greatly admired Tocqueville. But these two great figures, Raico makes clear, were far from alone in their respect for tradition. The Comte de Montalembert was a firmly committed Roman Catholic; by no means did he think that all religions of equal validity. "It is highly significant that Montalembert, as he categorically states, refuses to defend religious liberty on the basis of "the ridiculous and culpable doctrines that all religions are equally true and good in themselves, or that the spiritual authority does not obligate conscience."' (p. 152).

Given this view of religion, why was Montalembert a liberal? Given the unchangeable pluralism of contemporary society, it would be a hopeless project for Catholics to endeavor to establish Catholicism through the use of force directed against non-believers. Moreover, any attempt to do so would be dangerous. Once the principle of state intervention is admitted, would not anti-Catholics, should they gain power, try to suppress the Church? Far better, then, to adopt a principled position of non-intervention; in that way, freedom for all could be assured. Montalembert did not confine his liberalism to the advocacy of religious freedom. He strongly opposed socialism and was a prescient critic of the danger to freedom posed by a state educational monopoly. In the face of Raico's analysis, it would hardly do for Hayek to defend his dichotomy by pointing out that Montalembert was born in London.

Another influential figure who wreaks havoc with Hayek's schema is Gustave de Molinari. At first, one might surmise that Molinari's radical denial of the need for government would lead him to dismiss tradition as well. This was decidedly not the case. "This most 'extreme' of French or even of all European liberals (Auberon Herbert in Britain would be a close rival) displayed a warm sympathy for tradition and 'organic' culture, going so far as to criticize the Napoleonic Code for consolidating the 'reforms' of the Revolution by replacing the variegated customs of the provinces with a uniform legislation." (p. 157)

Mises stood foremost among twentieth-century advocates of classical liberalism, and Marxists have been unable adequately to respond to his challenges to their creed. Instead, they have all too often resorted to smears. In "Ludwig von Mises's *Liberalism* on Fascism, Democracy, and Imperialism," Raico answers one such attack on Mises, advanced by the British Marxist historian Perry Anderson.

Anderson noted that in *Liberalism*, published in Germany in 1927, Mises said this about Italian fascism: "It cannot be denied that [Italian] Fascism and similar movements aiming at the establishment of dictatorships are full of the best intentions and that their intervention has for the moment, saved European civilization." (p. 166). Was Mises, the supposed champion of freedom, really a fascist?

Raico's comment on this issue is simple and straightforward. Mises was of course not a fascist: his criticisms of that system were many, far reaching, and various. But Italy in the years after World War I really was threatened by socialist revolution, or at least many competent observers at the time believed; and Mussolini and his cohorts ended that danger. Anderson, by the way, is in the habit of smearing scholars he deems not far enough to the left. He called the Karl Wittfogel's great *Oriental*

Despotism "a vulgar charivari" (Anderson, *Lineages of the Absolutist State*, Verso, 1974, p. 487)

In "Eugen Richter and the End of German Liberalism," Raico describes the heroic struggle of the leader of the German liberals against Bismarck's welfare state. (He has written at length on German classical liberalism in his superb *Die Partei der Freiheit*.) Advocates of the welfare state often portray it as an effort to shield workers and the poor from the ravages of untrammeled capitalism. To the contrary, state-enforced welfare measures interfered with private welfare programs and threatened to initiate an unsustainable orgy of spending.

As Richter pointed out, "By hindering or restricting the development of independent funds, one pressed along the road of state-help and here awoke *growing claims on the State that, in the long run, no political system can satisfy.*" (p. 202, emphasis in original). Raico entirely concurs: "One might also reflect on a circumstance that today appears entirely possible: that, after so many fatal "contradictions" of capitalism have failed to materialize, in the end a genuine contradiction has emerged, one that may well destroy the system, namely the incompatibility of capitalism and the limitless state welfarism yielded by the functioning of a democratic order." (p. 202)

The book concluding chapter, "Arthur Ekirch on American Militarism," is a tribute to an outstanding historian who has traced the rise of militarism over the course of American history. Ekirch, like Raico, had a strong moral commitment to freedom; and he analyzed the rise of militarism, not as a dispassionate observer, but as a confirmed opponent.

In the course of his tribute to Ekirch, Raico accomplishes a remarkable feat. He offers a brilliant summary of the entire course of America's foreign policy, culminating in America's present position of world dominance. A few samples of his comments must here suffice. Of the great advocate of a strong navy, Alfred Thayer Mahan, he says, "Mahan was not much of a naval commander (his ships tended to collide), but he was a superb propagandist for navalism. His work on *The Influence of Sea Power Upon History, 1660–1783*, was seized upon by navalists in Germany, Japan, France, and elsewhere. It fueled the arms race that led to the First World War, and was no great blessing to mankind." (p. 214) On Theodore Roosevelt, he is no less unflattering: "Heaven only knows what Theodore Roosevelt is doing on that endlessly reproduced iconic monument on Mount Rushmore, right alongside Jefferson. He despised Jefferson as a weakling, and Jefferson would have despised him as a warmonger." (p. 214) For much more detail on this and cognate subjects, readers should consult Raico's outstanding *Great Wars and Great Leaders: A Libertarian Rebuttal*.

Ralph Raico is an extraordinary thinker and scholar. I first met him in 1979 and was at once impressed by his intelligence, his scholarship, and, not least, his humor. Thirty-two years later, these qualities remain impressive. I have learned a great deal from Ralph and am honored to have him as a friend.

David Gordon
Los Angeles
January 2012

1 Classical Liberalism and the Austrian School

Liberalism, today often called classical liberalism (but see the essay, "Liberalism: True and False," in the present volume) is based on the conception of civil society as by and large self-regulating when its members are free to act within the very wide bounds of their individual rights. Among these, the right to private property, including freedom of contract and exchange and the free disposition of one's own labor, is given a high priority. Historically, liberalism has manifested a hostility to state action, which, it insists, should be reduced to a minimum.

Austrian economics is the name given to the school, or strand, of economic science that began in 1871, with the publication of Carl Menger's *Principles of Economics* (Hayek 1968; Kirzner 1987; Salerno 1999). From a very early point and continuously, it has been linked—both by adherents and perhaps even more decisively by various opponents—to the liberal doctrine.[1] The purpose of this essay is to examine some of the connections that exist, or have been held to exist, between Austrian economics and liberalism.

---

1 One adherent of the school and historian of liberal ideas, Raimondo Cubeddu 1997, persuasively presents the doctrines of Austrianism, starting with methodological individualism and subjectivism, as the theoretical foundation of a new and intellectually much more potent form of liberalism in the twentieth century, the successor to the "classical liberalism" of earlier times.

Austrian Economics and *Wertfreiheit*

Writers have sometimes freely referred to "the Austrian ethical position" and the "moral and ethical stance" of the Austrian economists, denoting a position with strong (liberal) implications for politics (Shand 1984: 221; Reekie 1984: 176). At first glance, this is surprising, since Austrian economists have been at pains to affirm the *Wertfreiheit* (value-freedom or value-neutrality) of their teachings, and thus its conformity to the strictures of Max Weber on the character of scientific theories (Kirzner 1992b). Ludwig von Mises, for instance (1949: 881) stated that: "economics is apolitical or nonpolitical . . . it is perfectly neutral with regard to judgments of value, as it refers always to means and never to the choice of ultimate ends."[2]

This said, however, the fact is that all of the major figures in the development of Austrian economics habitually took positions on policy issues which they held to be somehow grounded in their economic doctrines. Mises, for instance, is widely recognized as probably the foremost liberal thinker of the twentieth century. In his *magnum opus*, *Human Action*, he shed light on the connection between value-free economics and liberal politics:

> While praxeology, and therefore economics too, uses the terms happiness and removal of uneasiness in a purely formal sense, liberalism attaches to them a concrete meaning. It presupposes that people prefer life to death, health to sickness, nourishment to starvation, abundance to poverty. It teaches men how to act in accordance with these valuations. . . . The liberals do not assert that men *ought* to strive after the goals mentioned above. What they maintain is that the immense majority prefer [them]. (1949: 154, emphasis in original)

According to Mises, then, economics teaches the *means* necessary for the promotion of the values most people endorse. Those means comprise, basically, the maintenance of a free market, private property

---

2 Lorenzo Infantino 1998: 114–30 discusses some interesting parallels between Mises and Max Weber in regard to methodological individualism, as well as the contrasts in their notions of rationality in human action.

economy. Thus, the economist *qua* economist passes no value judgments, including political value judgments. He only proposes *hypothetical* imperatives: if you wish to achieve A, and B is the necessary means for the achievement of A, then do B (Rothbard 1962, 2: 880–81). A question that will concern us is whether the division between Austrian theory and liberal principles is as surgically clean-cut as Mises seems to suggest.

Methodological Individualism

Methodological individualism has been a keystone of Austrian economics from the start (Christainsen 1994).[3] In his *Investigations*, Menger wrote:

> The *nation* as such is not a large subject that has needs, that works, practices economy, and consumes. . . . Thus the phenomena of "national economy" . . . are, rather, the *results* of all the innumerable individual economic efforts in the nation and . . . must also be theoretically interpreted in this light. . . .Whoever wants to understand theoretically the phenomena of "national economy" . . . must for this reason attempt to go back to their *true* elements, to the *singular economies in the nation*, and to investigate the laws by which the former are built up from the latter. (1985: 93; emphasis in original)

Methodological individualism was endorsed by the other leaders of Austrianism[4] to the point where Fritz Machlup (1981: 9) could list it

---

3 Erich Streissler 1990a.: 60 has even maintained that it is in this area that Menger's achievement is to be found, and not in co-initiating the marginalist revolution.
4 Eugen von Böhm-Bawerk, for instance, stated (1891: 380–81): "We must not weary of studying the microcosm if we wish rightly to understand the macrocosm of a developed economic order . . . we must seek an understanding of the phenomena of great things in the study of the world of small things." F.A. Hayek, who probably did more than anyone else to identify Austrianism with methodological individualism, wrote (1973: 8): "The consistent use of the intelligible conduct of individuals as the building stones from which to construct models of complex market structures is of course the essence of the method that Menger himself described as 'atomistic' (or occasionally, in manuscript notes, as 'compositive') and that later came to be known as methodological individualism."

as the first of "the most typical requirements for a true adherent of the Austrian school."

Probably because of the connotations of the noun, Austrians have stressed that what is at issue is *methodological* individualism. Israel Kirzner (1987: 148), in citing Machlup's criterion of Austrianism, warns that this is "not to be confused with political or ideological individualism"; it refers merely "to the claim that economic phenomena are to be explained by going back to the actions of individuals." Lawrence H. White (1990: 356), too, wishes to distance methodological individualism from any hint of politics. White criticizes Max Alter for alluding to a "political" battle in this connection, commenting: "in fact the phrase *methodological individualism* was coined precisely to distinguish it from other varieties of individualism, including the political variety."

But the interesting question is not whether the characteristic methodological principle of the Austrian school is *identical* with individualism in the political sense (usually more or less a synonym for liberalism). Obviously, it is not. The question is whether the principle itself has any political *ramifications*.

It is certainly possible for someone to adopt methodological individualism and not endorse liberalism (Böhm 1985: 252–53). Jon Elster, for instance, is able to insist on the necessity of methodological individualism in the social sciences, while continuing to view himself as a kind of Marxist (1985: 4–8).[5] Yet it is significant that Elster dismisses certain claims of Marx on the grounds of their incompatibility with methodological individualism. In general, it seems clear that the Austrian approach in methodology tends to preclude certain holistic ideologies that are also inconsistent with liberalism, such as classical Marxism and some varieties of racism and hyper-nationalism.[6] To this extent, then, it is not simply *methodological* individualism.

---

5 Elster makes the important point (1985: 5; emphasis in original): "It is not only our confidence in the explanation, but our understanding of it that is enhanced when we go from macro to micro, from longer to shorter time-lags. To explain is to provide a *mechanism*, to open up the black box and show the nuts and bolts, the cogs and wheels, the desires and beliefs that generate the aggregate outcomes."

6 The Austrian method also involves a universalism that has strong affinities with liberalism, in contrast to certain forms of conservatism. As Mises stated (1969: 38): "As against the

Political factors played a role in the debate over Austrian methodology from the start. The very fact that "nation" and "state" understood as holistic entities were not primaries in his system set Menger apart from important currents of economic thought in the German-speaking world of his time. Indeed, it was on the basis of Menger's methodology that Gustav Schmoller, leader of the German Historical School, instantly politicized the whole debate at the very start of the famous *Methodenstreit* (dispute over methods) (Bostaph 1978 and 1994). Reviewing the *Investigations*, Schmoller (1883:241) charged Menger with the cardinal sin of adhering to *Manchestertum* (laissez-faire), since his abstract and "atomistic" method might better be called "the Manchesterist-individualist" method.[7]

Friedrich von Wieser, together with Böhm-Bawerk the leader of the "second generation" of the Austrian school (after Menger), himself introduced a curious political note in discussing its origins. Wieser recalled how, as young economists, both he and Böhm-Bawerk had been struck by the contradiction in classical economics:

> While the chief accusation that was raised at the time against the classical economists in Germany concerned their [political] individualism, we found that they had become unfaithful to their individualistic creed from the start. As true individualists they would have had to explain the economy starting from the meaning of the individuals engaged in economic activity who were joined together in the economy . . . (1923: 87)

---

declarations of Schmoller and his followers, [the Austrians] maintained that there is a body of economic theorems that are valid for all human action irrespective of time and place, the national and racial characteristics of the actors, and their religious, philosophical, and ethical ideologies."

7 On the general philosophical background of the Austrian School, see especially Gordon 1993, also Smith 1994c. Pearson 1997: 31 attempts to minimize the differences between the German Historical School and the early marginalists (including the Austrians), maintaining that both were allegedly reacting against the Classical School (of mainly British political economy), rather than one another. His analysis fails to inspire confidence, however, since it is based on his assumption that the marginalists "displace[d] interest away from 'value,' that transcendent quality that had never quite lost the imprint of natural law, and toward 'price,' a frankly social phenomenon . . ."

Many decades later, F.A. Hayek in a sense concurred with Schmoller and Wieser. The central idea of his most extensive work on methodology, *The Counter-Revolution of Science*, is precisely the theoretical and historical connections between the denial of methodological individualism and the growth of socialism. Hayek assailed "methodological collectivism" for

> its tendency to treat wholes like "society" or the "economy," "capitalism" . . . or a particular "industry" or "class" or "country" as definitely given objects about which we can discover laws by observing their behavior as wholes. . . . The naive view which regards the complexes which history studies as given wholes naturally leads to the belief that their observation can reveal "laws" of the development of these wholes. (1955: 53, 73)

Furthermore, according to Hayek, the supposed discovery of such laws has resulted in the construction of philosophies of history on which major socialist projects have been erected—Marxism, of course, but particularly Saint-Simonianism, the system he dissects in his book. The followers of the early "utopian" socialist, Henri de Saint-Simon, were practitioners par excellence of scientism, the illegitimate application to the study of society of the methods of the natural sciences. And it is scientism—the negation of methodological individualism—that "through its popularizers has done more to create the present trend towards socialism than all the conflicts between economic interests . . ." (1955: 100–01). Opponents of liberalism, in criticizing Hayek for his methodological individualism, have also assumed that it was closely connected to his political philosophy.[8]

---

8 See Gellner 1968: 256 n. 4, where M. Ginsberg is cited: "those who refuse to accept methodological individualism . . . are well aware . . . of the dangers of concentrated power. But they deny that the only choice open to us is between a spontaneous competitive order on the one hand, and a system of all-pervading control on the other." See also Gellner's own comment on the same page: "[Methodological] individualists who attempt to save us, in the name of logic and liberty, from misconstruing our situation, are not wholly free at all times from suspicion that a little propaganda for *laissez-faire* is being hitched on to those very general issues."

Some Marxist critics have further criticized Austrian methodology for stunting our understanding of social reality. According to Ronald L. Meek, through the marginalist revolution in economic theory, "bourgeois" economics—including Austrianism—took refuge in a schema centering on the psychology of isolated, atomistic individuals. In this way, it (unconsciously) diverted attention from the crucial questions of *political economy* that had been the focus of classical economics, including Marxism. As a result, "real-life" issues, such as the division of the social product among competing classes—"those great problems of capitalist reality which worried the man in the street—have been systematically ignored" (1972: 505).

This Marxist complaint is misguided, however. The abstracting approach of Austrianism pertains—necessarily—to its theory. Some Austrians, it may be conceded, have neglected to *apply* their theory to the understanding of concrete, "real-life" issues. That this failing is not intrinsic to Austrian economics, however, was demonstrated—to cite only one example—by the outstanding Austrian economist, Murray N. Rothbard, who devoted much of his extremely productive career not only to "pure economics," but also to highly important questions of political economy, both on a theoretical level and in specific historical contexts (see, e.g., Rothbard 1963, 1970, 1995a, 1995b, 2002).[9]

Subjectivism

Austrian economics begins with and constantly emphasizes the action of the individual human being (Mises 1949: 11–29; Rothbard 1962, 1: 1–8). According to Ludwig Lachmann, for the Austrian school

> the thought design, the economic calculation or economic plan of the individual, always stands in the foreground of theoretical interest.... The significance of the Austrian school in the history

---

[9] In his account of the Great Depression (1963), as well as other works, Rothbard applies theory to help explain quite concrete historical events, often interpreting those events in the light of the "class" (or, "caste," in the stricter, Misesian-Rothbardian terminology) interests involved. See also the comment by Garrison and Kirzner (1989: 121) that, among other scientific merits, "Hayek's business cycle theory provided a basis for interpreting much of 19th- and 20th-century economic history."

of ideas perhaps finds its most pregnant expression in the statement that here man *as an actor* stands at the center of economic events. (1978: 47, 51; emphasis in original)[10]

This standpoint may be contrasted to that of neoclassical theory, of which Lachmann went so far as to declare: "Fundamentally, we cannot really speak of economic activity here. As in nature, people *react* to the current external conditions of their economic existence: they *do not act*." In support of this rather severe judgment, Lachmann cited the statement of Vilfredo Pareto: "The individual can disappear, provided that he leaves us this photograph of his tastes."[11] Incensed by such a depreciation of individual acting man, Lachmann assailed the "arid formalism" of neoclassical economics, which treats "the manifestations of the human mind in household and market as purely formal entities, on par with material resources" (1978: 51, 56, 181; emphasis in Lachmann).[12]

Israel Kirzner, too, has noted the uniqueness of the Austrian outlook. Both the earlier Ricardian and the current neoclassical economics exhibit a "mechanical quality," whereby "human aspirations, human errors, and human discoveries are downplayed, ignored, or simply

---

10 Cf. White 1984: 4: "The subjective approach to economic phenomena builds economic analysis upon the insight that every individual chooses and acts purposively. . . . This approach has been the hallmark of the Austrian School from its inception in the 1870s to the present day, although different members have defended their method in different ways." Cf. also Vaughn 1990: 382: "The human being that is the subject of Menger's study . . . cannot be summarized by a static and fully defined preference function. . . . He is an active creator both of himself and of his world. And creation is a process rather than a state of affairs."
11 In contrast to Pareto, in the Austrian view, consumers are viewed, not as fixed loci of consumption functions, but as sources of incessant change, who also play an entrepreneurial role (Mises 1949: 253–54). As for Pareto, despite the positivism and apparent "anti-individualism" of his methodology, he was all his life a fervent economic liberal; see Finer 1968 and the essay on "Ludwig von Mises's *Liberalism* on Fascism, Democracy, and Imperialism," in the present volume.
12 Cf. Kirzner's remarks 1976b: 59: "It is easy to see how foreign the notion of the 'automatic maintenance of capital' [the Clark-Knight concept] must have appeared to Mises. An approach that concentrates analytical attention—as Austrian economics does—on the purposive and deliberate decisions of individual human beings when accounting for all social economic phenomena must treat the notion of capital as a spontaneously growing plant as not merely factually incorrect but simply absurd."

assumed away."[13] Austrian economics, on the other hand, highlights the alertness, inventiveness, fallibility, and resourceful creativity of all the participants in the market process, especially in the case of the entrepreneur and the entrepreneurial function. This is a distinctive Austrian outlook which Kirzner traces back to Menger, whose originality consisted in his "vision of an economy created and shaped by human action" (Kirzner 1994, 1: xiv, xxiv).[14] For neoclassical economic theory, on the other hand, as one practitioner has ruefully admitted, entrepreneurs and entrepreneurship simply do not exist (Rosen 1997: 148–49).[15]

In this whole area there is a strong link to an important element of classical liberalism, as exemplified, for instance, in the early Wilhelm von Humboldt, Benjamin Constant, and Herbert Spencer.[16] In combating authoritarian ideologies, liberal thinkers focused on the individual human being per se (i.e., irrespective of class, race, etc.) as the fountainhead of creative response to an ever-changing world. From this they derived the basic liberal demand for as wide a latitude as possible for individual freedom of choice and action.

On the level of policy, Austrianism's individualist and subjectivist methodology tends, indirectly at least, to sway decisions in a liberal

---

13 Cf. the statement of the self-described Austrian "fellow traveler," Leland Yeager 1995: 219: "economics deals with human choices and actions, not with mechanistically dependable relations. The economy is no machine whose 'structure' can be ascertained and manipulated with warranted confidence." There are no constants in economics comparable to those in the natural sciences, and "no amount of cleverness with econometrics can make the nonexistent exist after all." See also Yeager 1997, where, after a judicious evaluation of Austrian economics, the author suggests some reasons for the relative neglect of the Austrian school by the mainstream of the profession.
14 See especially the works attempting to develop Misesian ideas on this topic by Israel M. Kirzner, beginning with Kirzner 1973; and the exposition by Rothbard 1997, 2: 245–53. Jaffé 1976 argues that decisive differences between the Austrian and neoclassical approaches that existed from the start have been overlooked because of the tendency to "homogenize" Menger, Jevons, and Walras as co-founders of "the marginalist revolution."
15 For an informative discussion of other contrasts between Austrianism and neoclassicism, see Huerta de Soto 1998.
16 Herbert Matis remarks (1974: 257) of the early Austrian school that "this new intellectual approach in economics was subjective, relative, and psychological, since it started from the human being and not from abstract concepts; it signified, therefore, to that degree a departure from classical liberalism." The confusions evident here are not untypical of the superficial treatment of liberalism by many writers on its history.

direction. Austrian economists are skeptical of the macroeconomic models devised by "mainstream economists," with their assumption that various global magnitudes act upon one another.[17] There appear to be affinities between a macroeconomic approach and anti-liberal policies. Hayek, for example, wrote, of the heightened interest in macroeconomic statistics associated with the Keynesian revolution:

> It was largely a growing demand for greater deliberate control of the economic process (which required more knowledge of the specific effects to be expected from particular measures) that led to the endeavor to use the obtainable statistical information as the foundation of such predictions. (1973: 12)[18]

It is, of course, possible for a macroeconomist to be a liberal—and even an Austrian. The most prominent contemporary example is Roger W. Garrison (see Garrison 2001 and the *Austrian Economics Newsletter* 2000). Jörg Guido Hülsmann (2001) has declared that modern (i.e., post-Ricardian) macroeconomics began with Böhm-Bawerk's *Capital and Interest*. But there, and in the later Austrian tradition, Hülsmann persuasively argues, the difference between macro- and microeconomics is merely nominal. It has to do with phenomena that can scarcely be affected by the choices of particular individuals and those where the effect of individual choices is crucial. Ultimately, however, *all* economic phenomena are generated by acting individuals, in the manner systematized in Mises's *Human Action*. Macroeconomics as understood and practised by the profession's mainstream produces the delusion of economic life as a great Machine, requiring constant manipulation by self-styled experts.

Austrians adopt a similarly skeptical outlook on welfare economics, which, they hold, also violates the principle of subjectivism. Israel

---

17 Cf., for instance, Edward G. Dolan's critique 1976b: 6, 11 of "mainstream economics": "it necessarily omits an important component of reality—the concept of purposive action," while Austrianism "insists on laying bare the true causal relationships at work in the social world and is not content to simply establish empirical regularities among dubious statistical aggregates." Austrianism offers "a microeconomic approach to macroeconomic problems."
18 See also the trenchant analysis in two essays on the subject by Rothbard 1997, 2: 180–84 and 217–25.

Kirzner writes: "Crucial to this theory is the attempt to aggregate, in some sense, the tastes, the purposes, or the satisfaction of individuals into an entity that it is the ideal of economic policy to maximize." Austrianism, on the other hand, provides an analytical framework "*that preserves the individuality of individual purposes,*" by the use of the concept of coordination of individual plans through market processes (Kirzner 1976a: 84–85, emphasis in original; see also the classic analysis by Rothbard 1997, 1: 211–54).

Individuality bears an intimate, perhaps even logical connection, to diversity, and Austrianism, in contrast to neoclassical economics, likewise accentuates the role of diversity in economic life: "The vice of formalism is precisely this, that various phenomena which have no substance in common are pressed into the same conceptual form and then treated as identical." (Lachmann 1978: 189)

To the degree that Austrian economics emphasizes the importance of omnipresent individual differences and diversity, a statist approach to policy becomes highly problematical. It is hard to avoid the conclusion that positive government action must always in varying degrees abstract from the differences in particular cases, entailing a high degree of uniformity and thus the likelihood of a mismatch with actual social circumstances. Thus, characteristic Austrian emphases—on the role of the economic actor's alertness to opportunities in his specific setting, on the market as a process of discovery, on the heterogeneity of the factors of production, on the ubiquity of significant differences among individuals—are so many points telling against the possibility either of socialist planning or of efficient state intervention in the economy.

The fear that clumsy and ponderous government activism would trample on "the individuality of individual purposes" was shared by a number of the great liberals of the past. Wilhelm von Humboldt, for instance, wrote (1969: 32): "The solicitude of a State for the positive welfare of its citizens must further be harmful in that it has to operate upon a promiscuous mass of individualities, and therefore does harm to these by measures which cannot meet individual cases."

Besides having implications for policy, the Austrian concern with the diversity of human beings and their situations is strongly congruent with liberalism's view of the nature of man.[19] The epigraph which John Stuart Mill placed at the beginning of his *On Liberty*, from Humboldt's *Limits of State Action*, epitomizes this liberal outlook: "The grand, leading principle towards which every argument unfolded in these pages directly converges is the absolute and essential importance of human development in its richest diversity" (quoted in Mill 1977: 213).

That *individuality* among human beings naturally leads to *inequality* is affirmed by both Austrian economics and liberal social philosophy, which insist on the legitimacy of widely differing levels of income and wealth. Mises, who believed in the innate physiological and intellectual inequality of human beings, stated outright that: "The inequality of incomes and wealth is an inherent feature of the market economy. Its elimination would entirely destroy the market economy." (1978a: 27–30; 1990: 190–201; 1949: 836). Lachmann condoned the inequality of social influence and power, declaring that "the market process is closely linked with what [Vilfredo] Pareto called 'the circulation of élites,' perhaps the most important of all social processes," and went on to brand "equalitarianism" as "the favorite myth of our century. No thinking person can fail to notice that as societies become more civilized, inequalities are bound to increase" (1978: 102, 108; see also Rothbard 1973b and 1997, 2: 3–35; and Bauer 1983).

---

19 Cf. the perceptive and important comment by Lawrence Birken (1988: 256): "Only with the emergence of marginalism was individual taste decidedly emancipated from the idea of universal need. With occasional exceptions, pre-marginalist thought had ignored or downplayed the significance of the idiosyncratic consumer, thus precluding the recognition of consumer preference as a mark of individuality. Early economic thought, functioning as a kind of secular morality which sought to uphold the idea of the 'normal,' conceived of need or utility in universal terms.... Only with the advent of marginalism do we see the emergence of a genuinely individualistic desire." Birken's analysis, however, would appear to apply much more to the Austrian than the neoclassical variant of marginalism.

Apriorism: Mises, Hayek, and Popper

The reliance on the deductive method that has always characterized Austrian economics culminated in the rigorously a priori approach of Ludwig von Mises and his followers (Rothbard 1997, 1: 28–77, 100–08; Hoppe 1995; Smith 1986, 1994a: 299–332, 1994b, and 1996). In this connection, the—rather startling—claim has been advanced that Mises's method is *inconsistent* with liberal principles.

In chiding Mises for his alleged illiberalism, T.W. Hutchison posited a sharp division in methodological principles between Mises and the later Hayek ("Hayek II," as he called him), suggesting that Hayek's own distinction between "true" and "false" individualism was pertinent to this division (1981: 223–24; Hayek 1948: 1–32). In Hayek's analysis, true individualism is identified with the British empirical tradition of social thought, while the false variety is tied to the French rationalist tradition stemming from Descartes. Hutchison cites Hayek:

> The antirationalistic approach, which regards man not as a highly rational and intelligent but a very irrational and fallible being, whose individual errors are corrected only in the course of a social process, and which aims at making the best of very imperfect material, is probably the most characteristic feature of English individualism. (Hutchison, 1981: 224)

Hutchison held that Hayek came at least implicitly to place Mises in the category of "false individualists," since, according to Hutchison (emphasis in original): "surely no '*true*' individualist will lay claim to knowledge of significant *a priori* propositions of 'apodictic certainty,' which are 'beyond the possibility of dispute,'" as did Mises. Siding with what he takes to be the position of the later Hayek, Hutchison continues:

> "False" as well as "True" Individualism has been very much present among modern Austrian views on the philosophy and method of economics . . . it is important that [the Austrians'] methodology, or epistemology, should be clearly, logically, and explicitly

compatible with their political principles. As well as its ethics, politics, and economics, freedom has its epistemology, which must surely be one of its most fundamental aspects and requirements. (1981: 224).[20]

A similar attack on Mises was launched by Milton Friedman, who stated that "the basic human value that underlies my own [political] beliefs" is "tolerance, based on humility. I have no right to coerce someone else, because I cannot be sure I am right and he is wrong." Accusing Mises (as well as Ayn Rand) of "intolerance in personal behavior," Friedman traced this supposed flaw in Mises's character to "his methodological doctrine of praxeology":

> ... his fundamental idea was that we knew things about "human action" (the title of his famous book) because we are human beings. As a result, he argued, we have absolutely certain knowledge of the motivations of human actions [sic][21] and he maintained that we can derive substantive conclusions from that basic knowledge. Facts, statistical or other evidence cannot, he argued, be used to test those conclusions. . . . That philosophy converts an asserted body of substantive conclusions into a religion. . . . Suppose two people who share von Mises's praxeological view come to contradictory conclusions about anything. How can they reconcile their difference? The only way they can do so is by a purely logical argument. One has to say to the other, "You made a mistake in reasoning." And the other has to say, "No, you made a mistake in reasoning." Suppose neither believes he has made a

---

20 Hayek himself lent some support to Hutchison's distinction between Mises and "Hayek II" in his foreword to a reprint of Mises's *Socialism* (Mises 1981: xxiii-xxiv), when he criticized Mises's claim that "all social cooperation [is] an emanation of rationally recognized utility," as both "factually mistaken" and an expression of Mises's "extreme rationalism." But the general thrust of this passage is to downplay his disagreement with Mises. Hayek states, for instance, that Mises "largely emancipated himself from that rationalist-constructivist starting point," and that "Mises as much as anybody has helped us to understand something which we have not designed."

21 Mises never claimed that the specific motivations of human action, in the psychological sense, were relevant to economics; rather it was a question of preferences as demonstrated in action.

mistake in reasoning. There's only one thing left to do: fight. (1991: 18)

How such an argument could emanate from such a distinguished source is simply baffling. Among other problems with it: Friedman's theory would predict the occurrence of incessant bloody brawling among mathematicians and logicians, the non-occurrence of which falsifies that theory in Friedman's own positivist terms. Friedman's position also entails that no religious person who felt certain about his religious beliefs could have any principled reason to respect the conflicting religious beliefs of others, which is absurd. Finally, Friedman's "explanation" of Mises's alleged personal "intolerance" fails to account for the personal "tolerance" of other practitioners of apriorism in economics.[22]

As for Hutchison, he really offers no argument at all for his strange attack on Mises.[23] Instead, there is the endorsement, without argument, of Hayek's very dubious distinction between "false," French individualism, and "true," British individualism, and of the confusing account of intellectual history Hayek builds on this imagined dichotomy. (See the essay on "Liberalism: True and False," in the present volume.)[24] Hutchison also makes the unsupported and no means obviously true assumption that "freedom" (presumably meaning liberal theory) must have a single epistemological (as well as ethical) foundation. Clearly,

---

22 It should be noted that Friedman expressed these views in a popular address. Still, it is difficult to see how his argument could be made substantially more rigorous or coherent. Friedman declares, for example, that we must "beware of intolerance [such as Mises supposedly displayed] if we're going to be really effective in persuading people," yet concedes, very graciously, that "there is no doubt in my mind that Ludwig von Mises has done more to spread the fundamental ideas of free markets than any other individual" (1991: 18). Friedman's brief account of Ayn Rand's allegedly a priori philosophy is simply uninformed and incorrect.
23 To those familiar with Mises's achievements (see Rothbard 1988; Hoppe 1993; Reisman 1998; Zlabinger 1994; Ebeling 1981), the attempt of Hutchison and others to minimize them is more ludicrous than troubling, e.g., Erich Streissler's assertion, regarding Mises (1990b: 109; see also 1988: 200) that, "not without truth, though certainly with little charity, [he] might be called the arch-lobbyist for entrepreneurial concerns in interwar Austria."
24 On the question of apriorism, it is worth noting that Hayek (1955: 221 n.1) wrote of John Locke that he regarded "the moral sciences" (ethics, political theory, etc.) "as *a priori* sciences comparable with mathematics and of equal certainty with it." The context makes it clear that Hayek is here passing a *favorable* judgment on Locke. It is doubtful whether either Hayek or Hutchison would have wished to classify Locke as "a false individualist."

Hutchison's candidate for *the* "epistemology of freedom" is the theory of knowledge of Karl Popper.

In touching on the intellectual relationship of Mises and Hayek, Hutchison claims that Hayek broke with Mises's "false" individualism and developed his epistemological ideas in the direction of Popper's position. Popper himself publicly alluded to this issue, when he claimed that Mises had seen in him "a dangerous opponent," who had perhaps robbed Mises "of the complete agreement of his greatest pupil, Hayek" (Popper 1992: 10). There is no reason, incidentally, to treat as proven Popper's unsupported speculations on Mises's motives for keeping his distance from him.

To what extent Hayek accepted Popper's methodological views remains unclear. In his Nobel lecture, in 1974, Hayek continued to argue that a fundamental difference exists between the subject matter of the natural and social sciences. Since the complexity of the phenomena studied in the latter usually renders empirical testing impossible, most attempts to apply the characteristic methods of the natural sciences in the social sciences are ruled out (Christainsen 1994: 14). Hutchison himself (1994: 233, n. 7) labels the claim that Hayek became a "falsificationist" as "exaggerated and misleading." One wonders, though, what a Popperian is supposed to be if not a falsificationist.[25]

But those who wish to maintain that Popper's methodology somehow undergirds the free society, understood as including economic freedom, are faced with a problem: Popper himself was wholly unaware of this supposed connection.

In his most famous work on social philosophy, *The Open Society and Its Enemies*, he asserts—*argues for* would be putting it much too strongly—that the state has an obligation not only to provide the usual welfare services, but beyond that to guarantee a livelihood to everyone willing to work, and, topping it all, to protect everyone from "inequitable arrangements" arising out of differential "economic power." Even in

---

25 For an incisive critique of Popperian falsificationism, see Gordon 1993: 34–41.

1974, Popper was advocating that the state should take over a controlling share of all "public companies" (Shearmur 1996: 51–52, 36).[26]

Most damaging to any claim that Popper represents authentic liberalism is the fact that he accepted the traditional mythology of industrial capitalism as a system of oppression of the working class, only gradually made tolerable by social reforms effected in part through socialist agitation. In *The Open Society and Its Enemies*, Popper wrote that Marx's protests against capitalist oppression "will secure him forever a place among the liberators of mankind." He contrasted Marx's "invincible humanitarianism and sense of justice" with the "cynical" defense of "shameless exploitation" of workers by "hypocritical apologists," i.e., the laissez-faire liberals of the time (1950: 310–12; see also 675 n. 13).[27] As late as 1973, he declared that, although he had decisive disagreements with Marx, he respected him highly "as a fighter for a better world" (1984: 167).

That Popper uncritically embraced the most negative interpretation of the industrial revolution is not surprising, considering that his source for the condition of workers in that period was Marx's *Capital* (Shearmur 1996: 52). But it is remarkable that Popper never reconsidered that interpretation, given that it was his friend Hayek himself among liberal theorists who led the fight to bring more historically correct views on this subject to the general public (Hayek 1954).[28] One wonders why

---

26 See also de Jasay 1991b. Gerard Radnitzky 1995: 49–84, especially 50, 64, 83, has criticized Popper's oft-repeated praise of Marx as a "humanist," as well as his political philosophy in general. He holds Popper's concessions to "a not thought-through social democracy" to have been a "survival strategy," which permitted him to find a wide readership for his views. This Radnitzky contrasts to Mises, who simply refused to compromise with the statist spirit of the times. Radnitzky's view paints Popper as a hypocrite and an opportunist, which does not seem right.

27 Popper's knowledge of the history of liberal thought was astonishingly deficient. He held, for instance, 1992: 10 that Hayek originated the notion that complete socialism entailed political enslavement (and that Mises derived it from Hayek). But this idea was a commonplace among late-nineteenth century liberals, as evidenced by Herbert Spencer's essay, "The Coming Slavery," Yves Guyot's La tyrannie socialiste, Eugen Richter's Pictures of a Social-Democratic Future, and other works.

28 On the influence of *Capitalism and the Historians*, see Taylor 1997: 162–64. In a learned study, Jeremy Shearmur (1996) has argued that, despite Popper's evident social-democratic attitudes, the implications of his ideas are more closely related to classical liberalism than

Popper, the fearless critical thinker, didn't just read *Capitalism and the Historians* and a few of the works cited in that collection.

Popper's case resembles that of another writer widely lionized as a great liberal, Isaiah Berlin. Berlin, too, endorsed the view that the industrial revolution and nineteenth century laissez-faire degraded and brutalized working people (Rothbard 1982: 216–17). Like Popper, Berlin seems to have had no inkling that, starting in the eighteenth century, Europe confronted an unprecedented population explosion, and that, as Rosenberg and Birdzell (1986: 147; see also Mises 1949: 613–19) put it, "the new factories and towns were a large part of the solution to Europe's problem . . . they were not part of the problem." From the 1920s on, economic historians like Clapham, Ashton, and Hartwell provided ample evidence for this judgment. Yet both Berlin and Popper were content to concur in archaic, politically inspired anti-capitalist myths—what Hayek called the socialist interpretation of economic history (1954: 7)—on the small matter of how the modern world came into being. It is most peculiar that, in spite of this, some persist in regarding Karl Popper and Isaiah Berlin as perhaps the premier liberal thinkers of the twentieth century.

Popper himself understood. Whatever the validity or scope of that claim, there is the anterior and more fundamental question—whether Popper's ideas on politics, based as they are on grossly incorrect historical and economic notions, are even important enough to warrant extended examination in the first place. Popper's superficiality in dealing with political issues is nowhere more obvious than in his 1956 *tour d'horizon* of the world scene, "The History of Our Time: An Optimist's View" (1962: 364–76). Here he declares that "our own social world is the best that has ever been"—neglecting, among other things, the Chinese, around one-fifth of the human race and then living under the Maoist terror regime. He not only implies, for no good reason, that the disappearance of "class differences" is desirable, but announces, absurdly, that in the United States (and elsewhere) "we have, in fact, something approaching classless societies." Similarly, in a tribute to Hayek (Popper 1997: 321, from a talk given in 1992), Popper recalls that often in conversations with Hayek, he criticized Mises's conduct of the fight against "what was then called . . . protectionism, or state-protectionism" (sic—presumably, Popper is referring to what everyone else calls interventionism), because "in a complex society, anything approaching a free market could only exist if it enjoyed the protection of laws, and therefore of the state. Thus the term 'free market' should always be placed in inverted commas, since it was always bound, or limited, by a legal framework and made possible only by this framework." On Popper's "logic," then, terms like "freedom of the press" and "religious freedom" should also always be placed in inverted commas, for the same reason.

Austrian Economic Theory

There is a sense in which economic theory per se, any analytical approach to economic questions, can be said to favor the market economy. Hayek remarked, regarding the attack on economics in the nineteenth century:

> The existence of a body of reasoning which prevented people from following their first impulsive reactions, and which compelled them to balance indirect effects, which could be seen only by exercising the intellect, against intense feeling caused by the direct observation of concrete suffering, then as now, occasioned intense resentment. (Hayek 1933: 125)

But Austrian economics has been so often and so closely tied to liberalism that it is plausible to seek the connection also in its distinctive economic theories.

The sustained theoretical attack on the possibility of rational economic planning under socialism initiated by Mises in the early 1920s and then led by him and Hayek doubtless played a major role, and rightly so, in associating the school with the liberal doctrine.[29] In the decades that followed, the common opinion among economists, that Mises and Hayek had been bested by their socialist adversaries, tended to confirm the sense that the Austrian position in general was antiquated and obsolete.[30] However, recent scholarship (Lavoie 1985; Boettke 1990; Steele 1992)—as well as certain well-known world events—has served to overturn the older verdict. Indeed, the revolution in thinking has prompted one scholar to remark that "it is really scandalous to observe how decades of ridicule poured upon Mises's 'impossibility thesis' [on rational planning under socialism] suddenly give way to an appreciation

---

29 On some differences between Mises and Hayek in connection with the famous debate, see Keizer 1994.
30 For a statement of this position, see März 1991: 101–05, where the author, in what purports to be a scholarly work, adopts the Marxist polemical tactic of characterizing Mises as having launched "the theoretical and ideological counter-offensive of the Austrian bourgeoisie" in his critique of socialist planning.

of his views as if they had been part of conventional wisdom all along" (Böhm, 1990: 231).[31]

That identifying the fatal flaw of central planning was a distinctively Austrian achievement is attested to by Sherwin Rosen, an economist in the neoclassical tradition. Rosen concedes that neoclassical theory was ill-equipped to discover the defects in the "market socialist" models put forth by Oskar Lange and others. So straitjacketed were many in the economics establishment by their own approach that they ignored and even ridiculed those who ventured to question the propagandistic reports of Communist economic "successes" (1997: 145).

A major criticism of the market economy from at least the time of Sismondi and the Saint-Simonians has been that it is inherently vulnerable to the business cycle. In sharp contrast, Austrian business cycle theory, originated by Mises and elaborated by Hayek, Rothbard, and others, begins by distinguishing savings-induced economic growth from growth produced by credit expansion. It is the latter that initiates the cycle of "boom-and-bust," by systematically distorting the signals that would otherwise provide for the smooth functioning of markets. As Rothbard states: "The unhampered market assures that a complementary structure of capital is harmoniously developed; bank credit expansion hobbles the market and destroys the processes that bring about a balanced structure." Since credit expansion is made possible by state action, the business cycle, so far from being a natural consequence of the free market and a heavy debit against it, is ultimately traceable to government action, especially in the era of central banking (Mises, 1949: 547–83; Rothbard 1963: 25–33, 35; and 1962, 2: 871–74; Garrison 1997a and 1997b).

Austrian economic theories are supportive of liberalism in other ways, as well. The analysis of the market as a *process* precludes certain characteristic interventionist or socialist moves, e.g., treating the sum of incomes of individuals and firms within a national jurisdiction as a kind of "national cake," which may be divided up at will. The same

---

31 Karen Vaughn 1994 maintains that the use by socialist writers of neoclassical theory to derive market socialist responses to the Austrian assault sensitized both Mises and Hayek to the distinctively Austrian components of their argument.

analysis also helps validate the social inequalities inherent in capitalism. As Mises declared unabashedly:

> The selective process of the market is actuated by the composite effort of all members of the market economy....The resultant of these endeavors is not only the price structure but no less the social structure, the assignment of definite tasks to the various individuals. The market makes people rich or poor, determines who shall run the big plants and who shall scrub the floors, fixes how many people shall work in the copper mines and how many in the symphony orchestras. (1949: 308)

Strong support for a liberal economic order is also provided by the theory put forward by Mises according to which the system of government intervention in economic transactions is inherently *unstable*, i.e., must resolve itself either into laissez-faire or into complete socialism. As the latter is not a viable economic order, Mises's argument amounts to establishing laissez-faire as the only stable regime for advanced economies (Mises 1977; see Ikeda 1997, including chapter 6, on the instability of the "minimal state"; Reisman 1998: 219–66; and Gordon 1997).

Another Austrian concept, of prices as surrogate information, also militates against interventionism. Streissler points out (1988:195) that Mises, building on Wieser, attacked interventionism for destroying "the mechanism of the creation and dissemination of information about economically relevant circumstances, i.e., market pricing," thus impeding economic efficiency.

Israel Kirzner's exploration of the "existential" conditions of the participants in market processes yields yet another close connection to the liberal position:

> For the science of human action, freedom is the circumstance which permits and inspires market participants *to become aware* of beneficial (or other) *changes* in their circumstances. . . . An understanding of Misesian economics thus permits us to see directly how it points unerringly to the social usefulness of political institutions which guarantee individual liberties and the

security of individual rights to life and property. (1992a: 248, emphasis in original)

But probably the clearest and most convincing grounds for associating Austrian economics with the free market has to do with the general conception of economic life propounded by the Austrians, beginning with Menger. In Hayek's view:

> It was this extension, of the derivation of the value of a good from its utility, from the case of given quantities of consumers' goods to the general case of all goods, including the factors of production, that was Menger's main achievement. (1973: 7)

This was the perspective that became standard with all of the founders. Kauder (1958: 418) notes that: "For Wieser, Menger, and especially for Böhm-Bawerk, the wants of the consumer are the beginning and end of the causal nexus. The purpose and cause of economic action are identical." Kirzner argues that it was this central vision that explains why, despite the particular and varying policy views of its founders (see below), Austrianism was perceived to be *the* economics of the free market. The founders' works

> expressed an understanding of markets which, *taken by itself*, strongly suggested a more radical appreciation for free markets than the early Austrians themselves displayed. It is this latter circumstance, we surmise, which explains how, when later Austrians arrived at even more consistently laissez-faire positions, they were seen by historians of thought as somehow simply pursuing an Austrian tradition that can be traced back to its founders. (1990: 93, emphasis in original)

Thus, Kirzner implicitly endorses the position Mises upheld in his reply to F.X. Weiss (see below). What is crucial is not the historically and personally conditioned policy views of the first Austrians, but the "overall vision of the economy" that was novel in Menger and shared by his successors. They saw the market economy as

Classical Liberalism and the Austrian School

a system driven entirely and independently by the choices and valuations of consumers—with these valuations transmitted "upwards" through the system to "goods of higher order," determining how these scarce higher-order goods are allocated among industries and how they are valued and remunerated as part of a single consumer-driven process. (Kirzner 1990: 99)[32]

In contrast to the classical economists, who perceived the capitalist system as producing the greatest possible amount of material goods, Menger's view was that it was "a pattern of *economic governance exercised by consumer preferences*." (Later, W.H. Hutt coined the term "consumer sovereignty" for this state of affairs.) As Kirzner points out, "it was this thoroughly Mengerian insight which nourished Mises's lifelong polemic against socialist and interventionist misunderstandings of the market economy" (Kirzner 1990: 99–100). And, it may be added, it was this fundamental insight into the nature of the private property system that discomfited and incensed Marxists and other socialists even to the present day.

Spontaneous Order in Society

Since liberalism is based on the recognition of the self-regulating capacity of civil society—of the social order minus the state—any social theory that centers on and explicates that capacity furnishes powerful support to the liberal viewpoint. Contemporary Austrians would find themselves in substantial agreement with Rothbard when he writes:

> the network of these free exchanges in society—known as the "free market"—creates a delicate and even awe-inspiring mechanism of harmony, adjustment, and precision in allocating productive resources, deciding upon prices, and gently but swiftly guiding the economic system toward the greatest possible satisfaction of the desires of all consumers. In short, not

---

32 Cf. Dasgupta 1985: 80: in contrast to classical economics, "consumption, not accumulation, appears in marginalist economics as the mainspring of economic activity. The new system, so to say, substitutes 'consumers' sovereignty' for 'capitalists' sovereignty.'"

only does the free market *directly* benefit all parties and leave them free and uncoerced; it also creates a mighty and efficient instrument of social *order*. Proudhon, indeed, wrote better than he knew when he called "Liberty, the Mother, not the Daughter, of Order." (1963, 2: 880, emphasis in original)

From an early point, Austrianism was noted for its emphasis on "spontaneous order" in society in a sense close to and even derivative of the writers of the Scottish Enlightenment. The societal arrangements are seen as mainly the product of the *unintended* consequences of self-seeking individual action, which in this way gives rise to social institutions that are beneficial though undesigned (Hayek 1967: 96–105; Hamowy 1987; and Vaughn 1987).

In his *Investigations*, Menger broaches the issue in Chapter 2, Book 3, devoted to "The Theoretical Understanding of Those Social Phenomena Which Are Not a Product of Agreement or of Positive Legislation, but Are Unintended Results of Historical Development." He poses the question: "How can it be that institutions which serve the common welfare and are extremely significant for its development come into being without a common will directed toward establishing them?" Menger points out that "Law, language, the state, money, markets, all these social structures are to no small extent the unintended result of social development,"[33] and goes on to provide a brilliant and famous explanation, based on methodological individualism, of the origin of money (1985: 146, 152–55; see also Menger 1981: 256–85).

In reviewing the *Investigations*, Gustav Schmoller criticized Menger for praising Edmund Burke, Savigny, and Niebuhr, who understood law as (in Schmoller's words) "the unreflective product of a higher wisdom, rather than as derived from the action of superior power [i. e., the state] . . . a transference of their doctrine to economics, Menger thinks, would have opened up 'an immeasurable area for fruitful activity,' in the direction of Burke." Schmoller comments bitingly:

---

33 It should be noted that by including the state in the same category as such social formations as language and markets, Menger is obscuring the crucial liberal distinction between state and civil society, coercion and voluntarism.

This lively sympathy for the mysticism of Savigny's folk-spirit arises obviously from the Manchesterist [i.e., laissez-faire] aversion to every conscious action of the collective organs of society. Just as law originates of itself, so should the economy be left to its own devices, conceived of as merely the play of egoistic and yet harmonious interests. (1883: 250)

Leaving aside the accusatory tone of this passage, one may concede that here Schmoller makes a plausible point. As presented by Austrian economists, spontaneous-order explanations may certainly serve to validate the liberal view of the functioning of society (although the writers Menger drew on are generally regarded as conservatives).

This is especially true of Hayek's work. Hayek even described Menger's question, how is spontaneous order possible, as "the central problem of the social sciences," since "the problem of the origin or formation and that of the manner of functioning of social institutions [is] essentially the same," a point not fully appreciated until Menger's exposition (Hayek 1955: 83; 1967: 101).

Hayek associated this view with the battle between liberalism and socialism:

From the belief that nothing which has not been consciously designed can be useful or even essential to the achievement of human purposes, it is an easy transition to the belief that since all "institutions" have been made by man, we must have complete power to refashion them in any way we desire. (1955: 83)

And yet it is by no means clear to what degree the Menger-Hayek view of the spontaneous origin—and, hence, in Hayek's interpretation, spontaneous functioning—of institutions is serviceable to liberalism. Menger himself posited a crucial qualification:

But never, and this is the essential point in the matter under review, may science dispense with testing for their suitability those institutions which have come about "organically." It must, when careful investigation so requires, change and better them according to the measure of scientific insight and practical experience at hand. No era may renounce this "calling." (1985: 234).[34]

Thus, a certain—undefined, but presumably considerable—area would seem to exist for "social engineering."

The real value of the notion of spontaneous order is probably best appreciated when it is contrasted to the approach of some key writers of the French Enlightenment, devotees of what may be called the "Lycurgus myth."

Lycurgus, the semi-mythical figure who supposedly originated the institutions of ancient Sparta, was widely admired in eighteenth century France. Those institutions all appeared to dovetail smoothly to generate the ideal type of human being, Spartan Man, selflessly and totally devoted to love of country. As Rousseau expressed it, Lycurgus made the citizens of Sparta into "beings above the level of humanity" (1962: 428–29; see also Parker 1965). He was Rousseau's chief model when he came to describe "the Lawgiver," in the *Social Contract*:

> The lawgiver is the engineer who invents the machine; the prince is merely the mechanic who sets it up and operates it. . . . Whoever ventures on the enterprise of instituting a people must be ready, as it were, to change human nature. . . . A sublime reason, which soars above the heads of the common people, produces those rules which the lawgiver puts into the mouth of the immortals. . . . The lawgiver's great soul is the true miracle which must vindicate his mission. (1968: 84–87)[35]

---

34 Emil Kauder 1965: 61 points out that Menger opposed religious bigotry, anti-Semitism, militarism, dueling, and the glorification of war, and "was very critical of the feudal pillars of the Habsburg monarchy—clergy, army, and nobility." A number of these are traditions or institutions which, it could well be argued, had developed "spontaneously."

35 In his last work on politics, *Considerations on the Government of Poland*, Rousseau, who is still viewed by many as a serious political thinker, continued his idolization of Lycurgus, while spelling out the totalitarian implications of his childish infatuation: "He showed them [the Spartans] their country unceasingly, in their laws, their games, their homes, their loves, their feasts. He did not allow them a moment to be by themselves alone. And from this continual constraint, ennobled by its object, was born that ardent love of country . . ." See Crocker 1973: 335.

This idea, that Lycurgus—or Numa Pompilius, or Moses, or some other super-human lawgiver—"instituted" a people, was shared by Mably and other influential *philosophes*, who could only grasp the emergence of useful patterns and structures in social life—of *order*—as the product of a designing mastermind. For the tradition that Hayek recommends, on the contrary, such order is best understood as coming about through a process of adaptive evolution. As Adam Ferguson wrote, in one of Hayek's favorite quotations: "nations stumble upon establishments which are indeed the result of human action, but not the execution of human design." Whatever the limitations of such a conception, it is clearly a great advance over the puerile notions of Rousseau and other *philosophes*.

The Ideological Background of the Rise of Austrian Economics

In keeping with his attempt to depict Austrian economic theory, and marginalism in general, as free of any political taint, Hayek declared:

> I can find no indication that Jevons, Menger, or Walras, in their efforts to rebuild economic theory, were moved by any desire to revindicate the practical conclusions that had been drawn from classical economics. Such indications as we have of their sympathies are on the side of the current movements for social reform. (1973: 3)

But here Hayek misses the point. The question is not whether Austrian (and marginalist) economics was a defense of laissez-faire against *social reform*, but whether it was a defense of the basic private property, market economy against *socialism*.

Hayek ignored the theoretical crisis that many felt existed in economics on the eve to the marginalist revolution. Friedrich von Wieser, for instance, testified in his biographical notice on Böhm-Bawerk that both scholars were deeply troubled as they began their careers as economists. Among the problems confronting them were what appeared to be the plain implications of the classical labor theory of value (see Rothbard 1995c, 2: 88–94). If that theory was true, then

Is not the socialist critique of current conditions, is not Karl Marx with his theory of surplus value, totally correct? Is not socialist theory just the completer of the classical idea, which the classical economists themselves did not have the courage to think through to the end?

Their "intellectual distress" was instantly alleviated, however, when they happened to discover Menger's *Principles*.[36] It should be stressed that Wieser gives no hint of bad faith. He states that both he and Böhm-Bawerk became convinced that socialism, in consistently applying the classical concept of value as stemming from labor, was *fallacious* (Wieser 1923: 88).

Frank A. Fetter was another scholar who saw the emergence of marginalism as a deliverance from an ideological impasse.

Fetter elaborated on the predicament of classical economics after the middle of the nineteenth century. Of Ricardo and his labor theory of value, he stated:

> with his sophistical arguments he had given to this really primitive conception the phenomenal authority of his name, and it was to go on exerting a tremendous and evil influence in ways then all unforeseen. Labor is the source of value (exchange value, virtually market price as he used it); labor is the cause of value; labor produces all wealth. Naturally follows the ethical and political conclusion: if labor produces all wealth then labor should receive all wealth. (1923: 597; see also Ross 1991)

John Stuart Mill's attempt to salvage Ricardo, Fetter continues, was quite unsatisfactory, "a broken reed against the surplus-value attack upon the system of private industry and private property." Then "Marxian socialism rose on the horizon" and quickly gained advocates, who often

---

36 Wieser maintained 1923: 91–92 that, before Menger, all the schools of economic thought "pursued the interests of one of the great economic parties . . . [and] sought evidence for their partisan interest." Very oddly, he even employs the Marxist terminology of "bourgeois" and "proletarian" economists, going so far as to assert that the "proletarian," i.e. socialist, economists, will be able to learn from Menger's economic theory, without "in any way giving up their fundamental standpoint"; rather, they will be able to "strengthen their standpoint."

supported their view with references to the Mill-Ricardian labor theory of value. "Well I remember the confidence and gusto with which this demonstration of the truth of Marxism was still presented by socialist speakers in the nineties, as I listened to them from Berlin to San Francisco."

Like Wieser, Fetter is quick to point out that no bad faith was involved in propagating the subjective theory.[37] Yet he asserts, as against Hayek, that even a "casual examination of the works of Jevons, Menger, Clark, and of their most influential colleagues reveals from first to last evidences of this undercurrent of interest in the political bearings of the value theory."[38] The story, however, ends happily from Fetter's point of view. The subjective-value theory left Marxism in the dust: "it would be difficult to find in the whole history of economic thought a more complete victory of one idea over another" (1923: 600–02, 605; on Fetter, see Herbener 1999).

From the opposing camp, a long line of socialist critics, from the 1890s on, pilloried marginalism as a mere rationalization for the exploitative capitalist system. The Italian socialist Achille Loria assailed the marginal approach for precluding "the possibility of a deep analysis of social relations" and eliminating "any theoretical threat against the established economic system" (Barucci 1972: 529). Karl Kautsky, the Pope of German Marxism before the First World War, took note of the Austrian challenge in the form of Böhm-Bawerk's work, declaring: "Böhm-Bawerk's and Marx's theories of value are mutually exclusive....

---

37 It was left for Erich Streissler among non-socialists to impute a class interest to the Austrian economists (1988: 200–01): "after the end of the monarchy the members of the School belonged to the old ruling class dispossessed of power and mostly expropriated through the hyperinflation which had abolished their rentier capital. No wonder they were particularly critical of the state."

38 Fetter 1923: 602 noted that the negative implications of the subjective theory for Marxian economics appears more clearly in Wieser's and Böhm-Bawerk's works, but maintained that "this application had, however, been recognized from the very beginnings of the subjective school." While he cites no particular evidence, he may have had in mind, for instance, Menger's critique of Rodbertus's claim that capitalists and landowners expropriate the product of labor and thus "live without working." To this Menger 1981: 168 n. 30 countered that they live "upon the services of their land and capital which have value, just as do labor services, both to individuals and to society."

That means, therefore: either-or" (cited in Chaloupek 1986: 198–99). Nikolai Bukharin (1927), who attended Böhm-Bawerk's lectures, labeled Austrianism "the economic theory of the rentier class."[39] Decades later, Ronald L. Meek claimed, citing Menger and Jevons, that "the founders [of marginalism] were very well aware of the dangerous uses which were currently being made of these doctrines [of classical economics] in certain quarters" (1972: 503).[40]

What the exact role the marginalist revolution was in overturning the labor theory of value is complicated, however, by the findings of scholars who have drawn attention to theoretical developments in continental Europe in the earlier nineteenth century. T.W. Hutchison rightly complained that:

> The history of economic thought in the first half or three-quarters of the nineteenth century was and still is often portrayed in very Anglo-centric terms, as though the theories which achieved for so long in Britain such an extraordinary dominance and authority…enjoyed a similar hold and authority elsewhere in Europe. This was not the case.[41]

---

[39] Streissler 1990a: 64 makes the peculiar statement that: "Perhaps Bukharin is not that far off the mark after all when he thinks it [Austrian economics] is the economics of the rentier." However, Günther Chaloupek, an author sympathetic to Marxism, is considerably closer to the mark when he states 1986: 221, in discussing Bukharin's critique of Austrianism: "But: if the marginal utility school drew attention to demand, this was certainly not in the first instance a symptom of the beginning of age of the rentier, but rather a reflex of the increased standard of living of the masses as well in the train of capitalist expansion."

[40] Joan Robinson, on the other hand, argued 1962: 52, emphasis in original, that while "the whole point of *utility* was to justify *laisserzfaire*," the theory had inherently egalitarian and redistributionist implications.

[41] That the approach to the history of economic thought centering on the British tradition from Smith to Mill must be abandoned is argued by Murray N. Rothbard (1976a). Rothbard persuasively claims 1976a: 53 that a more informed interpretation would see "Smith and Ricardo, not as founding the science of economics, but as shunting economics onto a tragically wrong track, which it took the Austrians and other marginalists to make right." Citing works by Marjorie Grice-Hutchinson and Raymond de Roover, Rothbard emphasizes the importance of medieval and early modern thinkers, particularly the Spanish Late Scholastics. These themes also pervade Rothbard's history of economic thought 1995c, where the Late Scholastics are treated in 1: 97–133. See also Jesús Huerta de Soto 1999.

Hutchison observes, for instance, that "the wages-fund theory had been demolished by Friedrich Hermann in 1832 and never gained significant support in Germany." German economists had already espoused the doctrine that value was founded on utility and income distributed to the factors of production on the basis of their productivity (1972: 443, 445).

Erich Streissler amplified Hutchison's argument, delving into works little known to Anglophone scholars, such as those of Hermann, Rau, and Mangoldt, and mining them for telling quotations, e.g., from Hermann, in 1832: the entrepreneur, in buying labor, "acts only as an agent of the consumers of the product. Only what the consumers give for the product constitutes the true remuneration of the service of the worker . . ."

So routine was the German rejection of the labor theory of value that Wilhelm Roscher, one of the founders of the "first" Historical School, could dismiss that theory as a "genuinely national English view" (1990a: 45n, 47n). Later, Karl Brandt, in reviewing Hufeland and other early nineteenth century German proponents of utility as the foundation of economic value, regarded them as continuing the French tradition of J.-B. Say (Brandt 1992: 169–84; see also Rothbard 1995c, 2: 1–45). So, even leaving aside the already centuries-old Late Scholastic tradition in economic thought and the well-known French and Italian writers of the eighteenth century, it appears that the supercession of the simplistic labor theory of value by a more sophisticated theory based on utility was well entrenched in standard continental texts, especially German ones, by the early 1800s.

But then the foregoing reports from Wieser, et al. on the state of economic theory on the eve of the "marginalist revolution" create a mystery. As Streissler notes (1990c: 164), Wieser and Böhm-Bawerk had studied in Germany and "imbibe[d] the old protoneoclassical German tradition at first hand." As for Fetter, while his studies in Germany date from a later period, he must surely have been aware of the earlier German texts. Thus, it is hard to understand the relief the three men expressed at the supposed definitive refutation of the labor theory of value and its socialist implications by Menger and the other marginalists, if that theory had already been superseded in the mainstream of German economic thought through most of the nineteenth century.

The Social Philosophy of the Austrian Economists

Erich Streissler (1987: 1) has maintained that what united the Austrian economists into a "school" was never any theoretical concept, such as marginal utility, but simply their liberal political ideas. While this may be an exaggerated, even eccentric, judgment, the divergent political views of the leaders of the school have certainly played some part in identifying it with liberalism.

Of the founders—Menger, Böhm-Bawerk, and Wieser—it is Wieser's views that seem to be the least problematical (Mayer 1929; Streissler 1986: 86–91).[42] Though not a socialist, Wieser firmly believed that the private property, market economy was rife with flaws that cried out for interventionist remedies. Robert B. Ekelund, Jr., has noted that, for Wieser, both consumers and workers were typically tyrannized by the possessors of great concentrations of wealth, and that in Wieser's view it was the duty of government to reduce the power of these property owners and provide for the "victims of acquisitive capitalism." Detecting power operating everywhere in market exchanges, Wieser even favored protective tariffs for less developed nations in order to counteract the economic and political domination of the wealthier countries. He tried to deploy marginal utility theory to justify not only progressive taxation, as Hayek noted, but also state subsidies for "projects productive of high total utility" (Ekelund 1992). There seems little reason to dissent from Streissler's characterization of Wieser as "a statist, who believed in the wisdom of the state machinery guided by a wise bureaucracy (coming from his own caste)" (1987: 14–15).[43]

---

42 Oscar Morgenstern 1927: 673–74, however, had a sharply different interpretation of Wieser's last work, *Gesetz der Macht*, and incongruously characterized Wieser as a "convinced pacifist."
43 Streissler 1986: 100 points out that Wieser's constant references to "the socialist state of the future" influenced his student Joseph Schumpeter in the latter's assessment of the probable course of historical development.

Wieser's last book, *The Law of Force*, intended as his *magnum opus*, has been open to widely varying interpretations (Streissler 1986: 86–91; Morgenstern 1927: 673–74; and especially Samuels in Wieser 1983: xiii–xxxvi). In any case, as a confusing hodgepodge in which all of history is explained and the whole future of mankind sketched through an obsessive application of the concepts of "power" and "leadership," this work is fundamentally outside the tradition of the Austrian school.[44] Menger's political orientation, on the other hand, has been the most studied and remains the most disputed.

Mises (1969: 18) conveyed the impression that Menger was more or less a classical liberal, asserting that he "heartily disapproved of the interventionist policies that the Austrian Government—like almost all governments of the epoch—had adopted." Streissler has also argued for a virtually laissez-faire Menger, seeing him as the source of the school's commitment to the free market.[45] Emil Kauder, on the other hand, saw Menger as a sympathizer with *Sozialpolitik* (social reform) and a critic of laissez-faire (1965: 62–64).[46]

Menger appears to have been exceedingly wary of expressing his policy views openly and unambiguously. Until recently, a chief source for his general ideas in this field was an article he published in the leading Viennese newspaper in 1891, titled, "The Social Theories of Classical Economics and Modern Economic Policy" (Menger 1935b). Here Menger, on the hundredth anniversary of the death of Adam Smith, attempts to rescue Smith's doctrine from grave misunderstandings. The major misinterpretation, he finds (in the manner of the later Lionel Robbins 1953) is that Smith has been wrongly accused of supporting laissez-faire, and

---

44 Even as regards Wieser's economic theory, Mises 1978b: 36 concluded that he "could not be called a member of the Austrian School, but was rather a member of the Lausanne School . . ." This viewpoint is cogently set forth in Hoppe and Salerno 1999.
45 Cf. Streissler's insightful remark 1987: 24: "Through Menger his school became a vessel of economic liberalism, at a time when in other countries it stood under an unlucky star. This school took over a then 'lost cause,' and nursed liberalism at the time of its deepest ebb—especially in the period between the wars."
46 Kauder 1965: 64 asserts of Menger: "He was not a consistent defender of free competition, and he was not a socialist, although his brother, the famous socialist Anton Menger, had some influence on him."

his doctrine unjustly amalgamated to that of the Manchester School. (Starting with the socialist agitator Ferdinand Lassalle, *Manchestertum*—"Manchesterism"—became in German-speaking countries the general term of abuse for the laissez-faire position.) It would be difficult for anyone reading Menger's piece to avoid the conclusion that he considered himself more of a *social* than a strictly *classical* liberal.

Streissler, however, has claimed (1987: 20–24; 1994) that a totally new light is cast on Menger's outlook by the notebooks kept by the Crown Prince Rudolf when he was tutored by Menger in 1876, and which were discovered in recent years by the Austrian scholar Brigitte Hamann (Menger 1994). In Streissler's judgment (1990b: 110), these notebooks "show Menger to have been a classical liberal of the purest water with a much smaller agenda for the state than even Adam Smith." It seems, however, that Streissler exaggerates the probative value of the notebooks (see the Note on Carl Menger's Social Philosophy, below).

Kauder maintained that the founders of the school, including Böhm-Bawerk, displayed an "uneasy swinging back and forth between freedom and authority in their economic policy," the result of contradictory forces working on their thought. On the one hand, they were "social *ontologists*. They believe that a general plan of reality exists. All social phenomena are conceived in relation to this master plan. . . . The ontological structure does not only indicate what is, but also what ought to be." Kauder takes as an example Böhm-Bawerk's *Positive Theory of Capital*, which demonstrates "the natural order under the laissez-faire mechanism. In 'beautiful harmony' the economic fabric is fitted together by marginal utility, discount theory of interest, and roundabout production, if the long run price (*Dauerpreis*) of free competition is reached" (Kauder 1958: 417, emphasis in original; see also Garrison 1999). This "social ontology"—an earlier version of Rothbard's conception of the market economy, cited above—is deeply congruent with the liberal vision.

But, according to Kauder, the underlying intellectual tradition in Austria was one of state paternalism, to the point where even the expression of the concept of a spontaneous economic order had been actively suppressed. The founders thus "tried to compromise between British [i.e., Smithian] and Austrian tradition." In the end, Böhm-Bawerk held that social stability was more important than progress, preaching a "social quietism akin to the ideals of the Austrian past" (Kauder 1958: 421–22).[47] To make matters worse, Stephan Böhm points out that "Böhm-Bawerk's outstanding achievement as Minister of Finance was the introduction of the progressive income tax on the total income of individuals." (1985: 256; see also Weber 1949: 667)[48]

Böhm-Bawerk himself conceded that the Austrian economists had not devoted much effort to practical questions of political economy in the first two decades of their activity, adducing as an excuse that "we must build the house before we can set it in order." He added, however, that "we have our opinions upon them, we teach them from our chairs, but our literary activities have thus far been bestowed almost exclusively upon theoretical problems." (Böhm-Bawerk 1891: 378)

What those opinions were at this point in his career Böhm-Bawerk divulged to some extent in another essay published at in 1891. Here he labels as slanderous Lujo Brentano's charge that the Austrian economists are indifferent to "the social question." On the contrary, Böhm-Bawerk insists, in his view there is "much that is lamentable and in need of reform in the present condition of society," and he looked on "an indifferent, *laissez-faire, laissez-passer* attitude" as completely misguided. In fact, he sympathizes "most warmly" with efforts at reform

---

[47] Paul Silverman, however, 1990: 85, 90–91 criticizes Kauder on the nature of the Austrian background of Menger's work (as well as on Menger's alleged methodological dependence on Aristotle). Silverman points up the importance in Austrian history of a school of liberal cameralists, including the key figure of Joseph von Sonnenfels, who posited "a system of preestablished social harmony which the state was to watch over and protect." Josef von Kudler, whose work on economics was the standard textbook in Austrian universities in the decades before the appearance of Menger's *Principles*, likewise displayed "a staunchly liberal outlook." In Silverman's view, the impact of the "Austrian tradition" on Menger was not in the direction of conservatism, spurring the search for a Metternichian stability; instead, it may mainly have worked to convey the notion of objective, rational ends for man in society. This set a limit to Menger's subjectivism, leading him, for instance, to differentiate real from imagined needs.
[48] Böhm 1990: 232 n. 2 suggests that Mises's extreme liberal viewpoint was out of step with the general position of the founders of Austrianism, who tended towards "a kind of 'enlightened conservatism' (in the European sense), or 'paternalistic conservatism'—allegations of laissez faire repeated ad nauseam notwithstanding."

in favor of the "economically oppressed," and, while he has not yet expressed himself on the subject in print, this, he writes, is what he always professes as a teacher (Böhm-Bawerk 1994: 112).

Later, in the 1930s, as the Austrian school gained in acceptance and prestige, attempts were made to enlist Böhm-Bawerk and the other founders as social reformers, and thus disassociate them from the principled economic liberalism of the then rising star of the school, Ludwig von Mises.

In a 1935 article, Wilhelm Vleugels defended the scientific usefulness of Austrian subjective value theory. At the same time he contended that it was perfectly compatible with the older German tradition that placed the needs of the national community above individual needs, a standpoint that at the time Vleugels wrote was, one might say, *de rigueur* in Germany. "If at the start [the writings of the Austrians] exhibited a certain tendency to consider the most important needs of the individual simultaneously as the most important needs of society, that tendency was forthwith surmounted" (Vleugels 1935: 550). Vleugels's major piece of evidence (besides statements by Wieser) is an essay by Böhm-Bawerk dating from 1886, to which the title, "Disadvantageous Effects of Free Competition," had been given.

In this essay, Böhm-Bawerk considers the claim that under conditions of free competition supply and demand are brought into the "most useful" and "socially most fruitful" equilibrium, creating "the socially greatest possible quantity of absolute [*rein*] utility." Surprisingly, the expositor of this viewpoint was Albert Schäffle, known for his social-reformist attitudes, and it is Böhm-Bawerk who holds it up to criticism. Böhm-Bawerk characterizes it as "deceptive," in that it rests upon a "confusion of high *relative* with high *absolute* gains from exchange." Hypothesizing an "ideal standard of measurement," Böhm-Bawerk maintains that a rich consumer who outbids a poor consumer for a given good may well gain less in utility than the poor consumer would have gained. While "cases of this kind occur, unfortunately, countless times in actual economic life," Böhm-Bawerk takes as his example Ireland in the 1840s. Then the indigenous population could not afford to pay the market price for grain, which was exported instead. The result was that the Irish starved and died, while the grain went, in part, to meet the demand of the rich for spirits and fine baked goods (1924: 476–77, 479). Böhm-Bawerk concludes:

> every unprejudiced person will recognize at once that here egoistic competition in exchange has certainly not led to the socially most fruitful distribution of the commodities wheat and corn, the distribution attaching to the greatest absolute [*rein*] utility for the vital preservation and development of the people [*Volk*]. (1924: 480)

Statements of this kind led Vleugels to declare that it was Austrian theory itself that had "scientifically brought about the collapse of the main basis of liberal theory and of the demand for laissez-faire erected upon it" (1937: 35). Later, Joan Robinson similarly argued that the implications of marginal utility theory were originally all in the direction of "progressive taxation and the Welfare State, if not more radical means [of intervening in] an economic system that allows so much of the good juice of *utility* to evaporate out of commodities by distributing them unequally" (1962: 52; emphasis in original).

Robinson's use of the term *juice* seems significant here, and points to the fundamental error of Vleugels (and Böhm-Bawerk) on this score. The assumption seems to be that marginal utility theory deals with a mental substance called "utility," a sort of effluvium that arises within individuals and is somehow or other susceptible of measurement. A throwback to Benthamite utilitarianism, this perspective implies that interpersonal comparisons of utility are not only possible but mandatory, if the aim is to "maximize" an aggregated "social utility."

But this whole approach falls to the ground once the reasoning of modern Austrian analysis is understood and accepted, that utility is always *ordinal*, never *cardinal*. It always refers to the individual's ranking of preferences in action, never to quantities of some kind of psychological substance that can be measured even for the acting individual, let alone among different individuals (Rothbard 1997, 1: 22–40; see also Kauder 1965: 215–17).

At all events, the citations from Böhm-Bawerk in the 1880s and 90s would appear to detach him rather decisively from the tradition of "doctrinaire" economic liberalism. Yet Erich Streissler is able to refer to him as "quite an extreme liberal . . . [with] a very extensive skepticism towards the state," one who shared Adam Smith's view of the state as both "bad" and "stupid." What is most intriguing is that Streissler's evidence derives from two newspaper articles published in 1914, the last year of Böhm-Bawerk's life.

Here Böhm-Bawerk criticized both the notion that coercive intervention (by labor unions) can circumvent economic law and the tendency of politicians to buy support and temporary social peace through massive expenditure of public monies. It appears, then, that it was Böhm-Bawerk's personal experience as Austrian finance minister that turned him into a caustic critic of political leaders and a skeptic of the governmental process itself (1987: 10–14). His thinking seems to have undergone an evolution based on first-hand observation of the political process, from an early focus on "market failure" to a more mature concern with the inevitably anti-social, "rent-seeking" aspects of state action. The question of Böhm-Bawerk's later views is of particular interest, as Streissler indicates: Mises attended Böhm-Bawerk's seminar in 1905–06, after the latter's last stint in government.

A few years before Vleugels's article was published, Franz X. Weiss, who had edited the collection of the smaller works of Böhm-Bawerk containing his 1886 essay, argued the same position as Vleugels—against Mises himself. At the 1932 meeting of the *Verein für Sozialpolitik* (Association for Social Policy, the major group of social scientists in German-speaking Europe) held in Dresden and attended by Mises, Hayek, and other leaders of the Austrian school, Weiss, too, attempted to distance Austrian economics from Misesian liberalism, citing various published statements from the older generation of Austrians. Among these were Menger's assertion that it was frivolous to accuse him of being a supporter of Manchesterism; Böhm-Bawerk's condemnation of "an indifferent policy of *laissez faire, laissez passer*"; and Wieser's view that the claim that there exist immutable natural laws of the economy impervious to state action "can hardly be taken seriously anymore."

His purpose, Weiss declared, was "to establish that a number of notable representatives [of the Austrian doctrine], among them its founders, did not draw from it the conclusions for economic policy that [Mises] believes he must draw." Mises's brief response to Weiss's critique: "I am not so pious towards authority [*autoritätsgläubig*] and quotation-minded [*zitatenfreudig*], and I base my argumentation on logic and not on exegesis." The interesting implication is that the political consequences of Austrian economics are to be gathered not from the particular views of its major early proponents, subject to the climate of opinion of their times, but from the inner logic of the system itself (Mises and Spiethoff 1933: 51–53, 131, 118).[49]

What writers like Weiss and Vleugels found unbearable about Mises was that, in Vleugels's words (1935: 538), he was "a scholar who is endeavoring to reanimate decisive errors of *Manchestertum*, in a refined form, to be sure, but still in all its extremism." These fundamental "errors" of the laissez-faire doctrine had, so it was thought, been safely buried once and for all in central Europe, if not throughout the civilized world. That Mises should presume to reopen the argument over the appalling and discredited ideas of laissez-faire was something his opponents, then and throughout his life, could never forgive him. It was Mises who revealed the intimate connections between Austrian economics and authentic liberalism.

Mises and Hayek

Beginning with Ludwig von Mises and F.A. Hayek, the links between liberalism and the Austrian School become intense and pervasive, since these two scholars were themselves at once the outstanding Austrian economists and the most distinguished liberal thinkers of the twentieth century. The American academic world, however, deemed

---

49 At the University of Vienna, Hans Mayer, who was all that was left of the Austrian school after the *Anschluss* with Nazi Germany, also held that Mises's radical liberal conclusions were not inherent in the school's teachings (Craver 1986: 10–11). This is easily understandable, given Mayer's position as a functionary of the new National Socialist regime. The tradition of attempting to disassociate Mises's "personal," "Manchester-liberal" world-view from "the objective findings of the Austrian school" was carried on by Weber 1949: 644.

none of this sufficient for them to be accorded the kind of positions to which they were clearly entitled.[50] They, and in particular Mises, were also responsible to a greater degree than is generally appreciated for the upsurge of the free-market philosophy in the second half of the century.[51]

But since the views of the two great men are so often amalgamated, it should be emphasized that not only did they differ to an extent on economic theory (Salerno 1993; see also Kirzner 1992c: 119–36), but, more pertinently to the theme of this essay, they exhibited a sharp distinction in the degree of their liberalism.

What follows refers to Hayek's *political* attitudes, not to his contributions to economic science. These were highly significant and valuable in the earlier part of his career, as he together with Mises built the theoretical foundations of the modern Austrian school.[52]

While Mises was a staunch advocate of the laissez-faire market economy (Mises 1978a; Rothbard 1988: 40; Hoppe 1993; Klein 1999),

---

50 Hans-Hermann Hoppe puts the matter very well. When Mises arrived in the United States in 1940, he was already "an international scientific celebrity," and his influential works, *The Theory of Money and Credit* and *Socialism* had been available in English for years. "But while every third-class European Marxist or 'Marxian' of the time found a respectable academic position without any difficulty, in the land of capitalism the American universities and intellectuals plainly and shamelessly turned a cold shoulder to Mises, the great theoretician of liberalism and capitalism." Mises finally obtained a position at New York University, but only as permanent guest professor, and the university did not pay his salary, which was covered from private sources. Hoppe 1993: 27–28, 30, 34 n. 24. Hayek's situation was analogous. While he did become a professor on the Committee on Social Thought, he was deemed unsuitable, not "scientific" enough (i.e., not sufficiently positivist) by the economics department of George Stigler and Milton Friedman, and his salary was likewise paid from outside sources.
51 Cf. Steele 1992: "The fact that there were capable liberal thinkers in Europe after World War II is mainly due to the influence of *Die Gemeinwirtschaft* [Mises's *Socialism*] during the inter-war years. There might not have been any West German 'economic miracle' without the existence of a handful of active people converted from socialism by Mises." See also Roll 1945: 176: "Hayek and his Viennese colleagues have been the leaders of an astonishing movement of revival [of individualism and liberalism] which in the early thirties began to appear also in England…There in nothing quite comparable to this movement in the United States."
52 See in particular Joseph T. Salerno's perceptive introduction to Hayek's *Prices and Production* and Other Works, "Hayek on the Business Cycle," *Mises Daily*, October 8, 2008.

Hayek was always more open to what he saw as the useful possibilities of state action. He had been a student of Wieser's, and, as he conceded, he was "attracted to him . . . because unlike most of the other members of the Austrian School [Wieser] had a good deal of sympathy with [the] mild Fabian Socialism to which I was inclined as a young man. He in fact prided himself that his theory of marginal utility had provided the basis of progressive taxation . . ." (Hayek 1983: 17).

Early in his career, Hayek stated that the lessons of economics will create a presumption against state interference, adding:

> However, this by no means does away with the positive part of the economist's task, the delimitation of the field within which collective action is not only unobjectionable but actually a useful means of obtaining the desired ends...the classical writers very much neglected the positive part of the task and thereby allowed the impression to gain ground that *laissez-faire* was their ultimate and only conclusion . . . (1933: 133–34)

This remained Hayek's standpoint throughout his long and richly productive scholarly life. It is regrettable, but typical, that a great many confused commentators continue to characterize him as a advocate of laissez-faire.[53] In fact, he always avoided using the term to describe his own views, quite unlike Mises, who gloried in it. Provocatively—and quite misleadingly—Hayek states that the supposed laissez-faire conclusions of classical economics " of course, would have been invalidated by the demonstration that, in any single case, State action was useful" (1933: 134). Here Hayek seems to have lost sight of a principle that otherwise loomed large in his thinking: that with such issues of social policy it could never be a question of "any single case," but rather of *general rules* and their overall effect.

---

53 On Hayek's position, see Shearmur 1997. The German "neo-liberal" Alexander Rüstow was one of many who could not differentiate the position of Hayek from that of "his master Mises," viewing both as "the last surviving examples" of the "old liberalism," fit to be placed in a museum; see Kathrin Meier-Rust 1993: 69–70. Meier-Rust herself (91) discusses the sharp differences between the German "neo-" and "Ordo-liberal," and the "classical laissez-faire champions" like Hayek.

Hayek habitually displayed a penchant for a considerable degree of *Sozialpolitik*.[54] In a radio debate in Chicago, following the publication of *The Road to Serfdom*, he not only stated that, "I have always said that I am in favor of a minimum income for every person in the country," but, pressed by two aggressive if uninformed leftist opponents, even made the astonishing assertion: "That the monetary system must be under central control has never, to my mind, been denied by any sensible person" (1994b: 114, 116). Some twenty years later, in the preface to a reprint of his book, Hayek admitted that at the time he wrote *The Road to Serfdom*, "I had not wholly freed myself from all the current interventionist superstitions and in consequence made various concessions which I now think unwarranted" (1994a: xxiv).[55] It may be that, besides his youthful inclination towards a mild Fabianism and his deep admiration for Friederich von Wieser, Hayek was influenced in this direction by the arrant statism that dominated intellectual life in Britain when he lived there in the 1930s and 40s, often involving starry-eyed admiration for the noble experiment underway in Soviet Russia. In any case, his divergence from the more consistent—or more "dogmatic"—variety of liberalism espoused by Mises endured to the end of his career.

Mises highlighted the possibilities of meeting the needs of the deserving poor through private charity and assailed Bismarckian schemes

---

54 See also Streissler 1987: 10: "pronounced liberals, at least in the eighteenth and nineteenth centuries, were rather averse to a redistributive function [of the state]. On the other hand, Friedrich von Hayek, for instance, is no longer of this opinion. He believes only that the pursuit of *Sozialpolitik* should not be attempted with the help of the market but through transfers independent of the market."

55 Hayek also later remarked that another error in *The Road to Serfdom* was his neglect of the significance of the experience of Soviet Communism, adding, rather oddly, that this was a fault "which is perhaps pardonable when it is remembered that when I wrote Russia was our wartime ally." This is a curious inversion of the strange criticism leveled at *The Road to Serfdom* by Erich Roll, in the *American Economic Review* (1945: 180): "Hayek might have stopped to reflect upon the very different development during the last few pre-war years in Germany and in the Soviet Union, and he might have had the grace, at the least, to acknowledge the very different manner in which the war itself has been conducted by the enemy and by our ally: we have yet to be shown that Maidanek is an inevitable corollary of a collective economy" (1945: 180). Evidently, Professor Roll and his equally ignorant editors at the *American Economic Review* had somehow never heard of the Ukrainian terror famine, the mass executions, or the system of forced labor camps known today as the Gulag, all conducted by our noble wartime ally, the model terror state of the twentieth century.

of social insurance (1949: 829–50, especially 832–36). Hayek, on the other hand, declared:

> though a few theorists have demanded that the activities of government should be limited to the maintenance of law and order, such a stand cannot be justified by the principle of liberty....It can hardly be denied that, as we grow richer, that minimum of sustenance which the community has always provided for those not able to look after themselves, and which cannot be provided outside the market, will gradually rise, or that government may, usefully and without doing any harm, assist or even lead in such endeavors.

As if that were not enough, Hayek raised the ante. Seemingly oblivious to any moral hazard or public choice considerations, he added:

> There is little reason why the government should not also play some role, or even take the initiative, in such areas as social insurance and education, or temporarily subsidize certain experimental developments. Our problem here is not so much with the aims as the methods of government action. (Hayek 1960: 257–58)

The state, Hayek insisted, is not solely "a coercive apparatus," but also "a service agency," and as such "it may assist without harm in the achievement of desirable aims which perhaps could not be achieved otherwise."[56] This opening to an extensive welfare state in cases where it "involves no coercion except for the raising of the means by taxation" (sic) (Hayek, 1978: 144), has been criticized by Anthony de Jasay. De Jasay cogently remarks that Hayek put his proposal "a touch naïvely," and adds:

> Here is a clear call, or what anyone might be excused for taking as one, to re-create something like the "Swedish model" under

---

56 Cf., e.g., Mises, 1949:149: "State or government is the social apparatus of compulsion and coercion. It has the monopoly of violent action. . . . The state is essentially an institution for the preservation of peaceful interhuman relations. However, for the preservation of peace it must be prepared to crush the onslaughts of peace-breakers."

the liberal banner. Horrified as Hayek would be by the imputation of such a proposal, his exposition is fully consistent with it, and must be classed as "loosely liberal" for that reason. (1991a: 15–16; see also 1996)[57]

Predictably, Hayek's endorsement of state activism in the "social" sphere has provided knowledgeable opponents of the laissez-faire position with a rhetorical argument of the form, "even F.A Hayek conceded . . ." (e.g., Battisti 1987: 264–65, where the author uses Hayek to undercut the minimal state position of Wilhelm von Humboldt).

Hayek and Mises may be contrasted in other respects as well. J.C. Nyiri points out that Hayek's social philosophy resembles not only the British Whig (moderate liberal) tradition, which Hayek explicitly recognized, but also that of Austrian *Altliberalismus* (Old Liberalism), which in some respects compromised liberalism even further than did Whiggism. As Nyiri states: "There is a haunting traditionalism, or conservatism, in Hayek's position . . ." Austrian *Altliberalismus* had a marked attraction for inherited institutions and a skepticism towards the concept of individual rights (whether understood as natural or positive). Many of its representatives were "definitely averse to unrestricted social mobility"—which mainly meant, in Austria-Hungary, the self-betterment of the Jews (Nyiri 1986: 104, 106).

In contrast, Mises was more radical in this as in other areas (see Rothbard 1981). While a strong proponent of traditional "bourgeois" (*not* aristocratic) culture, which he regarded as essentially harmonious with what we know of human nature, Mises understood that culture to be founded on a commitment to reason as a way of life.

Tributes to the faculty of human reason are strewn throughout his works, e.g., reason is "the mark that distinguishes man from animals and has brought about everything that is specifically human"; and, "Man has only one tool to fight error: reason" (Mises 1949: 91, 187; see also

---

57 Hans-Hermann Hoppe 1994: 67 has ventured to assert that "Hayek's view regarding the role of market and state cannot systematically be distinguished from that of a modern social democrat." But see the attack on Hayek for his rejection of the concept of social justice by a social democratic writer, in Plant 1994.

especially Salerno 1990). This stands in stark contrast to Hayek's disparagement of reason in his later works (especially Hayek, 1988).[58]

As for tradition, Mises's attitude was perhaps best expressed in *Theory and History*:

> History looks backward into the past, but . . . it does not teach indolent quietism; it rouses men to emulate the deeds of earlier generations. . . . Faithfulness to tradition means to the historian observance of the fundamental rule of human action, namely, ceaseless striving to improve conditions. It does not mean preservation of unsuitable old institutions and clinging to doctrines long since discredited by more tenable theories. (1957: 294, 296)[59]

Later Austrian economists, following in Mises's footsteps, have by and large adopted a more radical form of liberalism. One of the most prominent of them, Murray Rothbard (1970, 1973a; Block and Rockwell [eds.] 1988), surpassed even his mentor in his anti-statism. It is to a large degree due to Rothbard's "libertarian scholarship and advocacy" (Kirzner 1987: 149) that Austrianism is associated in the minds of many with a defense of the free market and private property to the point of the very abolition of the state and so of the total triumph of civil society (Hoppe 1987 and 1999; Lemieux 1988). It should be noted that Rothbard dealt extensively with questions of international relations, foreign policy, and war and peace, a dimension relatively neglected by other Austrians (e.g.,

---

58 Late in his life, Hayek 1994: 68, 72–73 referred to his "curious relationship" to Mises, from whom "I probably learnt more than from any other man." Here Hayek made the confusing claim that "Mises remained in the end himself a rationalist-utilitarian, and with a rationalist-utilitarianism, the rejection of socialism is irreconcilable. . . . If we remain strict rationalists, utilitarians, that implies that we can arrange everything according to our pleasure." At an earlier stage, Hayek's judgment of Mises had been much more positive. In 1952, Hayek wrote 1952: 729–30 of Mises that "since the early twenties [he] has been building a new edifice of liberal thought more consistently, more systematically, and more successfully than anyone else . . . his work resemble[s] that of the great social philosophers of the eighteenth century much more than the labors of a contemporary expert . . . he alone has given us a conclusive treatment of all economic and social thought," Hayek asserted, adding, "whether or not one concurs with him in every detail."

59 A comprehensive examination of what Hayek criticized as Mises's "extreme rationalism" (foreword to Mises, 1981: xxiii) is presented, with a critique of Hayek's position, in Salerno 1990.

Rothbard 1972, 1978; but see also Mises 1944). In this area, as in all others, Rothbard sought to further the core liberal ideal of combating the power of the state at every turn.

APPENDIX

A Note on Carl Menger's Social Philosophy

In analyzing the notebooks of Crown Prince Rudolf, Erich Streissler assumes that they reflect the policy views of the Crown Prince's tutor, Carl Menger. If that is so, Menger at this time harbored a very restrictive notion of the proper functions of the state, limiting them (beyond justice and defense) to remedying certain "externalities." "Only abnormal cases permit the intervention of the state; in the normal situations of economic life we shall always have to declare such a procedure to be harmful," Rudolf wrote. The state's duties are to be limited to implementing measures against the spread of cattle diseases; negotiating trade treaties with other states; building roads, railroads, canals, and schools; and imposing a maximum of fifteen hours a day on adult labor in factories and abolishing factory child labor altogether. (Streissler 1987: 22–23)

What to make then of Menger's later statements that appear to endorse *Sozialpolitik*? In dealing with the 1891 essay on Adam Smith, Streissler (1990b: 109–10; also Menger 1994: 13–14) distorts Menger's position in a passage which he himself quotes in German in a footnote. Streissler writes: "What [Menger] actually says is simply that Adam Smith did not consider justice always to be on the side of the employers in all their conflicts with and all their demands against their workers (obviously true!); and that Smith was not against all types of state actions in all cases (again obviously true)."

In the quotation he gives, however, this is what Menger says: "A. Smith places himself in all cases of conflict of interests between the poor and the rich, between the strong and the weak, *without exception*, on the side of the latter. . . . State intervention *in favor of* the poor and the weak is so little rejected by Smith, that he instead endorses it in all cases in which he expects a *favoring* . . . of the propertyless classes" (quoted in Streissler 1990b.: 109n., emphasis in Menger's original).

In defending Smith, Menger states that in fighting for the "poor" against the "rich" Smith went beyond support of the abolition of mercantilist measures harming the poor to outright advocacy of positive legislation. "Smith is even for legal determinations of the level of wages, insofar as they are set *in favor* of the workers, and declares such wage controls *always* just and fair. . . . Indeed, A. Smith goes so far as to designate *the profit on capital as a deduction from the full return to labor, and ground-rent even as the income of those* who wish to harvest where they have not sown." (Menger 1935b: 224, 230–31, emphasis in original) Menger treats J.-B. Say in the same manner. Say's—and Smith's—alleged support of tariffs to give an advantage to national industry is linked to the ideas of Friedrich List. Menger declares that the German social reform thinkers (the Socialists of the Chair, advocates of *Sozialpolitik*) were

> in part right in their fight against the representatives of capitalistic Manchesterism—the distorted image of classical economics, in regard to social policy—*not however against Smith and classical economics*. The final shape that classical economics assumed is not found in Cobden, Bright, Bastiat, Prince-Smith, and Schulze-Delitzsch, but in *John Stuart Mill*, that social philosopher who, next to Sismondi, must be characterized as the most important founder of the modern social reform [*social-politischen*] school, insofar as it has an objective scientific character. (Menger 1935b: 232–33, emphasis in original)

Further on, Menger explains the differing positions of the classical economists and the social reformers by referring to the conditions of their respective times. While the earlier economists sought to remove politically erected hindrances, now the stress has been on the positive intervention of the State, "a further development of the efforts for the betterment of the condition of the working class." (1935b: 234–55)

Menger had already disassociated himself from laissez-faire in 1884, in his rebuttal to Schmoller's review of his *Investigations*). Here Menger writes in a confusing and apparently contradictory manner. First he asserts that

> to be a supporter of the so-called Manchester school is, to be sure, no dishonor; it means only adhering to a series of scientific convictions, of which we can well characterize as the most important the proposition that the free play of individual interests best promotes the common good. Social philosophers intellectually much superior to Schmoller, men guided by the noblest love of truth, have professed themselves supporters of the above principle and the maxims of economic policy resulting from it. Menger 1935c: 92n.)

Menger goes on to say, however:

> If anything reconciles me to Schmoller's activity in the field of our science, odious in so many respects, then it is the circumstance that he is fighting with an unmistakable devotion on the side of honorable men against social evils and for the fate of the weak and the poor. This is a struggle in which, as different as the direction of my researches may be, my sympathies lie entirely on the side of such efforts. I may devote my meager power to the investigation of the laws in accordance with which the economic life of men is shaped; but nothing is further from the trend of my thinking than service in the interest of capitalism. No accusation of Schmoller's is more contrary to the truth, no reproach more frivolous, than that I am a supporter of the Manchester party ... (Menger 1935c: 93)[60]

---

[60] Menger adds in a footnote 1935c: 93 n.: "I certainly attack the so-called 'ethical' tendency in political economy in a number of places in my *Investigations*, while strictly distinguishing it from the 'social-political' [social reform] tendency in economic research." Streissler, incidentally, cites Menger's clash with Schmoller, but omits his praise of Schmoller's crusade for *Sozialpolitik* (Menger 1994: 24 n. 8).

Note that in this passage Menger implies that laissez-faire writers are in service to "the interest of capitalism."

Similarly, in 1906, Menger published in a Berlin newspaper an appreciation of John Stuart Mill on the hundredth anniversary of Mill's birth. Here he praises Mill for having devoted so much effort in his *Principles* to social questions, "and in this way attempted for England in many respects what a few decades later the so-called *Kathedersozialismus* [the Socialists of the Chair] tried to accomplish for German economics and Cauwès and Gide for the French." In doing this, Mill's work

> in particular contributed essentially to the fact that in the educated circles of all countries and in the public discussion today, social problems are to a far lesser degree than before comprehended from the standpoint of a one-sided class interest. (Menger 1935a: 290)

Once again, there is the implication that the laissez-faire position serves the interests of capitalists to the detriment of the rest of the community.

Streissler, incidentally, is quite misleading when he says (1990b:128) that, "J.S. Mill . . . was considered, at least by Menger, hardly better than a socialist." As the quotations from the essays of 1891 and 1906 show, Menger viewed Mill with great respect, as a social reformer whose work represented the culmination of classical economics.

Streissler tries to discount these later statements by Menger: "There is not a shred of evidence in his writing that [Menger] did change his position towards a more muted liberalism [after the period of the Crown Prince's notebooks]. His *general* pronouncements just appear more in favor of social policy; but he never gives *concrete* examples in conflict with the lecture notes." (1990b: 112, emphasis in original). But as Streissler himself writes of the founders of the Austrian school (1987:11), they "were all theoreticians and thus almost never wrote anything on their political views, although they certainly had quite pronounced views on economic policy." "Concrete examples" of Menger's overall policy views appear to be rare, except possibly as reported *indirectly*, in the notebooks.

On the other hand, Menger was surely aware that terms like *Sozialpolitik* and *Kathedersozialismus* denoted support for a quite activist state in economic affairs. If Menger was "a classical liberal of the purest water," as Streissler claims, why did he write so favorably of *Sozialpolitik* and *Kathedersozialismus*—to the point of conceding Schmoller's great services in furthering the cause of "social reform" in the midst of a diatribe against him?[61] Why did he attack Manchesterism so vehemently? Unless the explanation is to be found in political opportunism, these statements represent a great mystery, given Streissler's interpretation.

As against Menger's published statements spanning the years 1883–1906, Streissler sets what he takes to be implications of the notebooks of 1876. But it is clear from Streissler's own valuable researches that in certain respects the notebooks do not correspond to Menger's views (although they very probably reflect Menger's lessons to Rudolf): "The Crown Prince was taught pure classical wage theory, in absolute contrast to Menger's *Principles*. He is explicitly taught the 'Iron Law of Wages,' as F. Lassalle had termed this theory." Streissler's analysis culminates in what comes close to a *reductio ad absurdum*: "If one judges by the Notebooks Menger must have considered his innovations only unimportant frills on the great edifice of classical economics created by Adam Smith." (Menger 1994: 19–21)

Actually, Streissler himself suggests plausible grounds for Menger's teaching the Crown Prince a version of economics in which he himself did not believe, "in many instances . . . the exact opposite of what he had forcefully argued was the only possible correct theoretical position . . ." According to Streissler, Menger

> took the politically wise as well as the most economical course: he hardly presented his own ideas at all; he did not teach from his own published work. Instead he taught almost exclusively

---

61 By 1891 Menger (1935b: 244–45) also had some harsh criticisms of the policies of the social reformers: "The self-interest that the advocates of *Sozialpolitik* so utterly despise has not disappeared from the world. Rather, it has degenerated into a collectivist, national and class egoism, which strives not for the increase of the total product (of the object to be divided up!) but for as great a portion of the total product as possible for each individual social class."

from world-famous, i.e., from old books. . . . In this way, he guarded himself against possible criticism.

But in that case what reason is there to think that the notebooks unfailingly reflect Menger's "mature judgment?" (Menger 1994: 9, 6, 23)

Margarete Boos cites the letter Menger wrote to Kaiser Franz Josef, in which he outlined his political views. Here Menger distinguishes between the "individualists" and the "ethicists" (*Ethiker*); "the ethicists [also] hold freedom of economic activity to be the natural and normal state of affairs, but are aware of conflicts between individual and common interest in economic affairs, and attribute to the state…the right to influence economic affairs in the direction of the common interest." He himself, he writes, adheres to the "moderate school of the ethicists." Later, in an anonymous obituary for Rudolf published in a Vienna paper, Menger made a point of putting on record that the Crown Prince had been tutored from a point of view "as distant from Manchesterism as from protectionism." (Boos, 1986: 29, 31)

The fact is, as Boos points out, that Menger was under suspicion at the Imperial Court of being far too liberal. At an early point he was even subjected to police reports on his political inclinations. Thus, it may be that political opportunism—within the framework of a state where the expression of radical-liberal opinions could be highly damaging—really does explain, at least partially, Menger's endorsement of *Sozialpolitik* and his sometimes odd and contradictory statements on economic policy.

References

Barucci, Piero (1972) "The Spread of Marginalism in Italy, 1871–1890," *History of Political Economy* 4 (2) (Fall): 512–31.

Batemarco, Robert J. (1994) "Austrian Business Cycle Theory," in Boettke (ed.).

Battisti, Siegfried (1987) *Freiheit und Bindung. Wilhelm von Humboldts "Ideen zu einem Versuch, die Grenzen der Wirksamkeit des Staates zu bestimmen" und das Subsidiaritätsprinzip*, Berlin: Duncker and Humblot.

Birken, Lawrence (1988) "From Macroeconomics to Microeconomics: The Marginalist Revolution in Sociocultural Perspective," *History of Political Economy* 20 (2) (Summer): 251–64.

Birner, Jack and Rudy van Zijp (1994) (eds.) *Hayek, Co-Ordination and Evolution*, London: Routledge.

Block, Walter and Llewellyn H. Rockwell, Jr. (1988) (eds.) *Man, Economy, and Liberty: Essays in Honor of Murray N. Rothbard*, Auburn, Ala.: Ludwig von Mises Institute.

Boettke, Peter J. (1990a) *The Political Economy of Soviet Socialism: The Formative Years, 1918–1928*, Boston: Kluwer.

Boettke, Peter J. (1990b) "The Theory of Spontaneous Order and Cultural Evolution in the Social Theory of F.A. Hayek," *Cultural Dynamics* 3 (1): 61–83.

Boettke, Peter J. (ed.) (1994) *The Elgar Companion to Austrian Economics*, Aldershot, Eng.: Edward Elgar.

Boettke, Peter J. (1995) "Why Are There No Austrian Socialists? Ideology, Science, and the Austrian School," *Journal of the History of Economic Thought* 17 (Spring): 35–56.

Böhm, Stephan (1985) "The Political Economy of the Austrian School," in Piero Roggi (ed.) *Gli economisti e la politica economia*, Naples: Edizioni Scientifiche Italiane.

Böhm, Stephan (1990) "The Austrian Tradition: Schumpeter and Mises," in Hennings and Samuels (eds.)

Böhm-Bawerk, Eugen von (1891) "The Austrian Economists," *Annals of the American Academy of Political and Social Science* 1 (January): 361–84.

Böhm-Bawerk, Eugen von (1924) "Nachteilige Wirkungen des freien Wettbewerbs," in idem, *Gesammelte Schriften*, Franz X. Weiss (ed.), Vienna/Leipzig: Hölder-Pichler-Tempsky.

Böhm-Bawerk, Eugen von (1994 [1891]) "The Historical vs. the Deductive Method in Political Economy," in Kirzner (ed.), 1.

Boos, Margarete (1986) *Die Wissenschaftstheorie Carl Mengers. Biographische und ideengeschichtliche Zusammenhänge*, Vienna: Hermann Böhlaus.

Bostaph, Samuel (1978) "The Methodological Debate between Carl Menger and the German Historicists," *Atlantic Economic Journal* 6 (3) (September): 3–16.

Bostaph, Samuel (1994) "The Methodenstreit" in Boettke (ed.).

Brandt, Karl (1992) *Geschichte der deutschen Volkswirtschaftslehre, 1 Von der Scholastik bis zur klassischen Nationalökonomie*, Freiburg i.B.: Rudolf Haufe.

Bukharin, Nikolai (1927) *The Economic Theory of the Leisure Class*, New York: International Publishers.

Caldwell, Bruce J. (1984) "Praxeology and Its Critics: An Appraisal," *History of Political Economy* 16 (3) (Fall): 363–79.

Caldwell, Bruce J. (1986) "Towards a Broader Conception of Criticism," *History of Political Economy* 18 (4) (Winter): 675–81.

Caldwell, Bruce J. (1990) (ed.) *Carl Menger and His Legacy in Economics*, *History of Political Economy* 22 (annual supplement), Durham, N.C.: Duke University Press.

Chaloupek, Günther (1986) "Marxistische Kritik an der Österreichischen Schule," in Leser (ed.).

Christainsen, Gregory B. (1994) "Methodological Individualism," in Boettke (ed.)

Dasgupta, A.K. (1985) *Epochs of Economic Theory*, Oxford: Basil Blackwell.

Craver, Earlene (1986) "The Emigration of the Austrian Economists," *History of Political Economy* 18 (1) (Spring): 1–32.

Crocker, Lester G. (1973) *Jean-Jacques Rousseau: The Prophetic Voice (1758–1778)*, New York: Macmillan.

Cubeddu, Raimondo (1997) *Atlante del liberalismo*, Rome: Ideazione.

de Jasay, Anthony (1991a) *Choice, Contract, Consent: A Restatement of Liberalism*, London: Institute of Economic Affairs.

de Jasay, Anthony (1991b) "The Twistable is not Testable: Reflexions on the Political Thought of Karl Popper," *Journal des Économistes et des Études Humaines* 2 (4): 499–512.

de Jasay, Anthony (1996) "Hayek: Some Missing Pieces," *Review of Austrian Economics* 9 (1): 107–18.

Dolan, Edward G. (1976a) (ed.) *The Foundations of Modern Austrian Economics*, Kansas City: Sheed and Ward.

Dolan, Edward G. (1976b) "Austrian Economics as Extraordinary Science," in idem (1976a).

Eatwell, John, Murray Milgate and Peter Newman (eds.) (1987) *The New Palgrave: A Dictionary of Economics*, 4 vols., London: Macmillan.

Ebeling, Richard M. (1981) "Mises' Influence on Modern Economic Thought," *Wirtschaftspolitische Blätter* 28 (4): 15–24.

Elster, Jon (1985) *Making Sense of Marx*, Cambridge, Mass.: Cambridge University Press.

Ekelund, Robert B., Jr. (1992) "Power and Utility: The Normative Economics of Friedrich von Wieser," in Mark Blaug (ed.) *Eugen von Böhm-Bawerk (1851–1914) and Friedrich von Wieser (1851–1926)*, Aldershot, Eng.: Edward Elgar.

Fetter, Frank A. (1923) "Value and the Larger Economics. Rise of the Marginal Doctrine," *Journal of Political Economy* 31 (5) (October): 587–605.

Finer, S. E. (1968) "Pareto and Pluto-Democracy: The Retreat to Galapagos." *American Political Science Review* 62 (2) (June), 440–50.

Formaini, Robert (1990) *The Myth of Scientific Public Policy*, New Brunswick, N.J.: Transaction.

Foss, Nicolai J. (1994) *The Austrian School and Modern Economics: A Reassessment*, Copenhagen: Handelshøjskolens Forlag.

Friedman, Milton (1991) "Say 'No' to Intolerance," *Liberty* 4 (6) (July): 17–19.

Garrison, Roger W. (1997a) "Austrian Theory of Business Cycles," in David Glasner (ed.) *Business Cycles and Depressions: An Encyclopedia*, New York: Garland.

Garrison, Roger W. (1997b) "Mises, Ludwig Edler von (1881–1973)," in David Glasner (ed.) *Business Cycles and Depressions: An Encyclopedia*, New York: Garland.

Garrison, Roger W. (1999) "Eugen von Böhm-Bawerk: Capital, Interest, and Time," in Holcombe (ed.)

Garrison, Roger W. (2000) "An Austrian Macroeconomist: An Interview with Roger W. Garrison," *Austrian Economics Newsletter* (2000) 20 (4) (Winter).

Garrison, Roger W. (2001) *Time and Money: The Macroeconomics of Capital Structure*, London: Routledge.

Garrison, Roger W. and Kirzner, Israel M. (1989), "Friedrich August von Hayek," in Eatwell, et al. (1989).

Gellner, Ernest (1968) "Holism Versus Individualism," in May Brodbeck (ed.) *Readings in the Philosophy of the Social Sciences*, New York: Macmillan.

Gordon, David (1993) *The Philosophical Origins of Austrian Economics*, Auburn, Ala.: Ludwig von Mises Institute.

Gordon, David (1997) "Between Freedom and Socialism" (review of Sanford Ikeda's *Dynamics of the Mixed Economy*) *Mises Review* 3 (4): 1–5.

Grassl, Wolfgang and Smith, Barry (eds.) (1986) *Austrian Economics. Historical and Philosophical Background*, New York: New York University Press.

Hamowy, Ronald (1987) *The Scottish Enlightenment and the Theory of Spontaneous Order*, Carbondale, Ill.: Southern Illinois University Press.

Hayek, F.A. (1933) "The Trend of Economic Thinking," *Economica* 13 (May): 121–37.

Hayek, F.A. (1948) *Individualism and Economic Order*, Chicago: University of Chicago Press.

Hayek, F.A. (1952) "A Rebirth of Liberalism," *The Freeman* 2 (22) (July 28).

Hayek, F.A. (1954) (ed.) *Capitalism and the Historians*, Chicago: University of Chicago Press.

Hayek, F.A. (1955) *The Counter-Revolution of Science*, Glencoe, Ill.: Free Press.

Hayek, F.A. (1960) *The Constitution of Liberty*. Chicago: University of Chicago Press.

Hayek, F.A. (1967) *Studies in Philosophy, Politics, and Economics*, Chicago: University of Chicago Press.

Hayek, F.A. (1968) "Economic Thought: The Austrian School," *International Encyclopedia of the Social Sciences*, David Sills (ed.) 4, New York: Macmillan and the Free Press.

Hayek, F.A. (1973) "The Place of Menger's *Grundsätze* in the History of Economic Thought," in Hicks and Weber.

Hayek, F.A. (1978) *New Studies in Philosophy, Economics, and the History of Ideas*, London: Routledge & Kegan Paul.

Hayek, F.A. (1983) *Knowledge, Evolution, and Society*, London: Adam Smith Institute.

Hayek, F.A. (1988) *The Fatal Conceit. The Errors of Socialism*, W.W. Bartley III (ed.) *The Collected Works of F. A. Hayek*, 1, Chicago: University of Chicago Press.

Hayek, F.A. (1992) *The Fortunes of Liberalism. Essays on Austrian Economics and the Ideal of Freedom*. Peter Klein (ed.) *The Collected Works of F.A. Hayek*, 4, Chicago: University of Chicago Press.

Hayek, F.A. (1994a [1944]) *The Road to Serfdom*, "Preface to the 1976 Reprint," 50th Anniversary ed., Chicago: University of Chicago Press.

Hayek, F.A. (1994b) *Hayek on Hayek. An Autobiographical Dialogue*, Stephen Kresge and Leif Wenar (eds.), Chicago: University of Chicago Press.

Hayek, F.A. (1995) *Contra Keynes and Cambridge. Essays, Correspondence*, Bruce Caldwell (ed.) *The Collected Works of F.A. Hayek*, 9, Chicago: University of Chicago Press.

Hennings, Klaus and Warren J. Samuels, (1990) *Neoclassical Economic Theory, 1870 to 1930*, Boston: Kluwer.

Herbener, Jeffrey M. (1999) "Frank A. Fetter: A Forgotten Giant," in Holcombe (ed.)

Hicks, J. R. and Weber, W. (eds.) (1973), *Carl Menger and the Austrian School of Economics*, Oxford: Clarendon.

Holcombe, Randall G. (ed.) *15 Great Austrian Economists*, Auburn, Ala.: Ludwig von Mises Institute.

Hoppe, Hans-Hermann (1987) *Eigentum, Anarchie und Staat: Studien zur Theorie des Kapitalismus*, Opladen: Westdeutscher Verlag.

Hoppe, Hans-Hermann (1993) "Einführung: Ludwig von Mises und der Liberalismus," in Mises: 7–38.

Hoppe, Hans-Hermann (1994) "F.A. Hayek on Government and Social Evolution: A Critique," *Review of Austrian Economics* 7 (1): 67–93.

Hoppe, Hans-Hermann (1995) *Economic Science and the Austrian Method*, Auburn, Ala.: Ludwig von Mises Institute.

Hoppe, Hans-Hermann (1999) "Economics, Science, and Liberty," in Holcombe (ed.)

Hoppe, Hans-Hermann and Joseph T. Salerno (1999) "Friedrich von Wieser und die moderne Österreichische Schule der Nationalökonomie," in Herbert Hax (ed.) *Vademecum zu einem Klassiker der österreichischen Schule*, Düsseldorf: Verlag Wirtschaft und Finanzen.

Huerta de Soto, Jesús (1998) "The Ongoing *Methodenstreit* of the Austrian School," *Journal des Économistes et des Études Humaines* 8 (1) (March).

Huerta de Soto, Jesús (1999) "Juan de Mariana: The Influence of the Spanish Scholastics," in Holcombe (ed.)

Hülsmann, Jörg Guido (2001) "Garrisonian Macroeconomics," in *Quarterly Journal of Austrian Economics*.

Humboldt, Wilhelm von (1969 [1854]) *The Limits of State Action*, J.W. Burrow (ed.), J.C. Coulthard and J.W. Burrow (trs.), Cambridge, Eng.: Cambridge University Press.

Hutchison, T.W. (1972) "The 'Marginal Revolution' and the Decline and Fall of English Classical Economics," *History of Political Economy* 4 (2) (Fall): 442–68.

Hutchison, T.W. (1981) *The Politics and Philosophy of Economics. Marxians, Keynesians and Austrians*, New York: New York University Press.

Hutchison, T.W. (1994) *The Uses and Abuses of Economics: Contentious Essays on History and Method*, London: Routledge.

Ikeda, Sanford (1997) *Dynamics of the Mixed Economy: Towards a Theory of Interventionism*, London: Routledge.

Infantino, Lorenzo (1998) *Individualism in Modern Thought: From Adam Smith to Hayek*, London: Routledge.

Jaffé, William (1976) "Menger, Jevons and Walras De-Homogenized," *Economic Inquiry* 14 (4) (December): 511–24.

Kauder, Emil (1957) "Intellectual and Political Roots of the Older Austrian School," *Zeitschrift für Nationalökonomie* 17 (4) (December): 411–25.

Kauder, Emil (1965) *A History of Marginal Utility Theory*, Princeton, N.J.: Princeton University Press.

Keizer, Willem (1994) "Hayek's Critique of Socialism," in Birner and van Zijp.

Kirzner, Israel M. (1973) *Competition and Entrepreneurship*, Chicago: University of Chicago Press.

Kirzner, Israel M. (1976a) "Philosophical and Ethical Implications of Austrian Economics," in Dolan 1976a.

Kirzner, Israel M. (1976b) "Ludwig von Mises and the Theory of Capital and Interest," in Laurence S. Moss (ed.) *The Economics of Ludwig von Mises*, Kansas City: Sheed and Ward.

Kirzner, Israel M. (1987) "Austrian School of Economics," in John Eatwell, et al. (eds.), 1.

Kirzner, Israel M. (1990) "Menger, Classical Liberalism, and the Austrian School of Economics," in Caldwell 1990.

Kirzner, Israel M. (1992a) "Human Action, Freedom, and Economic Science," in John Robbins and Mark Spangler (eds.) *The Man of Principle: Essays in Honor of Hans Sennholz*, Irvington, N.Y.: Foundation for Economic Education.

Kirzner, Israel M. (1992b) "Austrian Economics and the Doctrine of *Wertfreiheit*. Paper presented to the Austrian Graduate Economics Colloquium of New York University.

Kirzner, Israel M. (1992c) *The Meaning of Market Process: Essays in the Development of Austrian Economics*, London: Routledge.

Kirzner, Israel M. (1994) (ed.) *Classics in Austrian Economics: A Sampling in the History of a Tradition*, 1, *The Founding Era*; 2, *The Interwar Period*; 3, *The Age of Mises and Hayek*, London: William Pickering.

Klein, Peter G. (1999) "F.A. Hayek: Austrian Economist and Social Theorist," in Holcombe (ed.).

Krohn, Claus-Dieter (1981) *Wirtschaftstheorien als politische Interessen. Die akademische Nationalökonomie in Deutschland 1918–1933*, Frankfurt: Campus Verlag.

Lachmann, Ludwig (1973) *Macro-Economic Thinking*, Menlo Park, Cal.: Institute for Humane Studies.

Lachmann, Ludwig (1978) *Capital, Expectations, and the Market Process: Essays on the Theory of the Market Economy*, Kansas City: Sheed and Ward.

Lavoie, Don (1985) *Rivalry and Central Planning. The Socialist Calculation Debate Reconsidered*, Cambridge, Mass.: Cambridge University Press.

Lemieux, Pierre (1988) *L'anarcho-capitalisme*, Paris: Presses Universitaires de France.

Leser, Norbert (1986) (ed.) *Die Wiener Schule der Nationalökonomie*, Vienna: Hermann Böhlaus Nachf.

Machlup, Fritz (1981) "Ludwig von Mises: The Academic Scholar Who Would Not Compromise," *Wirtschaftspolitische Blätter* 28 (4): 6–14.

März, Eduard (1991) *Joseph Schumpeter. Scholar, Teacher and Politician*, New Haven, Conn.: Yale University Press.

Matis, Herbert (1974) "Sozioökonomische Aspekte des Liberalismus in Österreich 1848–1918," in Hans-Ulrich Wehler (ed.) *Sozialgeschichte Heute. Festschrift für Hans Rosenberg zum 70. Geburtstag*, Göttingen: Vandenhoeck and Ruprecht.

Mayer, Hans (1929) "Friedrich Freiherr von Wieser," *Neue Österreichische Biographie 1815–1918*, Part 1, 6, Vienna: Amalthea.

Meek, Ronald L. (1972) "Marginalism and Marxism," *History of Political Economy* 4 (2) Fall, 499–511.

Meier-Rust, Katrin (1993) *Alexander Rüstow. Geschichtsdeutung und liberales Engagement*, Stuttgart: Klett-Cotta.

Menger, Carl (1935) *The Collected Works of Carl Menger*, 3 *Kleinere Schriften zur Methode und Geschichte der Volkswirtschaftslehre*, London: London School of Economics.

Menger, Carl (1935a [1906]) "John Stuart Mill," in Menger 1935.

Menger, Carl (1935b [1891]) "Die Social-Theorien der classischen National-Oekonomie und die moderne Wirthschaftspolitik, in Menger 1935.

Menger, Carl (1935c [1884]) *Die Irrthümer des Historismus in der deutschen Nationalökonomie*, in Menger 1935.

Menger, Carl (1981 [1871]) *Principles of Economics*, James Dingwall and Bert F. Hoselitz (trs.), New York: New York University Press.

Menger, Carl (1985 [1883]) *Investigations into the Method of the Social Sciences with Special Reference to Economics*, Louis Schneider (ed.), Francis J. Nock (tr.), New York: New York University Press.

Menger, Carl (1994) *Lectures to Crown Prince Rudolf of Austria*, Erich W. Streissler and Monika Streissler (eds.), Monika Streissler (tr.), with the assistance of David F. Good, Aldershot, Eng.: Edward Elgar.

Mill, John Stuart (1977) *Collected Works*, 18, *Essays on Politics and Society*, J.M. Robson (ed.).

Mises, Ludwig von (1933) *Grundprobleme der Nationalökonomie*, Jena: Gustav Fischer.

Mises, Ludwig von (1944) *Omnipotent Government*, New Haven, Conn.: Yale University Press.

Mises, Ludwig von (1949) *Human Action: A Treatise on Economics*, New Haven: Yale University Press.

Mises, Ludwig von (1957) *Theory and History*, New Haven, Conn.: Yale University Press.

Mises, Ludwig von (1969) *The Historical Setting of the Austrian School of Economics*, New Rochelle, N.Y.: Arlington House.

Mises, Ludwig von (1977 [1929]) *A Critique of Interventionism*, Hans F. Sennholz (tr.), New Rochelle, N. Y.: Arlington House.

Mises, Ludwig von (1978a [1927]) *Liberalism: A Socio-Economic Exposition*, Ralph Raico (tr.), Kansas City: Sheed, Andrews, and McMeel.

Mises, Ludwig von (1978b) *Notes and Recollections*, Hans F. Sennholz (tr.), South Holland, Ill.: Libertarian Press.

Mises, Ludwig von (1981 [1922]) *Socialism. An Economic and Sociological Analysis*, J. Kahane (tr.), F.A. Hayek (intr.), Indianapolis: Liberty Press.

Mises, Ludwig von (1990 [1961]) "On Equality and Inequality," in idem, *Money, Method and the Market Process: Essays by Ludwig von Mises*, Richard M. Ebeling (ed.), Normwell, Mass.: Kluwer Academic Publishers.

Mises, Ludwig von (1993 [1927]) *Liberalismus*. Hans-Hermann Hoppe (intr.), Sankt Augustin.: Academia Verlag.

Mises, Ludwig von and Arthur Spiethoff (1933) (eds.) *Probleme der Wertlehre*, Part II, Munich/Leipzig: Duncker and Humblot.

Morgenstern, Oscar (1927) "Friedrich von Wieser, 1851–1926," *American Economic Review* 17 (1) (March): 668–74.

Nyiri, J.C. (1986) "Intellectual Foundations of Austrian Liberalism," in Grassl and Smith (eds.)

O'Driscoll, Gerald P. (1986) "Money: Menger's Evolutionary Theory," *History of Political Economy*, 18 (4): 601–16.

Parker, Harold T. (1965 [1937]) *The Cult of Antiquity and the French Revolutionaries: A Study in the Development of the Revolutionary Spirit*, New York: Octagon.

Pearson, Heath (1997) *Origins of Law and Economics: The Economists' New Science of Law, 1830–1930*, Cambridge, Eng.: Cambridge University Press.

Plant, Raymond (1994) "Hayek on Social Justice: A Critique," in Birner and van Zijp (eds.).

Popper, Karl R. (1950) *The Open Society and Its Enemies*, Princeton, N.J.: Princeton University Press.

Popper, Karl R. (1962) *Conjectures and Refutations: The Growth of Scientific Knowledge*, New York: Basic Books.

Popper, Karl R. (1984) "The Frankfurt School: An Autobiographical Note," in Judith Marcus and Zoltán Tar (eds.) *Foundations of the Frankfurt School of Social Research*, New Brunswick, N.J.: Transaction.

Popper, Karl R. (1992) "The Communist Road to Self-Enslavement," *Cato Policy Report* 14 (3) (May/June) 1: 10–12.

Popper, Karl R. (1997) "Tribute to the Life and Work of Friedrich Hayek," in Stephen F. Frowen (ed.) *Hayek: Economist and Social Philosopher: A Critical Retrospect*, New York: St. Martin's.

Radnitzky, Gerard (1995) *Karl R. Popper*, Sankt Augustin: Friedrich-Naumann Stiftung.

Raico, Ralph (1992) "Prolegomena to a History of Liberalism," *Journal des Économistes et des Études Humaines* 3 (2/3): 259–72.

Raico, Ralph (1994) "Classical Liberalism and Austrian Economics," in Boettke (ed.).

Raico, Ralph (1996) "Mises on Fascism, Democracy, and Other Questions," *Journal of Libertarian Studies* 12 (1) (Spring): 1–27.

Reekie, W. Duncan (1984) *Markets, Entrepreneurs and Liberty: An Austrian View of Capitalism*, London: Wheatsheaf.

Robbins, Lionel (1953) *The Theory of Economic Policy in English Classical Political Economy*, London: Macmillan.

Robinson, Joan (1962) *Economic Philosophy*, Chicago: Aldine.

Roll, Erich (1945) "*The Road To Serfdom*" (review), *American Economic Review* 35: 176–80.

Rosen, Sherwin (1997) "Austrian and Neoclassical Economics: Any Gains from Trade?" *Journal of Economic Perspectives* 11 (4) (Fall): 139–52.

Rosenberg, Nathan and L.E. Birdzell, Jr. (1986) *How the West Grew Rich. The Economic Transformation of the Industrial World*, New York: Basic Books.

Ross, Dorothy 1991. *The Origins of American Social Science*. Cambridge, Eng.: Cambridge University Press.

Rothbard, Murray N. (1962) *Man, Economy, and State*, 2 vols. Princeton, N.J.: Van Nostrand.

Rothbard, Murray N. (1963) *America's Great Depression*. Princeton, N.J.: Van Nostrand.

Rothbard, Murray N. (1970) *Power and Market. Government and the Economy*, Menlo Park, Cal.: Institute for Humane Studies.

Rothbard, Murray N. (1972) "War Collectivism in World War I," in Ronald Radosh and Murray N. Rothbard (eds.), *A New History of Leviathan*. New York: E. P. Dutton.

Rothbard, Murray N. (1973a) *For a New Liberty*. New York: Macmillan.

Rothbard, Murray N. (1973b) "Egalitarianism as a Revolt against Nature," *Modern Age* 17 (4) (Fall): 348–57.

Rothbard, Murray N. (1976a) "New Light on the Prehistory of the Austrian School," in Dolan 1976a.

Rothbard, Murray N. (1976b) "Praxeology, Value Judgments, and Public Policy," in Dolan 1976a.

Rothbard, Murray N. (1978) "The Foreign Policy of the Old Right," *Journal of Libertarian Studies* 2 (1) (Winter): 85–96.

Rothbard, Murray N. (1979) *Individualism and the Philosophy of the Social Sciences*. San Francisco: Cato Institute.

Rothbard, Murray N. (1981) "The Laissez-Faire Radical: A Quest for the Historical Mises," *Journal of Libertarian Studies* 5 (3) (Summer): 237–53.

Rothbard, Murray N. (1982) *The Ethics of Liberty*, Atlantic Highlands, N.J.: Humanities Press.

Rothbard, Murray N. (1988) *Ludwig von Mises: Scholar, Creator, Hero*, Auburn, Ala.: Ludwig von Mises Institute.

Rothbard. Murray N. (1995a) *Making Economic Sense*, Auburn, Ala.: Ludwig von Mises Institute.

Rothbard, Murray N. (1995b) *Wall Street, Banks, and American Foreign Policy*, Burlingame, Cal.: Center for Libertarian Studies.

Rothbard, Murray N. (1995c) *An Austrian Perspective on the History of Economic Thought*, 2 vols., Aldershot, Eng.: Edward Elgar.

Rothbard, Murray N. (1997) *The Logic of Action*, 2 vols., Cheltenham, Eng.: Edward Elgar.

Rothbard, Murray N. (2002) *A History of Money and Banking in the United States: The Colonial Era to World War II*, Joseph T. Salerno (ed.), Auburn, Ala.: Ludwig von Mises Institute.

Rousseau, Jean-Jacques (1962 [1782]) "Considérations sur le gouvernement de Pologne," in idem, *The Political Writings*, C.E. Vaughan (ed.), 2, New York: John Wiley.

Rousseau, Jean-Jacques (1968 [1762]) *The Social Contract*, Maurice Cranston (tr.), Harmondsworth, Eng.: Penguin.

Salerno, Joseph T. (1990) "Ludwig von Mises as Social Rationalist," *Review of Austrian Economics*, 4: 26–54.

Salerno, Joseph T. (1993) "Mises and Hayek Dehomogenized," *Review of Austrian Economics* 6 (2), 113–46.

Salerno, Joseph T. (1999) "Carl Menger: The Founding of the Austrian School," in Holcombe (ed.).

Schmoller, Gustav (1883) "Zur Methodologie der Staats- und Sozial-Wissenschaften," *Schmollers Jahrbuch* 7 (3): 240–58.

Shand, Alexander H. (1984) *The Capitalist Alternative: An Introduction to Neo-Austrian Economics*, New York: New York University Press.

Shand, Alexander H. (1990) *Free Market Morality. The Political Economy of the Austrian School*, London: Routledge.

Shearmur, Jeremy (1996) *The Political Thought of Karl Popper*, London: Routledge.

Shearmur, Jeremy (1997) "Hayek, Keynes and the State," *History of Economics Review* 26 (Winter/Summer): 68–82.

Silverman, Paul (1990) "The Cameralist Roots of Menger's Achievement," in Caldwell (ed.).

Smith, Barry (1986) "Austrian Economics and Austrian Philosophy," in Grassl and Smith (eds.).

Smith, Barry (1994a) *Austrian Philosophy: The Legacy of Franz Brentano*, Chicago/Lasalle, Ill.: Open Court.

Smith, Barry (1994b) "Aristotelianism, Apriorism, Essentialism," in Boettke (ed.).

Smith, Barry (1994c) Review of David Gordon, *The Philosophical Origins of Austrian Economics*, *Review of Austrian Economics* 7 (2): 127–32.

Smith, Barry (1996) "In Defense of Extreme (Fallibilistic) Apriorism," *Journal of Libertarian Studies* 12 (1) (Spring): 179–92.

Steele, David Ramsey (1992) *From Marx to Mises. Post-Capitalist Society and the Challenge of Economic Calculation*, La Salle, Ill.: Open Court.

Streissler, Erich (1986) "Arma virumque cano. Friedrich von Wieser, The Bard as Economist," in Leser, 1986.

Streissler, Erich (1987) *Wie Liberal waren die Begründer der österreichischen Schule der Nationalökonomie?* Vienna: Carl Menger Institute.

Streissler, Erich (1988) "The Intellectual and Political Impact of the Austrian School of Economics," *History of European Ideas*, 9 (2): 191–204.

Streissler, Erich (1990a) "The Influence of German Economics on the Work of Menger and Marshall," in Caldwell (ed.).

Streissler, Erich (1990b) "Carl Menger on Economic Policy: The Lectures to Crown Prince Rudolf," in Caldwell (ed.).

Streissler, Erich (1990c) "Menger, Böhm-Bawerk, and Wieser: The Origins of the Austrian School, in Hennings and Samuels (eds.).

Streissler, Erich (1994), "Menger's Treatment of Economics in the Rudolf Lectures," introduction to Menger (1994).

Streissler, Erich and W. Weber (1973) "The Menger Tradition," in Hicks and Weber, 1973.

Taylor, Miles (1997) "The Beginnings of Modern British Social History?" *History Workshop Journal*, No. 43: 155–76.

Vaughn, Karen I. (1987) "Invisible Hand," in Eatwell, et al.

Vaughn, Karen I. (1994) *Austrian Economics in America: The Migration of a Tradition*, Cambridge, Mass.: Cambridge University Press.

Vleugels, Wilhelm (1935) "Die Kritik am wirtschaftlichen Liberalismus in der Entwicklung der deutschen Volkswirtschaftslehre," *Schmollers Jahrbuch* 59 (5): 513–52.

Vleugels, Wilhelm (1937) "Über Leistung, Schwächen und tatsächliche Bedeutung der deutschen (österreichischen) Nutzwertlehre," *Schmollers Jahrbuch* 61 (1. Halbband): 19–50.

Weber, Wilhelm (1949) "Wirtschaftswissenschaft und Wirtschaftspolitik in Österreich 1848 bis 1948," in Hans Mayer (ed.) *Hundert Jahre österreichischer Wirtschaftsentwicklung*, Vienna: Springer.

White, Lawrence H. (1984) *The Methodology of the Austrian School Economists*, Auburn, Ala.: Ludwig von Mises Institute.

White, Lawrence H. (1990) "Restoring an 'Altered' Menger," in Caldwell (ed.).

Wieser, Friedrich von (1923) "Karl Menger," *Neue Österreichische Biographie, 1815–1918*, Vienna: Wiener Drucke.

Wieser, Friedrich von (1983 [1926]) *The Law of Power: Das Gesetz der Macht, 1926*, Warren J. Samuels (ed.), W.E. Kuhn (tr.), Lincoln, Neb.: Bureau of Business Research, University of Nebraska.

Yeager, Leland B. (1995) "Why Subjectivism?" in Kurt R. Leube (ed.) *Die Österreichische Schule der Nationalökonomie, 2 Von Hayek bis White*, Vienna: Manzsche Verlag.

Yeager, Leland B. (1997) "Austrian Economics, Neoclassicism, and the Market Test," *Journal of Economic Perspective* 11 (4) (Fall): 153–65.

Zlabinger, Albert H. (1994) *Ludwig von Mises*, Königswinter: Friedrich Naumann Stiftung.

2 Liberalism: True and False

Introduction

In past decades, an immense amount of scholarly effort was devoted to the history of socialism, especially in its Marxist versions. Even the minutiae of socialist doctrine and agitation were examined, over and over again, in mind-numbing detail, and particular branches of the field, like "Marxist humanism," became minor academic industries. Such an imbalance in the allocation of scholarly resources would not perhaps have been irrational if one accepted the view—widespread among intellectuals of the time—that socialism was the predestined "radiant future of all mankind."

More recently, a change of focus has become evident. With the frustration of the traditional socialist project in the West and the failure and then collapse of "real existing" socialist regimes, it seems to have dawned on the scholarly world that more attention should be paid to the ideological foundations of our own civilization. Thus, liberalism—which Pierre Manent (1984: 9) rightly calls "the *basso continuo* of modern politics, of the politics of Europe and the West for about the past three centuries"—has increasingly become the subject of study, though still to a relatively modest degree, considering its intrinsic importance.

As yet no serious effort has been made to provide an overall account of the history of liberalism comparable to the highly praised, and deeply flawed, work of Guido de Ruggiero (1981), which, in any case, was limited to Europe, or, rather, to Britain, France, Germany, and Italy.[1] Such an account is very much needed and will doubtless be someday essayed. The remarks that follow may be regarded as prolegomena to such a general treatment of liberalism. They also represent an effort to advance the cause of theoretical coherence in an area of intellectual history that is increasingly recognized as vital.

Conceptual Mayhem

Understandably enough, the current disfavor into which socialism has fallen has spurred what Raimondo Cubeddu (1997: 138) refers to as "the frenzy to proclaim oneself a liberal." Many writers today have recourse to the stratagem of "inventing for oneself a 'liberalism' according to one's own tastes" and passing it off as an "evolution" from past ideas. "The superabundance of liberalisms," Cubeddu warns, "like that of money, ends up by debasing everything and emptying everything of meaning."[2]

In truth, a survey of the literature on liberalism reveals a condition of conceptual mayhem. One root cause of this is the frequent attempt to accommodate all important political groupings that have *called* themselves "liberal." This is an approach favored by some British scholars in particular, in whose conception of liberalism the doings and sayings of the British Liberal Party of the twentieth century weigh mightily (e.g., Eccleshall 1986; Vincent 1988).

There is no doubt that after around 1900 the Liberal Party in Britain veered increasingly in a statist direction. In the United States a similar transformation took place within the Democratic Party—once

---

[1] The original Italian edition dates from 1925. F.A. Hayek, with his characteristic generosity towards those outside the authentic liberal camp, refers (1954: 11) to "Ruggiero's justly esteemed" work, although he cites it in order to criticize the author's antiquated, ultra-pessimistic account of the industrial revolution.

[2] In a move characteristic of too many writers, Conrad Waligorski 1981: 2 eschews any "rigid and dogmatic [i.e., clear and consistent] definition of liberalism, because it would itself be illiberal."

"the party of Jefferson and Jackson"—at a somewhat later date. But such shifts, evident also in Continental parties that kept the liberal name, are easily explained by the dynamics of democratic electoral politics.

Faced with the competition of collectivist ideas, liberal parties produced a new breed of "political entrepreneurs," men skilled at mobilizing "rent-seeking" constituencies, i.e., those who use the state to enhance their economic position. In order to gain power, these leaders revised the liberal program to the point where it was "practically indistinguishable from democratic and social-reformist ideas, ending up by accepting the notion of the state as an instrument for redesigning society to produce particular ends." (Cubeddu 1997: 26)[3]

If one holds that the meaning of liberal must be modified because of ideological shifts within the British Liberal Party (or the Democratic Party in the United States), then due consideration must also be given to the National Liberals of Imperial Germany. They—as well as David Lloyd George and John Maynard Keynes—would have a claim to be situated in the same ideological category as, say, Richard Cobden, John Bright, and Herbert Spencer. Yet the National Liberals supported, among other measures: the *Kulturkampf* against the Catholic Church and the anti-socialist laws; Bismarck's abandonment of free trade and his introduction of the welfare state; the forcible Germanization of the Poles; colonial expansion and *Weltpolitik*; and the military and especially naval buildup under Wilhelm II (Klein-Hattingen 1912; Raico 1999: 86–151, and *passim*). Actually, if one simply went by party labels, the National Liberals would have *more* of a right to the title *liberal* than the authentically liberal German Progressives and *Freisinn*, whom they opposed, and the question of whether the National Liberals betrayed genuine liberalism in Germany could not even be raised.

A similar difficulty is presented by the case of Friedrich Naumann, regarded by many nowadays as the exemplary German liberal leader of the early twentieth century. Naumann's views paralleled those of the National Liberals in their later phase. He was a social imperialist par

---

3 As Ralf Dahrendorf cogently remarks, 1987: 174: "Liberal parties declined to the point of insignificance, unless they merely kept the name and changed their policies out of recognition, either in the direction of social democracy (Canada) or in that of conservatism (Australia)."

excellence, distinguishing himself by the frenzy of his campaign for colonies, a mighty navy, and the coming, yearned for war with England, until the emerging "constellation of forces"—i.e., the formation of the powerful Triple Entente of Britain, Russia, and France—revealed the fateful error of his cherished Weltpolitik (Raico 1999: 219–61; see also the essay on "Eugen Richter and the End of German Liberalism" in the present volume).[4] Must the definition and understanding of liberalism be stretched to include this "exemplary German liberal"? What, aside from standard Anglo-American intellectual parochialism, would stand in the way?

It is evident that mere self-description by politicians or political intellectuals cannot be decisive on this issue (Vierhaus 1982: 742). That Hitler *called* himself a kind of socialist, a National Socialist, creates no presumption that he must somehow be fitted into a history of socialism.[5]

A few authors have despaired of finding any common characteristics underlying the "liberalisms" of different national groups or even individual decades of modern history, though they continue to write as if there was *something* linking them (e.g., Wadl 1987: 13).[6] Most commentators, however, have attempted some demarcation of the concept, often through a listing of traits or of model figures.

In *The Liberal Imagination*, the New York literary critic Lionel Trilling characterized liberalism as, among other things, "a belief in

---

4 The case is similar with another highly regarded German "liberal," Walther Rathenau. See Raico 1999: 43–44.

5 However, certain of the views and policies Hitler espoused on state direction of the economy and the expansion of the welfare state suggest that he, as well as his model, Karl Lueger, may well have to be conceded a place in the history of at least of social welfarism. See Zittelmann 1990: 116ff., 145, 470, 489ff.

6 Similarly, Lothar Döhn 1977: 11, who claims that "all attempts at a universal, comprehensive conceptual determination of what liberalism is have failed," and then blithely goes on to speak of "non-liberal or anti-liberal elements" in theories and parties commonly considered liberal. Stuurman 1994: 32 asserts that liberalism is merely a "historical invention"; it possessed no coherent philosophy until after the revolutions of 1848, when it "appeared as a unified whole, a well-defined 'historical individual.'" Yet it is a fact that there were theoretical and political differences among thinkers usually considered to be liberals both before and after 1848, between, for instance, Jeremy Bentham and Benjamin Constant and John Stuart Mill and Herbert Spencer.

planning and international cooperation, especially where [Soviet] Russia is in question" (cited in Cranston 1967a: 460). Somewhat more plausibly, John Gray views liberalism as individualist, egalitarian, universalist, and meliorist, and goes on to distinguish equally valid "separate branches of a common [liberal] lineage" (1986: x–xi). Two libertarian philosophers, Douglas J. Den Uyl and Stuart D. Warner, maintain that the essential traits are liberty, the rule of law, representative government, and faith in progress (1987: 271). Gray and Den Uyl and Warner also furnish lists of "clear-cut," "unquestionable" liberals, which include, besides Locke, Kant, Herbert Spencer, and F.A. Hayek, thinkers like Keynes, Karl Popper, and John Rawls.

Yet such rosters leave the concept of liberalism so impoverished as to be useless. Canvassing the views of, say, Kant, Spencer, Popper, and Rawls yields no consensus on crucial issues, for instance, the welfare state or democracy (Ryan 1993: 291). It is highly significant that an unambiguous belief in private property is absent from both Gray's and Den Uyl and Warner's enumeration of essential traits.[7]

Private property, in fact, is and has always been the chief bone of contention in the debate. In recent years, with the emergence of a revitalized movement stressing property and the free market, a number of commentators have experienced acute embarrassment. While they feel they must take notice of this movement and occasionally concede that it may be a form of liberalism, they insist at the same time that it is *conservative*.[8]

---

7 When J. Salwyn Schapiro 1958: 88–90 came to catalogue liberalism's "lasting values," he included neither private property nor free trade. It is remarkable how even today many writers omit any discussion of private property in characterizing the doctrine. Here is an ideology that has shaped world history, but which, it seems, had nothing in particular to say about the conditions under which human beings work, survive, invest, and occasionally prosper.

8 Cf. Brunner 1987: 25–26, who persuasively argues that the standard treatment of the terms "liberal" and "conservative" in America "is almost an exercise in disinformation. The characteristic features of alternative visions of a desirable society are more usefully approached in terms of social and political institutions including, most particularly, the prevailing pattern of property rights." Brunner distinguishes among socialist, social democratic, liberal, and conservative positions. "The social democrat conception centers essentially on an extended and encompassing welfare state. . . . Private property rights, even in means of production, still remain. But these rights are typically restricted in various dimensions." The liberal conception "differs fundamentally from the other three positions by a severe constitutional limitation

Helio Jaguaribe, evidently a star of Brazilian political science, describes Hayek, Milton Friedman, and Ludwig von Mises (identified as the author of "the libel Socialism") as "extremely conservative" (1996: 31).[9] David Spitz likewise refers to the three thinkers as "conservatives," though what he could understand of their views is unclear, considering that he believes that Herbert Spencer was their "patron saint" (1982: 204, 206). A rather droll example of this definitional gambit is provided by the sociologist John A. Hall (1987: 37), who complains of "those modern conservative thinkers who confusingly [sic] call themselves liberals"—such as Milton Friedman.[10]

Nowhere is Max Weber's stricture more pertinent:

> The use of the undifferentiated collective concepts of everyday speech is always a cloak for confusion of thought and action. It is, indeed, very often an instrument of specious and fraudulent procedures. It is, in brief, always a means of obstructing the proper formulation of the problem. (Weber 1949: 110)

The result of ignoring Weber's warning is the terminological chaos acquiesced in by José Merquior (1991: 45–46):

---

on the range of admissible government activities. It also involves a much stricter constitutional anchoring of property rights."

9 Since Jaguaribe could hardly mean that these thinkers were deeply committed to the status quo and averse to radical change, the conclusion must be that in his view this movement is extremely conservative (and to that degree non-liberal) because it rejects the presumed goal of modern history, the universal welfare state.

10 Hall's blunder in stating Friedman's position deserves to be mentioned, as it is typical of the slovenliness of many writers when dealing with the ideas of free-market scholars. According to Hall, Friedman holds "that freedom and capitalism always go in tandem." But, as Friedman explicitly states in the work cited by Hall (Friedman 1962: 10): "History suggests only that capitalism is a necessary condition for political freedom. Clearly it is not a sufficient condition. . . . It is therefore clearly possible to have economic arrangements that are fundamentally capitalist and political arrangements that are not free." Gertrude Himmelfarb 1990: 324n concedes that in calling themselves the genuine liberals Friedman and Hayek are "more consistent" than their opponents who label these thinkers conservatives. She nonetheless holds that "the current usage must be respected as a reflection of the social reality." But what if the current usage is the product of a political strategy and itself produces conceptual incoherence? What is the "social reality" underlying this deceptive usage?

the meaning of liberalism changed a great deal. Nowadays what *liberal* generally means in continental Europe and Latin America is something quite different from what it means in the United States. Since Roosevelt's New Deal, American liberalism has acquired . . ." a social democratic tinge." Liberalism in the United States came close to liberal socialism …

To add to his muddle, Merquior suggests that the recent spread of free-market ideas signals yet *another* shift in the American meaning of liberal:

On the other hand, the meaning of liberalism in its current revival, both in the United States and elsewhere, has only a tenuous connection with the **mainstream U.S. meaning, and often even marks a departure from it.**[11]

One writer deserves special mention for his strategic boldness. Michael Freeden seeks to exclude belief in private property altogether from the contemporary meaning of liberalism. According to Freeden (1996: 19, 24, 35), private property was "previously a core liberal concept," but since the nineteenth century it has been "steadily gravitating to a more marginal position. . . . Property continued its migratory path from liberal center to periphery . . . the concept of property was released to gravitate towards a concept of need which supported the notion of universal individual welfare." Contemporary libertarians, whom some

---

11 Even in a literature so rich in stupified confusion, Merquior's contribution stands out. He denounces "minimal-state fanatics" who "do not hesitate to demand the dismantling of the welfare state, the adoption of private armies, even the use of private currencies." Note the inclusion among advocates of the minimal-state of the supporters of private armies (usually termed anarchists or anarcho-capitalists, a category that logically excludes believers in the minimal state), and also the implication that all these positions are self-evidently ludicrous. Merquior further argues, allegedly following Norberto Bobbio, that because democracy "is a consequence or at least an extension of liberalism" and because the welfare state is the product of "well articulated popular demands in the political market," the welfare state is a product of liberalism. But that would mean that any policies generated by the democratic process and widely supported, from laws against victimless crimes to militarism and wars of imperialist conquest, must be regarded as part of the liberal doctrine. Regarding Merquior's view that Hayek did not view the market as "the best means for distributing resources," since "a computer could do that better" (1996: 11, 16–17), any comment would be superfluous.

other writers classify as liberals or neoliberals, "must be excluded from the family of liberalisms" because they "stray from the evolutionary path liberalism has taken. . . . In the struggle over the legitimacy of words, libertarianism has so far failed to become a serious contender for the modern liberal mantle."

There are a number of problems with Freeden's gravitational-migrational position. What, for instance, does he intend to do with the term "economic liberalism"? On his analysis, it will have to denote the philosophy underlying the leveling welfare state.[12] And what of cognate terms, such as "liberalization of the economy"? Presumably, that must be taken to mean, not dismantling of government controls, but instead something like extending welfare benefits. Moreover, in Freeden's understanding, liberalism in its contemporary mode has nothing to say about the basic structure of the economy, aside from the requirement that it be fitted to meet the growing needs of welfare recipients.[13]

Anthony Arblaster, author of *The Rise and Decline of Western Liberalism* (1984)[14] has reassessed his earlier work with refreshing sincerity and candor. In the process, he reveals the mind-set of writers like Freeden as they "struggle" to impose their own meaning on the contested term. Confessing that he was mistaken in allotting only a few pages to "liberal political economy," Arblaster writes, regarding the views of Hayek and associated thinkers,

---

12 This was the recourse chosen by L.T. Hobhouse (1964: 88–109; see also Greenleaf 1983: 162–68), who includes under "economic liberalism": state ownership of land and ownership and operation of public utilities and key industries; high graduated income taxes and expropriation of "the social factor" in wealth creation; a "living wage" and extensive social security programs for all; and implementation of "the equation of social service and reward." Hobhouse gives no indication why this should be regarded as economic liberalism. Evidently it was sufficient that these policies were either being enacted by the British Liberal Party of his time or aimed at by its more radical wing. The program also provided a possible basis for the "Lib-Lab" political coalition Hobhouse favored.
13 Probably a minor consideration for Freeden is that his definition of liberalism does not translate. In French, for instance, *libéral* still means a believer in the free market economy, and *ultralibéral* a "doctrinaire" or "fanatical" believer in the free market, e.g., Frédéric Bastiat.
14 For a critique of his relentless attack on its subject by this interesting and provocative scholar see Raico 1989.

my account of the phenomenon was based on the only half-conscious assumption that "history" had rendered these ideas permanently obsolete, that their revival was almost an eccentricity, certainly a deviation from the main path of modern social and political development, which pointed steadily in the direction of the growth of state intervention in the economy, and of state responsibility for the welfare of its citizens.

Now our perspective must be "different and more somber." Contrasting "neo-liberal economic policies" with "the social democratic consensus," Arblaster holds that while the neoliberal project is "self-evidently reactionary," that "does not necessarily mean that it is not also a liberal one." He adds, reasonably enough: "Only if one adopts the North America [sic] equation of the term 'liberal' with 'progressive' or 'left-leaning' does that become impossible by definition" (Arblaster 1996: 165–66, 171).

Grappling with this issue causes even as accomplished a historian of ideas as Alan Ryan to flounder. Ryan (1993: 293–94, 296) concedes a place to Hayek within the category of contemporary liberals, but denies that *libertarianism* can be a variety of liberalism on the grounds that even classical liberals did not favor decriminalizing victimless crimes. But not only is this libertarian position clearly implied by, for example, Herbert Spencer's Law of Equal Freedom; it is also the stated view of Ludwig von Mises (1949: 728–29) and F.A. Hayek (1960: 451, n. 18).

To his credit, Ryan at least tries to differentiate "modern liberalism" from socialism. The former, he holds, "does not share the antipathies and hopes of a socialist defense of the welfare state . . . modern liberalism has no confiscatory ambitions" (295). But this attempt at a demarcation fails badly. The first part of Ryan's statement is hopelessly obscure, while the second underestimates both the degree to which social democrats have resignedly accepted the market economy as the indispensable milch cow for their welfare budgets and the greed of the "modern liberal" political class for the earnings of taxpayers.[15]

---

15 Cf. the remark of Paul Gottfried (2002: 26): "Restricted economic freedom can cohabit with an administrative state devoted to social experiments. Providing the capitalist goose is

The Role of John Stuart Mill

Much of the confusion prevailing in this field can be traced to John Stuart Mill, who occupies a vastly inflated position in the conception of liberalism entertained by English-speaking peoples.[16] This "saint of rationalism" is responsible for key distortions in the liberal doctrine on a number of fronts.[17] In economics, Mill opined that "the principle of individual liberty is not involved in the doctrine of free trade [economic liberalism]," provided ammunition for the protectionist arsenal, and accepted and even elaborated socialist arguments (Mill 1977: 293; Mises 1978a: 195; Raeder 2002: 357 n. 76 and 374 n. 23; and especially Rothbard 1995c 2: 277–85).[18]

Mill rejected the liberal notion of the long-run harmony of interests of all social classes, including entrepreneurs and workers, on the grounds that, "to say that they have same interest . . . is to say that it is the same thing to a person's interest whether a sum of money belongs to him or to someone else" (cited in Ashcraft 1989: 114). Following that odd and shortsighted reasoning would reveal a very large number of hitherto unsuspected conflicts of interest in society, e.g., between any two people who pass each other in the street. Indeed, in arguing that *anti*-capitalism is one of the hallmarks of liberalism, Alan Ryan (1993: 302) invokes none other than John Stuart Mill, who wrote (1965: 209): "The generality of laborers in this and most other countries have as little choice of occupation and freedom of locomotion . . . as they could . . .

---

not killed in the process, public administration can be both expansive and financially secure."
16 Elevating Mill to the status of model liberal thinker has also tended to reinforce the search for an underlying philosophical (in the narrower sense) basis in liberalism. This basis is often taken to include an empiricist epistemology and utilitarian ethics. But too many conflicting philosophical traditions—from Aristotelianism and Thomism to Kantianism and others—coexist within the history of liberalism for this to be credible. Cf. Bedeschi 1990: 1–2.
17 Mill's deviation from authentic liberalism comes out in his differences with Wilhelm von Humboldt, although according to Mill Humboldt was a major inspiration of *On Liberty*, which carries an epigraph from the latter's *Limits of State Action*. See Valls 1999, who, however, considers Mill the more realistic liberal.
18 Henry Sidgwick concluded that in the later editions of his *Principles* Mill was "completely Socialistic in his ideal of ultimate social improvement." Richard Cobden held that Mill's argument in favor of protection for "infant industries" "outweighed all the good which may have been caused by his other writings" (cited in Dicey 1963: 429 and n. 2).

on any system short of actual slavery"—this at a time when English and other "serfs" were migrating in the millions to the towns and cities and even to foreign lands.[19]

In international affairs, Mill repudiated the liberal principle of non-intervention in foreign wars, whose most trenchant exponent was Richard Cobden (1973). Where Cobden feared that such entanglements would undermine liberty at home, Mill provided interventionists with what has become a favorite argument: that a strong and free country like Britain has a moral obligation to come to the aid of peoples struggling for their freedom, if they are threatened by outside powers.[20] That such a standing policy of intervention would most likely compromise domestic freedom was not a problem that Mill, or those who have followed his lead, cared to address.

Worst of all was Mill's deformation of the concept of liberty itself. Liberty, it seems, is a condition that is threatened not only by physical aggression on the part of the state or other institutions or individuals. Rather, "society" often poses even graver dangers to individual freedom. This it achieves through "the tyranny of the prevailing opinion and feeling," the tendency "to impose, by other ways than civil penalties, its own ideas and practices as rules of conduct on those who dissent from them," to "compel all characters to fashion themselves upon the model of its own" (1977: 220). True liberty requires "autonomy," for

---

[19] Ryan slightly distorts Mill's statement by omitting the qualification "short of." As for Mill's mature views, a summary by a warm and famous sympathizer seems fair: "He came to look forward to a co-operative organization of society in which a man would learn to 'dig and weave for his country,' as he now is prepared to fight for it, and in which the surplus products of industry would be distributed among the producers. In middle life, voluntary co-operation appeared to him the best means to this end, but towards the close he recognized that his change of views was such as, on the whole, to rank him with the Socialists . . ." Hobhouse 1964: 62. One sees what Murray Rothbard had in mind in his heretical reference to Mill as "a woolly-minded man of mush" (1995c, 2: 277).

[20] David Manning 1976: 93 categorically asserts: "By the middle of the nineteenth century liberalism was as firmly committed to international support for national self-determination as it was to international free trade." Predictably, his evidence comes from Mill. Manning's assertion ignores the anti-interventionist Manchester School (and many others), whose influence on foreign policy thinking extended into the twentieth century.

adopting "the traditions or customs of other people" is simply to engage in "ape-like" imitation.[21]

Where others see men and women choosing goals laid out for them by institutions whose authority over them they freely accept, Mill perceives the extinction of freedom. In a striking and utterly preposterous illustration, the saint of rationalism writes: "An individual Jesuit is to the utmost degree of abasement a slave of his order" (1977: 308). One wonders what is supposed to follow from this. Must we form abolitionist associations to emancipate the willing "slaves" of the Society of Jesus? How should we go about selecting our John Brown to lead the storming of the slave-pits of Fordham and Georgetown universities? One also wonders by what right Mill and his alter ego Harriet Taylor could ever have imagined themselves entitled to legislate on the status of members of Catholic or Orthodox orders, of Orthodox Jews and devout Muslims, or of any other believers.[22]

His comment on the Jesuits illustrates a facet of Mill too rarely noticed: he was, in the words of Maurice Cowling, "one of the most censorious of nineteenth century moralists." He constantly passed judgment on the habits, attitudes, preferences, and moral standards of great numbers of people of whom he knew nothing. As Cowling dryly observes: "*Bigotry* and *prejudice* are not necessarily the best descriptions of opinions which Comtean determinism has stigmatized as outdated" (1963: 143–44, emphasis in original).

---

21 See Loren Lomasky's astute critique of the ideal of "autonomy," beloved of professional philosophers (1987: 42–45, 247–50), e.g.: "the advocacy of autonomy is typically accompanied by contempt for the actual. . . . One who is born to a particular family, nation, and religion is not thereby burdened with an anchor restricting his domain of choice but rather is the beneficiary of an inheritance of a manageable number of prospects for fashioning a worthwhile life."
22 Raeder 2002: 324–35 makes good use of the long review of Mill's *Autobiography* by Henry Reeve. Reeve, who had known Mill most of his life, was the editor of the *Edinburgh Review* and the translator of Tocqueville's *Democracy in America*. According to Reeve, one result of Mill's well-known peculiar and isolated upbringing and his and Harriet Taylor's later general avoidance of social intercourse was that Mill was "totally ignorant" of English life and society. Reeve added: "Mill never lived in what may be called society at all. . . . In later life he affected something of the life of a prophet, surrounded by admiring votaries…Mankind itself was to him an abstraction rather than a reality. He knew nothing of the world . . ."

In a posthumously published work, Joseph Hamburger (1999) examines the "dark side" of John Stuart Mill. Here Hamburger, who tells us that he long entertained the conventional view of Mill as a consummate proponent of individual freedom, analyzes Mill's On Liberty, but also his other writings and letters and the reports of his intimate friends. His conclusion is that the freedom of opinion espoused in On Liberty was largely part of Mill's grand strategy—to demolish religious faith, especially Christianity, and received mores, on the way to erecting a social order based on "the religion of humanity." True individuality would be incarnated in the future "Millian man," dreamt of by Mill and Harriet Taylor, a being in whom selfishness and greed would be replaced by altruism and the constant cultivation of the loftier faculties.

The pioneering revisionism of Cowling and Hamburger has been impressively confirmed by Linda C. Raeder. In her *John Stuart Mill and the Religion of Humanity* (2002), Raeder thoroughly examines all of Mill's major works and other relevant materials to uncover the pattern behind Mill's "self-avowed eclecticism" and his easy employment of "the idiom of the liberal tradition he knew so well." This pattern she finds in the early and permanent influence on Mill of philosophers Henri de Saint-Simon and Auguste Comte. The notion of progress entertained by these positivist thinkers was the steady advance to a this-worldly "religion of humanity" in which all of mankind would instinctively share. Mill's "aspirations for human beings were not for the flowering of their unique individuality but for their conformity to his personal ideal of value and service." In the end, Raeder concludes (338), Mill was no "true friend of liberty."

The fateful linking of liberalism to an adversarial stance vis-à-vis received religion, tradition, and social norms is due to John Stuart Mill more to than anyone else. It has unfortunately become standard. In a typical example, Owen Chadwick, Dixie Professor Emeritus of Ecclesiastical History at Cambridge, writes (1975: 22):

> A liberal was one who wanted more liberty, that is, more freedom from restraint; whether the restraint was exercised by police, or

by law, or by social pressure, or by an orthodoxy of opinion which men assailed at their peril. . . . The liberal thought that men needed far more room to act and think than they were allowed by established laws and conventions in European society.

Note how in this statement no distinction is made between state coercion on the one hand and social pressure, orthodox opinion, and conventions on the other. John Dunn states (1979: 29, emphasis in original):

If the central dispositional value of liberals is tolerance [sic], their central *political* value is perhaps a fundamental antipathy towards authority in any of its forms. . . . Dispositionally, liberalism has little regard for the past.

So much for Macaulay, Thierry, Lecky, Acton, and the other great liberal historians of the nineteenth century. Descriptions such as Chadwick's and Dunn's are much more expressive of the "antinomian"[23] mentality of contemporary Western academics than of liberalism historically.

Mill's view tends to erase the rather critical distinction between "incurring social disapproval and incurring imprisonment" (Burke 1994: 30),[24] and leads to pitting liberalism against innocent, non-coercive traditional values and arrangements, especially religious ones. It also forges an offensive alliance between liberalism and the state, even if perhaps contrary to Mill's intentions, since it is difficult to imagine how traditional norms could be uprooted except through the massive use of political power. Contemporary writers like Steven Lukes, committed to the Millian project of enjoining "autonomy," do not shrink from

---

23 The term was used in regard to "collectivist" liberals by Edward Shils 1989: 12–14.
24 See Burke's cogent discussion 1994: 28–30, where he criticizes Mill's tendency "to blur the dividing line between physical force and other kinds of pressure." See also Norman Barry (1996a: 50), who refers to "the kind of mindless and deliberate non-conformism recommended by John Stuart Mill . . . Under conditions of non-constraint, individuals are the makers of their own lives, whether or not they lead them as fully autonomous agents."

advocating this course, possibly unaware of its totalitarian implications, though it is difficult to see how.[25]

The "Old" vs. the "New" Liberalism

It is not disputed that the popular meaning of *liberal* has changed drastically over time. It is a well-known story how, around 1900, in English-speaking countries and elsewhere, the term was captured by writers who were essentially social democrats. Joseph Schumpeter (1954: 394) ironically observed that the enemies of the system of free enterprise paid it an unintended compliment when they applied the name liberal to their own creed, the opposite of what liberalism stood for from the start.

For a century now controversy has raged over the true meaning of liberalism (Meadowcroft 1996b: 2). Stephen Holmes (1988: 101) scoffs at the dispute as involving nothing more than "bragging rights." That does not stop him, though, from joining others of the camp Schumpeter referred to in fighting to secure the label for themselves. There is a profound truth in Thomas Szasz's proposition (1973: 20): "In the animal kingdom, the rule is, eat or be eaten; in the human kingdom, define or be defined." This is nowhere truer than in the political kingdom.

How did this momentous transformation of the term liberal—what Paul Gottfried (1999: 29) calls "a semantic theft"—come about?

This is the conventional interpretation: liberals from the eighteenth century on characteristically believed in laissez-faire. Beginning in the last decades of the nineteenth century, however, British thinkers like T.H. Green and L.T. Hobhouse (and their counterparts in the United

---

25 See Lukes 1973: 154–55, where the author writes of the need for government "to take an ever more active role in shaping and controlling the natural and social environment if equality and liberty are to be enhanced." One of the areas in which true liberty must be enhanced is religion, for religious belief, Lukes maintains, "is not compatible with the full development by individuals of their consciousness of themselves and their situation, and of their human powers." He concurs with Marx that the "abolition of religion as the *illusory* happiness of men, is a demand for their *real* happiness," etc. (Emphasis in Marx.) The government that is to undertake such social engineering, Lukes insists, must be "democratic and representative." Here Lukes runs into what proved to be a major obstacle for his predecessors in social engineering, Robespierre and Lenin among them: where could a truly democratic and representative government obtain the warrant to transform the retrograde people it intends to operate upon?

States, Germany, and elsewhere) realized that laissez-faire was totally inadequate to the conditions of modern society. Often inspired by John Stuart Mill—in Hobhouse's reverential words (1964: 63): "The teaching of Mill brings us close to the heart of liberalism"—they undertook to give liberalism a more up-to-date shape. As one expositor of the conventional view has written:

> The central value of the liberated individual, of man as far as possible his own sovereign, did not change; the understanding of that value and the means for achieving it did. (Smith 1968: 280)[26]

In particular, the state, which earlier liberals had feared as the enemy of individual liberty, was now correctly seen as a potent engine for furthering it in vital ways. The Old Liberalism gave way to the New.

The first thing to be pointed out is the political purpose behind the semantic change. It was to ease the way for the revolutionary extension of the state's agenda (ultimately, this has become in principle a *limitless* agenda). The crying need for such an extension, however, was grounded in a highly questionable theory, which is still operative. It is that the "old" liberalism of laissez-faire had been made obsolete by certain deep-seated changes in society. The pioneers of the "new liberalism" and their successors based their claims on the supposedly overwhelming power of business enterprise over consumers and workers. But, despite all their propaganda and that of their followers to the present day, such a power cannot be shown, empirically or theoretically, to exist. (Rothbard 1970: 168–73; Hutt 1954; Armentano 1982; Reynolds 1984: 56–68; DiLorenzo and High, 1988).

Moreover, and decisively, the standard rationale for speaking of a "new liberalism" is analytically flawed. For the *end* of achieving "the liberated individual" cannot be definitive of liberalism. Other ideologies,

---

26 This is from David G. Smith's entry on liberalism in *The International Encyclopedia of the Social Sciences*. It is a pity that such an important topic should have been left to Smith, whose treatment is often hopelessly confused: e.g., he claims that Ludwig von Mises cannot be considered a liberal because he was too "extreme" in leaving "the individual at the mercy of nature, society, and group and economic power," yet he labels J.-B. Say and Bastiat "liberal economists" (Smith 1968: 277, 280).

among them communist anarchism and many varieties of socialism, share that end.

Consider this statement by Eduard Bernstein, the founder of revisionist socialism (1909: 129, emphasis in original):

> The development and protection of the free personality is the goal of all socialist measures, even of those which superficially appear to be coercive. A closer examination will always show that it is a question of a coercion that *increases* the sum of freedom in society, that gives *more* freedom, and to a *wider* group, than it takes away.[27]

How does this differ from the standpoint of the "New Liberals" for the past century and more?[28] What divides liberalism from opposing ideologies is precisely its substantive program, the *means* it advocates—private property, the market economy, and the minimizing of the power of the state and of state-backed institutions.[29]

---

27 Cf. Pierre Angel 1961, especially 7, 9, 287, 332, 382–87, 411–15, and 420–33. Bernstein rejected Marxism's central economic concepts as well as state ownership and was resigned to the indefinite continued existence of the capitalist order. He insisted, however, that it should evolve into a "democratized" capitalism, with an expanding "social" legislation (he considered the Weimar "social state" a good start). Bernstein's revisionism ended by absorbing German socialism and for all practical purposes western socialism altogether, except for those who became known as Communists.

28 See also Lukes 1973: 12, where the author cites Jean Jaurès as asserting that "socialism is the logical completion of individualism," in that it realizes individualist ends through means more appropriate to the modern age. Lukes agrees, positing that "the only way to realize the values of individualism is through a humane form of socialism." We should be grateful to him for at least keeping individualism (in this context, the equivalent of political and economic liberalism) and socialism analytically distinct.

29 Cf. R.W. Davis (1995: vii–viii), in his foreword to the distinguished series, *The Making of Modern Freedom*: "We use freedom in the traditional and restricted sense of civil and political freedom—freedom of religion, freedom of speech and assembly, freedom of the individual from arbitrary and capricious authority over persons and property, freedom to produce and to exchange goods and services, and the freedom to take part in the political process . . ." Davis, the Director of the Center for the History of Freedom at Washington University, in St. Louis, the sponsor of the series, adds that this modern idea of freedom must be sharply differentiated from "the boundless calls for freedom from want and freedom from fear" of Franklin Roosevelt's Four Freedoms.

In Anglophone countries, those who anywhere else would be straightforwardly identified as social democrats or democratic socialists shy away from acknowledging their proper name. It is hard to avoid the conclusion that this is essentially a matter of political expediency. For some reason, labels suggestive of socialism have not been popular in countries of English heritage (cf. Gottfried 1999: 9).

This stark political fact was clear to Edward Bellamy, author of the socialist classic, *Looking Backward*. In 1888, in a letter to William Dean Howells, Bellamy weighed what to call his doctrine. He rejected the term, "socialist." That was a word he "never could well stomach," since it is foreign "in itself and equally foreign in all its suggestions." "Whatever German and French reformers may choose to call themselves, socialist is not a good name for a party to succeed with in America," he confided to Howells (Schiffman 1958: 370–71). Bellamy chose instead the name "nationalist." Others, on similar grounds, have preferred the label "liberal."

The social democratic commandeering of *liberal* met with great success, leading some laissez-faire liberals to incline towards describing themselves as *individualists* (Raico 1997). Amusingly, the next step was for socialists like John Dewey to try to capture that term as well. It turned out, according to Dewey, that there was an *old* individualism before the age of great corporations and modern social science; that kind must now be replaced by a *new* individualism (Dewey 1930). One product of this "new individualism" would be "a coordinating and directive council in which captains of industry and finance would meet with representatives of labor and public officials to plan the regulation" of the economy.

While this was obviously a replica of the corporate state that Mussolini was erecting in Italy, Dewey chose to ignore that parallel. The power center he proposed would have a voluntarist, and thus appropriately American, slant, as the United States set out constructively "upon the road which Soviet Russia is traveling" in such a deplorably destructive way (Dewey 1930: 118).[30] So, after the concept of *liberalism* was transformed to exclude adherents of the market economy and private property, now *individualism* was also to be redefined to the same end. Why, it's almost as if socialist propagandists like Dewey were trying simply to define the advocates of free enterprise out of existence—and debate—altogether.[31]

Liberalism and the Welfare State

It comes as no surprise that writers enamored of today's ever-expanding welfare state have attempted to amalgamate it to the liberal tradition, though few have been as creative as Maurice Cranston, who enlisted Lord Acton as a precursor of contemporary welfarism.[32] Stephen Holmes does not go so far, yet he maintains (1988) that the principles of "welfare liberalism are not only consistent with but, in some sense, follow directly from [classical] liberal principles themselves." His evidence is unconvincing. It consists mainly of two facts: that most classical liberals upheld minimal poor relief and that they favored protecting individual rights through tax-funded government agencies (the justice system and the military). Since industrialization produced "unprecedented forms of insecurity" (1988: 93), it was natural for liberalism to evolve in the direction of state welfare programs. Holmes also believes that the cosmopolitan nature of the liberal doctrine leads to "an international transfer plan whereby wealthy [Western] individuals helped support the poor wherever they lived" (1988: 97). The sly qualification "wealthy" should not go unnoticed.

---

30 A year later, Rexford Tugwell, of Roosevelt's "Brain Trust," wrote in *The New Republic* that "the interest of the liberals among us in the institutions of the new Russia of the Soviets has created a wide popular interest in 'planning.'" Cited in Gottfried 1999: 66.
31 Cf. Gottfried, ibid. 13: "When Dewey decided to characterize his proposed social reforms as 'liberal,' he had already tried out 'progressive,' 'corporate,' and 'organic.'"
32 See Cranston (1967b: 7–8), where he makes this absurd statement: "Lord Acton proposed to write a history of mankind in terms of its struggle towards freedom. . . . Acton seems to have meant by 'freedom'—freedom from the constraints of nature, freedom from disease and hunger and insecurity and ignorance and superstition." This Cranston calls the Progressive theory of freedom, which culminates in the welfare state.

Holmes seems to think, for no good reason, that market fluctuations, crop failures, etc.—i.e., economic insecurity—were a negligible matter before about the middle of the nineteenth century. He makes no mention of the moral hazard involved in state subsidies permitting "the poor"—nationally and internationally—to produce as many children as they wish. The assertion that such a subsidy scheme is implied in the thinking of eighteenth and nineteenth century liberals beggars belief. Even John Stuart Mill coupled support for relief for the poor with a proviso curtailing their freedom to procreate at will (Paul 1979: 181).[33] Confidence in Holmes's familiarity with classical liberal thought is not enhanced by his statement of "the standard Hayekian view," namely, that liberalism is "wholly incompatible with positive programs of public provision." Hayek, in fact, explicitly endorsed a wide program of public welfare provision (see The Constitution of Liberty, and Gordon 1998).[34]

Historically, the relationship between liberalism and the welfare state has been the opposite of one imagined by writers like Holmes.

When liberalism took shape in the eighteenth century as a comprehensive social philosophy, it presented itself as the antithesis of the mercantilist and cameralist system prevailing in Europe. The aim of that system is usually held to be the strengthening of the power of the monarchical state, especially its capacity to wage war. But this by no means excluded the goal of actively fostering the welfare of the king's subjects, particularly their economic wellbeing.[35] The Austrian minister

---

33 Ellen Paul adds, that in Mill's view, "without such a limitation on the recipients of public alms, future dependent populations would eat away the substance of society."

34 Holmes's argument that tax-funded provision of army, police, and judiciary are liberal concessions to welfarism, though still unconvincing, is more interesting. There are two possible rebuttals. First, that the classical liberals were, in fact, inconsistent, and that a thoroughgoing liberalism must eventuate in anarcho-capitalism. Second (and closer to traditional liberal thinking), that there is a qualitative difference between tax-funding for, on the one hand, an apparatus presumed to be indispensable to the survival of society (a state with an army, police, and justice system) and, on the other, for unlimited benefits to the "underprivileged."

35 Cf. Krieger 1963: 557, who writes (favorably) of mercantilism that it "sponsored the three kinds of activity commonly associated with the welfare state: regulation of the economically strong, support and direction of the economically weak, and the state's own enterprise where private initiative is wanting . . . whatever the ultimate motivation, the material well-being of the working population was a constant concern of the mercantilist statesman."

and leading cameralist writer, Joseph von Sonnenfels, for example, laid down the principle that: "Every citizen has a right . . . to claim from the state the greatest possible affluence" (Habermann 1997: 25; Kunisch 1986: 27–32). Paternal solicitude for the people was the supreme end of statecraft, according to Nicolas de la Mare, author of *Traité de police*, a work widely studied by Continental bureaucrats. De la Mare defined *police* (in German, *Polizei*) as "the science of governing men and doing them good, the method of rendering them, as much as possible, what they should be for the general interest of society." Its "unique object consists in leading man to the most perfect happiness which he is capable of enjoying in this life" (Raeff 1994: 319, 330 n. 48).

It was this "police science" that rationalized and helped generate the intricate network of laws, ordinances, edicts, and directives, the "excessive mania for regulation," of eighteenth century absolutism (Raeff 1994: 312). That its *intention* was allegedly benevolent made no difference to the liberals who assailed it as tyrannical (Habermann 1997: 17–65).[36] This was this system of control—of the economy as of the rest of social life—that the Physiocrat Mirabeau had in mind when he lashed out against "the rage to govern, the most disastrous disease of modern governments," the statement which Wilhelm von Humboldt (1969: 1) took as the motto for *The Limits of State Action*, the greatest work of German liberalism.

Liberalism thus grew up *in reaction against* the *Polizeistaat*—a word that, as it happens, translates best as *welfare state*. This first stage of the welfare state was followed by a

> second stage, influenced by the doctrines of the Enlightenment (natural law, laissez-faire, and the natural rights of the individual), [which] rejected paternalistic intervention by the state. It was to

---

36 Cf. Goetz Briefs 1930/31: 94–95. According to Briefs, liberalism arose as a reaction to the mercantilist attempt "to regard and treat economy and society as a branch of the public administration. Against this stands the thesis of liberalism: the state has no economic task. It also has no social task [aside from protection of liberty and property domestically and defense against foreign foes]. . . . In this way economy and society are separated out from the totality formed and composed by the state. This world runs by itself . . ."

be identified with the political democracy, liberalism, and laissez-faire of the nineteenth century. (Dorwart 1971: 2)

The third stage, in the heyday of which we are privileged to live, was inaugurated by the brilliant statesman and archenemy of liberalism, Otto von Bismarck. Bismarck's explicit aim was to prevent the workers from attaining middle class status through gradually accumulating private means and then passing them on to their children, in a steady intergenerational *embourgeoisement* of their families. Instead, members of the working class would be made ever dependent on state pensions, for which they were expected to show a fitting gratitude (Koch 1986: 30).[37] Bismarck's social legislation was bitterly opposed by the leading German liberals of his time, to no avail (Raico 1999: 154–79; and see the essay on "Eugen Richter and the End of German Liberalism," in the present volume).[38]

Recently, Paul Gottfried (1999; see also 2002) has contributed a penetrating analysis of the character of the contemporary welfare state:

> In Western Europe and North America, this state rests its power upon a multitiered following: an underclass and now middle-class welfariate, a self-assertive public sector, and a vanguard of media and journalistic public defenders. (1999: 139)

Under cover of the welfare state, and warmly seconded by their allies in the media and education, politicians, judges, and public administrators conduct an ongoing crusade against every form of inequality and "discrimination." Deploying the expanding power of the managerial and therapeutic state, the political class is engaged in an "assault on what the old liberals called civil society" (1999: 25).[39] The result is the calculated

---

37 This has, of course, been the end result of modern-day social security systems.
38 For all its many faults, Hirschman's *The Rhetoric of Reaction* (1991: 131–32) has the merit of pointing out the "tension" between the liberal tradition and the values underlying the modern welfare state. Hirschman notes that: "Perhaps this is the basic reason why social welfare policies were pioneered by Bismarck's Germany, a country singularly unencumbered by a strong liberal tradition."
39 Maurice Cowling (1990) has suggested the linkage between John Stuart Mill and today's "parties of civic and bureaucratic virtue," including militant environmentalists and radical feminists, in his introduction to the second edition of his 1963 work.

subversion of private property, equality before the law, and freedom of contract, speech, and association, the pillars of historic liberalism. The interventionist state, in the words of a German historian of state power, now claims the right to "shape society if necessary even against the will of the majority or at least of a large minority," and reveals itself as a "mere soft version of the total state" (Reinhard 1999: 467).[40] Today, the complaint that Herbert Spencer voiced over a century ago (1981: 23) rings truer than ever: "Such, then, are the doings of the party which claims the name of Liberal; and which calls itself Liberal as being the advocate of extended freedom!"

The Roots of Authentic Liberalism

That liberalism did not undergo a metamorphosis into a statist caricature of itself does not mean that it did not evolve. No argument is being offered here that the liberal idea suddenly sprang up at a certain point complete and fully matured. Neither can liberalism be approached as though it were a colloquy conducted among philosophers over the centuries.[41] Instead, it must be understood as a political and social doctrine and movement grounded in a distinctive culture and traceable to specific historical conditions.

That culture was the West—the Europe that arose in communion with the Bishop of Rome. The historical conditions were those of the Middle Ages. The history of liberalism is rooted in what economic historians sometimes call "the European miracle." More precisely, liberalism can be viewed as the slowly emerging ideological and political aspect of that "miracle."

---

40 Reinhard adds that "legitimation through the fiction of popular sovereignty allows intrusions of state power into society to appear as those of society into itself." Reinhard's whole analysis of the parallels between the welfare and totalitarian state (458–67), the culmination of his magisterial history of state power, is highly illuminating.

41 Even as learned a scholar as Pierre Manent suggests (1987: 8–11; emphasis in original) that liberalism "was thought and willed *before* being put into practice," and that it "assumes a conscious and 'constructed' project." His stress on the heavy reliance of the American founders on Montesquieu ignores other sources of American constitutionalism, such as English and colonial legal and political traditions, in turn conditioned by the distinctive societies in which they developed.

The essence of the European experience is that a civilization developed that felt itself to be a unity and yet was politically decentralized. The continent devolved into a mosaic of separate and competing jurisdictions and polities whose internal divisions themselves resisted central control. "There was, in other words, a type of laissez-faire built into Europe as a whole" (Hall 1987: 55). The relative ease of "exit" and sustained military competition furnished princes with strong incentives (not always determinative) to refrain from confiscations and other violations of property rights. In this process, a major role was played by the free towns in Italy, the Low Countries, Germany, and elsewhere, which became citadels of a self-governing, self-confident middle class, the nurturer and carrier of the commercial ethos.[42] Most important of all and unique to Europe was the existence of a powerful, independent, international Church.

The Role of the Medieval Church

Historically, in advanced societies the relationship between the religious and political authorities has been a symbiotic one. The priests sanctified, often deified the rulers, who in turn lavished financial and other privileges on them. In medieval Europe it was portentously different.

Lord Acton devoted his life and his immense learning to the study of the growth of liberty. Himself a Catholic, he was sensitive to the role of his Church in this epic story. Acton wrote, of the ongoing struggle between the secular powers and the Church over the appointment of bishops:

---

42 Some years back, it was much more common than it is now for classical liberalism to be contemptuously dismissed as the ideology of the rising, self-seeking bourgeoisie. According to Harry K. Girvetz (1963: 24, 60), the classical liberal program was "largely determined" by "the needs and aspirations of the merchants and manufacturers." Following Harold Laski, Girvetz quoted Arthur Young: "Everyone but an idiot knows that the lower classes must be kept poor or they will never be industrious." Taking Arthur Young rather than, say, Adam Smith or Condorcet as representative of eighteenth-century liberal thinking is so peculiar that it must be ascribed either to sheer, disqualifying ignorance or to bad faith, depending on how charitable one cares to be.

To that conflict of four hundred years we owe the rise of civil liberty ... although liberty was not the end for which they strove, it was the means by which the temporal and the spiritual power called the nations to their aid. The towns of Italy and Germany won their franchises, France got her States-General, and England her Parliament out of the alternate phases of the contest; and as long as it lasted it prevented the rise of divine right. (Acton 1956, 86–87)

Harold J. Berman has bolstered Lord Acton's analysis of the central role of the Catholic Church in generating Western liberty. With the fall of Rome and the eventual conversion of the Germans, Slavs, and Magyars, the ideas and values of Latin Christendom suffused the whole blossoming culture of Europe. Christian contributions range from the mitigation of slavery and a greater equality within the family to the concepts of natural law, including the legitimacy of resistance to unjust rulers. The Church's canon law exercised a decisive influence on Western legal systems: "it was the church that first taught Western man what a modern legal system was like." (1974, 59)

Berman, moreover, focuses attention on a critical development that began in the eleventh century: the creation by Pope Gregory VII and his successors of a powerful "corporate, hierarchical church...independent of emperors, kings, and feudal lords," and thus capable of foiling the relentless power-seeking of temporal authority (ibid. 56). In a major synthesis, *Law and Revolution*, Berman has highlighted the legal facets of the development whose economic, political, and ideological aspects other scholars have examined (Berman 1983): "Perhaps the most distinctive characteristic of the Western legal tradition is the coexistence and competition within the same community of diverse legal systems. It is this plurality of jurisdictions and legal systems that makes the supremacy of law both necessary and possible" (ibid. 10).

Berman's work is in the tradition of the great English scholar, A.J. Carlyle, who, at the conclusion of his monumental study of political thought in the Middle Ages, summarized the basic principles of medieval politics: that all—including the king—are bound by law; that a lawless ruler is not a legitimate king, but a tyrant; that where there is no justice there is no commonwealth; and that a contract exists between the ruler and his subjects (Carlyle and Carlyle 1950, 503–26).

Other recent scholarship has supported these conclusions. In his last, posthumous work, the distinguished historian of economic thought, Jacob Viner, noted that the references to taxation by St. Thomas Aquinas "treat it as a more or less extraordinary act of a ruler which is as likely as not to be morally illicit" (Viner 1978, 68–69). Viner pointed to the medieval papal bull, *In Coena Domini*, evidently republished each year into the late eighteenth century, which threatened to excommunicate any ruler "who levied new taxes or increased old ones, except for cases supported by law, or by an express permission from the pope" (ibid. 69). Throughout the Western world, the Middle Ages gave rise to parliaments, diets, estates-general, Cortes, etc., which served to limit the powers of the monarch. [13] A.R. Myers notes:

> Almost everywhere in Latin Christendom the principle was, at one time or another, accepted by the rulers that, apart from the normal revenues of the prince, no taxes could be imposed without the consent of parliament. . . . By using their power of the purse [the parliaments] often influenced the ruler's policies, especially restraining him from military adventures. (Myers 1975 29–30)

Popular rights, above all protection against arbitrary taxation, were defended by representative assemblies and often enshrined in charters that the rulers felt more or less obliged to respect. In the most famous of these, the Magna Carta, which the barons of England extorted from King John in 1215, the first signatory was Stephen Langton, Archbishop of Canterbury.

In a valuable synthesis of modern medievalist scholarship, Norman F. Cantor has summarized the heritage of the European Middle Ages:

> In the model of civil society, most good and important things take place below the universal level of the state: the family, the

arts, learning, and science; business enterprise and technological process. These are the work of individuals and groups, and the involvement of the state is remote and disengaged. It is the rule of law that screens out the state's insatiable aggressiveness and corruption and gives freedom to civil society below the level of the state. It so happens that the medieval world was one in which men and women worked out their destinies with little or no involvement of the state most of the time. (Cantor 1991, 416)

Thus, long before the seventeenth century, Europe had produced political and legal arrangements—a whole way of life—that set the stage for both individual freedom and the later industrial "take-off." Along with and reinforcing these institutions went a discourse based on natural law, entailing limitations on the prince's power. Highly important was the *desacralization* of the state. Karl Ferdinand Werner (1988) directs attention to the work of Friedrich Klinger, who already in 1941 pointed out how early Christian thinkers, specifically St. Augustine, had desacralized the state and thus radically altered the conception prevalent in Greco-Roman antiquity.

The last flowering of this natural law tradition was in Late Scholasticism, commonly associated with the school of Salamanca, whose key theoretical importance is coming to be appreciated (Rothbard 1995c, 1: 81–88, 99–131; Chafuen 1986).

The Attack of the Modern State and the Liberal Response

With the rise of centralizing, bureaucratic monarchies and royal absolutism, this unique political culture came under broad attack. The crucial incursions are those of the Spanish Habsburgs in the later sixteenth century in the Netherlands and of the Stuarts in seventeenth century England.

It is now that liberalism enters upon the scene. It appears from the start as a combative doctrine, in opposition to the centralizing and regimenting thrust of absolutism.

The political history of liberalism in the strict sense begins with John Lilburne and the Levellers in mid-seventeenth century England.

These dissenters were the first to present a comprehensive program including the separation of church and state, freedom of the press, abolition of state monopoly grants, local government, and the rejection of the socialist egalitarianism preached by groups like the Diggers (Wolfe 1944; Aylmer 1975).[43] From the time of the Levellers to the present day an unbroken tradition can be tracked, which, beyond all differences in modes of discourse and philosophical and theological presuppositions, is recognizably liberal.

Liberalism scored a major victory with the attainment of religious toleration (often for prudential reasons) and, finally, religious freedom, as it came to be acknowledged that in this area civil society could be left to fend for itself.[44] In general, liberalism as doctrine and movement was in continual interaction with social reality as it existed in western Europe and then British North America, growing *pari passu* as practice and theory uncovered the possibilities of beneficial spontaneous order in civil society.[45] With every liberal advance, "political philosophy and political economy processed, justified, and systematized these achievements" (Weede 1989: 33).[46]

---

[43] Cf. Murray Rothbard's judgment 1995c, 1: 313 that the Levellers were "the world's first self-consciously libertarian movement . . . while the economy was scarcely a primary focus of the Levellers, their adherence to a free market economy was a simple derivation from their stress on liberty and the rights of private property."

[44] Cf. Patterson 1997: 25–26: ". . . Locke's understanding of the need for toleration was broader and deeper than [John} Milton's. . . . And when Thomas Jefferson sat down in 1776 to prepare his speeches in connection with the disestablishment of the church in Virginia, he used Locke's *Letter concerning Toleration* as a stepping-stone for another advance in the theory of toleration. Jefferson's notes mark the leap of logic succinctly: 'It was great thing to go so far (as he [Locke] himself says of the parl. who framed the act of tolern.) but where he stopped we may go on.'"

[45] Cf. Hume 1985: 604–05 (emphasis in original): "It has also been found, as the experience of mankind increases, that the *people* are no such dangerous monster as they have been represented. . . . Before the United Provinces set the example, toleration was deemed incompatible with good government; and it was thought impossible, that a number of religious sects could live together in harmony and peace, and have all of them an equal affection to their common country and to each other. ENGLAND has set a like example of civil liberty . . ."

[46] Cf. Hardin 1993: 121: ". . . economic liberalism more or less grew. It was analyzed and understood retrospectively rather than prospectively. It came into being without a party or intellectual agenda. By the time Bernard Mandeville, Adam Smith, and others came to analyze it, they were analyzing characteristics of their own society. Insofar as they had programs, these

Among American historians, it is Joyce Appleby who has understood this interaction best. She comments on England in the seventeenth century, where economic writers discovered

> the underlying regularity of free market activity . . . and in so doing they had come upon a possibility and a reality. The reality was that individuals making decisions about their own persons and property were the determiners of price in the market. The possibility was that the economic rationalism of market participants could supply the order to the economy formerly secured through authority. (1987: 187–88)

Of the American colonies a hundred years later, Appleby writes:

> In the eighteenth century, two features of the market economy fascinated contemporaries: the reliance upon individual initiative and the absence of authoritarian direction. . . . A century and quarter of economic development had dramatically enhanced public opinion about voluntary human actions, and *society* was the word that emerged to represent the uncoerced relations of people living under the same authority. . . . It is this vision which animated the Jeffersonians. (1984: 22–23, emphasis in original)[47]

Three points require comment here.

First, it may be objected that this approach "privileges" the liberalism of certain nations, for instance, England, France, and the United States. In an age of egalitarianism run wild, this objection may strike some as a serious one. However, there is no reason to assume that all "liberalisms" are created equal—that Russian or Hungarian liberalism, for example, ought to be given equal weight with French liberalism in shaping our understanding of the essential meaning of the doctrine.

---

were for reforms of political practice to end elements of state-sponsored monopoly and protection." Hardin contrasts this with the "invention" of political liberalism.

47 Cf. Norman Barry 1991: 160: "Liberalism began in eighteenth-century Europe with the discovery that there are ordering mechanisms in society that maintain stability (or a kind of equilibrium) without central control."

Second, if, as is argued here, liberalism is a reflection of the society that generates it (and, in turn, shapes that society), then it is easily comprehensible that liberal movements in different national contexts will evince different characteristics. In a national culture in which the state traditionally played a dominant role, empirical liberalism, like much else, will be skewed in a statist direction.

Third, our understanding of the nature of liberalism does not so far decide anything regarding the *validity* of the liberal doctrine or the *feasibility* of a liberal social order. It may be that liberalism vastly overestimates the self-regulatory capacity of society. It is possible, for instance, that Keynesian management of aggregate demand and socialization of investment are necessary for the satisfactory functioning of the economy, or that supervision of culture by one or another religious authority is required for preserving a minimal morality.

More plausibly, it may well be that the liberal program of establishing a strictly limited state conceals a fundamental contradiction and, in the nature of things, inevitably makes way for a state armed with all-embracing powers. This has been persuasively argued by Hans-Hermann Hoppe (Hoppe 2001: 221–38), who states: "Contrary to the original liberal intent of safeguarding liberty and property, every minimal government has the inherent tendency to become a maximal government."

If any of these, or similar, theses prove to be correct, then liberalism could be shown to be fatally flawed. But such a demonstration would not change what liberalism was historically—what it understood itself to be and what it distinctively and characteristically was.

The historical phenomena that present themselves to anyone undertaking an account or appreciation of liberalism as a whole are daunting, to say the least. They involve the social, political, economic, legal, and intellectual histories of entire peoples over centuries. How are the strands that are relevant to liberalism to be separated out in this Himalayas of data? None of the usual methods appears to be satisfactory. They fail to provide us with what we require: an understanding of "liberalism as a *distinct* political doctrine, that we can tell apart from the others" (de Jasay 1991: 119, emphasis in original). A new approach seems called for.

Applying the Method of the Ideal Type

One possibility that has been suggested is utilizing Max Weber's notion of the "ideal type" (Briefs 1930/31: 101; Bedeschi 1990: 2–3).[48] Weber (1949: 90, 92, emphasis in original) describes it as follows:

> An ideal type is formed by the one-sided *accentuation* of one or more points of view and by the synthesis of a great many diffuse, discrete, more or less present and occasionally absent *concrete individual* phenomena, which are arranged according to those one-sidedly emphasized viewpoints into a unified *conceptual* construct (*Gedankenbild*). . . . It is a *utopia*. . . . When carefully applied, those concepts are particularly useful in research and exposition . . . there is only one criterion, namely, that of success in revealing concrete phenomena in their interdependence, their causal conditions, and their *significance*. The construction of abstract ideal types recommends itself not as an end but as a means.[49]

Ludwig Lachmann (who was dubious of its usefulness in economics, though not in history) comments on Max Weber's concept:

> "The ideal type is essentially a measuring rod. . . . By indicating the magnitude of approximation of an historical phenomenon to one or several of our concepts we can order these phenomena" [Weber]. In other words, the ideal type serves the purpose of ordering concrete phenomena in terms of their distance from it (Lachmann 1971: 26–27).[50]

---

48 Briefs states, of his use of "ideal-typical constructions," that they "throw into relief essential basic ideas of liberalism, without consideration of the qualifications that can be found in individual authors, are logically enhanced and thought out to the end."
49 Cf. Sadri 1992: 16 and 11–22: "a historical ideal type is the result of one-sided accentuation and stylization of historical facts . . . [it] is warped and lopsided, for it carries more logical consistency and less factual or historical detail than the reality it represents; and also because it favors certain elements of historical reality as 'relevant' and 'significant' to the exclusion of others."
50 See also the critique of Israel M. Kirzner 1976: 158–59, and Mises 1933: 71–88. The criticisms of Lachmann, Kirzner, and Mises are directed to what Raymond Aron 1970: 246–47 identified as the third kind of Weberian ideal-type, "rationalizing reconstructions of a particular

The ideal type of liberalism should express a coherent concept, based on what is most characteristic and distinctive in the liberal doctrine—what Weber refers to as the "essential tendencies" (1949: 91).[51] Historically, where monarchical absolutism had insisted that the state was the engine of society and the necessary overseer of the religious, cultural, and, not least, economic life of its subjects, liberalism posited a starkly contrasting view: that the most desirable regime was one in which *civil society—that is, the whole of the social order based on private property and voluntary exchange—by and large runs itself.*[52] For at least a century and a half, the idea that society and the state are rivals, that social power is diminished as state power grows, has been typical of those recognized as—or accused of—being the most "dogmatic," "doctrinaire," and "intransigent" of the liberals.[53]

---

kind of behavior." Here it is the first kind, "ideal types of historical particulars," that is being drawn on.

51 Hekman 1983: 32 stresses Weber's insistence on observing the "'logic' inherent in the concepts themselves. When Weber states that the features which make up the ideal type will be combined 'according to their compatibility,' his point is that concepts cannot be thrown together in arbitrary fashion. Ideal types are not the product of the whim or fancy of a social scientist, but are logically constructed concepts."

52 Cf. Karlson 1993: 77, who writes of civil society that its modern meaning "as a kind of sphere outside and distinct from the political sphere or the state, emerges slowly in the eighteenth and nineteenth centuries. One major influence came from natural rights theorists, such as Thomas Paine, who, inspired by Locke, argued that most actual governments continuously tend to threaten the individual freedom and natural sociability in civil society. The state is in this perspective at best seen as a necessary evil, and civil society is viewed as a largely self-regulating sphere where the good life may be reached." Hegel retained the contrast of civil society and state, while loading the former with a negative connotation. Karlson attempts to avoid what he sees as the normative slant of both of these approaches and defines civil society as: *"the non-political relationships and behavioral patterns between a large number of interdependent actors within a given political territory.* By 'non-political' is here meant social and economic arrangements, codes, and institutions that have evolved or exist without being directly created, upheld or enforced by the activities of the state, e.g. conventions, voluntary organizations, social norms and markets." (Emphasis in original)

53 Robert Skidelsky 1995: ix, defines collectivism—presumably the opposite of liberalism—as "the belief that the state knows better than the market, and can improve on the spontaneous tendencies of civil society, if necessary by suppressing them." He describes this as "the most egregious error of the twentieth century…this belief in the superior wisdom of the state breeds pathologies which deform, and at the limit, destroy, the political economies based on it."

One commentator who has grasped this is Ralf Dahrendorf, who writes of scholars like James Buchanan, Milton Friedman, and Robert Nozick that they were reverting to

> the original [liberal] project of asserting society against the state, the market against planning and regulation, the right of the individual against overpowering authorities and collectivities.

Dahrendorf adds, significantly: "Liberalism is not anarchism, but anarchism is in some ways an extreme form of liberalism" (1987: 174).[54]

Construction of the ideal type of liberalism would draw on emblematic expressions of the liberal affirmation of "society against the state."[55] Most succinct is the Physiocratic slogan, *"Laissez-faire, laissez-passer, le monde va de lui-même"* ("the world goes by itself"). Another is from Adam Smith:

> Little else is requisite to carry a State to the highest degree of opulence from the lowest barbarism, but peace, easy taxes, and a tolerable administration of justice; all the rest being brought about by the natural course of things. All governments which thwart this natural course, which force things into another channel, or which endeavor to arrest the progress of society at a particular point, are unnatural, and to support themselves are obliged to be oppressive and tyrannical. (Cited in Stewart 1996: 68)

Or the statement of Thomas Paine:

> Great part of that order which reigns among mankind is not the effect of government. It has its origin in the principles of society

---

54 Cf. Norman Barry 1996b: 58: "Economic liberalism finds its ultimate logical conclusion in the doctrine of anarcho-capitalism." Dahrendorf holds, however, that welfare liberalism is a valid continuation of the original liberal program.
55 As Weber wrote 1949: 95: "An ideal type of certain situations, which can be abstracted from certain characteristic social phenomena of an epoch, might—and this is indeed quite often the case—have also been present in the minds of the persons living in that epoch as an ideal to be striven for in practical life or as a maxim for the regulation of certain social relationships."

and the natural constitution of man. It existed prior to government, and would exist if the formality of government was abolished. (Paine 1969: 357)

Or the implications of the advice of Benjamin Constant:

Remain faithful to justice, which is of all the ages; respect freedom, which prepares all good things; consent to the fact that many things will develop without you; and entrust to the past its own defense and to the future its own accomplishment. (Constant 1957: 1580)

Since liberalism is essentially a doctrine of society's self-regulation—of its capacity to generate beneficial spontaneous order—a special role falls to economic theory, the best developed branch of social-scientific knowledge that has investigated phenomena of spontaneous social order.[56]

The elaboration of this ideal type would probably borrow heavily from the social theory of the French liberal school of J.-B. Say, Antoine Destutt de Tracy, and their followers. Here society is taken to be essentially an incalculable network of ever-changing voluntary exchanges. Government is limited to "the production of security," but has an inherent tendency to expand into exploiting the productive members of society (Raico 1993 and the essay "The Conflict of Classes: Liberal vs. Marxist Theories," in the present work).

In this way we may well be able to identify a central line of historical liberalism that would include, for instance, in America, Jefferson and the continuing radical Jeffersonian tradition; in France, Benjamin Constant, J.-B. Say, the *Industrialiste* school, and other writers for the *Journal des Économistes*; in England, Price, Priestly, Herbert Spencer, and the radical individualists of the late nineteenth century; in Germany,

---

56 Cf. the conclusion of one of the finest historians of liberalism (though not strictly a liberal himself), Albert Schatz 1907: 32: "little by little the idea will emerge and spread that the economic order is no more the artificial work of the legislator than the order that naturally reigns in the functioning of an organism is the work of the hygienist . . . that there is, in a word, a natural economic order and that this order is capable of being substituted for the artificial order of regulation. . . . The day that this idea is scientifically established one may say that the individualist [i.e., liberal] doctrine was born."

the late eighteenth century natural-law advocates of inviolable property rights and freedom of trade, the early Wilhelm von Humboldt, and John Prince Smith and his disciples; in Italy, Francesco Ferrara and the rest of the school of laissez-faire economists; and in Austria and America, Ludwig von Mises and those who have followed in his footsteps. Other movements and thinkers would be considered as they were situated nearer or further from this central line. Within this taxonomy, "new" or "modern" liberalism, like every other variety, would find its place.[57]

Focusing on the doctrine of society's self-regulation does not, of course, imply accepting that doctrine as true. Ideal-type analysis "has nothing to do with any type of perfection other than a purely *logical* one" (Weber 1949: 98–99, emphasis in original). In the end, it might turn out that the liberal world-view is, for better or worse, fundamentally mistaken. But even then, accounts of liberalism's history would still be interesting and important.

The suggested ideal type fulfills the requirement of fostering and guiding a research agenda. Divergences from the type would be studied to determine the particular historical and personal circumstances that conditioned them. Thus, the stronger state traditions in Germany and especially Russia, would be brought in, as would the felt deprivation of a national unity that could only be achieved by a militarily strong state in the German case. (The high proportion of German liberals in the nineteenth century who were state functionaries would not be overlooked.) On the issue of education, to take one instance, attention would be directed to the conditions faced by liberals like the Idéologues and Richard Cobden, who favored a role for the state, that may have been absent with others, such as Bastiat and Herbert Spencer, who opposed it.

Following such a procedure would avoid the recourse of "then there was this, and then there was that" over three hundred years. It would clearly delineate the features of a liberalism that evolved and spread but did not finally disintegrate into a mass of personal preferences

---

57 For a trenchant critique of varieties of the "new" liberalism and its modern descendents, see Conway 1995: 25–64.

and mental attitudes or into a politics indistinguishable from social democracy.[58]

References

Acton, John Emerich Edward Dalberg (1956). "The History of Freedom in Christianity," in *Essays on Freedom and Power*, Gertrude Himmelfarb (ed.), New York: Meridian.

Angel, Pierre (1961) *Eduard Bernstein et l'évolution du socialisme allemand*, Paris: Marcel Didier.

Appleby, Joyce (1978) *Economic Thought and Ideology in Seventeenth-Century England*, Princeton, N.J.: Princeton University Press.

Appleby, Joyce (1984) *Capitalism and a New Social Order: The Republican Vision of the 1790s*, New York: New York University Press.

Arblaster, Anthony (1984) *The Rise and Decline of Western Liberalism*, Oxford: Basil Blackwell.

Arblaster, Anthony (1996) "Liberalism After Communism," in Meadowcroft (ed.).

Armentano, Dominick T. (1982) *Antitrust and Monopoly: Anatomy of a Policy Failure*, New York: John Wiley and Sons.

Aron, Raymond (1970) *Main Currents in Sociological Thought*, 2, *Durkheim, Pareto, Weber*, Richard Howard and Helen Weaver (trs.), New York: Doubleday/Anchor.

Ashcraft, Richard (1989) "Class, Conflict, and Constitutionalism in J.S. Mill's Thought," in Rosenblum (ed.)

Aylmer, G. E. (ed.) (1975) *The Levellers of the English Revolution*, Ithaca, N.Y.: Cornell University Press.

Baechler, Jean, John A. Hall, and Michael Mann (eds.) (1988) *Europe and the Rise of Capitalism*, Oxford, Basil Blackwell.

---

58 The nadir of intellectual bewilderment in abolishing the distinction between liberalism and socialism may have been reached by Eccleshall 1986: 62, who states: "the task of creating a more liberal society now lies with those people who strive to lay the foundations of a socialist future within the existing framework of capitalism: with socialists who recognize, in the words of Marx and Engels, 'that mankind advances, not by leaps, but only step by step. . . . Only by degrees can private property be transformed into social property.'"

Barry, Norman (1991) "Liberalism," in Nigel Ashford and Stephen Davies (eds.) *A Dictionary of Conservative and Libertarian Thought*, London: Routledge.

Barry, Norman (1996a) "Classical Liberalism in the Age of Post-Communism," in Charles K. Rowley (ed.), *The Political Economy of the Minimal State*, Cheltenham, Eng.: Edward Elgar.

Barry, Norman (1996b) "Economic Liberalism, Ethics, and the Social Market," in Meadowcroft (ed.).

Bedeschi, Giuseppe (1990) *Storia del pensiero liberale*, Bari: Laterza.

Berman, Harold J. Berman, (1974) "The Influence of Christianity on the Development of Western Law." In idem, *The Interaction of Law and Religion*, 49–76. Nashville/New York: Abingdon Press. 1983.

Berman, Harold J. (1983) *Law and Revolution: The Formation of the Western Legal Tradition*. Cambridge: Harvard University Press.

Bernstein, Eduard (1909 [1899]) *Die Voraussetung des Sozialismus und die Aufgaben der Sozialdemokratie*, Stuttgart: J.H.W. Dietz Nachf.

Briefs, Goetz (1930/31) "Der klassische Liberalismus," *Archiv für Rechts- und Wirtschaftsphilosophie*, 24.

Brunner, Karl (1987) "The Sociopolitical Vision of Keynes," in David A. Reese (ed.) *The Legacy of Keynes*, San Francisco: Harper and Row.

Burke, T. Patrick (1994) *No Harm: Ethical Principles for a Free Market*, New York: Paragon House.

Carlyle, R.W., and A.J. Carlyle (1950), *A History of Medieval Political Theory in the West*, 6, *Political Theory from 1300 to 1600*, Edinburgh: Blackwood.

Chadwick, Owen (1975) *The Secularization of the European Mind in the Nineteenth Century*, Cambridge, Eng.: Cambridge University Press.

Chafuen, Alejandro A. (1986), *Christians for Freedom: Late-Scholastic Economics*, San Francisco: Ignatius Press.

Cobden, Richard (1973 [1903]) *Political Writings*, New York: Garland, 2 vols.

Constant, Benjamin (1957) *Oeuvres*, Alfred Roulin (ed.), Pléiade, Paris: Gallimard.

Conway, David (1995) *Classical Liberalism: The Unvanquished Ideal*, New York: St. Martin's.

Cowling, Maurice (1963) *Mill and Liberalism*, Cambridge, Eng.: Cambridge University Press.

Cowling, Maurice (1990) *Mill and Liberalism*, 2nd ed., Cambridge, Eng.: Cambridge University Press.

Cranston, Maurice (1967a) "Liberalism," in Paul Edwards (ed.) *The Encyclopedia of Philosophy*, 4, New York/London: Macmillan/Collier.

Cranston, Maurice (1967b) *Freedom: A New Analysis*, 3rd ed., London: Longmans.

Cubeddu, Raimondo (1997) *Atlante del liberalismo*, Rome: Ideazione.

Dahrendorf, Ralf (1987) "Liberalism," in Eatwell, et al. (eds.) 3.

Davis, R. W. (ed.) (1995) *The Origins of Modern Freedom in the West*, Stanford, Cal.: Stanford University Press.

de Jasay, Anthony (1991) *Choice, Contract, Consent: A Restatement of Liberalism*, London: Institute of Economic Affairs.

Den Uyl, Douglas J. and Stuart D. Warner (1987) "Liberalism in Hobbes and Spinoza," *Studia Spinozana 3*.

Dewey, John (1930) *Individualism Old and New*, New York: Minton, Balch.

Dicey, A. V. (1963 [1914]) *Lectures on the Relation between Law and Public Opinion in England during the Nineteenth Century*, London: Macmillan.

DiLorenzo, Thomas J. and Jack C. High (1988) "Antitrust and Competition, Historically Considered," *Economic Inquiry*, 26 (3) (July).

Döhn, Lothar (1977) "Liberalismus," in Franz Neumann (ed.) *Politische Theorien und Ideologien: Handbuch*, 2nd ed., Baden-Baden: Signal.

Dorwart, Reinhold August (1971) *The Prussian Welfare State Before 1740*, Cambridge, Mass.: Harvard University Press.

Dunn, John (1979) *Western Political Theory in the Face of the Future*, Cambridge, Eng.: Cambridge University Press.

Eatwell, John, Murray Milgate, and Peter Newman (eds.) (1987) *The New Palgrave. A Dictionary of Economics*, London: Macmillan, 4 vols.

Eccleshall, Robert (1986) *British Liberalism. Liberal Thought from the 1640s to 1980s*, London: Longman.

Freeden, Michael (1996) "The Family of Liberalisms: A Morphological Analysis," in Meadowcroft (ed.).

Friedman, Milton (1967) *Capitalism and Freedom*, Chicago: University of Chicago Press.

Gellner, Ernest and César Cansino (eds.) (1996) *Liberalism in Modern Times: Essays in Honor of José G. Merquior*, Budapest: Central European University Press.

Girvetz, Harry K. (1963) *The Evolution of Liberalism*, New York: Collier.

Goodin, Robert E. and Philip Pettit (eds.) (1993) *A Companion to Contemporary Political Philosophy*, Oxford: Blackwell.

Gordon, David (1998) "More Liberal than Thou," *Mises Review* 4 (1) (Spring).

Gottfried, Paul Edward (1999) *After Liberalism: Mass Democracy in the Managerial State*, Princeton, N.J.: Princeton University Press.

Gottfried, Paul Edward (2002) *Multiculturalism and the Politics of Guilt: Toward a Secular Theocracy*, Columbia, Mo.: University of Missouri Press.

Gray, John (1986) *Liberalism*, Minneapolis: University of Minnesota Press.

Greenleaf, W.H. (1983) *The British Political Tradition*, 2, *The Ideological Heritage*, London: Methuen.

Habermann, Gerd (1997) *Der Wohlfahrtsstaat: Geschichte eines Irrwegs*, 2nd ed., Berlin: Ullstein.

Hall, John A. (1987) *Liberalism: Politics, Ideology, and the Market*, Chapel Hill, N.C.: University of North Carolina Press.

Hamburger, Joseph (1999) *John Stuart Mill on Liberty and Social Control*, Princeton, N.J.: Princeton University Press.

Hardin, Russell (1993) "Liberalism: Political and Economic," *Social Philosophy and Policy*, 10 (2) (Summer).

Hayek, F.A. (1954) "History and Politics," in idem (ed.) *Capitalism and the Historians*, Chicago: University of Chicago Press.

Hayek, F.A. (1960) *The Constitution of Liberty*, Chicago: University of Chicago Press.

Hekman, Susan J. (1983) *Weber, the Ideal Type, and Contemporary Social Theory*, Notre Dame, Ind.: University of Notre Dame Press.

Himmelfarb, Gertrude (1990) *On Liberty and Liberalism: The Case of John Stuart Mill*, San Francisco: Institute for Contemporary Studies.

Hirschman, Albert O. (1991) *The Rhetoric of Reaction: Perversity, Futility, Jeopardy*, Cambridge, Mass.: Harvard University Press.

Hobhouse, L.T. (1964 [1911]) *Liberalism*, Oxford: Oxford University Press.

Holmes, Stephen (1988) "Liberal Guilt: Some Theoretical Origins of the Welfare State, in Moon (ed.)

Hoppe, Hans-Hermann (2001) *Democracy: The God that Failed. The Economics and Politics of Monarchy, Democracy, and Natural Order*, New Brunswick, N.J.: Transaction.

Humboldt, Wilhelm von (1968 [1854]) *The Limits of State Action*, J.W. Burrow (ed.), J.W. Burrow and Joseph Coulthard (trs.), Cambridge, Eng.: Cambridge University Press.

Hume, David (1985 [1777]) *Essays Moral, Political, and Literary*, Eugene F. Miller (ed.), Indianapolis, Ind.: Liberty Classics.

Hutt, W. H. (1954) *The Theory of Collective Bargaining*, Glencoe, Ill.: Free Press.

Jaguaribe, Helio (1996) "Merquior and Liberalism," in Gellner and Cansino (eds.)

Jones, E.L. (1987) *The European Miracle. Environments, Economies, and Geopolitics in the History of Europe and Asia*, 2nd ed., Cambridge, Eng.: Cambridge University Press.

Karlson, Nils (1993) *The State of State: An Inquiry Concerning the Role of Invisible Hands in Politics and Civil Society*, Uppsala: University of Uppsala, Dept. of Government and Political Science.

Kirzner, Israel M. (1976) *The Economic Point of View. An Essay in the History of Economic Thought* 2nd ed., Kansas City, Mo.: Sheed and Ward.

Klein-Hattingen, Oskar (1912) *Geschichte des deutschen Liberalismus*, 2, *Von 1871 bis zur Gegenwart*, Berlin-Schöneberg: Fortschritt (Buchverlag der "Hilfe").

Koch, Rainer (1986) "Liberalismus und soziale Frage im 19. Jahrhundert, in *Sozialer Liberalismus*, Karl Holl, Günter Trautmann, and Hans Vorländer (eds.), Göttingen: Vandenhoeck and Ruprecht.

Krieger, Leonard (1963) "The Idea of the Welfare State in Europe and the United States," *Journal of the History of Ideas* 24 (4) (October-December).

Kunisch, Johannes (1986) *Absolutismus*, Göttingen: Vandenhoeck and Ruprecht.

Lachmann, Ludwig (1971) *The Legacy of Max Weber. Three Essays*, Berkeley, Cal.: Glendessary Press.

Lukes, Steven (1973) *Individualism*, New York: Harper and Row.

Manent, Pierre (1987) *Histoire intellectuelle du libéralisme. Dix leçons*, Paris: Calmann-Lévy.

Manning, David (1976) *Liberalism*, New York: St. Martin's Press.

Meadowcroft, James (ed.) (1996a) *The Liberal Political Tradition: Contemporary Reappraisals*, Cheltenham, Eng.: Edward Elgar.

Meadowcroft, James (1996b) "Introduction," in idem (ed.).

Merquior, José G. (1991) *Liberalism Old and New*, Boston: Twayne.

Merquior, José G. (1996) "A Panoramic View of the Renaissance of Liberalisms," in Gellner and Cansino (eds.)

Mill, John Stuart (1963 [1848]) *Principles of Political Economy with Some of Their Applications to Social Philosophy, Collected Works*, 2, J.M. Robson (ed.), Toronto: University of Toronto Press.

Mill, John Stuart (1977 [1859]) *On Liberty*, in *Essays on Politics and Society, Collected Works*, 18, J.M. Robson (ed.), Toronto: University of Toronto Press.

Mises, Ludwig von (1933) *Grundprobleme der Nationalökonomie: Untersuchungen über Verfahren, Aufgaben und Inhalt der Wirtschafts- und Gesellschaftslehre*, Jena: Gustav Fischer.

Mises, Ludwig von (1949) *Human Action: A Treatise on Economics*, New Haven, Conn.: Yale University Press.

Mises, Ludwig von (1976 [1927]) *Liberalism: A Socio-Economic Exposition*, Ralph Raico (tr.) 2nd ed., Kansas City, Mo.: Sheed, Andrews, and McMeel.

Moon, J. Donald (ed.) (1988) *Responsibility, Rights, and Welfare: The Theory of the Welfare State*, Boulder, Colo.: Westview.

Myers, A.R. (1975) *Parliaments and Estates in Europe to 1789*, New York: Harcourt, Brace, Jovanovich.

Paine, Thomas (1969 [1792]) *The Rights of Man*, in *The Complete Works*, Philip S. Foner (ed.), New York: Citadel Press.

Patterson, Annabel (1997) *Early Modern Liberalism*, Cambridge, Eng.: Cambridge University Press.

Paul, Ellen Frankel (1979) *Moral Revolution and Economic Science: The Demise of Laissez-Faire in Nineteenth Century British Political Economy*, Westport, Conn.: Greenwood Press.

Raeff, Marc (1994) "The Well-Ordered Police State and the Development of Modernity in Seventeenth and Eighteenth Century Europe: An Attempt at a Comparative Approach," in idem, *Political Ideas and Institutions in Imperial Russia*, Boulder, Colo.: Westview.

Raeder, Linda C. (2002) *John Stuart Mill and the Religion of Humanity*, Columbia, Mo., University of Missouri Press.

Raico, Ralph (1989) Review of Arblaster's *The Rise and Decline of Western Liberalism*, *Reason Papers*, No. 14 (Spring).

Raico, Ralph (1993) "Classical Liberal Roots of the Marxist Doctrine of Classes," in *Requiem for Marx*, Yuri N. Maltsev (ed.), Auburn, Ala.: Ludwig von Mises Institute.

Raico, Ralph (1997) "Individualism," in *The Blackwell Encyclopedic Dictionary of Business Ethics*, Patricia H. Werhane and R. Edward Freeman (eds.), Oxford: Blackwell.

Raico, Ralph (1999) *Die Partei der Freiheit: Studien zur Geschichte des deutschen Liberalismus*, Jörg Guido Hülsmann (tr.), Stuttgart: Lucius and Lucius.

Reinhard, Wolfgang (1999) *Geschichte der Staatsgewalt: Eine vergleichende Verfassungsgeschichte Europas von den Anfängen bis zur Gegenwart*, Munich: Beck.

Reynolds, Morgan O. (1984) *Power and Privilege: Labor Unions in America*, New York: Universe.

Rosenberg, Nathan and L.E. Birdzell, Jr. (1986), *How the West Grew Rich. The Economic Transformation of the Industrial World,* New York: Basic Books.

Rosenblum, Nancy L. (ed.) (1989) *Liberalism and the Moral Life*, Cambridge, Mass.: Harvard University Press.

Rothbard, Murray N. (1970) *Power and Market: Government and the Economy*, Menlo Park, Cal.: Institute for Humane Studies.

Rothbard, Murray N. (1995) *An Austrian Perspective on the History of Economic Thought*, 2 vols., Aldershot, Eng.: Edward Elgar.

Ruggiero, Guido de (1981 [1927]) *The History of European Liberalism*, R.G. Collingwood (tr.), Gloucester, Mass.: Peter Smith.

Ryan, Alan (1993) "Liberalism," in Goodin and Pettit (eds.).

Sadri, Ahmad (1992) *Max Weber's Sociology of Intellectuals*, New York: Oxford University Press.

Schapiro, J. Salwyn (1958) *Liberalism: Its Meaning and History*, Princeton, N.J.: Van Nostrand.

Schatz, Albert (1907) *L'Individualisme économique et social. Ses origines, son évolution, ses formes contemporaines*, Paris: Armand Colin.

Schiffman, Joseph (1958) "Mutual Indebtedness: Unpublished Letters of Edward Bellamy to William Dean Howells," *Harvard Library Bulletin* 12 (3) (Autumn): 363–74.

Shils, Edward (1989) "Liberalism: Collectivist and Conservative," *Chronicles* 13 (7).

Skidelsky, Robert (1995) *The Road from Serfdom: The Economic and Political Consequences of the End of Communism*, London: Allen Lane/Penguin Press.

Smith, David G. (1968) "Liberalism," *International Encyclopedia of the Social Sciences*, David L. Sills (ed.), New York: Macmillan/Free Press.

Spencer, Herbert (1981 [1884]) "The New Toryism," in idem, *The Man vs. the State*, Indianapolis, Ind.: Liberty Press.

Spitz, David (1982) *The Real World of Liberalism*, Chicago: University of Chicago Press.

Stewart, Dugald (1966 [1793]) *Biographical Memoir of Adam Smith*, New York: Augustus M. Kelley.

Stuurman, Siep (1994) "Le libéralisme comme invention historique," in idem (ed.) *Les libéralismes, la théorie politique et l'histoire*. Amsterdam: Amsterdam University Press.

Szasz, Thomas S. (1973) *The Second Sin*, Garden City, N.Y.: Anchor/Doubleday.

Valls, Andrew (1999) "Self-Development and the Liberal State: The Cases of John Stuart Mill and Wilhelm von Humboldt," *Review of Politics* 61 (2) (Spring).

Vierhaus, Rudolf (1982) "Liberalismus," in Otto Brunner, et al. (eds.) *Geschichtliche Grundbegriffe: Historisches Lexikon zur politisch-sozialen Sprache in Deutschland* 3, Stuttgart: Klett-Cotta.

Vincent, Andrew (1988) "Divided Liberalisms?" *History of Political Thought* 9 (1) (Spring).

Viner, Jacob (1978) *Religious Thought and Economic Society*, Jacques Melitz and Donald Winch (eds). Durham, N.C.: Duke University Press.

Wadl, Wilhelm (1987) *Liberalismus und Soziale Frage in Österreich. Deutschliberale Reaktionen und Einflüsse auf die frühe österreichische Arbeiterbewegung (1867 – 1879)*, Vienna: Österreichische Akademie der Wissenschaften.

Waligorski, Conrad (1981) Introduction to Conrad Waligorski and Thomas Hone (eds.) *Anglo-American Liberalism: Readings in Normative Political Economy*, Chicago: Nelson-Hall.

Weber, Max (1949) *The Methodology of the Social Sciences*, Edward A. Shils and Henry A. Finch (trs. and eds.), Glencoe, Ill.: Free Press.

Weede, Erich (1989) "Ideen, Ideologie, und politische Kultur des Westens," *Zeitschrift für Politik* 36 (1) (March).

Werner, Karl Ferdinand (1988) "Political and Social Structures of the West, 300–1300," in Jean Baechler, et al. (eds).

Wolfe, Don M. (ed.) (1944) *Leveller Manifestoes of the Puritan Revolution*, New York: Thomas Nelson and Sons.

Zittelmann, Rainer (1990) *Hitler: Selbstverständnis eines Revolutionärs*, Stuttgart: Klett-Cotta.

3 Intellectuals and the Marketplace

Bankrolling Adam Smith?

Ronald Coase, Nobel Laureate in economics, relates an interesting incident highly revelatory of the state of mind of opinion moulders in the United States.

It concerns the natural gas shortage of the 1960s. Edmund Kitch, of the University of Chicago, had written a study demonstrating the part that short-sighted federal regulation played in the shortage, and presented his findings in a public lecture in Washington, D.C., in 1971. In Coase's words (1994: 49–50):

> Much of the audience consisted of Washington journalists, members of the staff of congressional committees concerned with energy problems, and others with similar jobs. They displayed little interest in the findings of the study but a great deal in discovering who had financed the study. Many seem to have been convinced that the law and economics program at the University of Chicago had been "bought" by the gas industry . . . a large part of the audience seemed to live in a simple world in which

---

This essay is adapted from a paper delivered at the general meeting of the Mont Pèlerin Society, in Cannes, September, 1994.

anyone who thought prices should rise was pro-industry and anyone who wanted prices to be reduced was pro-consumer. I could have explained that the essentials of Kitch's argument had been put forward earlier by Adam Smith—but most of the audience would have assumed that he was someone else in the pay of the American Gas Association.

In this episode we see a microcosm of the world habitually inhabited by anti-market intellectuals and those who have absorbed their teachings. The continued flourishing of this class of intellectuals remains an enduring puzzle and problem for classical liberals. The purpose of this essay is not to propose a definitive solution to the problem, but mainly to assemble and contrast some of the more salient positions advanced (mostly) by liberal scholars, as a step towards solving the puzzle. Finally, I will suggest which position appears to me to be the most plausible.

The Perennial Question

Forty-three years ago, at the 1951 meeting of the Mont Pèlerin Society at Beauvallon, a distinguished panel of scholars discussed the treatment of capitalism by the intellectuals.[1] The talks were assembled and published in a volume edited by F.A. Hayek, *Capitalism and the Historians*.

Arthur Schlesinger, Jr., (1954: 178) composed an entertaining screed on the work,[2] in the form of a review for, of all things, the prestigious *Annals of the American Academy of Political and Social Science*. "All the contributors to this queer volume seem to be driven by some

---

1 T.S. Ashton, "The Treatment of Capitalism by Historians," L.M. Hacker, "The Anticapitalist Bias of American Historians," and Bertrand de Jouvenel, "The Treatment of Capitalism by Continental Intellectuals." These were later supplemented by an additional essay by Ashton, a contribution by W.H. Hutt on the early nineteenth century factory system, and an introduction by F.A. Hayek on "History and Politics," and published by the University of Chicago Press, 1954.
2 A later, and less biased, judgment on the importance of the work is provided by Taylor 1997: 163: "During the following decade modern economic history took a dramatic swing away from the liberal-left consensus established by the Hammonds, Tawney, and the Webbs. The seminal text for this change of direction was the 1954 collection of essays compiled by F.A. Hayek, *Capitalism and the Historians . . .*"

curious sense of persecution," Schlesinger declared. *Capitalism and the Historians* is simply "a summons to a witch-hunt. Americans, one would think, have enough trouble with home-grown McCarthys without importing Viennese professors to add academic luster to the process." Harvard professor Schlesinger ended by denouncing the University of Chicago Press for publishing the book in the first place: "What conceivably could have persuaded a university press to publish this book is hard to imagine. This volume is one more example of what Senator Fulbright recently called 'that swinish blight so common in our time . . . anti-intellectualism.'"

Yes, of course: Hayek, Ashton, de Jouvenel, and the others, all swinish anti-intellectuals and witch-hunters, possibly afflicted with a touch of mental illness (a "sense of persecution"). The review is, in fact, a good example of how New Deal hacks like Schlesinger treated classical liberal thinkers when they were able to get away with it, even, inanely, trying to whip the University of Chicago Press into line.

Capitalism and the Historians

In his paper, Bertrand de Jouvenel described intellectuals as those who deal in the "mental images, representations of the universe . . . of the things and agents therein, of [man] himself and his relation to them." Since every society requires such representations, the importance of this group is very great (91).

It happens that a striking characteristic of modern intellectuals is their animosity towards the marketplace:

> An enormous majority of Western intellectuals display and affirm hostility to the economic and social institutions of their society, institutions to which they give the blanket name of capitalism. (103)

Why should this be? The reason cannot lie, de Jouvenel argues, in a puritanical disdain for social arrangements that satisfy the hedonistic demands of selfish individuals. Modern welfare democracy is also such an arrangement (although not as efficient in accomplishing its end), yet it is not subject to the same antagonism (95–96).

De Jouvenel claims, surprisingly, that "the intellectual's hostility to the businessman presents no mystery, as the two have, by function, wholly different standards." While the businessman's motto is the customer is always right, the intellectual's task is to preserve the highest standards of his field even against the weight of popular opinion (hence, the tendency to favor the painters, novelists, poets, film-makers, etc., "who are for intellectuals only"). (116–21).

There is no doubt that de Jouvenel has identified what is felt to be one of capitalism's major irritants. Many intellectuals find it impossible to resign themselves to the fact that, as Ludwig von Mises pointed out (1956: 9): "What counts in the frame of the market economy is not academic judgments of value, but the valuations actually manifested by people in buying or not buying."

But the attitude of the intellectuals can hardly be wholly accounted for by the mere fact that entrepreneurs serve the wishes of the public, rather than any loftier end—and for the same reason de Jouvenel himself gave earlier. In democratic welfare states, politicians and bureaucrats are also supposed to serve the public, rather than to struggle to preserve standards of excellence per se. Yet the intellectuals' enmity is rarely if ever directed against democracy, the welfare state, or its leaders and functionaries.

Thus, the problem remains. In a significant respect, the situation has deteriorated since the 1951 Mont Pèlerin meeting. Then, de Jouvenel could take for granted that even the modern leftist intellectual "takes pride in the achievement of technique [i.e., technology] and rejoices that men get more of the things which they want" (113). The same can hardly be said today, with the rise of a fanatical environmentalism and incessant attack on industrialism and the consumer society.

In 1972, twenty-one years after that panel at Beauvallon, R.M. Hartwell delivered a talk at the Mont Pèlerin meeting at Montreux, on "History and Ideology" (Hartwell 1974).[3] Hartwell, too, had occasion to remark on the "widely held aversion to the economic and political system which provided the institutional framework for modern economic

---

3 I am grateful to Professor Leonard P. Liggio for bringing this essay to my attention.

growth." As a historian, he naturally stressed the crucial role of historical myths, concocted and circulated by academic intellectuals, in nourishing this aversion.

Hartwell's lecture is especially noteworthy for drawing attention to the *systematic* character of the anti-capitalist onslaught, as experienced by the typical educated citizen of a western democracy, including those journalists cited above. History, he notes, "is only one element in a battery of self-reinforcing prejudice" against private property and the market economy. In literature, economics, philosophy, sociology, and other subjects, the student is continually subjected to data and interpretations that converge on a single point: the viciousness of private enterprise and the virtuousness of state intervention and state-supported labor unionism. "And what schools and universities propagate in formal education," Hartwell observes, "many other institutions reinforce"—particularly the churches, the creative arts, and the mass media (Hartwell 1974: 11–12).[4]

The Ever Changing Indictment

Now, twenty-two years later, we address, once again, the question of the intellectual and the marketplace.

This does not argue the futility of the question, however, but rather its central importance. In a sense, the Mont Pèlerin Society was *founded* to deal with the problem of the modern intellectual's antipathy to capitalism and the harmful consequences of that antipathy. Most of us here have now lived long enough to understand the truth of Schumpeter's assertion that "capitalism stands its trial before judges who have the sentence of death in their pockets." The only thing that changes, Schumpeter wrote, are the particulars (1950: 144). That ever-changing indictment is presented, over and over again, by the intellectuals.

In earlier times, they indicted capitalism for the immiseration of the proletariat, inevitable depressions, and the disappearance of the middle classes. Then, a little later, it was for imperialism and inevitable wars among the imperialist (capitalist) powers.

---

4 On the leftist leanings of American academics, see Lee 1994 and the surveys cited therein.

In more recent decades, the indictment again changed, as earlier accusations became too obviously untenable.

Capitalism was charged with being unable to compete with socialist societies in technological progress (Sputnik); with promoting automation, leading to catastrophic permanent unemployment; both with creating the consumer society and its piggish affluence and with proving incapable of extending such piggishness to the underclass; with "neo-colonialism"; with oppressing women and racial minorities; with spawning a meretricious popular culture; and with destroying the earth itself.[5] As George Stigler remarked: "A constant stream of new criticism—such as the problem of homeless families—is being invented, discovered, or heavily advertised."[6] The question remains: what is at the root of this ever-changing, never-ending indictment? What accounts for the intellectuals' unremitting hostility to the market economy?

To throw light on these questions, we must go beyond the specific accusations themselves. Israel Kirzner writes (1992: 96):

> Whatever the stated specific denunciations of capitalism, whatever the errors in economic analysis which are implicit in these denunciations, a thorough understanding of the anti-capitalist mentality cannot avoid ultimately coming to grips with the deep-seated prejudices and ingrained habits of thought which are, both consciously and unconsciously, responsible for the antipathy shown to the market system.

---

5 Cf. Bronfenbrenner 1981: 104: "Both the rise of environmental legislation and the post-thalidomide burgeoning of ostensible consumer protection have come since Schumpeter's death; both would have been grist for Schumpeter's mill." Philosopher Robert Nozick 1984: 134 wrote of an experience he often had in replying to criticisms that laissez-faire capitalism causes various evils, from monopoly and pollution to systematic overproduction or underproduction. After Nozick painstakingly refuted the stated charge, his interlocutor "drops the point and quickly leaps to another," child labor, racism, advertising, etc., etc. "Point after point is given up.... What is not given up, though, is the opposition to capitalism." Nozick concluded that the particular arguments are not important, since "there is an underlying *animus* against capitalism" (emphasis in original). This is an experience that many another advocate of the free market could also attest to.

6 Stigler 1989: 1. I am grateful to Dr. Claire Friedland, manager of the George J. Stigler archives, for her kindness in making this and other unpublished papers of Professor Stigler available to me.

Hayek on the Intellectuals and Socialism

F.A. Hayek was acutely concerned with our problem, since he, too, was wholly convinced of the importance of the intellectuals: "They are the organs which modern society has developed for spreading knowledge and ideas," he declares in his essay, "The Intellectuals and Socialism" (Hayek 1967). The intellectuals—whom Hayek characterizes as "the professional second-hand dealers in ideas"[7]—exercise their power through their domination of public opinion: "There is little that the ordinary man of today learns about events or ideas except through the medium of this class." Among other things, they often virtually manufacture professional reputations in the minds of the general population; and through their domination of the news media, they color and shape the information that people in each country have of events and trends in foreign nations. Once an idea is adopted by the intellectuals, its acceptance by the masses is "almost automatic and irresistible." Ultimately, the intellectuals are the legislators of mankind (178–80, 182).

With all this, Hayek's view of the intellectuals is flatteringly benign: their ideas are determined by and large by "honest convictions and good intentions" (184).[8] In "The Intellectuals and Socialism," Hayek does mention in passing the intellectuals' egalitarian bias; the analysis, however, is basically in terms of their "scientism." With his characteristic emphasis on epistemology, Hayek sees the revolt against the market economy as stemming from the methodological errors he identified and investigated at length in his brilliant study of the rise of French positivism, *The Counter-Revolution of Science* (1955).

Thus, in Hayek's view, the chief influence on the intellectuals has been the example of the natural sciences and their applications. As man has come to understand and then control the forces of nature, intellectuals have grown infatuated with the idea that an analogous

---

7 This definition by Hayek is somewhat idiosyncratic, in that it excludes the *originators* of ideas, e.g., among socialists, Saint-Simon and Marx.

8 At one point (182) Hayek does suggest that selfish personal interests might play a part in the intellectuals' attitude; he refers, without naming him, to Karl Mannheim and "the curious claim . . . that [the intellectual class] was the only one whose views were not decidedly influenced by its own economic interests." But he does not indicate why he considers this claim "curious."

mastery of social forces could produce similar benefits for mankind. They are under the sway of "such beliefs as that deliberate control or conscious organization is also in social affairs always superior to the results of spontaneous processes which are not directed by a human mind, or that any order based on a plan beforehand must be better than one formed by the balancing of opposing forces" (186–87). Hayek even makes the following astonishing statement (187):

> That, with the application of engineering techniques, the direction of all forms of human activity according to a single coherent plan should prove to be as successful in society as it has been in innumerable engineering tasks is too plausible a conclusion not to seduce most of those who are elated by the achievements of the natural sciences. It must indeed be admitted both that it would require powerful arguments to counter the strong presumption in favor of such a conclusion and that these arguments have not yet been adequately stated. . . . The argument will not lose its force until it has been conclusively shown why what has proved so eminently successful in producing advances in so many fields should have limits to its usefulness and become positively harmful if extended beyond those limits.

It is exceedingly difficult to follow Hayek's reasoning here. He appears to be saying that because the natural sciences have made great advances and because innumerable particular engineering projects have succeeded, it is quite understandable that many intellectuals should conclude that "the direction of all forms of human activity according to a single coherent plan" will be similarly successful.

But, in the first place, the advances of the natural sciences were not brought about in accordance with any overall central plan; rather, they were the product of many separate decentralized but coordinated researchers (produced analogously in some respects to the market process; see Baker 1945 and Polanyi 1951[9]). Second, from the fact that many

---

[9] These are both works with which Hayek was quite familiar, which makes his argument at this point more perplexing.

particular engineering projects have succeeded it does not follow that a single vast engineering project, one subsuming all particular projects, is likely to succeed; nor does it seem likely that most people will find such a claim plausible.

Why, then, is it natural, or logical, or easily comprehensible that intellectuals should reason from the triumphs of decentralized scientific research and of individual engineering projects to the success of a plan undertaking to direct "all forms of human activity"?[10]

In his review of Hayek's *The Road to Serfdom*, Joseph Schumpeter (1946: 269) remarks that Hayek was "polite to a fault" towards his opponents, in that he hardly ever attributed to them "anything beyond intellectual error." But not all the points that must be made can be made without more "plain speaking," Schumpeter declares.[11]

Schumpeter here implies an important distinction. Civility *in debate*, including the formal presumption of good faith on the part of one's adversaries, is always in order. But there is also a place for the attempt *to explain* the attitudes, for instance, of anti-market intellectuals (a form of the sociology of knowledge). In this endeavor, "politeness" is not precisely what is most called for. As regards the positivist intellectuals who argued from the successes of natural science to the need for central planning: it may well be that this false inference was no simple

---

10 In another essay, on "Socialism and Science," 1978: 295, Hayek refers to "the undeniable propensity of minds trained in the physical sciences, as well as of engineers, to prefer a deliberately created orderly arrangement to the results of spontaneous growth—an influential and common attitude, which frequently attracts intellectuals to socialist schemes. This is a widespread and important phenomenon which has had a profound effect on the development of political thought." It seems highly doubtful that surveys of political opinion among university professors in the United States, western Europe, or elsewhere, would find socialist opinions more common among physical scientists and engineers than in the humanities and social science faculties.

11 Hayek 1973: 161n. 18, 70, rebutted Schumpeter's criticism, asserting that it was not "'politeness to a fault' but profound conviction about what are the decisive factors" for his having attributed merely intellectual error to his opponents in *The Road to Serfdom*. Hayek reaffirmed that: "It is necessary to realize that the sources of many of the most harmful agents in this world are often not evil men but highminded idealists, and that in particular the foundations of totalitarian barbarism have been laid by honorable and well-meaning scholars who never recognized the offspring they produced." One wonders how Hayek could know this about the character of those who "laid the foundations of totalitarian barbarism."

intellectual error, but was facilitated by their prejudices and resentments, or perhaps their own will to power.[12]

In any case, Hayek's gentlemanly deference to anti-market intellectuals can sometimes be downright misleading. Consider his statement (1967: 193):

> Orthodoxy of any kind, any pretense that a system of ideas is final and must be unquestioningly accepted as a whole, is the one view which of necessity antagonizes all intellectuals, whatever their views on particular issues.

This, of a category of persons that in the twentieth century has notoriously included thousands of prominent apologists for Soviet Communism in all western countries, is indeed politeness "to a fault."[13] There was, after all, good reason, as late as the 1950s, for Raymond Aron (1957) to have written on *The Opium of the Intellectuals* and for H.B. Acton (1955) to have entitled what is probably the best philosophical critique of Marxism-Leninism, *The Illusion of the Epoch*.[14]

---

12 Cf. the comment by George Stigler 1989: 6: "a central reason for the dissatisfaction of the intellectuals with the enterprise system" is that "it does not give them a mechanism to coerce changes in the behavior of individuals." Cf. also Robert Skidelsky 1978: 83, who mentions, as one factor in the conversion of the younger American economists to Keynesianism, that, in the version propagated by Alvin Hansen, it provided a "rationale for the permanent direction of economic life by an élite of economists. . . . In the Keynesian political economy, public policy would be handed over to the professional economists, who alone would understand what needed to be done." Robert Higgs 1987a: 116 observes that American Progressives around 1900 found state intervention appealing because it implied a social organization supervised and directed by engineers, planners, technicians, and trained bureaucrats, and thus put "a wise minority in the saddle."

13 There is by now a substantial literature on the subject; see, for instance, Caute 1973. Richard Pipes 1993: 202 makes the interesting comment that: "The Bolshevik regime, for all its objectionable features, attracted them [intellectuals] because it was the first government since the French Revolution to vest power in people of their own kind. In Soviet Russia, intellectuals could expropriate capitalists, execute political opponents, and muzzle reactionary ideas." See also the challenge issued by Eugene D. Genovese (1994) to his fellow intellectuals to testify publicly on what they knew of the crimes of Soviet Communism and when they knew it.

14 Cf. O'Brien 1994: 344, who notes that "the overwhelming majority of [his] academic colleagues adopted an attitude of judicious agnosticism and relativism towards the horrors of the Stalinist and other Marxist regimes."

Nor was Communism the only nefarious orthodoxy to claim the loyalty of numerous intellectuals, as is shown by the cases of Martin Heidegger, Robert Brasillach, Giovanni Gentile, Ezra Pound, and many others. For a less complimentary but more realistic view of the integrity of modern intellectuals we may turn to the memoirs of the German historian, Golo Mann (1991: 534), who quotes from his diary of 1933: "18 May. [Josef] Goebbels in front of a writers' meeting in the Hotel Kaiserhof: 'We [Nazis] have been reproached with not being concerned with the intellectuals. That was not necessary for us. We knew quite well: if we first have power, then the intellectuals will come on their own.' Thunderous applause—from the intellectuals."[15]

Schumpeter on the Intellectual Proletariat

In chiding Hayek, Schumpeter suggested (1946: 269) that he might have learned a useful lesson from Karl Marx. Schumpeter's own interpretation reflects his lifelong engagement with Marxism. Like Marx, he offered a highly pessimistic prognosis for the capitalist system, though for mainly different reasons (1950: 131–45). But while Schumpeter holds that intellectuals will play a key role in capitalism's demise, he in no way relies on the scenario set forth in the *Communist Manifesto*.

There, Marx and Engels (1976: 494) announced that as the final revolution approaches, a section of the "bourgeois ideologists" will go over to the side of the proletariat. These will be the ideologists "who have worked their way up to a theoretical understanding of the historical

---

15 Benjamin Constant 1988: 137–38, in criticizing the French writers of the Revolutionary and Napoleonic period, described the intellectuals' penchant to identify with arbitrary power: "all the great developments of extrajudicial force, all the examples of recourse to illegal measures in dangerous circumstances have from century to century been recounted with respect and described with complacency. The author, sitting comfortably at his desk, hurls arbitrary measures in every direction. . . . For a moment, he believes himself invested with power just because he is preaching its abuse . . . in this way he gives himself something of the pleasure of authority; he repeats as loud as he can the great words of public safety, supreme law, public interest. . . . Poor imbecile! He talks to those who are only too glad to listen to him and who, at the first opportunity, will test out his own theories upon him." Constant's words may be viewed as a prescient gloss on Stalin's treatment of many of the Bolshevik intellectuals who had lent their aid to the creation of the Soviet terror state.

movement as a whole."¹⁶ Such a laughably self-serving description could hardly appeal to an inveterate skeptic like Schumpeter. Instead, his "Marxism" consisted in examining capitalism as a system with certain attendant sociological traits, and exposing the class interests of the intellectuals within that system.[17]

Compared to previous social orders, capitalism is especially vulnerable to attack:

> unlike any other type of society, capitalism inevitably and by virtue of the very logic of its civilization creates, educates, and subsidizes a vested interest in social unrest. (1950: 146)

In particular, it brings forth and nurtures a class of secular intellectuals who wield the power of words over the general mind. The capitalist wealth machine makes possible cheap books, pamphlets, newspapers, and the ever-widening public that reads them. Freedom of speech and of the press enshrined in liberal constitutions entails also "freedom to nibble at the foundations of capitalist society"—a constant gnawing away that is promoted by the critical rationalism inherent in that form of society. Moreover, in contrast to earlier regimes, a capitalist state finds it difficult, except under exceptional circumstances, to suppress dissident intellectuals: such a procedure would conflict with the general principles of the rule of law and the limits to the police power dear to the bourgeoisie itself (1950: 148–51).

The key to the hostility of intellectuals to capitalism is the expansion of education, particularly higher education.[18] This creates

---

16 The critique of Marxism as the camouflaged ideology of an intellectual would-be "new class" is part of the communist anarchist tradition, begun by Bakunin and continued by Machajski and others; see Dolgoff 1971 and Szelenyi and Martin 1991.

17 This approach, however, like the Marxist analysis of historical change in terms of class conflict, had numerous precursors among classical liberal thinkers; see the essay on "The Conflict of Classes: Liberal vs. Marxist Theories," in the present work.

18 Cf. Raymond Ruyer 1969: 155–56, who indicates the social and psychological problems resulting from prolonged state instruction (including "adult education") and the diffusion of "culture" under the aegis of the state. He concludes: "It is typical that the greatest progress that has come about in 'the democratic extension of culture' has been produced by private enterprise in the form of paperback books, in which the state did not involve itself, except to impose its usual taxes." A third of a century later, the same could be said of compact discs

unemployment, or underemployment, of the university-schooled classes; many become "psychically unemployable in manual occupations without necessarily acquiring employability in, say, professional work." The tenuous social position of these intellectuals breeds discontent and resentment, which are often rationalized as objective social criticism. This emotional malaise, Schumpeter asserts,

> will much more realistically account for hostility to the capitalist order than could the theory—itself a rationalization in the psychological sense—according to which the intellectual's righteous indignation about the wrongs of capitalism simply represents the logical inference from outrageous facts . . . (1950: 152–53)[19]

A major merit of Schumpeter's argument is that it elucidates an abiding feature of the sociology of radicalism and revolution: the hunt for government jobs. The interconnection between over-education, an expanding reservoir of unemployable intellectuals, the pressure for more bureaucratic positions, and political turmoil was a commonplace among European observers in the nineteenth century.[20] In 1850, the conservative author Wilhelm Heinrich Riehl (1976: 227–38) offered a remarkable analysis, in many ways anticipating Schumpeter, of the "intellectual proletariat" (*Geistesproletariat*). Even then Germany was producing each

---

and computers. Ruyer's work, quite unduly neglected, is a profound and elegant dissection of the intellectual's persistent resentment of the free market economy and capitalist society. In this respect, it stands in contrast to the recent book of Raymond Boudon (2004). Despite its promising title (*Why the Intellectuals do not Like Liberalism*) and occasional insights, Boudon's book proves to be superficial, e.g., in dating the intellectuals' turn against a liberal order from around 1950.

19 Schumpeter 1950: 155 highlights an important channel of the intellectuals' influence, by means of the state bureaucracies, which are "open to conversion by the modern intellectual with whom, through a similar education, they have much in common."

20 See O'Boyle 1970; also Levy 1987: 160, who writes of "the state-created intelligentsias of post-Restoration Europe [i.e., after 1815] which, outpacing economic growth, faced serious underemployment and played important roles in the revolutions of 1830 and 1848." In the Reichstag, Chancellor Otto von Bismarck (Raico 1999: 100) claimed that social revolutionaries in Russia consisted of the "diploma-proletariat," an excess produced by higher education which society could not absorb. The leaders were not workers, but consisted "in part of people of genteel education, many half-educated people . . . dissipated students and unsullied dreamers . . ."

year much more "intellectual product" than it could use or pay for, testifying to an "unnatural" division of national labor. This was a general phenomenon in advanced countries, Riehl maintains, resulting from the enormous industrial growth that was taking place. But the impoverished intellectual workers experience a contradiction between their income and their perceived needs, between their own haughty conception of their rightful social position and the true one, a contradiction which is far more irreconcilable than in the case of the manual laborers. Because they cannot "reform" their own meager salaries, they try to reform society. It is these intellectual proletarians who have taken the lead in social revolutionary movements in Germany. "These literati see the world's salvation in the gospel of socialism and communism, because it contains their own salvation," through domination of the masses.[21] Later revolutionary movements, whether of the left or the right, can be understood to a large extent as the ideologically camouflaged raid on the great state employment office. Carl Levy (1987: 180) has linked the expansion of the state from the later nineteenth century on to the growth in the numbers of the university-educated, who sought government jobs and utilized positivism as a facilitating ideology. Positivism

> stressed the need for expertise, special training, and trained intelligence . . . [fortified by] a desacralizing of tradition and the rapid expansion of the public sphere . . . [there proliferated] schemes for the organization of society which substituted for traditional elites and capitalist entrepreneurs a stratum of experts and/or the lay clerisy. Examples can be found among the Fabians and the ILP [Independent Labor Party], [Edward] Bellamy and other American authoritarian utopia builders, the Italian socialist professors, and the French socialist elites.

From this perspective, we obtain a deeper understanding of the claim that the welfare state "saved capitalism." What the welfare state has actually accomplished is to furnish a never-ending source of state jobs

---

21 Schumpeter does not mention Riehl in *Capitalism, Socialism, and Democracy* and refers to him once in his *History of Economic Analysis* (1954: 427 and 427 n. 20), but only in connection with Riehl's work in *Kulturgeschichte* (cultural history).

for the (mainly middle class) products of what is still referred to as university education, without, as in the nineteenth century, requiring a revolutionary assault.[22]

While there is doubtless a great deal of truth in Schumpeter's identification of the systemic surplus of intellectuals as a source of anti-capitalism, it also presents certain difficulties.

Such an overproduction—and consequent un- or under-employment—is a feature of non-capitalist societies, as well. Its effect is the *general* destabilization of regimes, as occurs from time to time in underdeveloped countries. A more detailed knowledge of the situation in former Communist societies might show that it was also implicated in their subversion and final overthrow.

More to the point: it is not so much the *unemployed* intellectuals who are the problem but the ones who *are* employed. Intellectuals unable to find suitable jobs may well provide a receptive subculture as well as occasional cannon fodder for revolutionary movements: among communist anarchists in the late nineteenth century, or in some third world countries more recently. In Germany after the First World War, artists and writers frozen out of the avant-garde culture of Weimar were prominent among the early National Socialists.

But Schumpeter's thesis does not hold for many other cases, probably the historically most significant ones. Émile Zola and Anatole France, Gerhart Hauptmann and Bertold Brecht, H.G. Wells and Bernard Shaw, John Dewey and Upton Sinclair were scarcely "unemployables" in the intellectual world. Today the "stars" of the mass news media of all the advanced countries—you would know their names in your own country; one could mention American "newspersons" who earn a million dollars a year or more, such being the savage inequalities of capitalism—are typically constant "nibblers" at the system of private

---

[22] Cf. Mises (1974: 47–48): "In dealing with the ascent of modern statism, socialism, and interventionism, one must not neglect the preponderant role played by pressure groups and lobbies of civil servants and those university graduates who longed for government jobs." In this connection, Mises mentions the Fabian Society in Britain and the *Verein für Sozialpolitik* (Association for Social Policy) in Imperial Germany.

enterprise. The question is rather why so many successful and highly influential intellectuals become carping critics of the free economy.[23]

The Two Approaches of Ludwig von Mises

If Schumpeter declined to be "polite to a fault" when it came to anti-market intellectuals, what is one to say of Hayek's own mentor, Ludwig von Mises?

No one surpassed Mises in the importance he attached to the power of ideas.[24] Thus, it was crucial to his social philosophy and historical interpretations to determine the basis of "the anti-capitalistic mentality," especially as represented among the intellectuals (Mises 1956).

Often Mises emphasizes invidious personal motivation—resentment and bitter envy—as the source of this attitude. Replacement of the society of status by the society of contract aggravated feelings of failure and inferiority. With equality of opportunity and all careers open to talent, lack of financial success becomes a judgment upon the individual. This is a burden he attempts to shift by scapegoating the social system (1956: 5–11). Intellectuals share this weakness, perhaps in an accentuated form. On occasion, Mises goes so far as to trace the "psychological roots of anti-liberalism" to mental pathology. The scapegoating of the social system by those unable to cope with the reality of their relative failure in life is, Mises claims, a mental disorder which psychiatry has so far neglected to classify. Engaging in a bit of volunteer psychiatric nosology, he ventures to label this condition "the Fourier complex" (1985: 13–17), after the early French socialist, Charles Fourier.

Although Mises's focus on envy and resentment is the best known of his attempts to explain the anti-capitalist mentality,[25] a second and

---

23 Doubt is cast on Schumpeter's fundamental analysis by Paul A. Samuelson 1981: 10, who points out that in Japan for decades "the continued omnipresence of Marxist terminology among journalists and teachers" has had no discernible effect on Japanese politics.
24 For instance, in 1932, Mises 1990: 96 stated: "All the misfortunes from which Europe has suffered in the last two decades have been the inevitable result of the application of the theories which have dominated the social and economic philosophy of the last fifty years."
25 On one of the very few occasions that he has taken notice of Mises's writings, Paul Samuelson 1981: 10, n. 3 writes of his "notion that those who can't hack it in the competitive commercial

different approach of his seems more fruitful. In an early essay titled "The Psychological Roots of the Resistance to Economics" (1933: 170–88), Mises launches a radical attack on the strand of traditional western morality that has stigmatized moneymaking. Citing Cicero's *De officiis* as an exemplary text, he identifies the contempt for moneymaking deeply ingrained in western culture as the source of the hostility towards capitalists, trade, and speculation "which today dominates our whole public life, politics, and the written word." This contempt, nurtured and sustained through the centuries under changing regimes, is the natural outgrowth of a class morality—specifically, the morality of the classes that are sheltered from the market by the circumstance that they live from taxes.[26] In our own day, it is a morality generated by "priests, bureaucrats, professors, and army officers," who look with "loathing and scorn" on entrepreneurs, capitalists, and speculators (1933: 181–82).[27]

Insight into the prevalence of this anti-market ethic helps explain (as Mises's other, envy-based approach does not) the anti-market attitudes often found even among the economically successful in the private sector, since "no one can escape the power of a dominant ideology." Thus, "entrepreneurs and capitalists themselves are swayed by the moral outlook that damns their activity." They suffer from a bad conscience and feelings of inferiority. This shows itself in, among other things, the support

---

struggle for existence become the whiners and complainers who seek to subvert the capitalistic order." This is also the only Misesian explanation mentioned by Nozick 1984: 138.

26 Friedrich Naumann, today a liberal icon in Germany, founded his National Social Association in 1896 to promote social welfare measures and an imperialist agenda. Eugen Richter, the chief authentic liberal political figure of the time, mocked Naumann's little group as a "pastor and school teacher party." Richter explained the deficient understanding of the market on the part of its members from the fact that they obtained their living from taxes. Raico 1999: 227. See also the essay on Richter in the present volume.

27 It should be pointed out that Mises had in mind Continental regimes, in which the clergy was customarily supported by state subsidies. De Jouvenel, in Hayek (ed.), 1954: 104, points out that modern intellectuals have taken over the task of the medieval clergy: they are "forever thrusting the condition of the poor before the eyes of the rich," and forever scolding the rich for being rich.

given to socialist movements by millionaires and their sons and daughters (1933: 184).[28]

Envy and Envy-Avoidance

A different slant on the anti-market attitudes of the economically successful is offered by another liberal scholar, Helmut Schoeck. In his *Envy* (1987), Schoeck presents an empirical examination of this pervasive yet elusive—and strangely under-investigated—phenomenon, in the light of evidence from anthropology, ethnology, social psychology, and history.[29]

Human beings are by nature prone to envy, springing from a primitive conception of causality that interprets the good fortune of others as having been achieved at a cost to oneself. People are equally subject, however, to a "universal fear of one's neighbor's envy and of the envy of the gods and spirits" (363, 308). Fear of the envy of others—of the "evil eye," for example—gives rise to "a primitive, pre-religious, irrational sense of guilt," and with it behavior patterns that aim at *envy-avoidance*.

In various societies varying means have evolved to cope with this sense of guilt and to ward off the retribution of the envious. With intellectuals in capitalist society, envy-avoidance often manifests itself in support for egalitarian causes. The diffuse dread of the envy of others, Schoeck finds, is "the root of that general, aimless sense of guilt which,

---

28 Drawing on Schumpeter, Robert Higgs 1987: 239 comments on one of the results of the cultural hegemony of the anti-capitalist intellectuals: "the bourgeoisie loses faith in its traditional values and ideals; its defense of the free-market system grows steadily weaker as it accommodates itself to a political environment that gives ever greater priority to social security, equality, and governmental regulation and planning." George Stigler 1984: 152–53 also held that, because of the influence of the intellectuals, capitalists have themselves become apologetic for their pursuit of profit. "To boast that large profits demonstrate great efficiency in producing existing products and introducing new ones is considered even by them [the capitalists] to be too archaic a form of thought for public consumption." Mises 1933: 183 suggests another reason for the intellectuals' rejection of economic theory, and, by implication, liberalism: they identify with "the demigods who make history," while economics demonstrates the strict limits to the power of these masters of mankind.

29 Choi 1993 equates envy with the demand for social justice, and sees it as stemming from an inability to understand the sources and functions of entrepreneurial profits. While suggestive and useful as far as it goes, this would seem to take too narrow a view of envy.

during the past hundred years, has exercised so disrupting and disorienting an influence. The pangs of guilt (social conscience), and the naive assumption that there could ever be a form of society that was either classless or otherwise non-provocative of envy, have been responsible for the adherence to leftist movements of large numbers of middle- and upper-class people . . ." (324). In adhering to movements that preach social and economic equality, they assuage their guilt and anxiety, for now they can feel they are helping to set up "a society in which no one is envious" (325).[30]

Schoeck's theory has the advantage of accounting also for the peculiar self-righteous "idealism" often displayed by leftist intellectuals, especially among the young:

> sensitivity to the envy of others is so deep-rooted in the human psyche that most people erroneously interpret the sense of redemption and peace, which they feel when they have made concessions to envy, as confirmation, not only of their moral superiority, but also of the expediency of their action in the reality of the here and now. (362)

We may add that the blessed release experienced by those who have, they feel, placed themselves safely beyond the envy of the resentfully dispossessed often turns to fury when they are faced with their class brethren who have casually spurned such psychological capitulation.

But How Relevant are the Intellectuals?

The authors considered so far have been agreed at least in assigning a great deal of weight in the ultimate determination of political events to intellectuals and the ideologies they generate. This was also the standpoint of Murray Rothbard, which he set forth theoretically (e.g., in Rothbard 1974: 72–76) and frequently explicated historically

---

30 Regarding the leftist orientation of the economically successful, Schoeck remarks (327) that: "a man will opt for a philosophically decked-out, long-term communist programme . . . all the more readily, the more unequal, distinguished, and exceptional is the position he already holds in society, in so far as he combines his privileged position with a sense of guilt."

(e.g., Rothbard 1989 and 1996). Virtually uniquely among free-market thinkers, Murray Rothbard was equally adept, where appropriate, at analyzing political change as the result of interest-group machinations—for example, in the case of the Federal Reserve (Rothbard 1994).

But the political relevance of the intellectuals has been challenged by another group of liberal scholars, most notably by George J. Stigler.[31]

Professor Stigler's justly famed wit was on target when he defined intellectuals (1975: 314) as "people who strongly prefer talking and writing to physical exertion." In this way, Stigler spurned the common but faulty inference that *intellectuals* are particularly *intelligent*. There is no necessary connection between the two categories: for the most part, what distinguishes an intellectual is his command of *a particular discourse*.[32]

Stigler was quite aware that, despite the many benefits they reap from the capitalist system, intellectuals have by and large been its implacable critics in all the sectors they dominate (Stigler 1984a: 143–58)[33]. Yet, while "there is a natural temptation to credit to them . . . the decline that has occurred in the public esteem for private enterprise and the

---

31 Norman Barry 1989: 55 (see also idem 1984) somewhat overstates the case when he refers to an "intellectual schizophrenia" in classical liberal thinking, which undertakes to explain the expansion of the public sector by the actions of "sinister interests," while crediting the triumph of the liberal cause to the advance of liberal "ideas." Actually, the position of most liberals who have addressed the problem may be best summed up by the statement of R.M. Hartwell 1989: 122: "Ideas count, and always have, for good or for ill." Barry's own suggestion 1989: 54, that "there is an interplay between ideas and interests and that the relative strengths of the two forces will depend upon the prevailing institutional arrangements in the society in question," is a fair summary of the customary liberal view.

32 Cf. the typically adroit *aperçu* of Raymond Ruyer 1969: 158: "One is an intellectual today . . . without any special aptitude for intellectuality, with an intelligence often inferior to that of a worker, an artisan, or a middling tradesman, and sometimes with an IQ manifestly close to the level of mental deficiency. In order to 'pass,' it is enough to have acquired the vocabulary of intellectuality."

33 Cf., ibid., 161: "The intellectual wishes to choose his way of life and also to choose his standard of living. He chooses freedom, outside of the economic circuit, but he does not renounce the benefits of this circuit. The men who work within the economy displease him, as the yokels displeased the aristocrats, who nonetheless lived on the labor of the yokels, or as the clothiers and shopkeepers of the seventeenth century were the butt of the sarcasms of high society and the 'persons of quality,' who in the end might refuse to settle their bills." It is a great pity that Ruyer's insightful and beautifully written book has not been translated into English, nor gained the appreciation it deserves.

large expansion of state control over economic life" (1982: 28–29), this temptation should be resisted. In his view, claims regarding the decisive influence of intellectuals and ideologies are unscientific, since such claims have never been quantified and subjected to empirical testing. In fact, there is a total lack of any theory of how ideologies originate and change (Stigler 1982: 35; 1984b: 3).

In contrast, Stigler proposes to attack the problem with the conventional analytical methods of (neoclassical) economics: hypotheses are to be formulated in quantifiable terms and tested against the data.

A central implication of economic theory is that "man is eternally a utility maximizer, in his home, in his office,—be it public or private—in the church, in his scientific work, in short, everywhere" (1982: 35). Just as they act on the market to maximize their personal utility, so "individuals consistently behave in a utility-increasing manner with respect to the use of the state" (1984b: 3), that is, in supporting measures that, in the aggregate, constitute the historical expansion of state power.

Very sensibly, Stigler warns against defining utility in such a way as to make the hypothesis tautological (1982: 26). Conceding that there is "no accepted content to the utility function," he proposes one, viz., that a person's utility "depend[s] upon the welfare of the actor, his family, plus a narrow circle of associates" (1982: 36).

How far this advances the argument is unclear, however. After all, a person's adherence to a given ideology is usually conditioned by his belief that it will, in some sense, promote his "welfare" and that of his family and close associates, so that reliance on utility functions does not automatically obviate the need to reckon with the impact of ideology.

In Stigler's view, the simplest way to test the role of ideology as a non-utility-maximizing goal is to ascertain whether the champions of a given ideology incur costs in supporting it.

> If on average and over substantial periods of time we find (say) that the proponents of "small is beautiful" earn less than comparable talents devoted to urging the National Association of Manufacturers to new glories, I will accept the evidence. But first let us see it. (1982: 35)

"Utility," then, appears, for all practical purposes, to mean maximization of income. This is reasonable from Stigler's viewpoint, since employing another value, for instance, maximization of *power*, would create insuperable difficulties for formalization and empirical testing in Stiglerian terms.

Stigler further holds that the desire of intellectuals to maximize their incomes (now including prestige and "apparent influence") explains their distribution along the political spectrum (1982: 34). He refers to Joseph Schumpeter as having partially accepted this position. But Schumpeter's (and Riehl's and others') ascription of economic motives to the intellectuals is of a very different order from Stigler's. As we have noted, Schumpeter held that economic factors (underemployment, etc.) tend to create a *mind-set* among intellectuals which is apt to generate anti-capitalistic ideologies that, in turn, spread throughout society. Stigler seems to maintain that economic factors operate upon individual intellectuals directly and immediately.

Stigler applies his notion of the relative unimportance of ideology in a general way to the repeal of the Corn Laws in England in 1846 usually considered a landmark victory of liberalism in its heroic phase. In this instance, it was not intellectuals like the classical economists, from Adam Smith on, nor even leaders like Richard Cobden and Robert Peel, who were responsible, but rather "a shift in political and economic power" (1975: 318–20).

Gary M. Anderson and Robert D. Tollison (1985) purport to provide a somewhat detailed study of the Anti-Corn League in the fashion of Stigler (as well as Gary Becker and others), which appears to avoid the ambiguities of Stigler's position.[34] While the authors do not

---

34 Stigler at one point writes 1975: 315 that the intellectual's role is not that of "simply meeting a well-defined demand for ideology by some important groups in the society. Groups and desired ideologies are neither clearly defined nor immutable through time, so the effective intellectual performs useful functions in detecting shifts of view, in filling in the details of the views, and in gradually adapting them to new circumstances." His tasks are "giving coherence to a set of positions or interests, of developing them into principles sufficiently broad to allow ready application to new issues and facts, of finding the natural allies and uncovering the submerged conflicts between groups"; these are "not routine or unimportant tasks." But Stigler's qualifications undermine his position to a substantial degree. If the

deny that "ideology played a role" in repeal, they declare that any basically ideological explanation should be avoided because of its untestability. Instead, they apply the framework of public choice analysis, focusing on the part played by the direct financial self-interest of some of the League's contributors and supporters. Yet it is far from clear how their own narrative, which piles up generally well-known facts with no attempt at quantification and formalization, is supposed to be "testable" in the rigorous sense they require. Droll is the authors' earnest presentation of the public subscription for Cobden and the awarding of a seat for Manchester in the House of Commons to John Bright as "the Payoff" of the two great liberal leaders.

George Stigler sometimes combined his deprecatory estimation of the influence of intellectuals with a similarly low evaluation of the influence of individuals altogether, including political leaders. As a general explanation of political change, Stigler's own hypothesis is that

> we live in a world of reasonably well-informed people acting intelligently in pursuit of their self-interests. In this world, leaders play only a modest role, acting much more as agents than as instructors or guides of the classes they appear to lead. (1982: 37)

As a rule, the effect of prominent leaders on history is "almost infinitesimal" (1975: 319). It is safe to say that this assessment would find little agreement from students of the careers of Mohammed, Napoleon, Bismarck, or Hitler—or of Lenin and Stalin.[35]

---

intellectuals have the job, among other things, of even *defining* interest groups, then their independent effect would seem to be considerable.

35 In a work tracing the Marxist-Leninist revolutionary vision that came to be shared by intellectual and military cadres in poor countries across the world, Forrest D. Colburn wisely observes 1994: 104, "for a satisfactory understanding of revolution, the revolutionary impulse itself has to be explained, and only the most reductionist theorist would argue that the radical urge to remake state and society is either completely 'rational' or 'self-interested' . . . this approach can perhaps explain the behavior of a Cuban bureaucrat or peasant, but it is a loss to explain Fidel Castro. His leadership of the Cuban Revolution cannot be explained solely as result of changes in objective conditions or material interests. His ideas—and he is full of them—are consequential because they surely shape his decisions. Explaining revolutionary elites' ideas is crucial, because in a revolution ideas are more than a kind of intervening variable that mediates interests and outcomes. Ideas transform perceptions of interests, sometimes

The Rise and Fall of Soviet Communism

Authors who minimize the impact of ideology in politics would have a hard time accounting for the rise, duration, and final demise of Communism in Russia. It is difficult to imagine what could explain crucial episodes in the history of Soviet Communism if ideology is relegated to a subordinate position. Such episodes include Lenin's own revolutionary career, the formation of the Bolshevik party, the coup d'état of October, 1917, the institution of "War Communism," victory in the civil war, and the fanatical dedication of the cadres who carried out the collectivization of agriculture and the terror famine.

In a major study, Martin Malia asserts (1994: 16) that "the key to understanding the Soviet phenomenon is ideology," specifically, Marxism-Leninism.

Malia traces the story back to the mid-nineteenth century. Russia, where civil society was weak and the state strong, provided fertile ground for the spread of socialist ideas. Liberal social theory the ideas of Locke, Hume, Adam Smith, Turgot, Jefferson, and others had never struck root. By the time an intelligentsia sprang up in Russia, European intellectuals, from whom the Russians derived most of their political views, had made capitalism into an object of horror. The chaos following the fall of the Tsar and the demoralization caused by the First World War permitted Lenin and his highly disciplined Bolsheviks to effect their coup d'état.

The Bolsheviks at once set about to realize the Marxist dream: to construct a free and prosperous society by abolishing private property and the market. But that task, Malia maintains, citing the Austrian School, in particular Mises and Hayek, was and is inherently impossible, an assault on reality (185, 515). From the start the Soviet Union was a "world-historical fraud" (15). The land that was supposedly in the vanguard of progressive humanity was, in truth, an arena of endless oppression, mass poverty, and boundless despair. Suppressing this reality, generating and propping up a *surreality*, became the job of the legions

---

wildly so. They shape actors' perceptions of possibilities, as well as their understanding of their interests."

of state-intellectuals at home, and, abroad, of the fellow-traveling intellectuals in every western country.[36]

The indoctrination first began on a vast scale with the civil war, and its target were the millions of recruits of the Red Army. Every known means of propaganda, from the printed word, lectures, and discussion groups to cabaret, plays, and movies, was used by the thousands of Bolshevik cadres who toured the fronts, with the explicit aim of turning the Russian peasant-soldier into "a conscious revolutionary fighter." The half-million Red Army soldiers who joined the Party in the course of the civil war became "the missionaries of the revolution," who "carried Bolshevism, its ideas and its methods, back to their towns and villages, where they flooded into Soviet institutions during the early 1920s" (Figes 1997: 602). The pervasive propaganda barrage continued for seven decades, testifying to the awareness of the Communist authorities that repression alone could never ensure their continued rule.[37]

Similarly, the collapse the Soviet regime can only be understood as a case study in the operation of ideology, in this case, of the end of an ideology's sway.

The subversion of the Leninist faith began after Stalin's death, with the "Thaw" introduced by Khrushchev. In the 1960s a few dissident intellectuals, often samizdat [independent, usually underground]

---

36 In contrast to Malia and others, Richard Pipes 1993: 502 holds that ideology was a "subsidiary factor . . . not a set of principles that either determined [the Communist ruling class's] actions or explains them to posterity." Pipes's reasoning, however, is seriously flawed: he claims, for instance, that Marxism could not have been complicit in Soviet crimes, because "nowhere in the West has Marxism led to the totalitarian excesses of Leninism-Stalinism." Here he ignores the fact that, in the West, socialist parties *abandoned* orthodox Marxism, opting instead for a "mixed economy" and the welfare state. In any case, his argument concerns ideology only as a determinant of the actions of the Communist rulers, not as a means of animating and controlling the people. Pipes further maintains that ideology played only a minor role in National Socialism. In this case he relies on the writings of Hermann Rauschning, who held, allegedly on the basis of his personal experiences, including intimate conversations with Hitler, that Nazism represented mere "nihilism." Rauschning's reports, however, are a highly questionable source and possibly fraudulent; see Tobias 1990. Moreover, it would be impossible today to find any knowledgeable person prepared to argue that the *ideology* of anti-Semitism played no role, or a minor one, in the Nazi massacre of the European Jews.
37 The use of the public school system for the mass indoctrination of the populace by all modern governments, but especially by totalitarian ones, is dealt with in Lott 1999.

publishers, sowed the seeds of doubt in small urban and university circles. Still, the great mass of Soviet citizens remained indoctrinated, until the declaration of perestroika and glasnost under Gorbachev.

Then the truth—of the crimes of Lenin as well as Stalin, the poverty prevailing in the socialist homeland, the true nature of the fantasy world woven by Soviet ideologists for decades—came to light. It was propagated by what Hayek called the "second-hand dealers in ideas," in the press, television, and radio (Shane 1994: 212–44). "By 1991 polls showed the majority of Soviet citizens and a substantial majority of urbanites had lost that basic faith in the system . . . the Soviet world-picture had been wrecked not by tanks and bombs but by facts and opinions, by the release of information bottled up for decades. . . . What changed minds was the cumulative, synergistic effect of a great deal of new information on a variety of subjects at once" (Shane 1994: 214–15, 221). The same swelling cascade of information shattered the faith of the Soviet ruling class itself, dissolving its sense of its own legitimacy and, finally, its will to coerce (Hollander 1999).

Importance of the Intellectuals Theoretically Reaffirmed

The position represented by Stigler has, in turn, been criticized by other liberal scholars, among them Douglass C. North. North freely concedes that public choice theory is invaluable in explaining much of political behavior: interest group pressures do account for a good deal of political decision-making (1981: 56). But to regard this as the whole story is to fall victim, in his view, to the "myopic vision" of neoclassical economics:

> Casual observation provides evidence that an enormous amount of change occurs because of large group action which should not occur in the face of the logic of the free rider problem. . . . Large groups do act when no evident benefits counter the substantial costs to individual participation; people do vote, and they do donate blood anonymously. . . . Individual utility functions are simply more complicated than the simple assumptions so far incorporated in neoclassical theory. (1981: 46–47)

Ideology, which, according to North, is ubiquitous, is "an economizing device by which individuals come to terms with their environment and are provided with a 'world view' so that the decision-making process is simplified." The fundamental aim of ideology "is to energize groups to behave contrary to a simple, hedonistic, individual calculus of costs and benefits."[38] And, aside from rare exceptions, ideologies develop under the guidance of intellectuals (North 1981: 49–53)

A crucial part of ideologies, ignored by scholars who minimize their significance, are judgments of right and wrong, just and unjust. In this connection, North presents an argument that might well give such scholars pause:

> If the concept [of just and unjust] is not crucial to the way in which choices are made, then we are left with the puzzle of accounting for the immense amount of resources invested throughout history in attempting to convince individuals about the justice or injustice of their position. (51)

In other words, if, as Stigler believed, people are reasonably well informed and act intelligently in pursuit of their self-interest, how are we to account for this massive and continual "misuse" of resources in contending over questions of right and wrong?

Robert Higgs is another knowledgeable critic of the Stiglerian position. In *Crisis and Leviathan* (1987a), he presents a detailed examination of the growth of the U.S. federal government in the twentieth century, highlighting the importance of intellectuals, "the specialists in the production and distribution of ideologies." "An understanding of ideology," he asserts, "is essential to an understanding of the growth of government" (1987a: 192, 36).[39]

---

38 Cf. Sartori 1969: 410: "in the ideological actor the 'logic of interest' combines with the 'logic of principles.' In fact, ideological politics represents a situation in which the utility scale of each actor is altered by an ideological scale. Hence, and much to the bewilderment of the pragmatist, in this case the logic of interest no longer suffices to explain, and even less to predict, political behavior."
39 Higgs (37) usefully defines ideology as "a somewhat coherent, rather comprehensive belief system about social relations," with four distinct aspects: cognitive, affective, programmatic, and solidary.

Higgs, too, believes that the conventional neoclassical approach is incapable of explaining a wide range of political behavior (1987a: 39–41). Drawing on widely accepted conclusions of social psychology, including those of Amartya Sen, he notes that individuals often act to confirm, enhance, and validate their "identity" or "self-image." For instance, "the kind of groups to which a person chooses to belong is closely connected with the kind of person he takes himself to be—a matter of prime concern to the typical person." This holds also for the political dimension of their self-image. Again, like North, Higgs stresses that in acting politically people are often truly concerned with what is right and wrong, just and unjust, issues that cannot be reduced to a narrow hedonistic calculus. Citing Schumpeter on the purely formal nature of the utility theory of value, which implies nothing regarding the *content* of people's wants, Higgs concludes that "one cannot demolish an ideological fortress with the weapons of neoclassical economics" (1987a: 42, 44; 1987b: 141–42).

Higgs's own methodology is strictly empirical, though not in any unrealistically quantitative sense. Since rhetoric is crucial to ideology, ideological changes can often be tracked by a careful examination of the rhetoric of opinion leaders. However, as everywhere in science, the method applied must be suited to the area of reality under study: "Although we cannot measure [ideology and ideological changes] as we would height or weight, we can learn a good deal about them qualitatively, and for certain purposes such knowledge may be adequate" (1987a: 48–51).

Higgs's insight that much political behavior involves the affirmation of one's self-image prompts the question: How do people acquire political identities which they then act to instantiate and confirm? A fountainhead of such identities is clearly the system of formal education.[40] From this point of view, it would prove highly instructive to examine how the educational establishments of western countries—especially higher education—function not only to convey the panoply

---

40 Cf. North 1981: 54: "The educational system in a society is simply not explicable in narrow neoclassical terms, since much of it is obviously directed at inculcating a set of values, rather than investing in human capital."

of anti-capitalist ideas, but also to impart a particular self-image to a significant proportion of the students it processes, a self-image which they will then live out—roughly, their identities as members of the adversary culture, the bearers of a lifelong animus against private enterprise.

The Role of Historical Myths

Hayek believed that historical writings have in all likelihood been the major medium for the spread of anti-market ideas among intellectuals. In his essay, "History and Politics," he notes the great impact of historical interpretations on political opinion, and speaks of "a socialist interpretation of history which has governed political thinking for the last two or three generations and which consists mainly of a particular view of economic history"—especially, of the industrial revolution. It is an interpretation most of whose tenets have long been shown to be mythical (Hayek [ed.] 1954: 3, 7). Hayek observes that the continued domination of this view, long discarded by scholars, presents a problem. In fact, today, forty years after Hayek wrote these lines, the obsolete "catastrophic" version of the industrial revolution continues to be cherished by the great majority.

It may be useful to focus on an example of another legend that has been a part of socialist pseudo-history, and that has now likewise been exploded.

For decades the prevailing view was that German big business played a central and essential role in the Nazi rise to power. Coincidentally, this interpretation echoed the official position of the Comintern (Communist International), set forth in the 1920s and 30s, according to which a generic "fascism," including its German variant, represented the naked fist of a bourgeoisie confronting the final proletarian assault.

For years socialists continued to tout the line that the financial and political support of German big business was to a great degree responsible for Hitler's coming to power—and, consequently, for World War II and all the atrocities it entailed. In the Federal Republic of Germany, intellectuals never tired of repeating Max Horkheimer's aphorism, couched in the patented portentousness of the Frankfurt School: "He who does not want to speak of capitalism should also be silent about fascism" (cited in Nolte 1982: 76). The view was shared and propagated, however, by many prominent non-socialist writers as well, Alan Bullock, Norman Stone, and H. Stuart Hughes, among them.

In 1985, in a work of superb scholarship, Henry Ashby Turner, Jr., of Yale, demonstrated that this interpretation was, simply, a myth. He relied on a multitude of primary sources ignored by other writers. Turner's own analysis is now accepted by practically all experts in the field. Whether he will have any more success in seeing his version passed on to the educated public than the economic historians of the industrial revolution have had remains to be seen.

Years ago, R.M. Hartwell had posed the question, why do we observe the persistence of historical accounts that are demonstrably false (Hartwell 1974: 2)?[41] Towards the end of his work, Turner reflects on why so many professional historians should have accepted the old fable of Hitler and the German industrialists so uncritically. His reply is: bias. "Bias, in short, appears over and over again in treatments of the political role of big business even by otherwise scrupulous historians" (Turner 1985: 350). He attempts to explain this dangerous prejudice (350–51):

> Professional historians generally have little or no personal contact with the world of business. Like so many intellectuals, they tend to view big business with a combination of condescension and mistrust.[42] . . . Since almost all of those who have concerned themselves with the relationship between the business community and Nazism have, to one degree or another, stood left or at least left of center in their political sympathies, a great many have found it difficult to resist the temptation to

---

[41] Another question of Hartwell's, why are most historians "softer on the 'left' than on the 'right'?" is also worth serious consideration.

[42] Cf. Pollard 2000: 1: "Making money is a dirty game. That sentence might almost sum up the attitude of English literature towards British business. Few writers have had first-hand experience of the world of commerce and industry. Their world is governed by the imaginative and the spiritual. It is no wonder therefore that they so often despise the other world that they see as materialistic . . ."

implicate big business . . . in the rise of Nazism. Although deliberate distortion figures in some publications on the subject, the susceptibility of most historians to the myths dealt with in this volume is attributable not to intellectual dishonesty but rather to the sort of preconceptions that hobble attempts to come to grips with the past.

Another way of putting Turner's explanation is in terms of one of the several components of the Marxist concept of ideology, as refined by Jon Elster (1985: 476, 487–90). The individual's comprehension of social relations is inevitably skewed by the particular position he himself occupies in the network of these relations, because he necessarily comes to understand "the whole from the point of view of the part."

Seen in this light, the root of the problem lies in the social position—the way of life—of the academic intellectual, whose views in turn profoundly shape and condition those of virtually all other intellectuals. Essentially, he is a mandarin, accustomed, to reiterate Mises's point, to living from an assured source of income—usually taxes, but the case is similar with guaranteed endowments. As such, he will rarely find it possible to appreciate or even begin to understand the way of life of capitalists, entrepreneurs, traders, and speculators, men and women who live and die by the vicissitudes of the market. Thus, the problem turns out to be one not so much of invidious personal motivation as of a socially determined distorted cognition.

In reply, one might object that it is academic intellectuals who, of all people, are morally and professionally obliged to free themselves from socially imposed blinders and to strive to see the free market order as it really is. That they have manifestly not lived up to this obligation is, however, merely another way of stating the problem we have been considering.

My own inclination is towards the "second" approach of Ludwig von Mises, focusing on the ingrained hostility to business and profit-making in our culture. This millenia-old antipathy continues to be spread by the highly influential classes sheltered from the market's threatening rigors, classes that will be with us for as far as we can see.

References

Acton, H.B. (1955) *The Illusion of the Epoch: Marxism-Leninism as a Philosophical Creed*, London: Cohen and West.

Anderson, Gary M. and Robert D. Tollison (1985) "Ideology, Interest Groups, and the Repeal of the Corn Laws," *Zeitschrift für die gesamte Staatswissenschaft* 14 (2): 197–212.

Aron, Raymond (1957) *The Opium of the Intellectuals*, Terence Kilmartin (tr.), London: Secker and Warburg.

Aronoff, Craig E., Randall B. Goodwin, and John L. Ward (eds.) (1984) *The Future of Private Enterprise* 1 *Challenges and Responses*, 3 *Ideas for a Changing World*, Atlanta, Ga.: College of Business Administration, Georgia State University.

Baker, John R. (1945) *Science and the Planned State*, New York: Macmillan.

Barry, Norman (1984) "Ideas *versus* Interests: The Classical Liberal Dilemma," in idem, et al., *Hayek's "Serfdom" Revisited*, London: Institute of Economic Affairs.

Barry, Norman (1989) "Ideas and Interests: The Problem Reconsidered," in Gamble, et al.

Boudon, Raymond (2004) *Pourquoi les intellectuels n'aiment pas le libéralisme*, Paris: Odile Jacob.

Bronfenbrenner, Martin (1981) "Schumpeter's Contributions to the Study of Comparative Economic System," in Helmut Frisch (ed.), *Schumpeterian Economics*, New York: Praeger.

Caute, David (1973) *The Fellow-Travellers: A Postscript to the Enlightenment*, New York: Macmillan.

Choi, Young Back (1993) "Entrepreneurship and Envy," *Constitutional Political Economy* 4 (3): 331–47.

Colburn, Forrest D. (1994) *The Vogue of Revolution in Poor Countries*, Princeton: Princeton University Press.

Coase, R.H. (1994) *Essays on Economics and Economists*, Chicago: University of Chicago Press.

Constant, Benjamin (1988) *Political Writings*, Biancamaria Fontana (ed. and tr.), Cambridge, Mass.: Cambridge University Press.

Denson, John V. (ed.) (1999) *The Costs of War: America's Pyrrhic Victories*, New Brunswick, N.J.: Transaction.

Dolgoff, Sam (1971) Introduction, *Bakunin on Anarchy: Selected Works by the Activist-Founder of World Anarchism*, idem (ed.), New York: Vintage.

Elster, Jon (1985) *Making Sense of Marx*, Cambridge, Eng.: Cambridge University Press.

Figes, Orlando (1997) *A People's Tragedy: The Russian Revolution 1891–1924*, New York: Viking/Penguin.

Gamble, Andrew, et al. (1989) *Ideas, Interests, and Consequences*, London: Institute for Economic Affairs.

Genovese, Eugene D. (1994) "The Crimes of Communism: What Did You Know and When Did You Know It?" *Dissent*, Summer.

Hartwell, R.M. (1974) *History and Ideology*, Menlo Park, Cal.: Institute for Humane Studies.

Hartwell, R.M. (1989) "The Political Economy of Policy Formation: The Case of England," in Gamble, et al.

Hayek, F.A. (ed.) (1954) *Capitalism and the Historians*, Chicago: University of Chicago Press.

Hayek, F.A. (1955) *The Counter-Revolution of Science: Studies on the Abuse of Reason*, New York: Free Press of Glencoe.

Hayek, F.A. (1967) *Studies in Philosophy, Politics, and Economics*, Chicago: University of Chicago Press.

Hayek, F.A. (1973) *Law, Legislation and Liberty*, 1, *Rules and Order*, Chicago: University of Chicago Press.

Hayek, F.A. (1978) *New Studies in Philosophy, Politics, Economics, and the History of Ideas*, Chicago: University of Chicago Press.

Higgs, Robert (1987a) *Crisis and Leviathan: Critical Episodes in the Growth of American Government*, New York: Oxford University Press.

Higgs, Robert (1987b) "Identity and Cooperation: A Comment on Sen's Alternative Program," *Journal of Law, Economics, and Organization* 3 (1) (Spring): 140–42.

Hollander, Paul (1999) *Political Will and Personal Belief: The Decline and Fall of Soviet Communism*, New Haven, Conn.: Yale University Press.

Kirzner, Israel M. (1992), "The Ugly Market," in Mark W. Hendrikson (ed.), *The Morality of Capitalism*, Irvington-on-Hudson, N.Y.: Foundation for Economic Education.

Lee, Dwight (1994) "Go to Harvard and Turn Left," in T. William Bixx and Gary M. Quinlivan (eds.) *The Cultural Context of Economics and Politics*, Lanham, Maryland: University Press of America.

Levy, Carl (1987) "Socialism and the Educated Middle Classes in Western Europe, 1870–1914," in Ron Eyerman, Lennart G. Svensson, and Thomas Söderqvist (eds.), *Intellectuals, Universities, and the State in Western Modern Societies*, Berkeley: University of California Press.

Lott, John R., Jr. (1999) "Public Schooling, Indoctrination, and Totalitarianism," *Journal of Political Economy*.

Malia, Martin (1994) *The Soviet Tragedy: A History of Socialism in Russia, 1917–1991*, New York: The Free Press.

Mann, Golo (1991) *Erinnerungen und Gedanken: Eine Jugend in Deutschland*, Frankfurt, a.M.: Fischer Taschenbuch Verlag.

Marx, Karl and Frederick Engels (1976), *Collected Works*, 6, *1845–48*, New York: International Publishers.

Meehl, Paul7 E. (1997) "The Selfish Voter Paradox and the Thrown-Away Vote Argument," *American Political Science Review* 71 (1) (March): 11–30.

Mises, Ludwig von, (1933) *Grundprobleme der Nationalökonomie*, Jena: Gustav Fischer.

Mises, Ludwig von (1956) *The Anti-Capitalistic Mentality*, Princeton, N.J.: Van Nostrand.

Mises, Ludwig von (1974) "Laissez-Faire or Dictatorship," in idem, *Planning for Freedom*, 3rd ed., Libertarian Press: South Holland, Ill.

Mises, Ludwig von (1985 [1927]) *Liberalism in the Classical Tradition*, Ralph Raico (tr.), 3rd ed., Irvington-on-Hudson, N.Y.: Foundation for Economic Education.

Mises, Ludwig von (1990) "The Great German Inflation," in idem, *Money, Method, and the Market Process*, Richard M. Ebeling (ed.), Norwell, Mass.: Kluwer.

Nolte, Ernst (1982) *Marxism, Fascism, Cold War*, Lawrence Kader (tr.), Atlantic Highlands, N. J.: Humanities Press.

North, Douglass C. (1981) *Structure and Change in Economic History*, New York: Norton.

Nozick, Robert (1984) "Why Do Intellectuals Oppose Capitalism?" in Aronoff et al. (eds.) 1.

O'Boyle, Lenore (1970) "The Problem of an Excess of Educated Men in Western Europe, 1800–1850," *Journal of Modern History* 42 (4) (December), 471–95.

O'Brien, D.P. (1994) "Hayek as an Intellectual Historian," in Jack Birner and Rudy van Zijp (eds.), *Hayek, Co-ordination and Evolution: His Legacy in Philosophy, Politics, Economics, and the History of Ideas*, London: Routledge.

Pipes, Richard (1993) *Russia Under the Bolshevik Regime*, New York: Alfred Knopf.

Polanyi, Michael (1951) *The Logic of Liberty: Reflections and Rejoinders*, London: Routledge and Kegan Paul.

Pollard, Arthur (2000) "Introduction," in idem (ed.), *The Representation of Business in English Literature*, London: Institute of Economic Affairs.

Raico, Ralph (1993) "Classical Liberal Roots of the Marxist Doctrine of Classes," in Yuri N. Maltsev (ed.), *Requiem for Marx*, Auburn, Ala.: Ludwig von Mises Institute.

Raico, Ralph (1999) *Die Partei der Freiheit: Studien zur Geschichte des deutschen Liberalismus*, Jörg Guido Hülsmann (tr.) Stuttgart: Lucius & Lucius.

Riehl, Wilhelm Heinrich (1976) *Die bürgerliche Gesellschaft*, Peter Steinbach (ed.), Frankfurt a.M.: Ullstein.

Rothbard, Murray N. (1974) "The Anatomy of the State," in Tibor R. Machan (ed.), *The Libertarian Alternative: Essays in Social and Political Philosophy*, Chicago: Nelson-Hall.

Rothbard, Murray N. (1989) "World War I as Fulfillment: Power and the Intellectuals," *Journal of Libertarian Studies* 9 (1) (Winter), 81–125. Reprinted in Denson (ed.) 1999.

Rothbard, Murray N. (1994) *The Case Against the Fed*, Auburn, Ala.: Ludwig von Mises Institute.

Rothbard, Murray N. (1996) "Origins of the Welfare State in America," *Journal of Libertarian Studies* 12 (2) (Fall): 199–229.

Ruyer, Raymond (1969) *Éloge de la société de consommation*, Paris: Calmann-Levy.

Samuelson, Paul (1981) "Schumpeter's *Capitalism, Socialism and Democracy*," in Arnold Heertje (ed.) *Schumpeter's Vision:* Capitalism, Socialism and Democracy *After 40 Years*, New York: Praeger.

Sartori, Giovanni (1969) "Politics, Ideology, and Belief Systems," *American Political Science Review* 63 (2) (June): 398–411.

Schlesinger, Arthur, Jr. (1954) Review of Hayek (ed.) *Capitalism and the Historians, Annals of the American Academy of Political and Social Science* 293 (May): 177–78.

Schoeck, Helmut (1987 [1969]) *Envy: A Theory of Social Behavior*, Indianapolis: Liberty Press.

Schumpeter, Joseph A. (1946) review of *The Road to Serfdom, Journal of Political Economy* 54 (3) (June).

Schumpeter, Joseph A. (1950) *Capitalism, Socialism, and Democracy*, 3rd. ed., New York: Harper.

Schumpeter, Joseph A. (1954) *History of Economic Analysis*, Elizabeth Boody Schumpeter (ed.), New York: Oxford University Press.

Shane, Scott (1994) *Dismantling Utopia: How Information Ended the Soviet Union*, Chicago: Ivan R. Dee.

Skidelsky, Robert (1978) "The American Response to Keynes," in A.P. Thirwall (ed.) *Keynes and Laissez-Faire*, London: Macmillan.

Stigler, George J. (1975) "The Intellectual and his Society," in Richard T. Selden (ed.), *Capitalism and Freedom: Problems and Prospects*, Charlottesville, Va.: University Press of Virginia.

Stigler, George J. (1982) *The Economist as Preacher and Other Essays*, Chicago: University of Chicago Press.

Stigler, George J (1984a) *The Intellectual and the Marketplace*, enlarged ed., Cambridge, Mass.: Harvard University Press.

Stigler, George J. (1984b) "Laissez-Faire: Policy or Circumstance?" with the assistance of Claire Friedland, unpublished paper.

Stigler, George J. (1989) "The Intellectuals and the Enterprise System," unpublished paper.

Szelenyi, Ivan and Bill Martin (1991) "The Three Waves of New Class Theories and a Postscript," in Charles C. Lemert (ed.) *Intellectuals and Politics: Social Theory in a Changing World*, Newbury Park, Cal.: Sage.

Taylor, Myles (1997) "The Beginnings of Modern British Social History," *History Workshop Journal* 43 (Spring): 155–76.

Tobias, Fritz (1990) "Auch Fälschungen Haben Lange Beine: Des Senatpräsidenten Rauschnings 'Gespräche mit Hitler,'" in Karl Corino (ed.), *Gefälscht! Betrug in Politik, Literatur, Wissenschaft, Kunst und Musik*, Frankfurt a.M.: Eichborn.

Turner, Henry Ashby, Jr. (1985) *German Big Business and the Rise of Hitler*, New York: Oxford University Press.

4 Was Keynes a Liberal?

Keynes and Neomercantilism

It is now common practice to rank John Maynard Keynes as one of modern history's outstanding liberals, the most recent "great" in the tradition of John Locke, Adam Smith, and Thomas Jefferson.[1] Like these men, it is generally held, Keynes was a sincere, indeed, exemplary, believer in the free society. If he differed from the "classical" liberals in a few obvious and important ways, it was simply because he tried to update the essential liberal idea to suit the economic conditions of a new age.

---

1 This is a modified version of an essay that originally appeared in *The Independent Review*, Fall, 2008.
Cf. the anthology by Bullock and Shock 1956. Numerous other scholars, such as E.K. Bramsted and K.J. Melhuish 1978 treat Keynes as a major twentieth century (and hence presumably more relevant) representative of the sequence that begins with the Levellers or Locke. The biographer of Locke, Maurice Cranston (1978: 101) categorizes Keynes, like Locke, as a liberal. B. Corry (1978: 26) goes so far as to term Keynes "essentially an economic liberal arguing for specific non-liberal measures solely in periods of unemployment . . ." Douglas Den Uyl and Stuart Warner (1987: 263) include Keynes in their list of "clear-cut" liberals, along with Adam Smith, Turgot, Benjamin Constant and others. John Gray (1986: xi) insists that Keynes's position is one that must be accommodated in defining the creed. Logically enough, Gray's definition of liberalism omits any mention of belief in private property. Anthony Arblaster (1984: 292), however, remarks that while Keynes was a "convinced Liberal," "it was, in the end, social democracy which inherited the legacy of his thought."

There is no doubt that throughout his life Keynes endorsed various broad cultural values, such as tolerance and rationality that are often referred to as "liberal," and, of course, he always *called* himself a liberal (as well as a Liberal, that is, a supporter of the British Liberal Party). But none of this carries great weight when it comes to classifying Keynes's political thought.[2]

Prima facie, Keynes as model liberal is already paradoxical on account of his embrace of mercantilist doctrine. When his major work *The General Theory of Employment, Interest, and Money* (Keynes 1973a) appeared, W.H. Hutt was about to send his *Economists and the Public* (1936) to press. In later years, Hutt would subject Keynes's system to detailed and withering scrutiny (Hutt 1963, 1979). At this point he could only hurriedly insert some initial observations. What struck Hutt most of all was that this renowned economist "would have us believe that the mercantilists were right and their classical [liberal] critics [e.g., Adam Smith] were wrong" (a position Keynes expounded in Chapter 23 of the *General Theory*).

Hutt was writing from the standpoint of economic science. Here we are dealing with the integrity of liberalism as a social philosophy. If, as I have argued elsewhere (Raico, 1989, 1992, 1999: 1–22), the liberal doctrine is characterized historically by a repudiation of the paternalism of the absolutist welfare state, this is even truer of its rejection of the mercantilist component in eighteenth century absolutism. How can a writer who tried to rehabilitate mercantilism be counted among the liberal greats?[3]

In defense of Keynes, Maurice Cranston (1978: 111) contended that no one would deny John Locke inclusion in the liberal ranks in spite of his adherence to mercantilism. Whether this was actually Locke's

---

2 Cf. Karl Brunner's conclusion (1987: 28) that, in his logically rigorous terminological schema, Keynes's "rejection of the liberal solution" is readily discoverable, since: "He finds the severe limitation imposed on government unacceptable. The matter requires, in his judgment, a thoroughly fresh approach."

3 Cf. Rowley 1987: 154, who writes that Keynes promoted "a belief in a fundamentally flawed, non-self-correcting market economy, continually in need of government intervention if it was not to degenerate into chaos. . . . Neomercantilism once again was waging war against the invisible hand, much as it had in pre-Smithian England."

standpoint is debatable; Karen Vaughn (1980) has furnished grounds for believing otherwise. But even if Locke had been a mercantilist it would lend no support to Cranston's argument. Locke is rightly viewed as a liberal great, *not* because of his views on economic theory and policy, whatever they may have been, but by virtue of his libertarian account of natural rights and what he believed followed from it.[4]

The Keynesian System

According to his supporters and himself, Keynes's turn to neo-mercantilism was necessitated by his discovery of fundamental flaws in classical economics. The classical theory, the claim goes, proved impotent to explain the causes either of Britain's chronic high unemployment in the 1920s or the Great Depression, while in the *General Theory* Keynes did both. This he accomplished by exposing the inherent gross defects of the undirected market economy, thereby effecting a "revolution" in economic thought.

Yet the particular crises Keynes reacted to were themselves produced by misguided government policies. The persistence of high unemployment in Britain is traceable in part to the decision of Winston Churchill as Chancellor of the Exchequer to return to gold at the unrealistic pre-war parity, and in part to the high unemployment benefits (relative to wages) available after 1920. The Great Depression resulted primarily from government monetary mismanagement, in particular, by the Federal Reserve in the United States. Both of these crises are amenable to explanation by means of "orthodox" economic analysis, requiring no theoretical "revolution" (Rothbard 1963; Johnson 1975: 109–12; Buchanan, et al., 1991; Benjamin and Kochin 1979).[5]

---

4 Despite the statement cited in note 162, Cranston (1978: 113) implicitly surrendered on the question of Keynes's fundamental liberalism: "Keynes really belonged with Francis Bacon, and the *philosophes*, and the utilitarians and the Fabians, to that class of intellectual which believes that intellectuals should rule." A number of more or less classical liberal writers have also held that Keynes could not be denied the title of liberal, see, e.g., Gottfried Habeler 1946: 193.

5 On the disastrous consequences of the exchange-rate error, see Harry Johnson (1975: 100, 122) who states: "Had the exchange value of the pound been fixed realistically in the 1920s—a prescription fully in accord with orthodox economic theory—there would have been no need

As Hutt noted, Keynes in the *General Theory* turned his back on all the recognized authorities, from Hume and Smith, through Menger, Jevons, and Marshall, to Wicksell and Wicksteed. Those thinkers, whatever the degree of their adherence to strict laissez-faire, at least held that the market economy contained self-correcting forces that rendered business fluctuations temporary. Discarding his "orthodox" predecessors (and contemporaries), Keynes aligned himself with what he himself dubbed that "brave army of heretics," Silvio Gesell, J.A. Hobson, and other social reformist and socialist critics of capitalism, whom mainstream economists had dismissed as crackpots (Friedman 1997: 7).

In a popular essay two years earlier, Keynes had already ranged himself on the side of these "heretics," the writers "who reject the idea that the existing economic system is, in any significant sense, self-adjusting.... The system is not self-adjusting, and, without purposive direction, it is incapable of translating our actual poverty into our potential plenty" (Keynes 1973b: 487, 489, 491). The *General Theory* was intended to provide the analytical framework to justify this position.

Changes in prices, wages, and interest rates, according to Keynes, do not fulfill the function ascribed to them in standard economic theory, of tending to generate a full-employment equilibrium. The level of wages has no substantial effect on the volume of employment; the interest rate does not serve to equilibrate savings and investment; aggregate demand is normally insufficient to produce full employment; and so on. The false assumptions, conceptual incoherences, and non sequiturs that

---

for mass unemployment, hence no need for a revolutionary new theory to explain it, and no triggering force for much subsequent British political and economic history.... Britain has paid a heavy long-run price for the transient glory of the Keynesian Revolution, in terms both of the corruption of standards of scientific work in economics and encouragement to the indulgence of the belief of the political process that economic policy can transcend the laws of economics with the aid of sufficient economic cleverness..." Regarding unemployment benefits, Benjamin and Kochin (1979: 468–72) point out that Edwin Cannan (an economist much admired by Hayek) was one of the few contemporaries to understand the part played by the dole in creating excess unemployment. For his pains, Cannan continues to be condemned by Keynesian writers such as Donald Winch as hard-hearted and lacking in compassion (ibid. 468, n. 40).

vitiate these extravagant claims have been frequently exposed (e.g., in Hazlitt 1959; Rothbard 1962, 2, *passim*; Hazlitt 1995; Reisman 1998: 862–94)[6]. As James Buchanan sums up the issue (Buchanan et al. 1991: 109): "There is simply no evidence to suggest that market economies are inherently unstable."

In any case, not every system retaining some elements of the private property market order can reasonably be considered liberal. In early modern history, there was, famously, a system that included private property and permitted markets to operate in a restricted and limited way. It insisted, however, on the overriding role of the state, without which economic life would collapse into anarchy. Economic liberalism arose as a reaction *against* this system, which is called mercantilism. Fascism, so far as its economic prescriptions went, would be another such system.

Equally crucial to the question at issue are the ways in which Keynes's errors undermined confidence in the free market order and opened the way for the colossal growth of state power.

Murray Rothbard noted that Keynes posited a world in which consumers are ignorant robots and investors are systematically irrational, driven by their blind "animal spirits." The conclusion was that the overall volume of investment had to be entrusted to a *deus ex machina*, a "class external to the market . . . the state apparatus" (Rothbard 1992: 189–91). This process Keynes refers to as "the socialization of investment." As he declares in the *General Theory*:

---

6 Some of the key errors were rooted in Keynes's methodology, his conclusion, for instance, that an unmanaged market economy was incapable of achieving intertemporal coordination. In the view of Roger Garrison 1985, the mechanisms by which such coordination is, in fact, brought about by market processes were concealed by Keynes's operating with higher levels of aggregation, while the real coordinating processes were set forth by Hayek. Hayek himself 1995: 246–47 believed that Keynes's most basic mistake was methodological, pursuing the "pseudo-exactness" of apparently measurable magnitudes, while disregarding the real interconnections of the economic system. Keynes's approach rested on the assumption that there exist constant functional relationships between total demand, investment, output, etc. In this way, it tended "to conceal nearly all that really matters," leading to the "obliteration of many important insights which we had already achieved and which we shall then have painfully to regain."

> I expect to see the State, which is in a position to calculate the marginal efficiency of capital-goods on long views and on the basis of the general social advantage, taking an ever greater responsibility for directly organizing investments. (1973a: 164)

Keynes argued for the creation of a National Investment Board; as late as 1943, he estimated that such an authority would directly influence "two-thirds or three-quarters of total investment" (Seccareccia 1994: 377).[7]

Robert Skidelsky (1988: 17–18) insists that in these instances Keynes did not have in mind the state in the sense of the central government, but rather those "semi-autonomous bodies within the State" of which he spoke in 1924, "bodies whose criterion of action within their own field is solely the public good as they understand it, and from whose deliberations motives of private advantage are excluded." (Keynes 1972: 288–89)

Skidelsky, however, appears oblivious to the problems of this high-sounding conception. Keynes never specified how such bodies were to operate, never gave any reason to believe they would be in a position to calculate the "marginal efficiency of capital" (a thoroughly confused concept, in any case; see Hazlitt 1959: 156–70; Anderson 1995: 200–05), and never indicated by what subtle means they would be kept untainted by motives of private (including personal ideological) advantage.[8] Moreover, since Keynes granted that these "autonomous bodies" would be "subject in the last resort to the sovereignty of the democracy as expressed through Parliament," how could they be prevented from effectively becoming agencies of the central state?

If liberalism's core doctrine is that, given institutional adherence to the rights of life, liberty and property, civil society can be counted on by and large to run itself, and if the showcase example in liberalism's brief

---

7 See also Seccareccia 1993, where the author rebuts the common view of Keynes as a would-be or actual savior of capitalism.

8 Cf. Brunner 1987: 47: "None of [Keynes's] essays ever elaborates in the slightest the content of this proposal [to socialize investment]. We do not know in what form the socialization should be implemented. The institutional choices are never examined . . . [and we have no way] to assess the consequences of such socialization."

is the capacity of the undirected market economy to function satisfactorily, then the "Keynesian Revolution" signaled the abandonment of liberalism.

Within a very few years, Keynesianism triumphed among economists prominent in the academy and government, becoming after World War II the official doctrine in advanced countries. It was mandated by the administrators of the Marshall Plan and their allies in the United Nations Economic Commission for Europe and of the European Recovery Program. Italy, for instance, "was constantly urged to reflate by both these agencies" (de Cecco, 1989: 219–21).[9] While West Germany, under the leadership of Ludwig Erhard and advised by economists like Wilhelm Röpke, resisted, in Britain both major parties championed Keynesian demand management as the means to full employment, now the principal goal. In the United States, the Employment Act of 1946 recognized the primary responsibility of the federal government for ensuring maximum employment through fiscal operations. The results of this revolution were disastrous.

Prior to Keynes, budget balancing had at least been the goal of the governments of civilized countries. Keynesianism reversed this "fiscal constitution." By making governments responsible for "counter-cyclical" fiscal policy while ignoring the tendency of shortsighted politicians to accumulate deficits, it set the stage for the unprecedented levels of taxation and public debt of the decades following the Second World War (Buchanan 1987; Rowley 1987; Buchanan et al. 1991).

It is sometimes maintained that Keynes was "not a Keynesian," in the sense that he cannot be held responsible for the application of his theory by his followers. Yet, with what other "great" or "model" liberal do we have a coterie of highly influential acolytes who interpreted him in a sharply anti-liberal sense? As Michael Heilperin (1960: 125) sardonically observed: "If [Keynes] was a liberal, then he was that extraordinary

---

9 The author adds, concerning the role of the Christian Democrats for decades, that they "helped the technocrats maintain their hold over the economy. They became the arch-defenders of the IRI," the vast state holding company that was by far the largest firm in Italy (1989: 222).

kind of liberal whose practical recommendations consistently promote collectivism."

Rules or "Discretion"?

In contrast to earlier absolutist and later collectivist ideologies, liberalism is characterized by its insistence on *rules*, in political as in economic life (cf. Hayek 1973: 56–59). The rule of law as the foundation of the *Rechtsstaat* is an obvious example, as is the doctrine of *laissez-faire*, which even John Stuart Mill felt obliged to pay lip service to as a (readily defeasible) principle ("Laissez-faire, in short, should be the general practice . . ."). Maximum flexibility and leeway in the exercise of power is not a trait that commends itself to liberals. A government of laws, not of men is a well-known liberal slogan.[10]

Murray Rothbard (1992: 177) noted that Keynes was opposed, as it were, to principle *on principle*.[11] It is no exaggeration to say that he was constitutionally averse to rules, or "dogmas," as he often called them. This attitude dominated Keynes's thinking throughout his life. In 1923, he declared:

> when great decisions are to be made, the State is a sovereign body of which the purpose is to promote the greatest good of the whole. When, therefore, we enter the realm of State action, everything is to be considered and weighed on its merits. (Keynes 1971a: 56–57)

In his last years, he found "much wisdom" in the proposition that the state should "fill the vacant post of entrepreneur-in-chief," only "interfering with the ownership or management of particular businesses . . . on the merits of the case and not at the behest of dogma" (Keynes 1980: 324). In a letter to F.A. Hayek, apropos of Hayek's recently

---

10 It is another, theoretically perhaps more important, question whether these goals of liberalism could ever have been compatible with the continued existence of an institution based on monopoly power and the authority to tax, i.e., the state. On this question, see the pioneering work of Hans-Hermann Hoppe 2001, especially 229–34.

11 Cf. Bruce Caldwell 1995: 41: "Keynes was famous, and not just among economists, for changing his mind. Indeed, mutability was part and parcel of his public persona . . ."

published *The Road to Serfdom*, Keynes chided him for not realizing that "dangerous acts can be done safely in a community which thinks and feels rightly, which would be the way to hell if they were executed by those who think and feel wrongly" (1980: 387–88).

This, Robert Skidelsky (1988:15) claims, is the heart of Keynes's "second revival of liberalism" (after the earlier "New Liberalism" of the Hobhouse school): Keynes aimed to "superimpose a managerial philosophy . . . a philosophy of *ad hoc* intervention based on disinterested thought . . ." Alec Cairncross (1978: 47–48) states that: "He hated enslavement by rules. He wanted governments to have discretion and he wanted economists to come to their assistance in the exercise of that discretion." Yet it is precisely the *ad hoc* nature of Keynes's approach, his faith in a strangely disembodied "disinterested thought" and his predilection for government "discretion" unencumbered by principled limits that run straight against the grain of the liberal doctrine.[12]

Authentic liberalism has traditionally harbored a deep distrust for the agents of the state, on the grounds that they lack either competence or detachment or both. Keynes's airy reliance on economic experts whose sage advice would be put into effect by self-denying politicians flies in the face of this wholly warranted suspicion and all of the historical and theoretical evidence supporting it. In contemporary terms, it contradicts the teachings associated with the school of public choice.[13]

---

12 In an appreciation of Keynes, *The Economist* 1993: 110 perversely declared that "a theme that recurs in his work is a preference (echoing Hayek, please note, whose work he praised) for rules over discretion in economic policy . . ."
13 Cf. Rowley 1987a: 119, 123, where the author describes Keynes as being "about as far away from the approach of modern public choice as an individual conceivably could be," and accuses him of ignoring "the dangerous discretion that his theories had placed in the hands of vote-seeking politicians." Donald Winch 1989: 124, a defender of Keynes against the charge of statism, seems to concede that the logic of Keynesian thought leads in a statist direction: "When the technocratic interpretation of state capacity associated with Keynes himself is mixed with politics, can Keynes' own minimalist [sic] position be sustained? Are not left-Keynesians (and their monetarist opponents for that matter) correct in believing that the logic of Keynesianism leads to greater intervention, such that what may have begun as macroeconomic management requires extension into microeconomic intervention to ensure success?"

Keynes's Utopia

Keynes was often given to ruminations on the nature of the future society. Since his writings are rife with inconsistencies,[14] it has been possible for some of his followers to contend that what Keynes basically wanted was merely "to wed full employment to classical liberalism . . . his model was very much 'capitalism plus full employment,' and he was relatively sanguine about the feasibility of macro-control'" (Corry 1978: 25, 28).

Throughout Keynes's career, however, there are clear indications of a longing for a much more radical social order, in his words, a "New Jerusalem" (O'Donnell 1989: 294, 378 n. 27). He confessed that he had played in his mind "with the possibilities of greater social changes than come within the present philosophies" even of Fabian socialist thinkers like Sidney Webb. "The republic of my imagination lies on the extreme left of celestial space," he mused (1972: 309).

Light is shed on this somewhat obscure avowal by numerous statements strewn over decades. Taken together, they confirm the argument of Joseph Salerno (1992) that Keynes was a *millenialist* a thinker who viewed social evolution as pursuing a preordained course to what he conceived to be a happy ending: a utopia (O'Donnell 1989: 288–94).

Keynes looked forward (1980: 369) to a condition of "equality of contentment amongst all" (whatever that might conceivably mean), where the problem facing the average person will be "how to occupy the leisure, which science and compound interest will have won for him, to live wisely, agreeably, and well" (1972: 328). Technological progress, fueled by socialized investment, will automatically guarantee adequate consumer goods for all. It is at that point that the serious questions of living will arise:

---

14 See the peculiar judgment on Keynes by Thomas Balogh 1978: 67: "His strength and infinite, yet tantalizing, charm lay in being able to discard views (and people) at the drop of a hat." This does not seem far from Rothbard's characterization of Keynes as an intellectual "buccaneer."

The natural evolution should be towards a decent level of consumption for everyone; and, when that is high enough, towards the occupation of our energies in the non-economic interests of our lives. Thus we need to be slowly reconstructing our social system with these ends in view. (1982a: 393)

Leaving aside the question of who will decide when the level of consumption is high enough: what techniques did Keynes imagine existed to bring about such a restructuring of society? As always when he pondered his desired future, specifics are nonexistent.[15] What is clear is that in the future utopia the state will be the incontestable leader.[16] Putting an end to "economic anarchy," the new "régime [will be one] which deliberately aims at controlling and directing economic forces in the interests of social justice and social stability" (1972: 305).[17]

The state, according to Keynes, will even decide on the optimal level of population. Regarding eugenics, Keynes occasionally gave the appearance of indecision: "the time may arrive a little later when the community as a whole must pay attention to the innate quality as well as to the mere numbers of its future members" (1972: 292; Salerno 1992: 13–14). At other times, he was quite definite: "The great transition in human history" will begin "when civilized man endeavors to assume conscious control in his own hands, away from the blind instinct of

---

15 Keynes's approach here is characteristic of critics of the market economy. As Roger Garrison 1993: 478 observes: "His failure to explain in any detail just how this ideal system would work is consistent with socialist thought in general, which has always focused on the perceived failings of the actual system rather than on the allegedly superior workings of the imagined one."

16 Cf. O'Donnell 1989: 299–300: "At bottom, Keynes's prescription was that the state should act as the guardian, supervisor, and promoter of civilized society...it was an active supervisor with an ethically directed program of gradual evolutionary change, including modification of the rules of the game."

17 In this same famous essay, "Am I a Liberal?" Keynes *also* asserts, with his usual muddle when it comes to his social philosophy, that he is merely striving for "novel measures for safeguarding capitalism" (1972: 299).

mere predominant survival" (1983: 859),[18] a view curiously reminiscent of Leon Trotsky's at around the same time.[19]

So, the state—in its guise as "civilized man"—will channel and oversee the reproduction of the human race as well.

In all these matters, the state will, in turn, be guided by wise and farseeing intellectuals of Keynes's own sort.[20] How could it be otherwise? Left to their own devices, the great majority of people are virtually helpless. As Keynes declared: "Nor is it true that self-interest generally *is* enlightened; more often individuals acting separately to promote their own ends are too ignorant or too weak to attain even these." (1972: 288; emphasis in original) Since he held that in economic questions "the right solution will involve intellectual and scientific elements which must be above the heads of the vast mass of more or less illiterate voters" (1978: 295), one wonders how much of "the sovereignty of the democracy" could possibly continue to exist in Keynes's utopia.

Naturally enough, given his own tastes, the arts played a central role in his vision. He complained of the niggardliness of state subsidies to the arts that was defended by "the sub-human denizens of the Treasury." Such a policy was incompatible with any loftier conception of "the duty and purpose, the honor and glory [sic] of the State." Art subsidies were a means for the State to fulfill its duty to elevate "the common man,"

---

18 On another occasion, Keynes reiterated the need to confront the problem of overpopulation "with schemes conceived by the mind in place of the undesigned outcome of instinct and individual advantage. . . . It is many generations since men as individuals began to substitute moral and rational motive as their spring of action in the place of blind instinct. They must now do the same thing collectively." (Keynes 1977: 453

19 The Bolshevik leader Leon Trotsky 1960: 254–55 expressed similar eugenic views, although in a more "Promethean" spirit, on the "great transition" to the future utopia: "The human species, the coagulated *homo sapiens*, will once more enter into a state of radical transformation, and in his [sic] own hands will become an object of the most complicated methods of artificial selection and psycho-physical training. . . . The human race will not have ceased to crawl on all fours before God, kings, and capital, in order later to submit humbly before the dark laws of heredity and a blind sexual selection!" See the essay, "Leon Trotsky: the Ignorance and the Evil," in my collection, *Great Wars and Great Leaders: A Libertarian Rebuttal.*

20 See Bernard Corry's comment (1993: 37–38): "Politicians were seen by Bloomsbury as an uneasy mix of fools, opportunists, and knaves; so what are we left with to steer the country? Some sort of intellectual establishment, closely allied to academia (or rather a small part of it with Cambridge roots!), who could give dispassionate, expert advice and control . . . Keynes had a Bloomsbury belief in the power and duty of the intelligentsia to advise and control events . . ."

to lead him to feel himself "finer, more gifted, more splendid, more carefree" (Keynes in Moggridge 1974: 34–35). During the war, Keynes served as a leading spokesman for what afterwards became the Arts Council. "Death to Hollywood" was his slogan. He was immensely gratified to be able to report, implausibly enough, that 3,000 English factory workers in the Midlands had reacted with "wild delight" to a ballet performance (Keynes in Moggridge 1974: 41, 48). In the future, besides state subsidies, there would be inculcation of art appreciation in the schools: going to plays and visiting art galleries "will be a living element in everyone's upbringing, and regular attendance at the theatre and concerts a part of organized education" (1982b: 371).

The utter banality of this state-sponsored crusade for aesthetic Uplift—a key to the realization of Keynes's utopia—is exceeded only by its spirit–crushing dreariness.

Keynes and the Totalitarian "Experiments"

Further grounds for doubting Keynes's liberalism can be found in his attitude in the 1920s and 30s towards the continental "experiments" in planned economy.

At certain times Keynes displayed an outlook on German National Socialist and Italian Fascist economic policy surprising in a supposed model liberal thinker. Two texts are at issue here: the preface to the German edition of the *General Theory* (Keynes 1973a: xxv–xxvii), and the essay, "National Self-Sufficiency" (Keynes 1933; 1982: 233–46).

In the preface, Keynes observes that he is deviating from "the English classical (or orthodox) tradition," which, he notes, never totally dominated German thought.

> The Manchester School and Marxism both derive ultimately from Ricardo.[21] . . . But in Germany there has always existed a

---

21 This is typical of Keynes's ignorant and cavalier way with the history of economic thought. Ricardian economics exercised no influence on the thought of Cobden and Bright, leaders of the Manchester School; see Grampp 1960: 7, 106–07. On Keynes's distortion of Malthus as a precursor of his own position, see Rothbard 1995: 105–06. On Keynes's ignorance of and lack of interest even in the precursors of his own theories, see Garvey 1975.

large section of opinion which has adhered neither to the one nor to the other....Perhaps, therefore, I may expect less resistance from German than from English readers in offering a theory of employment and output as a whole, which departs in important respects from the orthodox tradition. (1973a: xxv–xxvi)

To entice his readers in National Socialist Germany even further, Keynes adds:

much of the following book is illustrated and expounded mainly with reference to the conditions existing in the Anglo-Saxon countries. Nevertheless the theory of output as a whole, which is what the following book purports to provide, is much more easily adapted to the conditions of a totalitarian state, than is the theory of the production and distribution of a given output produced under conditions of free competition and a large measure of laissez-faire. (1973a: xxvi)

Roy Harrod in his earlier biography (1951) chose not mention this preface at all.[22] Robert Skidelsky refers to it as "unfortunately worded," and leaves it at that (1992: 581). Alan Peacock writes of the passage (without quoting it) that Keynes indicated "that the then German (Nazi) government would be more sympathetic to his ideas on the employment-creating effects of public works than the British government" (1993: 7). This, however, runs contrary to the clear meaning of the text: it is not that the Nazi leaders chanced to be more sympathetic to one of Keynes's particular proposals, but that, in Keynes's view, his theory "is much more easily adapted to the conditions of a totalitarian state." Peacock adds "there is some dispute over whether or not the preface was accurately translated." But that issue in no way affects the excerpt quoted here, which is from Keynes's English manuscript.[23]

---

22 Michael Heilperin, in a long footnote (1960: 127, n. 48), commented on the absence of any reference to this preface in Harrod's work, the major biography of Keynes at the time he wrote. In view of the suppression of academic and other freedoms in Nazi Germany, Heilperin called Keynes's ingratiating text "an indelible blot on his record as a liberal."
23 The dispute involves some sentences that appear in the German edition but not in Keynes's manuscript; but these do not seem to inculpate Keynes any further, except for the use of the

Nazi economic thinkers sometimes used references to Keynes to support the explicitly anti-liberal economic policies of National Socialism. Otto Wagener, who headed a Nazi economics research bureau before the seizure of power, gave Hitler a copy of Keynes's book on money, because it was "a very interesting treatise," conveying the feeling that the author was "far on the road to us, without being familiar with us and our viewpoint" (Barkai 1977: 55, 57, 156). Publication of the German edition of *The General Theory* received critical reviews from publications that had managed to keep their distance from the official Nazi economic line, while a Nazi apologist at Heidelberg welcomed it "as a vindication of National Socialism." Keynes himself remarked that the German authorities had permitted publication "on paper rather better than usual, and the price was not much higher than usual" (Skidelsky 1992: 581, 583).

A weightier instance of the difficulty of classifying Keynes as a liberal is his essay on "National Self-Sufficiency" (Keynes 1933, 1982: 233–46).[24] Here laissez-faire and free trade are treated with characteristic Bloomsbury derision. In the dismal past they had been viewed "almost as a part of the moral law," a component of the "bundle of obsolete habiliments one's mind drags round" (Keynes 1933: 755). Very different, however, is Keynes's posture towards the doctrines that were all the rage as he wrote. "Each year it becomes more obvious that the world is embarking on a variety of politico-economic experiments," as the presumptions of nineteenth century free trade are abandoned. What are these "experiments"? They are those underway in Russia, Italy, Ireland, and Germany. Even Britain and America are striving for "a new plan."

---

phrase "pronounced national leadership [*Führung*]" with a positive connotation. In any case, it seems likely that Keynes approved of the additions. See Bertram Schefold 1980: 175–76.
24 The version in *The Collected Writings* is from *The New Statesman and Nation*, July 8 and 15, 1933. The essay was first published, however, in *The Yale Review*. Quotations here are from this version, Keynes 1933. Heilperin (1960: 111) states that this essay "can well be regarded, for all its brevity, as one of Keynes's most significant writings," and observes that Keynes downplays the totalitarian character of the regimes he discusses: "They were experimenting that was the wonderful thing about it!" Here Heilperin captures the essential spirit of this piece and of Keynes's thought over several years.

Keynes is oddly agnostic on the chances for success of these various projects:

> We do not know what will be the outcome. We are—all of us, I expect—about to make many mistakes. No one can tell which of the new systems will prove itself best. . . . We each have our own fancy. Not believing that we are saved already [sic], we each should like to have a try at working out our own salvation. (761–62)

He concedes that "in matters of economic detail, as distinct from the central controls," he favors "retaining as much private judgment and initiative and enterprise as possible" (762). But

> we all need to be as free possible of interference from economic changes elsewhere, in order to make our own favorite experiments towards the ideal social republic of the future . . . (763)

At the time Keynes wrote this article, the doctrine of "national self-sufficiency" that he was preaching was often identified with National Socialism and Italian Fascism. When Franklin Roosevelt "torpedoed" the London Economic Conference of June, 1933, the President of the Reichsbank Hjalmar Schacht smugly told the *Völkischer Beobachter* (the official newspaper of the Nazi Party) that the American leader had adopted the economic philosophy of Hitler and Mussolini: "Take your economic fate in your own hand and you will help not only yourself but the whole world" (Garraty 1973: 922).

Keynes admits that many errors are being committed in all the contemporary essays in planning. While Mussolini may be "acquiring wisdom teeth," "Germany is at the mercy of unchained irresponsibles—though it is too soon to judge her."[25] Keynes reserves his harshest criticism for Stalin's Russia, perhaps a historically unprecedented example of "administrative incompetence and of the sacrifice of almost everything

---

25 This and similar criticisms of Nazi Germany were omitted in the German translation of the essay, evidently with Keynes's permission; see Borchardt 1988. Although Borchardt is aware of *The Yale Review* version, he cites the essay from *The Collected Writings* and thus overestimates its liberal tenor.

that makes life worth living to wooden heads" (766). "Let Stalin be a terrifying example to all who seek to make experiments," Keynes declares. (769)

Yet his critique of Stalin—who had just condemned millions to death in the terror famine and was filling Lenin's Gulag with additional millions—is oddly oblique and off center. What the Soviet and the other socio-economic experiments require above all is "bold, free, and remorseless criticism." But

> Stalin has eliminated every independent, critical mind, even those sympathetic in general outlook. He has produced an environment in which the processes of mind are atrophied. The soft convolutions of the brain are turned to wood. The multiplied bray of the loud-speaker replaces the soft inflections of the human voice. The bleat of propaganda bores even the birds and the beasts of the field into stupefaction. (769)

"Wooden heads . . . brains turned to wood . . . bores . . . into stupefaction." The reader may judge for himself whether this critique—redolent of John Stuart Mill's harping on the all-importance of endless discussion and debate—is adequate to the deeds of Josef Stalin and Soviet power as of 1933.

Finally, there is a passage in this essay as it appeared in its first version, in *The Yale Review*, which is omitted from *The Collected Writings*[26]:

> But I bring my criticisms to bear, as one whose heart is friendly and sympathetic to the desperate experiments of the contemporary world, who wishes them well and would like them to succeed, who has his own experiments in view, and who in the last resort

---

26 It should have appeared in Keynes 1982: 244, after: "For I must not be supposed to be endorsing all those things which are being done in the political world today in the name of economic nationalism. Far from it." The version in *The Collected Writings* likewise omits a few other passages, of negligible importance, that appear in the *Yale Review*. The editor of this volume in no way indicates that the version included differs from the one published in The *Yale Review*; moreover, he incorrectly gives the issue of the *Yale Review* in question as "Summer 1933."

prefers anything on earth to what the financial reports are wont to call "the best opinion in Wall Street." (Keynes 1933: 766)[27]

Skidelsky's comment (1992: 483) on this essay is brief and bland: "As Keynes noted in his 'National Self-Sufficiency' articles [the essay appeared in two parts in *The New Statesman and Nation*], social experiments were in fashion; all of them, whatever their political provenance, envisaged a much enlarged role for government, and a greatly restricted role for free commerce." This hardly seems sufficient.

The question at this point is this: how can someone who expressed a wistful sympathy for the "experiments" of the Nazis, Fascists, and Stalinist Communists, and whose threadbare Bloomsbury mockery was reserved for the freely functioning society of laissez-faire be considered a clear-cut example of a liberal, or any liberal at all?[28]

Soviet Communism

Questions are also raised by the tone and substance of some of Keynes's more extended remarks on Soviet Communism. Following a trip to the Soviet Union in 1925, he published, *A Short View of Russia* (1972: 253–71). Skidelsky calls this, with astonishing implausibility, "one of the most searing attacks on Soviet communism ever penned" (1994: 235).

It is true that Keynes perceives some grave flaws of the Soviet regime, especially the persecution of dissenters and the general oppressiveness. But these he holds to be in part the fruit of revolution and of "some beastliness in the Russian nature—or in the Russian and Jewish

---

27 Keynes reiteration during the 1920s and 30s of the wonderfulness of social engineering "experiments" finally becomes almost laughable. Another example: in *The End of Laissez-Faire* ([1926] 1972: 290, emphasis supplied), he wrote: "I criticize doctrinaire State Socialism, not because it seeks to engage men's altruistic impulses in the service of society, or because it departs from *laissez-faire*, or because it takes away from man's natural liberty to make a million, or *because it has courage for bold experiments*. All these things I applaud."

28 Throughout his career Keynes was, of course, a relentless critic of the laissez-faire principle. *The End of Laissez-Faire* (Keynes 1972: 272–94) is perhaps his most famous polemical essay. It was reviewed at the time by the Italian (by no means "doctrinaire") liberal economist Luigi Einaudi (1926). Einaudi's critique of Keynes and reaffirmation of the value of laissez-faire in practice is discussed in the essay on "The Centrality of French Liberalism," in the section on "Laissez-faire as Political Guideline," in the present volume.

natures when, as now, they are allied." It is "one face" of the "superb seriousness of Red Russia." Such seriousness can be dour, "crude and stupid and boring in the extreme," witness the Methodists (270)—another Bloomsbury touch. Keynes gives no sign that despotism might be the natural consequence, the entirely predictable result, of such a concentration of power in the state as the Bolsheviks had effected in Russia. This view has been a mainstay of liberal thought from at least the time of Montesquieu and Madison, through Mises and Hayek, and on to the present day. One would expect a liberal to highlight the point.

Instead, Keynes gushes over the Soviets' will to engage in bold "experiments" in social engineering. In Russia, "the method of trial-and-error is unreservedly employed. No one has ever been more frankly experimentalist than Lenin." As for the catastrophically failed "experiments" of the first years of Bolshevik rule, which had compelled the shift from "war communism" to the then-current system of the New Economic Policy (NEP), Keynes describes them in the most anodyne terms: earlier "errors" had now been corrected and "confusions" dissipated (262).[29] Keynes is dazzled by the regime's character as "the laboratory of life," and concludes that Soviet Communism has "just a chance" of success. Still, he asserts in this "searing attack," "even a chance gives to what is happening in Russia more importance than what is happening (let us say) in the United States of America" (270).[30]

What was at the root of Keynes's sympathy for the Soviet experiment? A hint is given at the beginning of his essay, when Keynes playfully suggests that the Archbishop of Canterbury might deserve to be called a "Bolshevist," "if he seriously pursues the Gospel precepts." (Jesus Christ as the first Chekist?) What moves Keynes most deeply is the "religious"

---

[29] "Errors" and "confusions" seem hardly adequate terms for what a recent historian of Soviet Communism has characterized as "the titanic descent into chaos" of those years, with the death of millions; see the chapter on "War Communism: A Regime is Born, 1918–1921," in Malia 1994: 109–39; also the illuminating analysis in "'War Communism'—Product of Marxian Ideas," Roberts 1971: 20–47.

[30] Keynes adds (271) that Soviet Russia is very much to be preferred to Tsarist Russia, from which "nothing could ever emerge." This is an amazingly dimwitted judgment, especially in view of Keynes's love of the arts. Old Russia can, of course, boast of great achievements in many fields, including music, dance, and, above all, literature, unequaled by its Soviet successor.

element in Leninism, whose *"emotional and ethical essence centers about the individual's and the community's attitude towards the love of money"* (259; emphasis in the original). The Communists have transcended "materialistic egotism" and brought about "a real change in the predominant attitude towards money.... A society of which this is even partially true is a tremendous innovation":

> in the Russia of the future it is intended that the career of money-making, as such, will simply not occur to a respectable young man as a possible opening, any more than the career of a gentleman burglar or acquiring skill in forgery or embezzlement.... Everyone should work for the community—the new creed runs—and, if he does his duty, the community will uphold him. (260–61)

In contrast to this inspiring religiosity, "modern capitalism is absolutely irreligious," lacking in any sense of solidarity and public spirit:

> it seems clearer every day that the moral problem of our age is concerned with the love of money, with the habitual appeal of the money motive in nine-tenths of the activities of life, with the universal striving after individual economic security as the prime object of endeavor, with the social approbation of money as the measure of constructive success, with the social appeal to the hoarding instinct as the foundation of the necessary provision for the family and for the future. (268–29)

This preference for Communist over capitalist morality was to remain with Keynes for years.

In 1928, Keynes paid a second visit to Russia, which produced a less favorable assessment. But while Skidelsky (1992: 235–36) assures us that "the romance was clearly over," that is another of his little exercises in disinformation. The romance continued at least to 1936, with Keynes's review of *Soviet Communism*, by his friends Sidney and Beatrice Webb. None of those who argue for Keynes's liberalism has frankly confronted his quite unambiguous pronouncement,[31] included in a brief radio talk delivered for the BBC in June, 1936, in the "Books and Authors" series (1982: 333–34).

The only work that Keynes deals with at any length is the Webbs' recently published massive tome, *Soviet Communism*. (The first edition carried the subtitle, *A New Civilisation?*; in later editions, the question mark was dropped.) As leaders of the Fabian Society, the Webbs had toiled for decades to bring about a socialist Britain. In the 1930s, they turned into ardent propagandists for the new regime in Communist Russia—in Beatrice's words, they had "fallen in love with Soviet Communism" (Muggeridge 1968: 245). What she called "love" their nephew by marriage, Malcolm Muggeridge 1973: 72, labeled "besotted adulation." During their three-week visit to Russia, where, Sidney boasted, they were treated like "a new type of royalty," the Soviet authorities supplied them with the imaginary facts and figures for their book (Cole 1946: 194; Muggeridge 1968: 245). The Stalinist apparatchiks were well satisfied with the final result. In Russia itself, *Soviet Communism* was translated, published, and promoted by the regime; as Beatrice smugly declared: "Sidney and I have become ikons in the Soviet Union" (Muggeridge 1973: 206).[32]

Ever since it first appeared, *Soviet Communism* has been seen as probably the prime example of the aid and comfort lavished by literary fellow travelers on the Stalinist terror state. If Keynes had been a liberal and a lover of the free society, one would expect his review, despite his friendship with the authors, to be a scathing denunciation. But the opposite is the case. As Beatrice was pleased to note, Maynard, "in his

---

31 Logically, it should have been discussed by Skidelsky in volume two of his biography, which covers the period to 1937. But while he mentions the Webbs' *Soviet Communism*, he does not touch on Keynes's radio review; Skidelsky 1994: 488. It is passing strange that nowhere in his immense, three-volume biography of Keynes does Skidelsky find space even to mention this highly incriminating piece. It is also absent from his essay on Keynes and the Fabians (1999). The talk is mentioned in O'Donnell 1989: 377, n. 13.
32 Even Beatrice's friend and biographer, Margaret Cole (Cole 1946: 199) stated that the book, while containing some criticisms, was "in some sense, an enormous propaganda pamphlet, defending and praising the Soviet Union." This was not meant as a criticism, since, as is evident from her biography, Cole shared the Webb's admiration for Stalinism.

attractive way, boomed our book in his recent radio talk" (Webb 1985: 370).

In fact, Keynes advised the British public that *Soviet Communism* was a work "which every serious citizen will do well to look into":

> Until recently events in Russia were moving too fast and the gap between paper professions and actual achievements was too wide for a proper account to be possible. But the new system is now sufficiently crystallised to be reviewed. The result is impressive. The Russian innovators have passed, not only from the revolutionary stage, but also from the doctrinaire stage. There is little or nothing left which bears any special relation to Marx and Marxism as distinguished from other systems of socialism. They are engaged in the vast administrative task of making a completely new set of social and economic institutions work smoothly and successfully over a territory so extensive that it covers one sixth of the land surface of the world.

There is, yet again, fulsome praise for Soviet "experimentation":

> Methods are still changing rapidly in response to experience. The largest scale empiricism and experimentalism which has ever been attempted by disinterested administrators is in operation. Meanwhile, the Webbs have enabled us to see the direction in which things appear to be moving and how far they have got. (Keynes 1982b: 333–34)

Britain, Keynes feels, has much to learn from the Webbs' work:

> It leaves me with a strong desire and hope that we in this country may discover how to combine an unlimited readiness to experiment with changes in political and economic methods and institutions, whilst preserving traditionalism and a sort of careful conservatism, thrifty of everything which has human experience behind it, in every branch of feeling and of action. (334)

One should note, incidentally, the studied backtracking and basic confusion typical of much of Keynes's social philosophizing—an "unlimited readiness to experiment" is somehow to be combined with "traditionalism" and "careful conservatism."

By 1936 no one had to depend on the Webbs' deceitful propaganda for information on the Stalinist system. Eugene Lyons, William Henry Chamberlin, Malcolm Muggeridge himself, the world's conservative, social democratic, Catholic, and left-anarchist press had revealed the grim truth about of the charnel house presided over by Keynes's "innovators" and "disinterested administrators."[33] Anyone willing to listen could learn the facts regarding the terror famine of the early 1930s, the vast system of slave labor camps, and the near-universal misery that followed on the abolition of private property. For those not blinded by "love," the evidence was unmistakable that Stalin was perfecting the model killer-state of the twentieth century.

The Hatred of Money

What explains Keynes's praise for the Webbs' book and the Soviet system? There can be little doubt that the major reason is, once again, his deep-seated aversion to profit-seeking and moneymaking, an attitude shared by the Fabian couple.

According to their friend and fellow Fabian, Margaret Cole, the Webbs looked on Soviet Russia as, morally and spiritually, "the hope of the world" (Cole 1946: 198). For them, "most exciting" of all was the role of the Communist Party, which, Beatrice held, was a "religious order," engaged in creating a "Communist Conscience." By 1932, Beatrice could announce that: "It is because I believe that the day has arrived for the changeover from egotism to altruism—as the mainspring of human life—that I am a Communist" (cited in Nord 1985: 242–44). In *Soviet Communism*, the Webbs gush over the replacement of monetary incentives by the rituals of "shaming the delinquent" and Communist self-criticism (Webb and Webb 1936: 761–62). Up to the very end of her

---

33 Eugene Lyons's comments on the Webbs' admiration for the "strong faith" and "resolute will" of those who carried out the liquidation of the kulaks, among other mass murders, can be found in Lyons 1937: 284. See also the remarks by Robert Conquest 1986: 317–18, 321. In his novel, *Winter in Moscow,* Muggeridge (1934) described the world of the foreign fellow traveler who visited the Soviet Union; it was more often "New Liberals" and Fabians rather than non-Communist socialists who were duped by the Soviet regime, he observed.

life, in 1943, Beatrice was still lauding the Soviet Union for "its multiform democracy, its sex, class, and racial equality, its planned production for community consumption, and above all its penalization of the profit-making motive" (Webb 1948: 491). And, after her death, Keynes eulogized her as "the greatest woman of the generation which is now passing."[34]

Like the Webbs, Keynes identified religiosity with the individual's self-abnegation for the good of the community. In economic terms, this translated into working for non-pecuniary rewards, in this way transcending the sordid motivation of "nine-tenths of the activities of life" in capitalist societies. For Keynes, as for the Webbs, this was the essence of the "religious" and "moral" element they detected and admired in Communism.

In his passion to malign moneymaking, Keynes even resorted to calling on psychoanalysis for support. Fascinated like most of the Bloomsbury circle by the work of Sigmund Freud, Keynes valued it above all for the "intuitions" which paralleled his own, especially on the significance of the love of money. In his *Treatise on Money*, Keynes refers to a passage in a 1908 paper by Freud, in which he writes of the "connections which exist between the complexes of interest in money and of defaecation" and the unconscious "identification of gold with faeces." (Freud 1924: 49–50; Keynes 1971b: 258 and n. 1; Skidelsky 1992: 188, 234, 237, 414).[35] This psychoanalytical "finding"—by the man Vladimir Nabokov correctly identified as the Viennese Fraud—permitted Keynes to assert that love of money was condemned not only by religion but by "science" as well. Thus, besides constituting "the central ethical problem of modern society" (cited in O'Donnell 1989: 377, n. 14), the preoccupation with money was also a fit subject for the alienist.

---

34 In a letter to George Bernard Shaw (Skidelsky 2001: 168). Skidelsky adds, somewhat cryptically, that, though Keynes had arranged for an admiring obituary of Beatrice, he "still hankered after an appreciation of her economics." (ibid. 527, n. 76) It is entertaining to consider what the economic thought of this silly woman could have consisted in.
35 Obviously, if one were to proceed as Keynes did, one would have to probe Keynes's own unconscious mind for the disreputable sources both of his involvement with the subject of money throughout his professional career, and of his intense, affect-laden rejection of the money motive.

Keynes looked forward to the time when the love of money as mere possession "will be recognized for what it is, a somewhat disgusting morbidity, one of those semi-criminal, semi-pathological propensities which one hands over with a shudder to the specialists in mental disease" (Keynes 1972: 329). Sad to say, in all of this rubbish Keynes finds no space to elaborate on the treatment he anticipates such specialists will mete out to the deranged persons diagnosed as suffering from this mental affliction.

In Keynes's pro-Soviet remarks and in the lack of any concern about them among his devotees, we find, once again, the grotesque double standard that continues to be nearly universal (Applebaum 1997; Malia 1999; Courtois 1999). If in the mid-1930s a celebrated writer had expressed himself towards Nazi Germany in the occasionally benevolent terms Keynes used for the Soviet Union, he would have been pilloried and his name would reek to this day. Yet as evil as the Nazis were to become, in 1936 their victims amounted to a small fraction of the victims of the Soviet regime.[36]

In fact, the case of Keynes is worse than that of someone who merely praised Hitler, say, for alleged successes in curing the unemployment problem or restoring German self-respect, or for whatever other "achievements" National Socialism might have claimed. The real analogue to Keynes, in his mixture of criticism and sympathy in regard to Soviet Communism, would be a writer who decried the persecutions and suppression of freedom of thought under the Nazis, while praising them for their "awareness" of the "racial question," from which we might derive some hope for the future. For the very thing that Keynes found admirable in Soviet Russia—the iron will to suppress moneymaking and the profit motive—was the main source of the horrors.

---

36 In a letter dated May 2, 1936 (1961, 403), H.L. Mencken, who was often as astute politically as he was witty in general, wrote: "I am against the violation of civil rights by Hitler and Mussolini as much as you are, and well you know it. . . . You protest, and with justice, every time Hitler jails an opponent, but you forget that Stalin and company have jailed and murdered a thousand times as many. It seems to me, and indeed the evidence is plain, that compared to the Moscow brigands and assassins, Hitler is hardly more than a common Ku Kluxer and Mussolini almost a philanthropist."

As adherents of a variant of Marxism, Lenin, and after him, Stalin, shared Marx's loathing of money. The aim of Communism was to abolish money, along with profit-seeking and private exchange—the whole market system—that money made possible. Soviet Communism selected its prey chiefly from among those marked by their love of money and profits: the bourgeoisie and the landlords of the old regime; the "speculators" and "hoarders" of the years of "war communism" and the first Red Terror; then the NEPmen and "kulaks" of the period of collectivization and the introduction of the Plans (Leggett 1981; Conquest 1986; Malia 1994: 129–33). How could Keynes have overlooked the link between individual wealth-seeking and state-inflicted torment that was the rule in Soviet Russia—particularly considering that, in the book he reviewed in his radio address, the authors glorify Stalin's decision to proceed to "the liquidation of the kulaks as a class"(Webb and Webb 1936: 561–72)?

A notable feature of Keynes's complimentary comments on the Soviet system here and elsewhere is their total lack of any *economic* analysis. Keynes was blithely unaware that there might exist a problem of *rational economic calculation* under socialism. This was a question that had already occupied continental scholars for some time, and was the focus of lively discussion at the London School of Economics.

The year before Keynes's radio address, a volume appeared in English edited by F.A. Hayek, *Collectivist Economic Planning* (Hayek 1935), which featured a translation of the seminal 1920 essay by Ludwig von Mises, "Economic Calculation in the Socialist Commonwealth." At the London School, Hayek was already giving a course of "The Problems of a Collectivist Economy," starting in 1933–34. A seminar directed by Hayek, Lionel Robbins, and Arnold Plant, chiefly devoted to the same subject, had been offered in 1932–33 (Moggridge 2004).

Keynes gives no indication he had the slightest inkling of the debate or was even in the least interested in the question.[37] Instead, what

---

37 As late as 1944, in a letter to Hayek commenting on *The Road to Serfdom*, Keynes stated: "The line of argument you yourself take depends on the very doubtful assumption that planning is not more efficient. Quite likely from the purely economic point of view it is efficient" (Keynes 1980: 386). That Keynes could have referred to this as an "assumption"

matters for Keynes is the excitement of the Soviet experiment—was there ever any other economist, or purported liberal thinker, who so often invoked "excitement" and "boredom" as criteria for judging social systems?—the awe-inspiring scope of the social changes directed by those "disinterested administrators," and the path-breaking ethical advance of abolishing the profit motive.

Does this mean that Keynes was at any point ever a Communist? Of course not. But his clearly expressed sympathy with the Soviet system (as well as, to a much lesser extent, with other totalitarian states), when added to his state-furthering economic theory and his state-dominated utopian vision, should embarrass those who unhesitatingly, and ignorantly, enlist him in the liberal ranks. Viewing Keynes as "the model liberal of the twentieth century"—or as any liberal at all—can only render an indispensable historical concept incoherent.

References

Anderson, Benjamin (1995 [1949]), "Digression on Keynes," in Hazlitt (ed.): 185–206.

Applebaum, Anne (1997) "A Dearth of Feeling," in Hilton Kramer and Roger Kimball (eds.), *The Future of the European Past*, Chicago: Ivan R. Dee.

Arblaster, Anthony (1984) *The Rise and Decline of Western Liberalism*, Oxford: Blackwell.

Balogh, Thomas (1978), "Keynes and Planning," in Thirwall.

---

indicates that he never became aware of—or else refused to think about—the great debate over economic calculation under socialism. The total lack of economic analysis in his reports from Soviet Russia brings to mind Karl Brunner's conclusion (1987: 47) on Keynes's notions of social reform: "One would hardly guess from the material of the essays that a social scientist, even economist, had written [them]. Any social dreamer of the intelligentsia could have produced them. Crucial questions . . . are never faced or explored." There may well be truth in the judgment of his good friend Beatrice Webb (1985: 371), in 1936: "Keynes is not serious about economic problems; he plays a game of chess with it in his leisure hours. The only serious cult with him is aesthetics . . ." For an evaluation of Keynes as "the consummate artist," aside from the scientific implications of his theory, see Buchanan (1987).

Barkai, Avraham (1977) *Das Wirtschaftssystem des Nationalsozialismus: Der historische und ideologische Hintergrund, 1933–1936*, Cologne: Berend von Nottbeck.

Benjamin, Daniel K. and Levis A. Kochin (1979) "Searching for an Explanation of Unemployment in Interwar Britain," *Journal of Political Economy* 87 (3) (June).

Borchardt, Knut (1988) "Keynes' 'Nationale Selbstgenügsamkeit' von 1933: Ein Fall von kooperativer Selbstzensur," *Zeitschrift für Wirtschafts- u. Sozialwissenschaften*, 108: 271–85.

Bramsted, E. K. and K. J. Melhuish (eds.) (1978) *Western Liberalism: A History in Documents from Locke to Croce*, London/New York: Longman.

Brunner, Karl (1987) "The Sociopolitical Vision of Keynes," in Reese (ed.): 23–55.

Buchanan, James (1987) "Keynesian Follies," in Reese (ed.): 130–45.

Buchanan, James, with R.E. Wagner and John Burton (1991) "The Consequences of Mr. Keynes," in James Buchanan, *Constitutional Economics*, Oxford: Blackwell.

Bullock, Allan and Maurice Shock (eds.) (1956) *The Liberal Tradition: From Fox to Keynes*, Oxford: Clarendon.

Cairncross, Alec (1978) "Keynes and the Planned Economy," in Thirlwall (ed.): 36–58.

Caldwell, Bruce (1995), "Introduction" to Hayek: 1–48.

Cole, Margaret (1946) *Beatrice Webb*, New York: Harcourt, Brace.

Conquest, Robert (1986) *The Harvest of Sorrow: Soviet Collectivization and the Terror-Famine*, New York: Oxford University Press.

Corry, B. (1978) "Keynes in the History of Economic Thought: Some Reflections," in Thirwall (ed.): 3–34.

Courtois, Stéphane (1999) "Introduction: The Crimes of Communism," in Courtois et al.: 1–31.

Courtois, Stéphane, et al., *The Black Book of Communism: Crimes, Terror, Repression*, Jonathan Murphy and Mark Kramer (trs.), Mark Kramer (consulting ed.), Cambridge, Mass.: Harvard University Press.

Crabtree, Derek and A. P. Thirwall (eds.) (1993) *Keynes and the Role of the State*, New York: St. Martin's.

Cranston, Maurice (1978) "Keynes: His Political Ideas and Their Influence," in Thirwall (ed.): 101–15.

de Cecco, Marcello, (1989) "Keynes and Italian Economics," in Hall (ed.): 195–229.

Den Uyl, Douglas J. and Stuart Warner (1987) "Liberalism in Hobbes and Spinoza," *Studia Spinozana* 3 (1987): 262–318.

The Economist (1993) "The Search for Keynes" (December 26, 1992–January 8).

Einaudi, Luigi (1926) "La fine del 'laissez-faire'" *La Riforma Sociale*, 3rd series, 37 (11–12) (November-December).

Freud, Sigmund (1924) "Character and Anal Eroticism, *Collected Papers*, 2, Joan Riviere (tr.) London: Hogarth Press and the Institute of Psycho-Analysis.

Friedman, Milton (1997) "John Maynard Keynes," Federal Reserve Bank of Richmond, *Economic Quarterly* 83 (2) (Spring).

Garraty, John A. (1973) "The New Deal, National Socialism, and the Great Depression," *American Historical Review* 78 (October).

Garrison, Roger W. (1985) "Intertemporal Coordination and the Invisible Hand: An Austrian Perspective on the Keynesian Vision," *History of Political Economy* 17 (2) (Summer): 307–21.

Garrison, Roger W. (1993) "Keynesian Splenetics: From Social Philosophy to Macroeconomics," *Critical Review* 6 (4): 471–91.

Garvey, George (1975) "Keynes and the Economic Activists of Pre-Hitler Germany," *Journal of Political Economy* 83 (2) (April): 391–405.

Grampp, William D. (1960) *The Manchester School of Economics*, Stanford, Cal.: Stanford University Press.

Gray, John (1986) *Liberalism*, Minneapolis: University of Minnesota Press.

Habeler, Gottfried (1946) "The Place of the General Theory of Employment, Interest, and Money in the History of Economic Thought," *Review of Economic Statistics* 28 (1) (February).

Hall, Peter A. (1989) (ed.) *The Political Power of Economic Ideas: Keynesianism Across Nations*, Princeton, N.J.: Princeton University Press.

Harrod, Roy F. (1951) *The Life of John Maynard Keynes*, New York: Harcourt, Brace.

Hayek, F.A. (ed.) (1935) *Collectivist Economic Planning*, London: Routledge and Kegan Paul.

Hayek, F.A. (1973) *Law, Legislation, and Liberty*, 1 *Rules and Order*, Chicago: University of Chicago Press.

Hayek, F.A. (1995) *Contra Keynes and Cambridge: Essays, Correspondence*, in *Collected Works*, 9, Bruce Caldwell (ed.), Chicago: University of Chicago Press.

Heilperin, Michael A. (1960) "The Economic Nationalism of John Maynard Keynes," in idem, *Studies in Economic Nationalism*. Geneva: Droz, and Paris: Minard.

Hazlitt, Henry (1959) *The Failure of the "New Economics": An Analysis of Keynesian Fallacies*, Princeton, N.J.: Van Nostrand.

Hazlitt, Henry (1995 [1960]) (ed.) *The Critics of Keynesian Economics*, Irvington, N.Y.: Foundation for Economic Education.

Hoppe, Hans-Hermann (2001) *Democracy: The God that Failed. The Economics and Politics of Monarchy, Democracy, and Natural Order*, New Brunswick, N.J.: Transaction.

Johnson, Harry G. (1975) "Keynes and British Economics," in Milo Keynes (ed.), *Essays on John Maynard Keynes*, Cambridge, Eng.: Cambridge University Press.

Keynes, John Maynard (1933) "National Self Sufficiency," *Yale Review*, 22 (4) (June): 755–69.

Keynes, John Maynard (1974) "Art and the State," "Arts in Wartime," and "The Arts Council: Its Policy and Hopes," 33–39, 40–43, 44–48.

Keynes, John Maynard, *The Collected Writings*, London: Macmillan, Cambridge University Press and St. Martin's Press for the Royal Economic Society: (1971a) 4, *A Tract on Monetary Reform*, Elizabeth Johnson and Donald Moggridge (eds.)

(1971b) 6, *A Treatise on Money: 2. The Applied Theory of Money*, Elizabeth Johnson and Donald Moggridge (eds.).

(1972) 9, *Essays in Persuasion*, Elizabeth Johnson and Donald Moggridge (eds.).

(1973a) 7, *The General Theory of Employment, Interest and Money*, Elizabeth Johnson and Donald Moggridge (eds.).

(1973b) 13 *The General Theory and After: Part I Preparation*, Donald Moggridge (ed.)

(1977) 17, *Activities 1920–1922. Treaty Revision and Reconstruction*, Elizabeth Johnson (ed.).

(1980) 27, *Activities 1940–1946. Shaping the Post-War World: Employment and Commodities*, Donald Moggridge (ed.).

(1982a) 21, *Activities 1931–1939. World Crises and Policies in Britain and America*, Donald Moggridge (ed.).

(1982b) 28, *Social, Political and Literary Writings*, Donald Moggridge (ed.).

(1983) 12, *Economic Articles and Correspondence. Investment and Editorial*, Donald Moggridge (ed.).

Leggett, George (1981) *The Cheka: Lenin's Secret Police*, Oxford: Clarendon Press.

Lyons, Eugene (1937) *Assignment in Utopia*, New York: Harcourt, Brace.

Malia, Martin (1994) *The Soviet Tragedy: A History of Socialism in Russia, 1917–1991*, New York: Free Press.

Malia, Martin (1999) "Foreword: The Uses of Atrocity," in Courtois, et al.: ix–xx.

Mencken, H. L. (1961) *Letters*, Guy J. Forgue (ed.) New York: Knopf.

Moggridge, D. E. (1974) *Keynes: Aspects of the Man and His Works*, New York: St. Martin's Press.

Moggridge, D. E. (2004) Review of Bruce Caldwell, *Hayek's Challenge: An Intellectual Biography of F.A. Hayek* www.eh.net/bookreviews/library/0820.shtml.

Muggeridge, Kitty and Ruth Adam (1968) *Beatrice Webb: A Life, 1858–1943*, New York: Knopf.

Muggeridge, Malcolm (1934) *Winter in Moscow*: London: Eyre and Spottiswoode.

Muggeridge, Malcolm (1973) *Chronicles of Wasted Time. Chronicle I: The Green Stick*, New York: William Morrow.

Nord, Deborah Epstein (1985) *The Apprenticeship of Beatrice Webb*, Amherst, Mass.: University of Massachusetts Press.

O'Donnell, R. M. (1989) *Keynes: Philosophy, Economics, and Politics: The Philosophical Foundations of Keynes's Thought and their Influence on his Economics and Politics*, New York: St. Martin's.

Peacock, Alan (1993) "Keynes and the Role of the State," in Crabtree and Thirwall (eds.).

Raico, Ralph (1989) Essay-review of Anthony Arblaster, *The Rise and Decline of Western Liberalism*, *Reason Papers* 14 (Spring): 167–79.

Raico, Ralph (1992) "Prolegomena to a History of Liberalism," *Journal des Économistes et des Études Humaines* 3 (2/3) (Sept.): 259–72.

Raico, Ralph (1999) *Die Partei der Freiheit: Studien zur Geschichte des deutchen Liberalismus*, Jörg Guido Hülsmann (tr.), Stuttgart: Lucius and Lucius.

Reese, David A. (ed.) (1987) *The Legacy of Keynes*, San Francisco: Harper and Row.

Reisman, George (1998) *Capitalism*, Ottawa, Ill.: Jameson.

Roberts, Paul Craig (1971) *Alienation and the Soviet Economy: Toward a General Theory of Marxian Alienation, Organizational Principles, and the Soviet Economy*, Albuquerque, N. M.: University of New Mexico Press.

Rothbard, Murray N. (1962) *Man, Economy, and State*, 2 vols. Princeton, N.J.: Van Nostrand.

Rothbard, Murray N. (1963) *America's Great Depression*, Princeton, N.J.: Van Nostrand.

Rothbard, Murray N. (1992) "Keynes, the Man," in Mark Skousen (ed.), *Dissent on Keynes. A Critical Appraisal of Keynesian Economics*, New York: Praeger.

Rothbard, Murray N. (1995) *Classical Economics: An Austrian Perspective on the History of Economic Thought*, Aldershot, Eng.: Edward Elgar.

Rowley, Charles K. (1987) "The Legacy of Keynes: From the General Theory to Generalized Budget Deficits," James M. Buchanan, Charles K. Rowley, and Robert D. Tollison (eds.) *Deficits*, Oxford: Blackwell: 143–69.

Salerno, Joseph T. (1992) "The Development of Keynes's Economics: From Marshall to Millenialism," *Review of Austrian Economics* 6 (1): 3–64.

Schefold, Bertram (1980) "The General Theory for a Totalitarian State? A Note on Keynes's Preface to the German Edition of 1936," *Cambridge Journal of Economics* 4.

Seccareccia, Mario (1993) "On the Intellectual Origins of Keynes's Policy Radicalism in the *General Theory*," *History of Economic Ideas*, I (2): 77–104.

Seccareccia, Mario (1994) "Socialization of Investment," Philip Arestis and Malcolm Sawyer (eds.) *The Elgar Companion to Radical Political Economy*, Aldershot, Eng: Edward Elgar: 375–79.

Skidelsky, Robert (1988) "Keynes's Political Legacy," in Omar F. Hamouda and John N. Smithin (eds.) *Keynes and Public Policy After Fifty Years*, 1, *Economics and Policy*, New York: New York University Press.

Skidelsky, Robert (1994) *John Maynard Keynes*, 2, *The Economist as Saviour, 1920–1937*, New York: Penguin.

Skidelsky, Robert (1999) "Doing Good and Being Good," *Times Literary Supplement*, (March 26): 13–15.

Skidelsky, Robert (2001) *John Maynard Keynes*, 3, *Fighting for Freedom, 1937–1946*, New York: Viking.

Thirlwall, A. P. (ed.) (1978) *Keynes and Laissez-Faire*, London: Macmillan.

Trotsky, Leon (1960 [1924]) *Literature and Revolution*, Ann Arbor, Mich.: University of Michigan Press.

Vaughn, Karen I. (1980) *John Locke: Economist and Social Scientist*, Chicago: University of Chicago Press.

Webb, Beatrice (1948) *Our Partnership*, Barbara Drake and Margaret I. Cole, (eds.) London: Longman.

Webb, Beatrice (1985) *The Diary of Beatrice Webb*, 4: *1924–1943*. *"The Wheel of Life,"* Norman and Jeanne MacKenzie (eds.) Cambridge, Mass.: Harvard University Press.

Webb, Sidney and Beatrice Webb (1936) *Soviet Communism: A New Civilisation?* 2, New York: Charles Scribner's Sons.

Winch, Donald (1989) "Keynes, Keynesianism, and State Intervention," in Peter A. Hall (ed.) *The Political Power of Economic Ideas: Keynesianism Across Nations*, Princeton, N.J.: Princeton University Press.

5 The Conflict of Classes: Liberal vs. Marxist Theories

Few ideas are as closely associated with Marxism as the concepts of class and class conflict. It is, for instance, impossible to imagine what a Marxist philosophy of history or theory of revolution would be in the their absence. Yet, as with much else in Marxism, these concepts remain ambiguous and contradictory.[1] An example: while Marxist doctrine supposedly grounds classes in the process of production, *The Communist Manifesto* asserts in its famous opening lines:

> The history of all hitherto existing society is the history of class struggles. Freeman and slave, patrician and plebeian, lord and serf, guild-master and journeyman, in a word, oppressor and oppressed, stood in constant opposition to one another . . .[2]

On examination, however, these opposed pairs turn out to be, either wholly or in part, not economic, but legal, categories.[3]

---

[1] Cf., a contemporary Marxist theoretician, Charles Bettelheim 1985 22, who concedes that Marx "did not arrive at a unique and coherent conception of classes and of class conflict."
[2] Karl Marx and Friedrich Engels, *Selected Works in Three Volumes* (Moscow: Progress Publishers, 1983), 1, 108–09.
[3] According to Pitirim Sorokin (1947), Marx never presented a consistent conception of social class; the groups mentioned at the beginning of the *Manifesto*, for instance, include "castes, feudal orders, oppressors and oppressed of all kinds, hierarchies of the medieval corporation."

Neither Marx nor Engels ever resolved the contradictions and ambiguities in their theory in this area. The last chapter of the third and final volume of Marx's *Capital*, published posthumously in 1894, is titled, "Classes."[4] Here he states: "The first question to be answered is this: What constitutes a class?" "At first glance" it would seem to be "the identity of revenue and sources of revenue." That Marx finds inadequate, since "from this standpoint, physicians and officials, e.g., would also constitute two classes." Distinct classes would also be yielded by

> the infinite fragmentation of interest [sic] and rank into which the division of social labour splits labourers as well as capitalists and landlords—the latter, e.g., into owners of vineyards, farm owners, owners of forests, mine owners and owners of fisheries.

At this point, there is a note by Engels: "Here the manuscript breaks off." This was not on account of Marx's sudden demise, however. The chapter dates from a first draft composed by Marx between 1863 and 1867, that is, sixteen to twenty years before his death.[5] Engels's explanation is that "Marx used to leave such concluding summaries until the final editing, just before going to press, when the latest historical developments furnished him with unfailing regularity with proofs of the most laudable timeliness for his theoretical propositions."[6] This explanation would be more convincing if in the intervening years before his death Marx had elsewhere provided a clear definition of classes consistent with the other parts of his theory. In fact, the terms "class" and "classes" as they appear throughout the works of Marx and Engels are totally muddled.[7]

Marx, in Sorokin's view, was well aware of this central defect in his theory, and his abruptly terminated chapter in the last volume of *Capital* was a failed attempt to remedy it. The enduring confusion among Marxists regarding the meaning of class, Sorokin held, may also be traceable to Marx's own intellectual confusion. Cf. Mises 1957: 113: "Marx obfuscated the problem by confusing the notions of caste and class."
4 Karl Marx, *Capital: A Critique of Political Economy*, 3, *The Process of Capitalist Production as a Whole*, Friedrich Engels (ed.) (New York: International Publishers, 1967), 885–86.
5 Ibid. Friedrich Engels, "Preface," 3.
6 Ibid. 7.
7 Horst Stuke 1976. Stuke lists (70–71) some fifty different, mutually contradictory uses of the terms in the founding works of Marxism.

Nonetheless, it remains the case that Marxism is so closely identified with the ideas of classes and of conflicts among them that an important chapter in the history of political thought has been virtually forgotten.

Few economists are as often and as highly celebrated for their knowledge of modern intellectual history as Albert O. Hirschman. Yet Hirschman is obviously at a total loss when confronted with a clear statement of the *liberal* doctrine of class conflict, in Vilfredo Pareto's *Cours d'économie politique* (1896–97). Here Pareto speaks of the struggle to appropriate the wealth produced by others as "the great fact that dominates the whole history of humanity." To Hirschman's ear this "sounds at first curiously—perhaps consciously—like the *Communist Manifesto*." But Pareto quickly "distances himself from Marxism" by using the term "*spoliation*," and by ascribing spoliation, or plunder, to the dominant class's control of the state machine. (Hirschman 1991: 55) Evidently, Hirschman has not the slightest inkling that Pareto was presenting, in the customary terminology, a generations-old liberal analysis that goes back at least to the first decades of the nineteenth century.

Not only was the notion of class conflict a commonplace for decades before Marx began to write, but a quite different theory of class conflict had been worked out which itself played a major role in the genealogy of Marx's ideas.

Marxism's Debt to the Liberal Doctrine

Adolphe Blanqui was the protégé of J.-B. Say and succeeded him in the chair of political economy at the Conservatoire des Arts et Métiers. In what is probably the first history of economic thought, published in 1837, Blanqui wrote:

> In all the revolutions, there have been but two parties confronting each other; that of the people who wish to live by their own labor, and that of those who would live by the labor of others. . . . Patricians and plebeians, slaves and freemen, guelphs and ghibellines, red roses and white roses, cavaliers and roundheads, liberals

and serviles [in Spain], are only varieties of the same species. (Blanqui 1837: x, emphasis in original)[8]

Blanqui quickly makes clear what he understands to have been at issue in these social conflicts:

> So, in one country, the fruit of labor is taken from the workman by taxes, under pretence of the welfare of the state; in another, by privileges, declaring labor a royal concession, and making one pay dearly for the right to devote himself to it. The same abuse is reproduced under forms more indirect, but not less oppressive, when, by means of custom-duties, the state shares with the privileged industries the benefits of the taxes imposed on non-privileged classes. (Blanqui1 837: x–xi).

Blanqui was by no means the originator of this liberal analysis of the conflict of classes; rather, he drew on a perspective that was widespread in liberal circles in the first decades of the nineteenth century (see below). Marx and Engels were well aware of the existence of this earlier notion. In a letter written in 1852 to his follower, Joseph Weydemeyer, the first exponent of Marxism in the United States,[9] Marx asserts:

> no credit is due to me for discovering the existence of classes in modern society or the struggle between them. Long before me bourgeois historians had described the historical development of this class struggle and bourgeois economists the economic anatomy of the classes.[10]

---

8 Cf., Nolte 1983: 599 n. 79, where he observes that Engels attacked what he called Blanqui's "miserable history of economics" in a newspaper article shortly before he composed *The Principles of Communism*, which Marx drew upon in composing the *Manifesto*.
9 Marx to J. Weydemeyer, March 5, 1852, Karl Marx and Friedrich Engels, *Selected Correspondence* (Moscow: Progress Publishers, 1965), 67–70.
10 Ibid. 69. Marx here states that his own contributions are restricted to having shown that classes are not a permanent feature of human society, and that the class struggle will lead to the dictatorship of the proletariat and thence to a classless society. Charles Bettelheim 1985: 69 agrees with Marx on this point: "Lacking these elements ["polarization, historical tendency, final result"] we are faced with a conception already long defended by numerous historians who recognize the existence of class struggles and their action upon the course of history."

The two most prominent "bourgeois historians" whom he names are the Frenchmen, François Guizot and Augustin Thierry;[11] two years later, Marx referred to Thierry as "the father of the 'class struggle' in French historiography."[12]

This "bourgeois" genealogy of the Marxist theory of class conflict was freely conceded by Marx's early followers. Towards the end of his life, Engels suggested that so little did individuals count in history as compared to the great underlying social forces, that even in the absence of Marx himself, "the materialist conception of history" would have been discovered by others; his evidence is that "Thierry, Mignet, Guizot, and all the English historians up to 1850" were striving towards it.[13] Franz Mehring, Plekhanov, and other Marxist writers in the period of the Second International emphasized the roots of the Marxist class conflict doctrine in the liberal historiography of the French Restoration.[14] Lenin also credited "the bourgeoisie," not Marx, with having originated

---

11 The third is the much less significant English writer, John Wade. Later in the letter, Marx refers to the economists Ricardo, Malthus, Mill, Say, et al., who revealed how the "economic bases of different classes are bound to give rise to a necessary and ever-growing antagonism among them." It is worth noting that in the same letter, Marx ridicules the view of "the fatuous [Karl] Heinzen," that "the existence of classes [is connected with] the existence of political *privileges* and *monopolies* . . ." (emphasis in original).
12 Marx to Engels, July 27, 1854. *Selected Correspondence*, 87.
13 Engels to H. Starkenburg, January 25, 1894. Karl Marx and Friedrich Engels, *Selected Correspondence*, 468.
14 In his classic biography of Marx, Franz Mehring 1962, 75 traces this conception to Marx's period in Paris in 1843–44, when he immersed himself in the historiography of the French Revolution: "The study of the French Revolution led him on to the historical literature of the 'Third Estate,' a literature which originated under the Bourbon restoration and was developed by men of great historical talent who followed the historical existence of their class back into the eleventh century and presented French history as an uninterrupted series of class struggles. Marx owed his knowledge of the historical nature of classes and their struggles to these historians . . . Marx always denied having originated the theory of the class struggle." David McLellan telescopes the process described by Mehring when he states 1973: 95: "It was his [Marx's] reading of the history of the French Revolution in the summer of 1843 that showed him the role of class struggle in social development." Neither Guizot nor Thierry concentrated their analysis on the Revolution; in any case, it is much more likely that it was their emphasis on class struggle as a constant, spanning centuries of medieval and modern history that impressed Marx.

the theory of the class struggle.¹⁵ Strangely, even this lengthy, one could say, star-studded chapter in the history of *socialist* ideas is *terra incognita* to the eminent historian of economic thought, Professor Albert O. Hirschman.¹⁶

Sources of *Industrialisme*

Of the French historians mentioned by the Marxist writers, only Augustin Thierry in his younger days had delved deeply into the subject and had, in fact, participated in shaping a consistent, radical-liberal analysis of classes and class conflict. The purpose of this essay is to sketch the background and content of this remarkable analysis, discuss some points that arise in connection with it, and direct attention to some variations that appeared later and elsewhere. The possibility that it might prove considerably superior to Marxism as an instrument for interpreting social and political history will also be considered.

---

15 Cf. Lenin 1943: 30: "The theory of the class struggle was not created by Marx, but by the bourgeoisie before Marx and is, generally speaking, *acceptable* to the bourgeoisie." (Italics in original.) The second part of Lenin's statement, however, is problematical.

16 Needless to say, Professor Hirschman is equally blithely ignorant that the use of the concept of "spoliation" was as common among the Italian as among the French laissez-faire liberals. Here are a few examples: Francesco Ferrara, "Introduzione" [1851], Federico Bastiat, *Armonie Economiche* (Turin: Unione Tipografico, 1945), 53 paraphrasing Bastiat: "Socialism and protectionism were nothing but two cheeks of the same face: Thiers and Proudhon, Odier and Blanc [conservatives and socialists] had a single source and a single common intention. The spirit of spoliation [*spogliazione*] produced both of them..." The noted economist and close friend of Pareto, Maffeo Pantaleoni, wrote, in "Il secolo ventesimo secondo un individualista" [1900], in idem, *Scritti varii di economia* (Milan/Palermo/Naples: Remo Sandron, 1909), 2: "The public powers, which historically have already been most effective instruments of spoliation in the hands of the nobilty, first, and then of the bourgeoisie, will now become the means of procuring bread and circuses for the people." A. de Viti de Marco, *Due Commemorazioni: Angelo Messedaglia, Maffeo Pantaleoni* (Rome: Attilio Sampaolesi, 1927), 49, wrote that Pantaleoni was enraged by the collectivist and interventionist features of the post-World War I Italian political scene, including "the demagoguery of taxation [*la demogogia tributaria*], organized by the alliance of all the parasitic groups for the speedier spoliation of the well-to-do and the savers and the free [i.e., non-unionized] workers—that is of the *producers*..." (emphasis in original). In 1889, the Italian free-trade journal, *L'Economista*, was clearly operating with the same conceptual framework when it declared its support for a movement that would place on its banner the slogan: "'defense of the taxpayer and consumer'—in this motto is contained a whole program." Emilio Fanzina, "La 'buona stampa' liberista e le premesse ideologisce del liberismo di sinistra agli inizi del periodo crispino (1887–1890), *Critica Storica*, new series, 11, No. 2 (June 1974), 84.

Liberal class conflict theory emerged in a polished form in France, in the period of the Bourbon Restoration, following the defeat and final exile of Napoleon. From 1817 to 1819, two young liberals, Charles Comte and Charles Dunoyer, edited the journal *Le Censeur Européen*; beginning with the second volume (issue), another young liberal, Augustin Thierry, collaborated closely with them. The *Censeur Européen* developed and disseminated a radical version of liberalism, one that continued to influence liberal thought up to the time of Herbert Spencer and beyond. It can be viewed as a core-constituent—and thus one of the historically defining elements—of authentic liberalism (see "Liberalism, True and False, in the present work). In this sense, a consideration of the world-view of the *Censeur* group is of great importance in helping to give shape and content to the protean concept of *liberalism*. Moreover, through Henri de Saint-Simon and his followers and other channels, it had an impact on socialist thought as well. Comte and Dunoyer called their doctrine *Industrialisme,* Industrialism.[17]

There were several major sources of Industrialism. One was Antoine Destutt de Tracy, the last and most famous of the Idéologue school of French liberals, whose friend, Thomas Jefferson, arranged for the translation and publication of his *Treatise on Political Economy* in the United States before it appeared in France.[18] Destutt de Tracy's definition of society (1970: 6) was crucial:

> Society is purely and solely a continual series of exchanges. It is never anything else, in any epoch of its duration, from its commencement the most unformed to its greatest perfection. And this is the greatest eulogy we can give to it, for exchange is an admirable transaction, in which the two contracting parties always

---

17 Professor Leonard P. Liggio has the great merit of having recognized the significance of the Industrialist writers and has pioneered the modern study of their thought; see his highly important article 1977, (the scope of which is considerably wider than is suggested by the title), and the relevant works cited in the endnotes, as well as idem 1990; also Dunoyer 1880; Harpaz, 1959; Halévy 1965; Allix 1910.

18 What appealed to Jefferson was Destutt de Tracy's condemnation of government squandering of social wealth through public debt, taxation, banking monopolies, and public spending, which paralleled his own anti-Hamiltonian views; cf. Kennedy 1978: 228.

both gain; consequently, society is an uninterrupted succession of advantages, unceasingly renewed for all its members.

Destutt de Tracy's position was that "commerce is society itself. ... It is an attribute of man. ... It is the source of all human good ..."[19] Commerce was a "panacea," in the words of a student of his thought, "the world's civilizing, rationalizing, and pacifying force."[20]

Charles Comte, Dunoyer, and Augustin Thierry and his brother Amédée were frequent guests at Destutt de Tracy's salon in the rue d'Anjou, a center of liberal social life in Paris. Here they mingled with Stendhal, Benjamin Constant, Lafayette, and others.[21]

Constant's work, *De l'esprit de conquête et de l'usurpation* ["On the Spirit of Conquest and of Usurpation"], which appeared in 1813, is another source of Industrialist thought. Dunoyer credits Constant with being the first to distinguish sharply between modern and ancient civilization, thus opening up the question of the distinctive aim of the modern age and the form of organization appropriate to that aim.[22] From the reactionary author Montlosier was derived the view of the importance of conquest in the predominance of the nobility over the commoners. The liberal reaction against the militarism and despotism of the Napoleonic period also played a part.[23]

The Role of Jean-Baptiste Say

There is little doubt, however, that the chief intellectual influence on Industrialism was J.-B. Say's *Traité de l'économie politique*, the

---

19 Ibid.180. This leads Kennedy, for some reason, to refer to Destutt de Tracy's position as a form of "economic determinism."
20 Ibid.183.
21 Ibid. 270–72. At a later point, Kennedy refers to Augustin Thierry and Dunoyer as among Destutt de Tracy's "old friends"; ibid. 290. See also Cheryl B. Welch, *Liberty and Utility: The French Idéologues and the Transformation of Liberalism* (New York: Columbia University Press, 1984), 157–58. Augustin Thierry, in his review of Destutt de Tracy's *Commentaire sur L'Esprit des Lois de Montesquieu*, states: "the principles of the *Commentaire* are also ours." *Censeur Européan*, 7 (1818), 220.
22 Dunoyer 1880, 175–76; Ephraïm Harpaz, "'Le Censeur Européen,'" 197.
23 Allix, "J-B. Say et les origines de l'industrialisme," 305.

second edition of which appeared in 1814 and the third in 1817.[24] Comte and Dunoyer probably became personally acquainted with Say during the Hundred Days of Napoleon's brief return to France, in the spring of 1815. Together with Thierry, they were participants at Say's salon.[25] (Comte later became Say's son-in-law.) The third edition of Say's *Traité* was accorded a two-part review of over 120 pages in the *Censeur Européen*.[26] Say held that wealth is comprised of what has value, and value is based on utility:

> [The different ways of producing] all consist in taking a product in one state and putting it into another in which it has more utility and value ... in one way or another, from the moment that one creates or augments the utility of things, one augments their value, one is exercising an industry, one is producing wealth.[27]

All those members of society who contribute to the creation of values are deemed productive, but Say awards pride of place to the entrepreneur. He was one of the first to realize the boundless possibilities of a free economy, led by creative entrepreneurs. As one commentator summarizes his message:

> The productive power of industry is limited only by ignorance and by the bad administration of states. Spread enlightenment and improve governments, or, rather, prevent them from doing harm; there will be no limit that can be assigned to the multiplication of wealth.[28]

---

24 Ibid. Michael James, "Pierre-Louis Roederer, Jean-Baptiste Say, and the Concept of Industry," *History of Political Economy*, 9, No. 4 (Winter 1977), 455–75, argues for Say's indebtedness to the Idéologue Roederer for some important concepts, but grants that it was Say who directly and powerfully influenced the *Censeur Européen* group.
25 Harpaz, "Le Censeur Européen," 204–05.
26 *Censeur Européen*, I (1817), 159–227, II (1817), 169–221.
27 Jean-Baptiste Say, *Cathéchisme d'Économie Politique, ou Instruction Familière* (Paris: Crapelet, 1815), 14. Note the stress on utility, typical of continental thinkers, in contrast to the labor theory of value of the British.
28 Allix, "J.-B. Say et les origines de l'industrialisme," 309. Cf. Harpaz., 356: "The immense progress of modern material civilization is sketched, or at the very least suggested, in the twelve volumes of the *Censeur Européen*."

There exist, however, categories of persons who simply consume wealth rather than produce it. These unproductive classes include especially the army, the government, and the state-supported clergy[29]—what could be called the "reactionary" classes, associated with the Old Regime.

But Say was quite aware that anti-productive and anti-social activity was also possible, indeed, altogether common, when otherwise productive elements employed state power to capture privileges:

> But personal interest is no longer a safe criterion if individual interests are not left to counteract and control each other. If one individual, or one class, can call in the aid of authority to ward off the effects of competition, it acquires a privilege and at the cost of the whole community; it can then make sure of profits not altogether due to the productive services rendered, but composed in part of an actual tax upon consumers for its private profit; which tax it commonly shares with the authority that thus unjustly lends its support. The legislative body has great difficulty in resisting the importunate demands for this kind of privileges; the applicants are the producers that are to benefit thereby, who can represent, with much plausibility, that their own gains are a gain to the industrious classes, and to the nation at large, their workmen and themselves being members of the industrious classes, and of the nation.[30]

Thus, while there is a harmony of interest among producers (between employers and workers, for instance), a natural conflict of interests obtains between producers and non-producers, including those members of the producing classes when they choose to exploit

---

29 Allix, "J.-B. Say et les origines de l'industrialisme, 341–44.
30 Jean-Baptiste Say, *A Treatise on Political Economy, or the Production, Distribution, and Consumption of Wealth*, tr. from the 4th ed., C. R. Prinsep ([1880] New York: Augustus M. Kelley, 1964), 147. It has been persuasively argued that Say was an important source for the modern theory of "rent-seeking"; Patricia J. Euzent and Thomas L. Martin, "Classical Roots of the Emerging Theory of Rent Seeking: the Contribution of Jean-Baptiste Say," *History of Political Economy*, 16, No. 2 (Summer 1984): 255–62. As they point out, Say was quite familiar with why "those engaged in any particular branch of trade are so anxious to have themselves made the subject of regulation . . ." Cf., *Treatise*, 176–77.

government-granted privilege. As one scholar has put it, the cry of Say and of his disciples could be, "Producers of the world, unite!"[31]

The Social Philosophy of the *Censeur Européen*

The essential achievement of Comte, Dunoyer, and Thierry in the *Censeur Européen* was to have taken the ideas of Say and other earlier liberals and forged them into a fighting creed.[32]

Industrialism casts itself as a general theory of society. Taking as its starting point acting man, who strives to satisfy his needs and desires, it posits that the purpose of society is the creation of "utility" in the widest sense: of the goods and services useful to man in the satisfaction of his needs and desires. In acting to meet these, man has three means available: he may take advantage of what nature offers spontaneously (this occurs only in rather primitive circumstances); he may plunder the wealth that others have produced; or he may labor to produce wealth.[33]

In any given society, a sharp distinction can be drawn between those who live by plunder and those who live by production. The first are characterized in various ways by Comte and Dunoyer, including "the idle," "the devouring," and "the hornets"; the second, are termed, among other things, "the industrious" and "the bees." To attempt to live without producing is to live "as savages."[34] The producers are "the civilized men."[35]

Cultural evolution has been such that whole societies may be designated as primarily plundering and idle, or productive and industrious. Thus, Industrialism is not merely an analysis of social dynamics,

---

31 Allix, "J.-B. Say et les origines de l'industrialisme," 312.
32 As Dunoyer 1880: 179 put it: "If it is doubtful that these writers had perceived the political consequences of their observations relative to industry, these observations cast a new light upon politics that was singularly favorable to its progress. Their writings fell into the hands of several men who were making this science their special study, and effected a revolution in their ideas. Such was notably the effect these writings produced in the authors of the *Censeur*."
33 Charles Comte, "Considérations sur l'état moral de la nation française et sur les causes de l'instabilité de ses institutions," *Censeur européen*, I, 1–2, 9. The similarity to Franz Oppenheimer's analysis is clear. See his *The State*, John Gitterman (tr.), C. Hamilton (intr.) New York: Free Life, 1975.
34 Charles Comte, "Considérations sur l'état moral," 11.
35 Ibid. 19.

but also a theory of historical development. Indeed, much of Industrialist theory is embedded in its account of historical evolution.

The "Industrialist Manifesto"

The history of all hitherto existing society is the history of struggles between the plundering and the producing classes. Following Constant, plunder through warfare is said to have been the method favored by the ancient Greeks and Romans. With the decline of the Roman Empire in the West, Germanic barbarians established themselves, through conquest, as the lords of the land: feudalism developed, especially in France after the Frankish invasion and in England after the Norman Conquest. It was essentially a system for the spoliation of domestic peasants by the warrior elite of "noblemen."[36] Under feudalism, there was

> a kind of superordination that subjected the laboring men to the idle and devouring men, and which gave to the latter the means of existing without producing anything, or of living nobly.[37]

Throughout the Middle Ages, the nobility exploited not only its own peasants but especially the merchants who passed through their territories. The nobles' castles were nothing but thieves' dens.[38] With the rise of the towns in the eleventh century, one may even speak of "two nations" sharing the soil of France: the plundering feudal elite and the productive commoners of the towns.

To the rapacious nobility there eventually succeeded the equally rapacious kings, whose "thefts with violence, alterations of the coinage, bankruptcies, confiscations, hindrances to industry" are the common stuff of the history of France.[39] "When the lords were the stronger, they viewed as belonging to them everything they could lay hold of. As soon

---

36 Ibid. 9.
37 Charles Comte, "De l'organisation sociale considérée dans ses rapports avec les moyens de subsistance des peuples," *Censeur Européen*, 2 (1817), 22.
38 Charles Comte, "Considérations sur l'état moral," 14. Thierry's famous work on the Norman Conquest is already foreshadowed in this early essay of Comte's, in his attack on William the Conqueror. ibid. 19–20.
39 Ibid. 20–21.

as the kings were on top, they thought and acted in the same way."[40] With the growth of the wealth produced by the commoners, or Third Estate, additional riches were available for expropriation by the parasitic classes. Comte is particularly severe on royal manipulation of money and legal tender laws, and quotes a seventeenth century writer on how "discountings [les escomptes] enriched the men of money and finance at the expense of the public."[41]

In modern times, the main types of the idle classes have been the professional soldiers, monks, the nobles, bourgeois who were ennobled, and governments.[42]

"Peace and Freedom"

A pro-peace position was central to the Industrialist point of view; in fact, the motto on the title page of each issue of the *Censeur Européen* was: *Paix et Liberté*—Peace and Freedom.

The Industrialist attack on militarism and standing armies was relentless and savage. Dunoyer states that the "production" of the standing armies of Europe has consisted in "massacres, rapes, pillagings, conflagrations, vices and crimes, the depravation, ruin, and enslavement of the peoples; they have been the shame and scourge of civilization." Particularly anathematized were wars engendered by mercantilism, or "the spirit of monopoly . . . the pretension of each to be industrious to the exclusion of all others, exclusively to provision others with the products of its industry." In the course of a jeremiad against the imperialist policy of the English, Dunoyer states, significantly:

> The result of this pretension was that the spirit of industry became a principle more hostile, more of an enemy of civilization, than the spirit of rapine itself.

Monasticism, in the Industrialist view, encouraged idleness and apathy (but see my criticism below). In modern times, the nobles, no longer

---

40 Ibid. 21.
41 Ibid. 22.
42 Charles Dunoyer, "Du système de l'équilibre des puissances européenes," *Censeur Européen*, 1, 119–26.

able to live by directly robbing the industrious, began to fill government positions, and lived by a new form of tribute, "under the name of taxes."[43] Members of the bourgeoisie who achieved noble status no longer tended to their own businesses and, in the end, had no means of subsistence but the public treasury. Finally, governments "have very rarely furnished society with the equivalent of the values they received from it for governing."[44]

The Industrialist writers anticipated that as society approaches perfection they would witness the ultimate triumph of their cause. Comte looked forward to "the extinction of the idle and devouring class" and the emergence of a social order in which "the fortune of each would be nearly in direct ratio to his merit, that is, to his utility, and almost without exception, none would be destitute except the vicious and useless."

State Functionaries as Exploiters

The class of contemporary exploiters that the Industrialist writers examined most closely was the government bureaucrats. As Comte put it:

> What must never be lost sight of is that a public functionary, in his capacity as functionary, produces absolutely nothing; that, on the contrary, he exists only on the products of the industrious class; and that he can consume nothing that has not been taken from the producers.[45]

---

43 Charles Comte, "De l'organisation sociale," 33.
44 Charles Dunoyer, "Du système de l'équilibre," 123. Dunoyer goes on to state (124): "If, in precisely rendering this service [protection of liberty and property to the members of society], it makes them pay more than it is worth, more than the price at which they could obtain it for themselves, everything it takes in addition is something truly subtracted from them, and, in this respect, it acts according to the spirit of rapine." It will be noted that Dunoyer is faced with a problem here, in so far as he assents to monopoly government with taxing powers. The same is true regarding his assertion (125) that the government, in providing security, "should not have obliged them [the citizens] to pay more than it should naturally cost." This is a chink in the Industrialist logic that the free-market anarchist Gustave de Molinari soon exposed.
45 "De l'organisation sociale," 29–30.

True to the Industrialist concentration on the "economic" element, Dunoyer examined "the influence exercised on the government by the salaries attached to the performance of public functions."[46] In the United States—always the model Industrialist country (they were writing in the early nineteenth century)—official salaries, even for the president, are low. Typically, American officials receive an "indemnity" for their work, but nothing that could be called a "salary."[47] In France, on the other hand, it is not the fact that the exercise of power has been made into "a lucrative profession" that shocks public opinion, but its being monopolized by a single social class.[48]

Public expenditures, however, bear almost an inverse relationship to the proper functioning of government. In the United States, where government costs some 40 million francs a year, property is more secure than in England, where it costs more than 3 billion.[49] The characteristics of public employment are the reverse of those of private business. For instance,

> ambition, so fertile in happy results in ordinary labor, is here a principle of ruin; and the more a public functionary wishes to progress in the profession he has taken up, the more he tends, as is natural, to raise and increase his profits, the more he becomes a burden to the society that pays him.[50]

As increasing numbers of individuals aspire to government jobs, two tendencies emerge: government power expands and the burden of taxation and government expenditures grows. In order to satisfy the new hordes of office-seekers, the government extends its scope in all directions. It begins to concern itself with the people's education, health, intellectual life, and morals, sees to the adequacy of the food supply, and regulates industry, until "soon there will be no means of escape

---

46 "De l'influence qu'exercent sur le gouvernement les salaires attachés à l'exercice des fonctions publiques," *Censeur européen*, XI, 75–118.
47 Ibid. 77.
48 Ibid. 78.
49 Ibid. 80.
50 Ibid. 81–82.

from its action for any activity, any thought, any portion" of the people's existence.[51] Functionaries have become "a class that is enemy to the wellbeing of all the others."[52]

Since the exploitation of government jobs has ceased to be the private preserve of the aristocracy it has become the object of everyone in society.[53] In France there are perhaps "ten times as many aspirants to power than the most gigantic administration could possible accommodate.... Here one would easily find the personnel to govern twenty kingdoms."[54]

With the emphasis on state functionaries, a new and surprising interpretation of the Great Revolution is presented by the Industrialist writers. The Declaration of the Rights of Man and of the Citizen of 1791 proclaimed admission to government jobs as a natural and civil right: "one can say that the French Revolution was only a war the aim of which was to decide by whom the [government] positions would be occupied, or, rather, to decide if the nation was to be exploited by men of the noble caste or by men coming from the industrious class."[55]

---

51 Ibid. 86.
52 Ibid. 88.
53 Ibid. 89.
54 Ibid. 103.
55 "De l'organisation sociale,"pp. 34–35. This was also the interpretation of the 1789 Revolution adopted by Gustave de Molinari. See the essay on "The Centrality of French Liberalism," in the present volume. Some years after Dunoyer wrote, Molinari personally witnessed the frenzied hunt for government jobs when he accompanied Frédéric Bastiat to the Hôtel de Ville on the day following the proclamation of the Second Republic, in February, 1848. Bastiat wished to make sure that the new government would approve publication of the journal he planned to publish. At the Hôtel de Ville, Molinari recalled, they encountered "the mob of conquerors hurrying to gather the fruits of the victory. Those who saw [Bastiat] bravely plunge into the densest part of the turbulent mob and make an incredible effort to reach the *Holy of Holies*, where the new distributors of government jobs were standing, probably thought that he was going to solicit some important position, since one had to be looking to become an ambassador or at least a commissioner to dare to venture, that day, into the midst of the immense revolutionary saturnalia. But Bastiat did not go to ask for the favor of living at the expense of his fellow citizens. He went simply to request authorization to enlighten them. Despite his superhuman efforts, Bastiat did not succeed in completely piercing the thick wall of the supplicants, and [his new periodical] *La République Française* appeared without authorization." Cited in Georges de Nouvion, *Frédéric Bastiat: sa vie, ses oeuvres, ses doctrines*, Paris: Guillaumin, 1905.

Similarities with Marxism

The focus of the *Censeur* liberals on the ravenous exploitation of the productive classes by the growing class of state functionaries opens another point of contact with Marxism. As has been sometimes noted,[56] Marxism contains two rather different views of the state: most conspicuously, it views the state as the instrument of domination by exploiting classes that are defined by their position within the process of social production, e.g., the capitalists. Sometimes, however, Marx characterized the state itself as the independently exploiting agent. Thus, in *The Eighteenth Brumaire of Louis Bonaparte*, he writes, quite in the Industrialist spirit:

> This executive power, with its enormous bureaucracy and military organization, with its ingenious state machinery, embracing wide strata, with a host of officials numbering half a million, besides an army of another half million, this appalling parasitic body, which enmeshes the body of French society like a net and chokes all its pores, sprang up in the days of the absolute monarchy.

All regimes assisted in the growth of this mammoth parasite, according to Marx. He adds:

> Every common interest was . . . snatched from the activity of society's members themselves and made an object of government activity, from a bridge, a schoolhouse, and the communal property of a village community, to the railways, the national wealth, and the national university of France. . . . The parties that contended in turn for domination [in revolutions] regarded the possession of this huge state edifice as the principal spoils of the victor . . .[57]

---

56 Richard N. Hunt, *The Political Ideas of Marx and Engels: I, Marxism and Totalitarian Democracy, 1818–1850* (Pittsburgh: University of Pittsburgh Press, 1974), 124–31; David Conway, *A Farewell to Marx: An Outline and Appraisal of his Theories* (Harmondsworth: Penguin, 1987), 162–64.

57 "The Eighteenth Brumaire of Louis Bonaparte," in Marx and Engels, *Selected Works*, 170–71.

In a later work, *The Civil War in France*, Marx writes of "the State parasite feeding upon, and clogging, the free movement of society."[58]

Thus, the conception of the "parasite-state" is clearly enunciated by Marx. It is incorrect, however, to maintain that Marx originated this conception,[59] since, as we have seen, several decades before Marx the *Censeur Européen* group had already singled it out as the major example of in modern society of the plundering and "devouring" spirit.

Interestingly, another similarity between Industrialism and Marxism is in the doctrine of ideology (in the Marxist sense). According to the Industrialist view, there are ideas and values that serve the interests of the productive and of the exploiting classes, respectively. Comte mentions the typically feudal judgment, that those who sweat for their wealth are viewed as ignoble while those who "gain it by shedding the blood of their fellows" are glorious; such an essentially barbaric idea, he asserts, had to be hidden and veiled by placing it in the context of classical antiquity.[60]

Comte even indicates what the existence of what could be called "false consciousness," that is, the harboring by members of one class of ideas contrary to their interests and useful to the interests of an opposing class. He states:

> The war waged by the slaves against their masters has something base to our eyes.
>
> These are men who fight so that the product of their industry should not be the spoils of those who enslaved them; it is an ignoble war. The war waged by Pompey against Caesar charms us; its object is to discover who will be the party who will tyrannize the world; it takes place between men equally incapable of subsisting by their own efforts; it is a noble war. If we trace our

---

58 "The Civil War in France," in ibid. 293.
59 Hunt, *The Political Ideas of Marx and Engels*, 124.
60 Comte, "De l'organisation sociale," 29–30.

The Early Thierry and Industrialism

In the period of his association with the *Censeur Européen*, Augustin Thierry[62] shared the Industrialist philosophy of Comte and Dunoyer, with perhaps even more radical emphases. His review-essay on Destutt de Tracy's *Commentaire sur l'Esprit des Lois de Montesquieu* is particularly important in this connection. Thierry seconds Destutt de Tracy's firm adherence to laissez-faire:

> Government should be good for the liberty of the governed, and that is when it governs to the least possible degree. It should be good for the wealth of the nation, and that is when it acts as little as possible upon the labor that produces it and when it consumes as little as possible. It should be good for the public security, and that is when it protects as much as possible, provided that the protection does not cost more than it brings in. . . . It is in losing their powers of action that governments improve. Each time that the governed gain space, there is progress.[63]

As against Montesquieu, Thierry sides with Destutt de Tracy: "commerce consists in exchange; it is society itself"; and "taxation is always an evil."[64]

Thierry demolishes a perenniel slur on the participants in a market economy when he quotes with approval from Destutt de Tracy's *Commentaire*:

> As for the alleged greediness that commerce, rightly understood, inspires in those who make it their social estate: it is a vague reproach, which should be classed with the most insipid and

---

61 Ibid. 36–37n.
62 On Thierry, see Augustin-Thierry 1922; Carroll 1951; Smithson 1973; and Gossman 1976.
63 Augustin Thierry, "Commentaire sure L'Esprit des Lois de Montesquieu," *Censeur européen*, 7 (1818), 228, 230.
64 Ibid. 205–06.

meaningless rantings. Greediness consists in ravishing the goods of another through violence or cunning, as in the two noble professions of conqueror and courtier. But the merchant, like all other industrious men, seeks his benefit only in his talent, in virtue of freely arrived at agreements, and appealing to faith and the laws.[65]

The functions of government are to ensure security, "whether there is a danger from outside or whether the mad and idle threaten to disturb the order and peace necessary for labor." In a simile freighted with meaning in the rhetoric of Industrialism, Thierry asserts that any government that exceeds these limits ceases to be a government properly speaking:

> its actions can be classed with the action exerted upon the inhabitants of a land when it is invaded by soldiers; it degenerates into domination, and that occurs regardless of the number of men involved, of the arrangement in which they order themselves, or what titles they take . . .[66]

Sharing the horror of militarism of the other Industrialist authors, Thierry quotes Destutt de Tracy with approval on "the absurd and ruinous wars which have been too often waged to maintain the empire and exclusive monopoly over some faraway colonies." This is not true commerce, he declares, but "the mania for domination."[67]

Thierry goes on to sketch a radical-liberal program of very great scope indeed. First of all, the spirit of the free communes of the Middle Ages, which battled the plundering nobility, must be revived; that spirit will inspire men "to oppose the league of civilization to the league of dominators and the idle." The intellectual movement will be allied to a great social movement:

> An invisible and ever-active power, labor, spurred on by industry, will precipitate at the same time all of the populations of Europe

---

65 Ibid. 217.
66 Ibid. 244.
67 Ibid. 218.

into this general movement. The productive force of the nations will break all its fetters. . . . Industry will disarm power, by causing the desertion of its satellites, who will find more profit in free and honest labor than in the profession of slaves guarding slaves. Industry will deprive power of its pretexts and excuses by recalling those the police keep in check to the enjoyments and virtues of labor. *Industry will deprive power of its income, by offering at less cost the services which power makes people pay for.* To the degree that power will lose its actual force and apparent utility, liberty will gain and free men will draw closer together (emphasis supplied).[68]

Appropriately enough, in view of the remarkable sentence italicized in the above passage, Thierry unequivocally enunciates the cosmopolitanism of a liberalism tending to sheer libertarian anarchism. States are merely "incoherent agglomerations that divide the European population . . . dominions formed and increased by conquests or by diplomatic donations." Eventually, the bonds linking men to states will be shed. Then

the passage from one society to another will scarcely be felt. Federations will replace states; the loose but indissoluble chains of interest will replace the despotism of men and of laws; the tendency towards government, the first passion of the human race, will cede to the free community. The era of empire is over, the era of association begins.[69]

Thierry highlights the role of historical writing in aiding in the great struggle. "We are the sons of these serfs, of these tributaries, of these bourgeois that the conquerors devoured at will; we owe them all that we are." History, which should have transmitted memories of this tradition to us, "has been in the pay of the enemies of our fathers. . . . Slaves emancipated only yesterday, our memory has for a long time

---

68 Ibid. 256–57.
69 Ibid. 257–58.

recalled to us only the families and acts of our masters."⁷⁰ As if presaging his own work on the chartered towns of the Middle Ages, he adds:

> If a skillful and liberal pen were finally to undertake our history, that is, the history of towns and associations . . . all of us would see in it the meaning of a social order, what gives it birth and what destroys it.⁷¹

Critique of Industrialism

As for a critique Industrialism, a few problems may be indicated here.

First, it is likely that by sidestepping the issue of rights—property, Comte claims, is better called a "fact," or even a "thing," than a right—the Industrialist writers set the stage for difficulties arising later on in their theory.

Second, by concentrating on production rather than on exchange of rightful property, they create false targets of attack. Thus, "monks"—they really mean the religious orders altogether—are deemed "idlers," placed in the same category as feudal lords and brigands, and, quite deliberately, no distinction is made among paupers between those who live on voluntary charity and those who live from state aid.⁷² It would seem that the Industrialists did not understand the implications of their own insistence on the existence of "immaterial" as well as "material" values.

Finally, in regard to the state: again, by speaking blithely of production rather than voluntary exchange, the Industrialists appear to be trying to avoid the tricky issue of the "production" of a good—security—that is forced upon "the consumer."

---

70 Ibid. 251–52.
71 Ibid. 255.
72 Charles Comte, "De la multiplication des pauvres, des gens à places, et des gens à pensions," *Censeur Européen*, 7, 1n.

Guizot and Mignet

Although François Guizot has often been placed in the same category as Thierry as a historian of class conflict, especially by Marxists, his views were crucially different. Guizot had no connection with the *Censeur* group, being a supporter instead of the *juste milieu* (roughly, golden mean) views of the *Doctrinaire*, Royer-Collard. As a leader of the Doctrinaires (of whom it has been said that no school of thought ever deserved the name less), Guizot lacked any guiding theory, such as Industrialism, to apply in his historical works. Always an eclectic, he wrote for a while in the 1820s in the then popular idiom of classes and class conflict. But he never held that one of the competing classes would or *should* triumph. On the contrary, the struggle, according to Guizot, was already in his own day eventuating in a grand synthesis, whereby aristocracy and Third Estate would combine in the "French Nation."[73]

As a thinker—and, of course, in his political role—Guizot was essentially oriented towards the state. A major purpose of his account of French history was to show that "the bourgeoisie and the power of the Crown were not only allies but forces pressing towards each other."[74] He thoroughly endorsed the historical collaboration of Crown and the Third Estate, which reached a kind of apotheosis in the July Monarchy of Louis Philippe (1830–48), particularly under Guizot's own ministry.

Over the years, Guizot's influence on Thierry grew, and it was all in the direction of highlighting the historical contribution of *all* "classes" to the creation of *la Grande Nation*, especially the assistance

---

73 Shirley M. Gruner, *Economic Materialism and Social Moralism*, The Hague/Paris: Mouton, 1973, 108–10, aptly summarizes Guizot's standpoint: He "liked to be popular and therefore liked to be considered up-to-date in his ideas. Nor does he wish to appear 'unscientific.' Therefore he never denies anything outright but seeks to modify a little here and there so that finally nothing is left of it. There is no head-on opposition…This is in fact the whole problem of Guizot—his indecisive decisiveness so that not only in history but in politics the basically constitutional conservative appears at times to long for the trappings of a radical liberal." Gruner shrewdly adds that "it has also been in the interest of certain groups, for instance the Communists of 1848 [including presumably Marx and Engels], to suggest that there was not much difference between Guizot and the other 'bourgeois' liberals."
74 Gerhard (1960), 305.

accorded the Third Estate by the Monarchy in its rise to recognition and preeminence.

This tendency in Thierry's work culminates in his *Essai sur l'Histoire de la Formation et des Progrès du Tiers État* (see my critique below), which appeared as the introduction to a collection of documents whose publication was inspired by Guizot.

François Mignet, a friend of Thierry and fellow historian, is also often mentioned as another of the liberal precursors of Marxist class conflict theory. But although Mignet did, of course, write of the struggles of the aristocracy and the Third Estate during the Revolution, an immense gulf separated him from the original class conflict analysis of the Industrialists. A sort of *reductio ad absurdum* of the glorification of the bourgeoisie in and of itself, irrespective of its connection with production, was reached by Mignet when in 1836 he wrote of the French Revolutionary armies (emphasis supplied):

> All the old aristocratic armies of Europe had succumbed to these bourgeois, at first disdained and then feared, who, forced to take up the sword and having made use of it as before of the word, as previously of thought, had become heroic soldiers, great captains, and had added to the formidable power of their ideas *the prestige of military glory and the authority of their conquests*.[75]

Mignet also chided Charles Comte for his deprecation of the "Great Men" of history. Comte's views here were part of the attempted Industrialist "transvaluation of all values," whereby, for example, a small manufacturer or a shepherd was to be more highly valued than destructive conquerors like Caesar or Pompey. But Mignet was of a more Hegelian, not to say more pedestrian, turn of mind. According to him, Comte

> forgot that the greatest advances of humanity have had as their representatives and defenders the greatest captains . . . that Napoleon's sword had, for fifteen years, led to the principle of

---

75 François Mignet, "Le comte Sieyès: Notice," *Notices et portraits historiques et littéraires*, I (Paris: Charpentier, 1854), 88.

modern equality penetrating all of Europe. He likewise disputed the difficult art of governing the peoples . . .⁷⁶

Friend and collaborator of Adolphe Thiers, who was virtually the personification of the corrupt bourgeois state in nineteenth century France, and like Thiers a glorifier of Napoleon, Mignet simply inhabited a different intellectual world from Say, Comte, Dunoyer, and the young Thierry.

Thierry's Defection

Eventually, Thierry exchanged his sophisticated Industrialist analysis of class conflict for a considerably coarser one. At some point, he came to believe that the Industrialist view "falsified" history by subjecting it to too rigid a theoretical scheme.⁷⁷

> The type of general and purely political considerations to which I had confined myself up until then seemed to me for the first time too arid and limited. I felt a strong inclination to descend from the abstract to the concrete, to envisage the national life in all its facets and to take my point of departure in solving the problem of the antagonism of the different classes of men in the bosom of the same society the study of the primitive races in their original diversity.⁷⁸

The "tinge of politics was effaced," Thierry explains, as he devoted himself more to "science."⁷⁹ In fact, he did not cease altogether to write as the historian of the oppressed and downtrodden, as the chronicler,

---

76 François Mignet, "Charles Comte: Notice," ibid. II, 102.
77 "After much time and labor lost in thus obtaining artificial results, I perceived that I was falsifying history by imposing identical formulas on totally different periods." Augustin Thierry, *Dix Ans d'Études Historiques* (Paris: Furne, 1851 [1834]), 3. He adds that, after his first essays on English history, in the *Censeur Européen*, he began to feel the need to leave to each epoch its originality: "I changed style and manner; my former rigidity became more supple . . ." ibid. 6–7. Of his earlier radical-liberal views, he says: "I aspired enthusiastically towards a future of which I had no very clear idea . . ." [*vers un avenir, je ne savais trop lequel* . . .] ibid. 7.
78 Ibid. 8.
79 Ibid. 12.

first, of the sufferings of the defeated "races" like the Saxons at the time of the Norman Conquest, then of the rise to power and pride of the despised Third Estate in France.

But Thierry's treatment of class conflict in his more famous works is defective and, ultimately, fatally flawed. When he deals with the history of France in the medieval and early modern period, for instance, the industrious, creative element of society is identified *tout court* with the "Third Estate," the exploiting idlers and parasites with the feudal nobility and its descendants alone. Thus, critical distinctions existing *within* the Third Estate, or bourgeoisie, of the sort that Say had already exposed, are omitted. The earlier analytical dividing line between those who act on the market, through exchange, and those who use force above all through the state disappears. In this way Thierry sinned against his own methodological principle: "The great precept that must be given to historians is to distinguish instead of confounding" (cited in Stadler 1955: 283).

The Final Stage

In Thierry's last major work, *Essay on the History of the Formation and Progress of the Third Estate*, virtually nothing is left of the original Industrialist doctrine. Instead, we are presented with what amounts to a case study in complacent and self-satisfied Whiggish historiography. It turns out that the events and figures of some 700 years of French history have all conspired to bring about the triumph of what is now Thierry's ideal, the modern, centralized French state, based on equality before the law, to be sure, but rich in power and historical glory, as well.

Over and over again, the French kings are praised for having worked to elevate the Third Estate, largely by providing bureaucratic jobs for its members, and, in the traditional manner, for have "created" France. Richelieu is eulogized both for his foreign and domestic policies, equally admirable, and for "multiplying for the commons, besides offices, places of honor in the State."[80] Colbert, the architect of French predatory

---

80 Thierry, *Essai sur l'Histoire de la Formation et des Progrès du Tiers État* (1894 [1853]) Paris: Calmann Lévy, 172.

mercantilism, is glorified as a commoner who planned "the industrial regeneration of France," and is applauded for his distribution of its tax-funded largesse to writers, scholars, and "all classes of men."[81] One could go on.

How to explain this radical shift of perspective? The chief reason is to be sought in Thierry's experience of the socialist agitation of 1848 including the violence of the June Days, and the specter of social revolution haunted him to the end of his life. He was anxious that the socialist troublemakers should not be able to draw sustenance from his work on the role of classes in French history. In the Preface to the *Essay*, Thierry implies that now, in 1853, there is no further need for the concept of classes: "the national mass" is "today one and homogeneous." Only "the prejudices spread by systems that tend to divide" the homogeneous nation into "mutually hostile classes" could suggest otherwise.[82] The present-day antagonism between bourgeoisie and workers, which some wish to trace back for centuries, is "destructive of all public order." Thus, ironically, one of the thinkers who was a major inspiration for the socialist concept of class conflict ended by categorically denying any class conflict in the modern world, and he did so in part out of fear of the dangers posed now that it had been reshaped by the socialists.[83] He put this in the form of the statement that there could no longer be a history of the Third Estate—now the Third Estate was in reality, as the Abbé Siéyes had announced it programmatically in 1788, "everything."[84]

---

81 Ibid. 195.
82 Ibid. 1–2.
83 Marx discusses Thierry's *Essai* in the letter to Engels cited in note 211. Interestingly, he commends Thierry for describing "well, if not as a connected whole: (1) How from the first, or at least after the rise of the towns, the French bourgeoisie gains too much influence by constituting itself the Parliament, the bureaucracy, etc., and not as in England through commerce and industry. This is certainly still characteristic even of present-day France." *Selected Corr.* 88.
84 Augustin Thierry, "Preface," *Essai sur l'Histoire de la Formation det des Progrès du Tiers État*.

The Liberals and the July Monarchy

The July Monarchy of Louis Philippe, which came to power in 1830, was notorious for its corruption on behalf of the bourgeoisie, especially in the form of massive and blatant jobbery (see, e.g., Cormenin de la Haye 1846). This was the regime of which Alexis de Tocqueville wrote:

> [The middle class] entrenched itself in every vacant government job, prodigiously augmented the number of such jobs, and accustomed itself to live almost as much upon the Treasury as upon its own industry.[85]

Many of the liberals were major beneficiaries of the new regime, rewarded for the support they had given, and continued to give, to Louis Philippe. Dunoyer was made prefect in Moulins and Stendhal consul at Trieste, while Daunou was reappointed as director of the National Archives.[86] Others of the liberal party under the Restoration did as well or better. Guizot, of course, was one of the chief figures of the new order. With Mignet, Thiers, Villemain, he "shared the highest offices of the state, the most brilliant favors of the regime."[87] Thierry himself, however, now blind and in poverty, was reduced to pleading for assistance, until Guizot awarded him a small pension.[88]

Thus, any analysis of the reasons behind the conservative drift of many French liberals after 1830—and of their abandonment of the dangerous idea of class conflict in their own time—would have to take account not only of the growing threat of socialism, but also of the new links to power and wealth that the "liberal" regime of Louis Philippe afforded them.

---

85 Alexis de Toqueville, *Recollections*, Alexander Teixeira de Matos (tr.) J.P. Mayer (ed.), New York: Meridian, 1959. 2–3.
86 Allix, 318–19.
87 A. Augustin-Thierry, Augustin Thierry, 1795–1856 (Paris: Librairie Plon, 1922) 114.
88 Ibid. 112f.

Other Liberal Class Conflict Theories

The Industrialist doctrine of class conflict was by no means the first or only treatment of this question in the history of liberal theory. A theoretically purer approach is perhaps to be found in a parallel American tradition of political thought. In the United States, some of the Jeffersonians and Jacksonians also grappled with the question of class, in the politically relevant sense, and came to conclusions reminiscent of the Industrialist school. John Taylor of Caroline, William Leggett, and John C. Calhoun were keen observers and critics of the social groups—the classes—which they saw as utilizing political power in order to exploit the rest of society, the producers.

John Taylor was outraged by the betrayal of the principles of the Revolution by a new aristocracy based on "separate legal interests," the bankers privileged to issue paper money as legal tender and the beneficiaries of "public improvements" and protective tariffs. American society has been divided into the privileged and the unprivileged by this "substantial revival of the feudal system."[89]

Two decades later, in the 1830s, the northern radical, William Leggett, denounced the same exploiting classes. A thoroughgoing Jeffersonian and disciple of Adam Smith and J.-B. Say, Leggett held that the principles of political economy are the same as those of the American Republic: Laissez-faire, Do not govern too much. This system of equal rights was being overthrown by a new aristocracy, among whom Leggett particularly singled out the state-connected bankers for attack.

> Have we not, too, our privileged orders? our scrip nobility? aristocrats, clothed with special immunities, who control, indirectly, but certainly, the power of the state, monopolise the most copious source of pecuniary profit, and wring the very crust from the hard hand of toil? Have we not, in short, like the wretched serfs of Europe, our lordly master? ... If any man doubts how these

---

89 Eugene Tenbroeck Mudge, *The Social Philosophy of John Taylor of Caroline: A Study in Jeffersonian Democracy* (New York: AMS Press, 1968 [1939]), 151–204, passim.

questions should be answered, let him walk through Wall-street.[90]

The American aristocracy naturally favored a strong government, including control of banking. Leggett, in contrast, demanded "the absolute separation of government from the banking and credit system."[91]

John C. Calhoun, in his *Disquisition on Government*, focused attention on the taxing powers of the state, "the necessary result" of which

> is to divide the community into two great classes: one consisting of those who, in reality, pay the taxes and, of course, bear exclusively the burthen of supporting the government; and the other, of those who are the recipients of their proceeds through disbursements, and who are, in fact, supported by the government; or, in fewer words, to divide it into tax-payers and tax-consumers. But the effect of this is to place them in antagonistic relations in reference to the fiscal action of the government and the entire course of policy therewith connected.[92]

Liberal class conflict rhetoric was often applied in the later nineteenth century; in England, it as a recurrent theme in the agitation for repeal of the Corn Laws, used by Cobden, Bright, and others. It underlies the attack by William Graham Sumner on the "plutocrats," capitalists who use the state rather than the market to enrich themselves.

Bringing the State Back In

Today a revival appears to be underway of the concept of the state as the creator of classes and class conflict. A group of scholars

---

90 William Leggett, *Democratick Editorials: Essays in Jacksonian Political Economy*, Lawrence H. White (ed.) (Indianapolis: Liberty Press, 1984), 250–51. See also Lawrence H. White, "William Leggett: Jacksonian Editorialist as Classical Liberal Political Economist," *History of Political Economy*, 18, No. 2 (Summer 1986), 307–24.
91 William Leggett, *Democratick Editorials*, 142.
92 John C. Calhoun, *A Disquisition on Government and Selections from the Discourse*, C. Gordon Post (ed.) Indianapolis: Bobbs-Merrill, 1953, 17–19.

including Theda Skocpol has produced an anthology with the significant title, *Bringing the State Back In*.[93] In an introductory chapter, Skocpol speaks of "an intellectual sea change" taking place, by which the "society-centered ways of explaining politics and governmental activities" popular in the 1950s and 60s are being reversed, and government itself is looked upon as "an independent actor."

We must recognize, she argues, the capacity of the state to act independently of the various groupings of "civil society" more systematically than is allowed by the Marxist notion of "relative autonomy." In particular, in regard to relations with other states, a state may often act in ways that cannot be explained by its concern for private interests, even for collective private interests. Skocpol notes that while state actions are often justified by reference to their appropriateness for the long-run interests of society or the benefits that accrue to various social groups (which would tend to shift the center of attention once more to society), "autonomous state actions will regularly take forms that attempt to reinforce the authority, political longevity, and social control of the state organizations whose incumbents generated the relevant policies or policy ideas." Citing Suzanne Berger, Skocpol stresses that the view that social "interests" determine politics is one-sided and shallow, if for no other reason than because

> "the timing and characteristics of state intervention" affect "not only organizational tactics and strategies," but "the content and definition of interest itself." . . . Some scholars have directly stressed that state initiatives create corporatist forms . . . the formation, let alone the political capacities, of such purely socioeconomic phenomena as interest groups and classes depends in significant measure on the structures and activities of the very states the social actors, in turn, seek to influence.[94]

---

93 Theda Skocpol, *Bringing the State Back In* (1985), Cambridge, Eng.: Cambridge University Press. The title derives from an earlier essay by Skocpol.
94 A scholar who stressed the role of the state in creating corporatist forms and hence "class interest" (although he preferred the term "caste" to "class") was Ludwig von Mises; see his *Theory and History: An Interpretation of Social and Economic Evolution* (New Haven: Yale University Press, 1957), 113–15. Mises, who examined this topic thirty years ago, is not

Class Conflict in Marxist Regimes

From a scientific point of view, the liberal theory—which locates the source of class conflict in the exercise of state power—has another pronounced advantage over the conventional Marxist analysis: liberal theory is able to shed light on the structure and functioning of Marxist societies themselves. "The theory of the Communists," as Marx wrote, may be summed up in the single sentence: Abolition of private property."[95] Yet, Communist societies, which have essentially abolished private property, are hardly on the road to the abolition of classes. This has led to some deep soul-searching among Marxist theoreticians and justified complaints regarding the inadequacy of a purely "economic" analysis of class conflict to account for the empirical reality of the socialist countries.[96] Yet the liberal theory of class conflict is ideally suited to deal with such problems in a context where access to wealth, prestige, and influence is determined by control of the state apparatus.

References

Allix, Edgard (1910) "J.-B. Say et les origines d'industrialisme," *Revue d'Économie Politique* 24: 304–13, 341–62.

Augustin-Thierry, A. (1922) *Augustin Thierry (1795–1856), d'après sa correspondance et ses papiers de famille*, Paris: Plon-Nourrit.

Bettelheim, Charles (1985) "Reflections on Concepts of Class and Class Struggle in Marx's Work," Carole Biewener (tr.), in Stephen Resnick

---

mentioned by Skocpol. See also Murray N. Rothbard, *Power and Market: Government and the Economy* (Menlo Park: Institute for Humane Studies, 1970), 12–13, where Rothbard writes: "It has become fashionable to assert that 'Conservatives' like John C. Calhoun 'anticipated' the Marxian doctrine of class exploitation. But the Marxian doctrine holds, erroneously, that there are 'classes' on the free market whose interests clash and conflict. Calhoun's insight was almost the reverse. Calhoun saw that it was the intervention of the State that in itself created the 'classes' and the conflict." Rothbard also prefers the term "caste": "castes are State-made groups, each with its own set of established privileges and tasks." ibid. 198, note 5.

95 "Manifesto of the Communist Party," in Karl Marx and Friedrich Engels, *Selected Works*, 47.

96 George Konrad and Ivan Szelényi, *The Intellectuals on the Road to Class Power*, Andrew Arato and Richard E. Allen (trs.) (New York/London: Harcourt Brace Jovanovich, 1979) xiv-xvi, 39–44, and passim.

and Richard Wolff (eds.) *Rethinking Marxism: Struggles in Marxist Theory. Essay for Harry Magdoff and Paul Sweezy*, Brooklyn, N. Y.: Autonomedia.

Blanqui, Jérôme-Adolphe (1837) *Histoire de l'Économie Politique en Europe depuis les anciens jusqu'à nos jours*, Paris: Guillaumin.

Calhoun, John C., (1953) *A Disquisition on Government and Selections from the Discourse*, C. Gordon Post (ed.) Indianapolis: Bobbs-Merrill.

Carroll, Kieran Joseph (1951) *Augustin Thierry (1795–1856)*, Washington, D.C.: Catholic University of America Press.

Conway, David (1987) *A Farewell to Marx: An Outline and Appraisal of his Theories*, Harmondsworth, Eng.: Penguin.

Cormenin de la Haye, Louis-Marie "Timon" (1846) *Ordre du Jour sur la Corruption Électorale*, 7th ed., Paris: Pagnerre.

Destutt de Tracy, Antoine Louis Claude (1970 [1817]) *A Treatise on Political Economy*, Thomas Jefferson (tr.), New York: Augustus M. Kelley.

Dunoyer, Charles (1880) "Notice Historique sur l'Industrialisme," in *Oeuvres 3 Notices de l'Économie Sociale*, Paris: Guillaumin.

Euzent, Patricia J. and Martin, Thomas L. (1984) "Classical Roots of the Emerging Theory of Rent Seeking: the Contribution of Jean-Baptiste Say," *History of Political Economy* 16 (2) (Summer).

Gerhard, Dietrich, (1960) "Guizot, Augustin Thierry, und die Rolle des Tiers État in der französischen Geschichte," *Historische Zeitschrift*, 190, 2.

Gossman, Lionel (1976) *Augustin Thierry and Liberal Historiography*, Beiheft 15, *Theory and History*.

Gruner, Shirley M. (1973) *Economic Materialism and Social Moralism*,The Hague/Paris: Mouton.

Halévy, Élie (1965 [1907]) "The Economic Doctrine of Saint-Simon," in idem, *The Era of Tyrannies: Essays on Socialism and War*, R. K. Webb (tr.), Garden City, N.Y.: Anchor/Doubleday.

Harpaz, Ephraïm (1959) "'Le Censeur Européen': Histoire d'un Journal Industrialiste," *Revue d'Histoire Économique et Sociale*, 37 (2): 185–218, (3) 328: 57.

Hirschman, Albert O. (1991) *The Rhetoric of Reaction: Perversity, Futility, Jeopardy*, Cambridge, Mass.: Harvard University Press.

Hunt, Richard N. (1974) *The Political Ideas of Marx and Engels: I Marxism and Totalitarian Democracy, 1818–1850*, Pittsburgh: University of Pittsburgh Press.

James, Michael, "Pierre-Louis Roederer, Jean-Baptiste Say, and the Concept of Industry," *History of Political Economy* 9 (4) (Winter 1977).

Kennedy, Emmet (1978) *A Philosophe in the Age of Revolution: Destutt de Tracy and the Origins of "Ideology,"* Philadelphia: American Philosophical Society.

Konrad, George and Szelényi, Ivan (1979) *The Intellectuals on the Road to Class Power*, Andrew Arato and Richard E. Allen (trs.), New York: Harcourt Brace Jovanovich.

Leggett, William (1984) *Democratick Editorials: Essays in Jacksonian Political Economy*, Lawrence H. White (ed.), Indianapolis: Liberty Press.

Lenin, V. I. (1943 [1917]) *State and Revolution*, New York: International Publishers.

Liggio, Leonard P. (1977) "Charles Dunoyer and French Classical Liberalism," *Journal of Libertarian Studies* 1 (3) 153–78

Liggio, Leonard P. (1990) "The Concept of Liberty in Eighteenth and Nineteenth Century France," *Journal des Économistes et des Études Humaines* 1 (1) (Spring).

Marx, Karl and Friedrich Engels (1963 [1930]) *The Communist Manifesto*, D. Ryazanoff (ed.) New York: Russell and Russell.

McLellan, David (1973) *Karl Marx: His Life and Thought*, New York: Harper and Row.

Mehring, Franz (1962 [1918]) *Karl Marx: The Story of His Life*, Edward Fitzgerald (tr.), Ann Arbor: University of Michigan Press.

Mignet, François "Le comte Sieyès: Notice," *Notices et portraits historiques et littéraires*, I (Paris: Charpentier, 1854), 88.

François Mignet, François "Charles Comte: Notice," *Notices et portraits historiques et littéraires*, II (Paris: Charpentier, 1854), II, 102.

Mises, Ludwig von (1957) *Theory and History: An Interpretation of Social and Economic Evolution*, New Haven: Yale University Press.

Mudge, Eugene Tenbroeck (1968 [1939]) *The Social Philosophy of John Taylor of Caroline: A Study in Jeffersonian Democracy*, New York: AMS Press.

Nolte, Ernst (1983) *Marxismus und Industrielle Revolution*, Stuttgart: Klett-Cotta.

Oppenheimer, Franz (1975 [1907]) *The State*, John Gitterman (tr.), New York: Free Life.

Rothbard, Murray N. (1970) *Power and Market: Government and the Economy*, Menlo Park, Cal.: Institute for Humane Studies.

Say, Jean-Baptiste (1964 [1880]) *A Treatise on Political Economy, or the Production, Distribution, and Consumption of Wealth*, from the 4th ed., C. R. Prinsep (tr.), New York: Augustus M. Kelley.

Say, Jean-Baptiste (1815) *Cathéchisme d'Économie Politique, ou Instruction Familière*, Paris: Crapelet

Skocpol, Theda (1985) *Bringing the State Back In*, Cambridge, Eng.: Cambridge University Press.

Smithson, Rulon Nephi (1973) *Augustin Thierry: Social and Political Consciousness in the Evolution of Historical Method*, Geneva: Droz.

Sorokin, Pitirim (1947) "Qu'est-ce qu'une classe sociale?" *Cahiers Internationaux de Sociologie*, 2: 68–71.

Stuke, Horst (1976), "Bedeutung und Problematik des Klassenbegriffs: Begriffs- und sozialgeschichtliche Überlegungen im Umkreis einer historischen Klassentheorie," in Ulrich Engelhardt, Volker Sellin, and Horst Stuke (eds.) *Soziale Bewegung und politische Verfassung: Beiträge zur Geschichte der modernen Welt*. Stuttgart: Ernst Klett.

Thierry, Augustin (1851) *Dix Ans d'Études Historiques*, Paris: Furne.

Thierry, Augustin, (1859 [1853]) *Essai sur l'Histoire de la Formation et des Progrès du Tiers État* Paris: Firman-Didot.

Tocqueville, Alexis de (1959), *Recollections*, Alexander Teixeira de Mattos (tr.). J. P. Mayer, ed., New York: Meridian.

Welch, Cheryl B. (1984) *Liberty and Utility: The French Idéologues and the Transformation of Liberalism*, New York: Columbia University Press.

White, Lawrence H. (1986) "William Leggett: Jacksonian Editorialist as Classical Liberal Political Economist," *History of Political Economy* 18 (2) (Summer): 307–24.

6 The Centrality of French Liberalism

Introduction

In his invaluable history of economic thought, Murray Rothbard notes, with some asperity, the misguided account that has economic theory begin with Adam Smith—whose "reputation almost blinds the sun"—and triumphantly continue with Malthus, Ricardo, and John Stuart Mill. This nearly universal concentration on the British writers, Rothbard maintains, obliterates the far more fruitful Continental tradition represented by the Late Scholastics in Spain and, particularly, by the French school of Cantillon, Turgot, J.-B. Say, and Frédéric Bastiat.[1]

It is the thesis of this essay that a similar point can be made for the study of the history of European liberalism, the political economy and political philosophy so closely connected with the development of economic thought. As regards the nineteenth century at least, the importance of Britain in the history of liberal thought has usually been exaggerated, while the contributions of French thinkers—often notably relevant to present day concerns—have as a rule been either minimized or overlooked completely.

---

1 Murray N. Rothbard, *An Austrian Perspective on the History of Economic Thought*, 1, *Economic Thought before Adam Smith*, 345, 435, 441–48. See also the important essay by Joseph T. Salerno, "The Neglect of the French Liberal School in Anglo-American Economics: A Critique of Received Explanations," *Review of Austrian Economics*, 2 (1988), 113–56.

This is especially true of the writers of the journal, the *Censeur Européen*, Charles Comte, Charles Dunoyer, and Augustin Thierry, in the early nineteenth century. They provided what is probably the most detailed and analytical treatment of the millenia-long struggle between the predatory, state-oriented social strata and their victims among the producing strata. This subject is dealt with in the essay, "The Conflict of Classes: Liberal vs. Marxist Theories," in the present volume.

Hayek's "True and False Individualism"

Unfortunately, an element of great confusion has been introduced into the study of French liberalism through some of the writings of F.A. Hayek, principally his influential essay, "Individualism: True and False."[2] In this rather baffling work, Hayek attempts to distinguish two traditions of individualism (or liberalism). The first, basically a British and empirical line of thought, represents genuine liberalism; the second, French (and Continental), is a no true liberal tradition, but rather a rationalistic deviation that leads "inevitably" to collectivism. This follows from the contrasting social theories underlying the two approaches. Where the first appreciated the truth regarding social institutions, that they originated and developed "spontaneously," the second held them to be the product of deliberate human "contrivance or design."

The problems with Hayek's treatment are legion, and many of them are addressed in the essay on "Liberalism: True and False," in the present volume. Later, in *The Constitution of Liberty* (56), when Hayek notes some eighteenth natural rights theorists—including Priestley, Price, Paine, and Jefferson—he asserts that they "belong entirely" to the rationalist tradition of liberalism. No evidence is presented that these thinkers held that social institutions are "designed" by all-knowing

---

2 In F.A. Hayek, *Individualism and Economic Order* (Chicago: University of Chicago Press, 1948), 1–32. See also the chapter on "Freedom, Reason, and Tradition," in idem, *The Constitution of Liberty* (Chicago: University of Chicago Press, 1960), 54–70. The confusion in "Individualism: True and False" begins with the motto from Alexis de Tocqueville that Hayek places at the beginning of his essay: "From the eighteenth century and from the revolution, as from a common source, two rivers had sprung: the first led men to free institutions, while the second led them to absolute power." There seems no reason to think that the distinction Tocqueville makes here corresponds to the one that Hayek develops in his essay.

legislators, which he takes to be the hallmark of that tradition.[3] Strangely, it is this strand of natural rights thinking that is supposed to have led to "totalitarian democracy."[4]

Some might uncharitably suspect Hayek of a terminal Anglophilia which tended to blind him to some obvious facts. He himself wrote: "I sometimes feel that the most conspicuous attribute of liberalism . . . is the view that moral beliefs concerning matters of conduct which do not interfere with the protected sphere of other persons do not justify coercion." (*The Constitution of Liberty*, 402.) But it was in France, with the Napoleonic Code, that religious equality was established decades before it "evolved" in Britain; and the same Code decriminalized voluntary sexual acts between adults a century and a half before the British government ventured to publish the Wolfenden Report.

If Hayek's analysis were correct, it would be hard to account for the fact that the liberal intellectual tradition in France through the nineteenth and into the twentieth century retained a vigor and purity it could boast of nowhere else. Indicative of this is that in France the term "liberalism" even today suggests what in Anglophone countries

---

3 Bastiat, in his well-known essay, "The Law," complains of how "strongly rooted in our country" is the idea that "mankind is merely inert matter, receiving from the government life, organization, morality, and wealth . . ." He lists and critiques a number of French authors on the virtual omnipotence of the legislator. Among them, however, are only two who are generally included in the liberal tradition, Condillac—and one of Hayek's favorites, Montesquieu. Frédéric Bastiat, *Selected Essays on Political Economy*, George B. de Huszar, (ed.), Seymour Cain (tr.) (Irvington, N.Y.: Foundation for Economic Education, 1964) 70–83. Leonard P. Liggio, in "Evolution of French Liberal Thought: From the 1760s to the 1840s," *Journal des Économistes et des Études Humaines*, 1, No. 1 (Winter 1989), 145–46, notes that critics of French political centralization were heavily indebted to the French liberal thinkers who had experienced it first hand and were its most trenchant analysts.

4 Ibid. Oddly enough, a few pages later (*The Constitution of Liberty*, 60), Hayek posits as "the logical outcome of the rational laissez-faire doctrine" not totalitarianism or collectivism, but anarchism. It should be pointed out that Hayek is mistaken in calling upon J.L. Talmon's *The Origins of Totalitarian Democracy* (London: Secker and Warburg, 1955) for support of his thesis. The authors mainly dealt with in that work are Rousseau, Mably, and the Jacobins, chiefly Robespierre and Saint-Just. None of these can be considered liberals. The burden of the few pages (44–45) that Talmon devotes to the Physiocrats is that they offered "an astonishing synthesis of economic liberalism and political absolutism," the latter deriving from their fear that any dilution of royal "legal despotism" would lead to a triumph of anti-social special interests.

must generally be qualified as "classical liberalism." In this essay some of the important and distinctive insights of nineteenth century French liberalism will be sketched and their remarkable pertinence to many current political issues highlighted.

The Place of Benjamin Constant

Benjamin Constant is, I would maintain, the representative figure not only of French but of European, liberalism in the nineteenth century.[5] Émile Faguet was only somewhat exaggerating when he said of Constant that he "invented liberalism."[6] Fortunately, Constant is one exception (Tocqueville is the other) to the deplorable neglect of French nineteenth century liberal thinkers. Isaiah Berlin, the philosopher of pluralism, has championed the importance of Constant, calling him "the most eloquent of all defenders of freedom and privacy."[7] As Constant studies have flourished in recent years, it has grown increasingly clear that Constant was, above all, the political philosopher of *modernity*.

What is the essential character of the modern world, and what is the political system suited to that distinctive character? Constant was led to consider this question by his experiences as a young man during the Great Revolution. That Revolution had been born in the quest for liberty. But, as Constant saw it the Revolution manifested a fatal flaw. The Terror cannot be explained merely as the result of circumstance. There was a theory behind it: in Constant's view, it was the idea of Ancient Liberty misapplied to the modern age.

Constant's discussion of the ancient polis, or city-state, is celebrated. Max Weber took what he called "the brilliant Constant hypothesis" to be a perfect example of the concept of "ideal-type."[8] Briefly, according to Constant, Ancient Liberty was the ideal of the classical republics of Greece and Rome, and, in the modern time, of writers like

---

5 Hayek awards this honor to Tocqueville and Lord Acton, both of whose writings, despite other great merits, show a defective understanding of economic liberalism.
6 Émile Faguet, *Politiques et moralistes du XIXe siècle* (Paris: Boiven, 1891) 255.
7 See his "Two Concepts of Liberty," in Isaiah Berlin, *Four Essays on Liberty* (Oxford: Oxford University Press, 1969) 126.
8 Max Weber, *The Methodology of the Social Sciences*, Edward A. Shils and Henry A. Finch (trs.) (Glencoe, Ill.: Free Press, 1949) 104.

Rousseau and Mably.⁹ It held that freedom consists in the citizens' exercise of political power. It is a *collective* notion of freedom, and it is compatible with—even demands—the total subordination of the individual to the community. While each citizen would be subordinate to the whole, he would have his share in the exercise of total power over the community's members.

Ancient Liberty had its roots in the society of those times, a society of slavery and incessant warfare. The idea of Modern Liberty, too, has its roots in its own distinctive society, one based on free labor and peaceful commerce. Constant asks, "What is it that in our time an Englishman, a Frenchman, an inhabitant of the United States of America, understand by the word, 'liberty'":

> It is for each to be subject to nothing but the laws, not to be arrested, nor imprisoned, nor put to death, nor mistreated in any way as a consequence of the arbitrary will of one or more individuals. It is for each the right to speak his opinion, to choose his line of work and to practice it; to dispose of his property, and even to abuse it; to go, to come, without obtaining permission, or giving an account of his motives or undertakings. It is for each the right to join with other individuals, whether to confer on his interests, or to profess the religion that he and his associates prefer, or simply to fill his days and hours in a way more fitted to his inclinations and his fantasies. Finally, it is the right of each to influence the administration of government . . .¹⁰

The fatal error of Rousseau and the Jacobins was to attempt to resurrect the ancient ideal in the modern world. Since the modern world has produced an entirely different sort of human personality—what we

---

9 Benjamin Constant, "De la Liberté des Anciens comparée à celle des Modernes," *Cours de Politique Constitutionnelle*, Édouard Laboulaye (ed.) (Paris: Guillaumin, 1872) 2, 537–60.
10 Ibid. 540–41. John Gray, in his *Liberalism* (Minneapolis: University of Minnesota Press, 1986), 20, cites this passage but omits any reference to property rights, an error caused by Gray's reliance on the defective translation of this Constant text contained in Guido de Ruggiero's *History of European Liberalism*. Unfortunately, Gray's blunder has been repeated by subsequent authors who have relied on his book.

know as "the individual," in a sense unknown to the ancients—the result could only be catastrophe.[11]

But the Jacobin project did not end in 1794. In fact, the essence of the totalitarian movements of the twentieth century was the goal of realizing a collective freedom and creating a uniform and collective type of human being (Soviet Man, National Socialist Man, etc.). As the philosopher of an irreducible pluralism, Constant was the great critic of all such totalitarian pretensions *avant la lettre*.

Moreover, Constant's analysis has a direct bearing on western countries today, which have become the arena of what have been called the culture wars, on the analogy to the wars of religion of earlier centuries. Conflicting groups wish to make use of the state power to realize their own cultural—religious, moral, ethical, even aesthetic—values. Those on the "right" promote "traditional" or "family" values, while "leftists" push for the spread of "progressive," "egalitarian," or "enlightened" ideas. Both sides contend for mastery of important parts of the state apparatus, the public schools above all, but also the media (in countries where radio and television are departments of the government), and the centers for state funding of culture. The struggle is often bitter, especially when, as in the case of the public schools, it is the minds of children that is at stake. Again, what is involved in all of this is an attempt, less savage than during the French Revolution, to ensure uniformity of culture and moral values through state coercion.

Constant was the first great liberal thinker who was compelled to wage an intellectual battle on two fronts, a situation that became typical of liberalism in the nineteenth century and into our own time. His enemies were the Jacobin and socialist descendants (for the most part) of Jean-Jacques Rousseau on the one side, and, on the other, the theocratic conservatives such as de Maistre and de Bonald.

---

11 The importance of Constant's analysis of the Revolution has been recognized in a major work of synthesis, François Furet and Mona Ozouf (eds.) *A Critical Dictionary of the French Revolution*, Arthur Goldhammer (tr.) (Cambridge, Mass.: Harvard University Press, 1989). The thought of Constant and of his frequent collaborator, Madame de Staël, permeates this work.

As against the egalitarians and socialists who aimed to overthrow tradition, especially in religion, Constant appreciated the importance of *voluntary* traditions, those generated by the free activity of society itself. In this respect, Constant was much superior to John Stuart Mill, whose distaste for all of the inherited ways of mankind has misled Anglo-American liberalism in highly unfortunate directions (see the essay on "Liberalism: True and False" in the present volume). Constant emphasized the value of these old ways in the struggle against state power. Having lived through the Reign of Terror and the Napoleonic dictatorship, he was one of the first to understand the power of the modern state. Any element of social life that might act as a barrier to it was welcome in his eyes. Anticipating Tocqueville, and, in our century, thinkers like Bertrand de Jouvenel and Robert Nisbet, Constant wrote:

> The interests and memories which are born of local customs contain a germ of resistance which authority suffers only with regret, and which it hastens to eradicate. With individuals it has its way more easily; it rolls its enormous weight over them effortlessly, as over sand.[12]

As for the conservatives, they attempted to erect the Christian notion of Original Sin into the theoretical underpinning for a system of oppression, arguing for a strong state to keep a firm check on natural man. Constant was willing to grant some plausibility to the notion of the natural corruption of human nature. But how could this be turned into a warrant for an authoritarian state? Were the politicians born of an Immaculate Conception? As Constant wrote:

> [There is a] bizarre notion according to which it is claimed that because men are corrupt, it is necessary to give certain of them all the more power . . . on the contrary, they must be given less power, that is, one must skillfully combine institutions and place within them certain counterweights against the vices and weaknesses of men.[13]

---

12 Benjamin Constant, *Cours de Politique Constitutionnelle*, 2, 170–71.
13 Benjamin Consant, *Commentaire sur l'ouvrage de Filangieri* (Paris: Dufart, 1824) 27.

While under the Jacobins, the state power had been thrown into the scales to produce a society based on Rousseauian values, under the Restoration, conservatives sought to use the state power to instill Catholic and theocratic values, which was no less objectionable to Constant. As he put it: "If I reject violent and forced improvements, I equally condemn the maintenance, by force, of what the progress of ideas tends to improve and reform insensibly."[14] He summed up the necessary attitude on the conflict of cultural values inevitable in the modern world:

> Remain faithful to justice, which is of every age; respect liberty, which prepares all good things; consent to the fact that many things will develop without you; and confide to the past its own defense, to the future its own accomplishment.[15]

The resolution, then, of the culture wars is similar to that of the wars of religion: let the government keep out of the matter, let society arrange these matters for itself.

Political Centralization

A major theme developed by the French liberals is the danger of centralized power. The causes and consequences of the vast concentration of power in the hands of the state has preoccupied many of the deepest students of modern society, from Ortega y Gasset and Bertrand de Jouvenel (especially in his classic, *On Power*), to Robert Nisbet and Michael Oakeshott. On this question the great French source—indeed, the great source among political thinkers altogether—is Alexis de Tocqueville.

In France, as Tocqueville showed in his historical works, the modern bureaucratic state was built by the kings and continued by the Revolution and Napoleon.

When Tocqueville first came to the United States at the age of twenty-six, he was amazed by the virtual absence of any sign of the state. America seemed to him a country without a government, and he praised

---

14 Benjamin Constant, *Cours de Politique Constitutionnelle*, 2, 172n.
15 Benjamin Constant, "De l'esprit de conquête et de l'usurpation," *Oeuvres*, Alfred Roulin, (ed.) Pléiade edition (Paris: Gallimard, 1957) 1580.

her for it. Here Tocqueville was continuing the love affair of French liberalism with the United States that began in the Enlightenment and continued for generations. (Sometimes, it must be admitted, the French became rather uncritical admirers, as in their adulation of Abraham Lincoln and the Union cause during the War Between the States.[16])

Too much has been made of Tocqueville's concern with "the tyranny of the majority" in the first volume of *Democracy in America*, perhaps because this motif is what caught the eye of John Stuart Mill in his enthusiastic review of that first part. Of more permanent interest is the analysis in the second volume, of the dangers of state centralization when linked with modern democracy and the striving of the masses for ever-growing material satisfactions. At the conclusion of *Democracy in America* Tocqueville presents what must be one of the most terrifying images in the whole history of political thought:

> I seek to trace the novel features under which despotism may appear in the world. The first thing that strikes the eye is an innumerable multitude of men, all equal and alike. . . . Above this race of men stands an immense and tutelary power, which takes upon itself alone to secure their gratifications and watch over their fate. That power is absolute, minute, regular, provident, and mild. It would be like the authority of a parent if, like that authority, its object was to prepare men for manhood; but it seeks, on the contrary, to keep them in perpetual childhood: it is well content that the people should rejoice, provided that they think of nothing but rejoicing. For their happiness such a government willingly labors, but it chooses to be the sole agent and the only arbiter of that happiness; it provides for their security, foresees and supplies their necessities, facilitates their pleasures, manages their principal concerns, directs their industry...what remains, but to spare them all the care of thinking and all the trouble of living?[17]

---

16 See Serge Gavronsky, *The French Liberal Opposition and the American Civil War* (New York: Humanities Press, 1968).
17 Alexis de Tocqueville, *De la Démocratie en Amérique*, II, bk. 4, ch. vi.

It is astonishing that fifty years before the birth of the modern welfare state in Bismarckian Germany, Tocqueville was already describing—and critiquing—it.[18]

Following Tocqueville, the French liberals never ceased focusing attention on the dangers of state centralization. Indeed, in the speech that Henri-Dominique Lacordaire, along with Montalembert the outstanding leader of the French Catholic liberals (see below) delivered upon his election as Tocqueville's successor at the Académie Française, he lashed out at the radical-democratic movement in Europe for aiding and abetting state centralization:

> The European democrat, idolater of what he calls the State, takes the human being from his cradle in order to offer him as a sacrificial victim to the public Omnipotence. He holds that the child, before belonging to the family, belongs to the City [i.e., the political organization], and that the City, that is, the people represented by those that govern them, has the right to form his mind on a uniform and legal model. He holds that the commune, the province, and every other association, even the most indifferent, depends on the State, and cannot act, nor speak, nor sell, nor buy, nor, finally, exist, without the intervention of the State and in the degree determined by it, in this way making the most absolute civil servitude the entrance way and the foundation of political liberty.[19]

"Tolerance" and Belief in the Modern World

It is widely agreed that an important part of liberalism is the notion of the neutrality of the state in matters of culture and values. In the liberal view, the state must limit itself to procedural questions,

---

18 Stephen Holmes, "Constant and Tocqueville: An Unexplored Relationship," *Annales Benjamin Constant*, no. 12 (1991) 39, writes of Tocqueville's portrayal of the future despotism: it sounds "like the welfare state as libertarians conceive and deride it." It would be interesting to know in which respects Holmes believes that Tocqueville's vision differs from the reality of the modern welfare state in its essential character and tendencies.

19 Henri-Dominique Lacordaire, *Notices et Panégyriques* (1886) (Paris: Poussielgue), 345.

insuring all individuals against the infringement of their rights by force, and otherwise leaving them free to develop concrete value systems in voluntary association with others.

A number of critics of liberalism have charged that this principle of state-neutrality tends to degenerate into the notion that all moral and cultural values are, in fact, "relative," non-binding, and even non-existent in any meaningful sense (or else—which probably amounts to the same thing—all equally true or valid). But if all value systems, all religions, for instance, are seen as equally worthy not only of toleration but of endorsement and acceptance, this will necessarily sap and ultimately destroy any firm, heartfelt commitment to concrete values. In this way, spiritual life will be impoverished, and milder or more serious social and personal pathologies promoted.

Such an association of liberalism with moral relativism, however, is in no way necessary. In part, at least, it appears to be traceable to nothing more than the ambiguity of the term "liberal." It is as if one were to claim that a (political) liberal is necessarily committed to a "liberal" education, i.e., has to condemn an education centered on engineering, for instance.

But the view that links liberalism with acceptance of what is commonly called moral relativism has sometimes gained support from self-described liberals, among them Stephen Macedo.[20] Macedo grants that what he calls "liberal justice" (respect for the rights of others) implies "tolerance" for divergent lifestyles, ethical choices, etc. This is not, however, sufficient, in his view. "A merely 'tolerant' community does not really stand out as one that is flourishing as a community." For a community to flourish "in a distinctively liberal way," "liberal virtues" are also required." We must "sympathize" with alien "projects and commitments, with choices different from our own, careers and lifestyles not seriously considered before."

> Liberal citizens who acquire the capacity to sympathize with widely divergent ways of life acquire a range of "live options,"

---

20 Stephen Macedo, *Liberal Virtues. Citizenship, Virtue and Community in Liberal Constitutionalism* (Oxford: Clarendon Press, 1990).

and become open to change. Live options incite self-examination, self-criticism, and experimentation. Live options multiply with . . . the acceptance of "off-beat" careers and of different sexual orientations, with the breakdown of gender-based stereotypes, and with the acceptance of divorce and remarriage.[21]

Liberalism, according to Macedo, tends to "temper or attenuate the devotion to one's own projects and allegiances, by encouraging persons to regard their own ways as open to criticism, choice, and change . . ." This must be welcomed, since, "if social practices and moral norms are to promote rather than constrain liberty they must have certain substantive characteristics, they must embody attitudes of tolerance [in the wider sense] and openness to change rather than pressures to conformity." "Quiet obedience, deference, unquestioned devotion, and humility, could not be counted among the liberal virtues," Macedo states.[22] In his conception of liberalism, it "holds out the promise, or the threat, of making all the world like California."[23]

Finally, in declaring that "the liberal ideal will not appeal to those who seek a final, definitive answer to the great question of how to live,"[24] Macedo forecloses the possibility that adherence to liberalism is perfectly compatible with firm faith in a rigorous religious tradition.

The French Liberal Catholics on Tolerance and Pluralism

This was a question that was addressed by an unduly neglected but, again, highly relevant school of thought in nineteenth France, the Catholic liberals, whose best representative was the Count de

---

21 Ibid. 266–67.
22 Since he asserts this without qualification, Macedo seems to imply that these traits are somehow antithetical to or out of keeping with liberalism in all cases, presumably including deference to one's parents, unquestioned devotion to one's family, and humility before God.
23 Ibid. 267, 270, 278.
24 Ibid. 280. Since all this openness, willingness to experiment, endorsement of differing lifestyles, etc., is supposed to stimulate the growth of the individual, it is remarkable that Macedo holds at the same time that "there is no tension between being at home in a tradition or set of practices and the development of one's individuality." Ibid. 270.

Montalembert.²⁵ These thinkers helped introduce a new phase in the evolution of liberalism. Earlier liberals, like the Idéologues, had been generally anti-religious, and especially anti-Catholic. The *Censeur Européen*, for instance, was thoroughly Voltarian in its treatment of the Catholic Church, waging "a merciless war against the revived religious orders, the reopening of the seminaries, the extension of religious instruction and the activities of the missionaries," and ceaselessly denigrating "conversions, and mass ordinations."²⁶ In part under the influence of Benjamin Constant, the attitude of liberalism began to change.

In 1830, a group of Catholic liberals founded the journal *L'Avenir* [The Future}, to advocate religious freedom and to work towards a reconciliation of Catholicism and liberalism. For these writers, the all-important consideration was the character of society in the nineteenth century, "with its opinions so varied and contradictory, its diverse beliefs, its immense and inexorable need for tolerance and liberty"²⁷—what would today be called the "pluralism" of modern society. One implication of this modern pluralism was that any faction, like the Catholics, that might attempt to curtail the freedom of others could not be sure that their own freedom would not in turn be curtailed when their opponents came to power.²⁸

One of the editors of *L'Avenir*, Charles Forbes René de Tryon, Count de Montalembert, went on to become the leader of the movement. The most famous presentation of his views was at a Catholic congress held in Malines, Belgium, in August, 1863.²⁹ Belgium was of

---

25 See C. Constantin, "Libéralisme catholique," in A.Vacant, et al. (eds.), *Dictionnaire de la Théologie Catholique* (Paris: Letouzey, 1926), 9, cols. 506–629; and George Armstrong Kelly, *The Humane Comedy: Constant, Tocqueville and French Liberalism* (Cambridge: Cambridge University Press, 1992), 114–133. I am grateful to Professor Leonard P. Liggio for his great service in directing attention to the importance of this group.
26 Ephraïm Harpaz, "*Le Censeur Européen:* Histoire d'un journal quotidien," 147–49.
27 Quoted in C. Constantin, "Libéralisme catholique," col. 530. In the same passage, it demanded "freedom of labor and of industry."
28 Ibid. cols. 536–37. The conception of power as always a two-edged sword was a major argument used by Constant against state interference in religious and cultural questions.
29 His two speeches are reprinted in Charles Forbes René de Tryon, Comte de Montalembert, *L'Église libre dans l'état libre* (Brussels: *La revue belge et étrangère*, 1863). See also C. Constantin, "Libéralisme catholique," cols. 585–90.

great significance to Montalembert and his associates, since there Catholics (including the bishops) had joined with liberals in establishing full religious freedom in the constitution of 1831.[30]

In his two speeches, Montalembert places his plea for religious freedom within a historicist framework, reminiscent of Constant's analysis of freedom ancient and modern. Just as Constant does not suggest that freedom as the ancients conceived of it was "wrong," so Montalembert does not unequivocally condemn the religious intolerance practiced in previous centuries. Rather, his position on the Church's use of coercion in past ages is somewhat ambivalent. While he feels "an invincible horror for all the tortures and all the violence done to humanity on the pretext of serving or defending religion," it is a fact that Europe owes its Christian character to the Church's past relationship with the state. Yet, European society has outgrown the need for such a relationship, and "even admitting that the system of force in the service of faith . . . has produced some grand results in the past, it is impossible to deny that it is doomed to hopeless impotence in the century in which we live." Moreover, too often in the past, the Church paid for its privileged access to power by being required to act as an accomplice or servant to the temporal rulers.[31]

He is not, he claims, engaged in theoretical, still less in theological, disputation. He speaks solely as a politician and historian. "I invoke facts, and I draw purely practical lessons." Given the character of the modern world, "nothing is more impossible today than to reestablish even a shadow of feudalism or theocracy." Liberty is an absolute necessity for the Church; this is his overriding concern. Indeed, he describes his own career as having been "totally consecrated to the defense of the rights and the liberties of Catholicism." But "the Church can no longer be free except in the bosom of general freedom. No special freedom, and that of the Church less than any other, can exist today except under

---

30 Ibid. cols. 522–24. The constitution provided for state subsidies to religious groups, however.
31 Montalembert, *L'Église libre dans l'état libre* 47, 52, 63–65.

the guarantee of the common liberty. It was otherwise in the great centuries of Christian history," but times have changed, irrevocably.[32]

The Jacobin and Napoleonic dictatorships had given European, and especially French, liberals an inkling of the possibilities of massed power in the hands of the modern state. Montalembert quotes a prescient passage from Ignaz von Döllinger, the teacher of Lord Acton, who maintained that the unitary despotism of the Roman Empire was much less threatening to the liberty of the soul and to Christian faith than the absolutism of the modern state. The first Caesars had no censorship, secret or even ordinary police, official education, bureaucracy, telegraph, railroads, nor any of the infinite resources that civilization now puts at the service of tyranny. Today religion is necessary as an individual-moral, as well as an institutional, bulwark against the crushing power of the modern state. What else is capable of inspiring the individual "with the moral force, the virile patience, the invincible perserverance, the uncompromising independence which we will have more and more need of to hold our own against the torrent"? In particular, religious faith is needed to defend private property in this age of envious democracy, because, Montalembert notes ironically, if inaccurately, "to believe in property when one does not believe in God, one must be a proprietor."[33]

It is highly significant that Montalembert, as he categorically states, refuses to defend religious liberty on the basis of "the ridiculous and culpable doctrines that all religions are equally true and good in themselves, or that the spiritual authority does not obligate conscience." He distinguishes sharply between "dogmatic intolerance" and "civil tolerance," "the one necessary to eternal life and the other necessary to modern society." François Guizot is cited:

> The principle of religious liberty, as every truly Christian man must understand and practice it, in no way touches on the unity, the infallibility of the Church.... It consists solely in recognizing the right of the human conscience not to be governed, in its

---

32 Ibid. 7, 12–15.
33 Ibid. 26, 30–31.

relations with God, by human [i.e., state] decrees and punishments.[34]

Modern society is divided into two camps, believers and non-believers: while each maintains its own viewpoint, they must learn to live with each other. "As for me," Montalembert asserts, "I hold every man to be my ally who, whatever may be his belief or banner, wishes for my freedom as for his own, and who does nothing to prevent me from praying, speaking, writing, giving alms, associating myself, and teaching, as I wish." Again, distinguishing the dogmatic from the political level he states:

> Our Lord, speaking of himself, says: "Who is not for me is against me." But, speaking to his disciples, he tells them: "Who is not against you is for you." It is a rule as essential to follow in public life as in spiritual life.

He ends his speeches at Malines by an act of deference and humility, doing his "duty as a Catholic, by submitting all of my expressions as well as all of my opinions to the infallible authority of the Church."[35]

Some years later, Gustave de Molinari, who had evidently attended the 1863 congress at Malines, reported in detail on Montalembert's speeches in a highly laudatory review.[36] He noted that following its enthusiastic reception of Montalembert's remarks, the Catholic assembly adopted a series of resolutions, including one Molinari found "particularly significant":

---

34 Ibid. 44–45. Compare C. Constantin, "Libéralisme catholique," cols. 506, 509, 531, where the author points out that it is an error to identify the position of Catholic liberalism, in the sense advocated by Montalembert, with the liberal Protestant standpoint. The former "never wished to be and never has been dogmatic liberalism, whose fundamental principle is the absolute sovereignty of the individual reason. Instead, the Catholic liberal movement was and is "solely political and social." The Catholic liberals insisted that in matters of religious dogma they were as orthodox as the most intransigent of their opponents within the Church. *L'Avenir*, the journal of the movement, insisted that "perfect civil tolerance" does not in the least imply "dogmatic tolerance." The Church "at no point renounces its doctrine, which it preaches, defends, and propagates," while recognizing the same right in other faiths.
35 Montalembert, *L'Église libre dans l'état libre* 84–85.
36 Gustave de Molinari, "Les Congrès Catholiques," *Revue des Deux Mondes*, 3rd series, 11 (1875), 411–30.

It is in the interest of Catholics as of all citizens who sincerely wish for liberty to substitute as much as possible for the intervention and omnipotence of the state the creative energy and principle of expansion of the spirit of association.[37]

Molinari commended the Catholic liberals for attacking "the system of protection applied to religion." Just as freetraders argued that protectionism undermined industrial efficiency and prosperity, so it can be argued that religious "protectionism," as in the Spain of his time, has been deleterious to religion, while "competition" among religions has been beneficial. It is no wonder, Molinari added, that the Belgian organ of the free trade movement congratulated Montalembert on his speeches, calling him the "Cobden of religious liberty." Molinari concluded by looking forward to the time when "the alliance of Catholicism and liberty" would become "a fruitful reality."[38]

Montalembert's Principled Anti-Statism

Montalembert was not simply an advocate of religious freedom within a modern pluralist society; his anti-statism was wide-ranging. He was a strong believer in private property and opponent of socialism.[39] A careful student of Tocqueville, he was as firm an enemy of centralization and state bureaucracy as any French thinker of the nineteenth century. Decentralization—which he defines, rather in the spirit of the Tenth Amendment to the United States Constitution, as the sum of "liberties, local and personal, municipal and provincial"[40]—must be promoted in every possible way. Bureaucracy in modern societies is a

---

37 Ibid. 420–21. Molinari noted that at the following year's meeting in Malines, the Congress strongly recommended the introduction or development of the teaching of political economy in Catholic schools.

38 Ibid. 427–28, 430. On the use of the free trade analogy on behalf of liberty of conscience by British writers, see George H. Smith, *Atheism, Ayn Rand, and Other Heresies* (Buffalo: Prometheus, 1991) 122–26.

39 This is not to suggest that Montalembert was a thorough or consistent liberal in economic affairs. See, for instance, his speech to the National Legislative Assembly, December 13, 1849, "Impôt des boissons," Montalembert, *Discours* (Paris: Jacques Lecoffre, 1860), 3, 1848–1852, 296–339, in opposition to Bastiat's proposal to end the tax on wine.

40 "La décentralisation," in Montalembert, *Oeuvres polémiques et diverses*, (Paris: Jacques Lecoffre, 1868) 3, 385.

"virus," and the state has become a "secular idol." The French must learn to withdraw themselves from the tutelage of this "colony of functionaries" sent from Paris that inhabits "the capital of every department, district, and canton," and which "represents a kind of dominant or conquering caste, charged, like the English in Hindustan, with thinking, speaking, and acting for a population of incapable natives."[41]

A particular object of Montalembert's attack was the state monopoly in secondary and university education.[42] As things stand now, he held, children undergo a process designed to convert them to values and views at odds with those of their parents. The world-view of the public school teachers differs radically from that of the French people as a whole. The teachers, like their university professors, preach a skepticism and corrosive rationalism that continually undermine the social order resting on religion, the family, and private property. Youth, and the people at large, is being deprived of religion and nothing put in its place, except socialism.

In a passage that surprisingly anticipates Joseph Schumpeter's analysis of the role of the intellectuals in subverting capitalism, Montalembert attacks an overdeveloped educational system for producing a mass of half-educated graduates, "suited for everything and good at nothing," who will inevitably become future office-seekers, thus necessitating a vast expansion of state functions: they will then "be hurled upon public jobs, that is, on the budget, as upon a prey."
If it were up to him, Montalembert declares, there would be no state education at all: "the state has only too much responsibility as it is."

Since France is constitutionally required to provide public education, he proposes that instead of being centralized and directed from Paris it should be organized by the departments into which the country was divided. Control should be exercised by councils including members elected by fathers of families according to universal suffrage. In this way, "society" rather than the state would direct the education of children. Everything possible must be done to thwart the educational

---

41 Ibid. 388–90.
42 Cf., e.g., the speeches of January 17, 1850, February 4, 1850, and February 12, 1850, in Montalembert, *Discours*, 3, 1848–1852: 340–85, 385–89, and 390–417.

"monopolizers, [who] in the name and under the colors of the state," tear children away from their parents "in order to close them up in intellectual prisons and keep them there until the very traces of the beliefs of their parental homes are obliterated from their souls . . ."[43]

The position of the Catholic liberals like Montalembert bears a strong resemblance to the one brilliantly presented in the work of H. Tristram Engelhardt, Jr.[44] In dealing with the major questions of bioethics, Engelhardt has occasion to consider the place in liberal society of ethical systems that are rooted in religious and other outlooks that demand a good deal of rigor and impermeability to alternative value systems.

Like Montalembert, Engelhardt insists that he is offering no "manifesto on behalf of secular pluralist ethics," but rather simply acknowledging its "inevitability." In contrast to the ancient Greek polis or medieval European society, in the present age "a large-scale state must act as a neutral vehicle for spanning numerous communities with often diverse views of the good life."[45] Yet, such a bland enervated ethical neutrality is not appropriate for individuals:

> It is only within the embrace of a particular community that one learns whether it is right or wrong, worthwhile or not, to do the things one has a secular moral right to do. The domain of secular ethics does not exhaust the universe of ethical reflection. . . . It is within particular moral worlds that one lives and finds full meaning in life . . . a full and concrete moral life.[46]

The solution lies in distinguishing between "ethics as a procedure and ethics as content." This yields a "two-tiered moral life . . . (1) that of a content-poor secular ethics, which has the ability to span numerous divergent moral communities, and (2) the particular moral communities

---

43 Montalembert, *L'Eglise libre dans l'état libre* 25.
44 H. Tristram Engelhardt, Jr., *The Foundations of Bioethics* (New York: Oxford University Press, 1986).
45 Ibid. viii, 48.
46 Ibid. 49–50.

within which one can achieve a contentful understanding of the good life."⁴⁷

Competing moral visions, so long as they "are pursued within the morality of mutual respect . . . need to be tolerated, even if they are not endorsed or supported." In the spirit of Montalembert, Engelhardt concludes: "One shows sufficient tolerance for the overarching procedural restraints of liberal society by walking to the property line of one's peaceably established moral enclave, one's Communist commune or one's Amish community . . . insofar as one does not carry the imposition of one's viewpoint beyond that line . . ."⁴⁸

Gustave de Molinari: Reactionary Anarchist

The dean of the laissez-faire French economists in the last decades of the nineteenth century and virtually until his death in 1911 was the Belgian-born Gustave de Molinari.⁴⁹ Molinari is most famous for his doctrine of "competing governments"—he has been called "the first anarcho-capitalist"⁵⁰—and while he allegedly modified his position in later years, there is no doubt that he was always an unbending advocate of laissez-faire. Yet this "doctrinaire," who would seem to fit perfectly into Hayek's category of "French rationalist," evidenced views on history and politics that place him in surprisingly close proximity to a kind of hard-core conservatism.⁵¹

---

47 Ibid. 53–54.
48 Ibid. 385–86.
49 On Molinari, see the treatments by David M. Hart, "Gustave de Molinari and the Anti-statist Liberal Tradition," *Journal of Libertarian Studies*, Part I, 5, No. 3 (Summer 1981): 263–90; Part II, 5, No. 4 (Fall 1981): 399–434; and Part III, No. 1 (Winter 1982): 83–104; and Murray N. Rothbard, *Classical Economics*, 453–55. On Molinari's most influential disciple, see idem., "Vilfredo Pareto, Pessimistic Follower of Molinari," in ibid. 455–59.
50 Ibid. 453 See the bibliography in Pierre Lemieux, *L'anarcho-capitalisme* (Paris: Presses Universitaires de France, 1988), 23–24.
51 The reviewer of Molinari's *Les soirées de la rue Saint-Lazare. Entretiens sur les lois économique et défense de la propriété*, in the *Journal des Économistes*, 24, No. 104 (November 15, 1849) 368–69, praises him for his stinging critique of the typical socialist—"this pygmy puffed up with pride who would try to substitute his own work for that of the creator"—and for his characterizing the principle of socialism as "recklessly arrogant." This would seem, except for the much more aggressive phrasing, to be rather close to Hayek's own conception of socialism as "the fatal conceit."

The first and best known expression of Molinari's anarcho-capitalism is an article in the *Journal des Économistes*, in 1849,[52] the starting point of which already causes problems for Hayek's typology. Molinari distinguishes between two schools of social philosophy: the first holds that human associations, since they are "organized in a purely artificial way by primitive legislators," can be "modified or remade by other legislators, to the degree that social science progresses." Molinari clearly believes this view, which, according to Hayek is the essence of "constructivist rationalism," to be nonsense. The opposing school, the one to which Molinari obviously adheres, maintains that "society is a purely natural fact," and "moves by virtue of pre-existing general laws."

Common observation confirms that among the needs that must be satisfied in society is security—the protection of the life, liberty, and property of each of individual. It is clearly in the interest of the members of society to "procure security at the lowest possible price." With all goods, whether material or immaterial, free competition guarantees that consumers will obtain goods at the lowest price. Thus, "the production of security should, in the interest of the consumers of this immaterial good, remain subject to the law of free competition." From this it follows that "no government should have the right to prevent another government from establishing itself in competition with it, or to oblige the consumers of security to turn exclusively to it for this commodity."

Under the present regime, the providers of security are able, through the use of force, to establish a monopoly and impose a "surcharge" (*surtaxe*) on the consumers, by charging a price for their commodity that is "higher than its value." The government industry becomes highly profitable, and the natural consequence is the form of "competition" for "customers" characteristic of monopoly government: war. Monopoly provision leads to a situation where "justice becomes costly and slow, the police vexatious, individual liberty ceases to be respected, the price of security is abusively high and unequally levied." In contrast,

---

[52] Gustave de Molinari, "De la production de la securité," *Journal des Économistes*, 22, No. 95 (February 15, 1849) 277–90.

competition among "governments" would have the predictable benefits of lowering prices and stimulating improvement in the product.[53]

Drawing on both natural rights and economic (utilitarian) arguments, Molinari accuses other economists, in particular that paragon of laissez-faire, Charles Dunoyer, of inconsistency in repudiating this approach out of hand (while he commends Adam Smith for recognizing the benefits of competition among courts of law[54]). In fact, other French liberals, including Dunoyer and Bastiat, criticized Molinari's theoretical elimination of "monopoly government," and he seems to have had no followers on this issue in the France of his time.

Interestingly, in this early essay Molinari already demonstrates an antipathy to democracy which some would consider out of place in such a radical thinker, explicitly setting individual rights, including especially property rights, above majority rule. He considers the case in which a socialist majority is sent to the legislative assembly and a socialist president is elected. "Suppose that this majority and this president, invested with the sovereign authority, decrees, as M. Proudhon has demanded, the levying of a tax of three billion on the rich, in order to set up work for the poor, is it likely that the minority will submit itself peacefully to this iniquitous and absurd—but legal and *constitutional*—spoliation? No, without a doubt it would not hesitate to ignore *the authority* of the majority and defend its property [emphasis in original]."[55]

In his historical writings and in contrast to French liberals of a more "British" persuasion (in Hayek's terminology), like Constant,

---

53 Ibid. 281–282, 289. In connection with the controversial question of how a system of "competing governments" would work, Molinari sketches some of the requirements of his system, both for the suppliers of security and for its consumers. The latter would be obliged to subject themselves to the penalties on offenses against person and property imposed by the government they have chosen, as well as to submit to "certain inconveniences" the object of which is to facilitate the government's apprehension of criminals. Ibid. 288.
54 In *The Wealth of Nations*, Bk. 5, chap. 1.
55 Molinari, "De la production de la sécurité," 287. Molinari's disciple, Vilfredo Pareto, advocated acting according to this principle when it came to an actual historical case, viz., the predatory conduct of socialist local governments in Italy before the Fascist seizure of power; see Ralph Raico, "Mises on Fascism, Democracy, and Other Questions," *Journal of Libertarian Studies*, 12, 1 (Spring 1996), 19–20. A modified version of this appears in my essay, "Mises's *Liberalism* on Fascism, Democracy, and Imperialism," in the present volume.

Guizot, and Toqueville, Molinari came to see no redeeming features in the Revolution of 1789. Traditionally, French liberals had credited the Revolution with certain reforms (especially in its earlier, pre-Jacobin phase, "1789" rather than "1793"), such as abolishing internal tariffs and establishing religious freedom. But, Molinari maintains, "if the Revolution had not broken out, the reforms attributed to it would have been pursued peacefully for their useful qualities, and these reforms would then have been definitive."[56] This is a view of the Old Regime and the Revolution that in important respects differs little from the one later presented by the historian Pierre Gaxotte, an intellectual luminary of the royalist and far-right group, *Action française*.[57]

The Revolution put an abrupt end to this organic evolution and initiated a massive shift of power to the state. "Military serfdom"— involuntary military service, roundly condemned by Turgot, Condorcet, and nearly all the other pre-revolutionary economists—had nearly disappeared in France. The Revolution universalized conscription: "This retrogression in the regime of [military] serfdom would suffice of itself to outweigh all the progressive reforms, real or imagined, that are customarily set to the credit of the revolution." This "blood tax" was retained by the Restoration, since the upper and middle classes could easily purchase exemption through paying for replacements. Here was another example of class-legislation, as was the *livret*, or book listing previous employments, now mandatory on laborers, and the prohibition of workers' organizations. The end result of the Revolution has been "to diminish the sum of liberties enjoyed by the French and at least to double the weight of the government of France."[58]

This most "extreme" of French or even of all European liberals (Auberon Herbert in Britain would be a close rival) displayed a warm sympathy for tradition and "organic" culture, going so far as to criticize the Napoleonic Code for consolidating the "reforms" of the Revolution by replacing the variegated customs of the provinces with a uniform

---

56 Gustav de Molinari, *L'évolution politique et la Révolution* (Paris: C. Reinwald, 1884) 271–74.
57 Pierre Gaxotte, *La révolution française* (Paris: Plon, 1936), 2 vols.
58 Molinari, *L'évolution politique et la Révolution*, 280–81, 285, n. 1, 287, n. 1, 289–90.

legislation: "In many respects the ancient customs, adapted over centuries to the populations they ruled and successively perfected by way of experiment, left a much greater area to individual liberty and established the responsibility attaching to liberty with more equity." Molinari even assailed "the system of weights and measures, invented by professors of mathematics, in contempt of the experience and needs of those engaging in exchange," and imposed by the Revolution.[59]

Much to his honor, Molinari indicted the Revolution for its "war of extermination" against the Catholic and royalist population of the Vendée, in western France.[60] He estimated that the attempted genocide claimed some 900,000 victims; in any case, the number was in the hundreds of thousands. This horrific, bloody episode had been blotted out of the accounts of earlier, less forthright French liberals (as it has been by pro-Revolution historians ever since). It may be that these liberals were anxious not to provide ammunition to their conservative foes. More likely, their strange silence is owing to the fact that these victims of state mass-murder were, after all, Catholic and royalist.

In the long run, Molinari maintained, the most destructive result of the Revolution was to remove any curb to "the appetite for exploitation" of the bourgeoisie. This is what the famous achievement of "equality before the law" in large part amounted to. "The Revolution left the field clear to the middle class, and the latter did not neglect to turn the situation to its profit, by replacing the privileges suited to the interests of the nobility and clergy by other privileges suited to their own." A new class was put "in possession of the apparatus for concocting laws and regulations." The hereditary monarch had at least to some extent a personal interest in preserving the state from ruin and in promoting its prosperity.[61]

Molinari applies the class conflict theory which by his time had become a cornerstone of French liberal ideas, but, unlike earlier thinkers,

---

59 Ibid. 272. As Dr. David Gordon has pointed out to me, Herbert Spencer also opposed state-imposed standards of weights and measures.
60 Ibid. 333, n. 1
61 Ibid. 278–79, 290, 295–97.

he does not exempt the regimes that passed for liberal in French politics.[62] The "liberal" July Monarchy was the the creature of the bourgeoisie, which aimed "from now on to fix the exploitation of the state firmly in their own hands." The liberal party "was the expression of those in the governing class that had issued from the revolution." The middlle classes profited from tariffs, government contracts, state subsidies for railroads and other industries, state-sponsored banking, and the jobs available in the ever-expanding state bureaucracy itself. Soon, a radical movement emerged, as "the swelling profits of an exploitation spreading every day and branching out more and more excited the envy of the classes excluded from the feast." The final term is arrived at with universal manhood suffrage, where the whole population must be bought off.[63] Molinari's relentlessly scathing and cynical analysis of representative government and advancing democracy suggests that his anarcho-capitalism was a product not only of economic and natural rights theory, but also of his interpretation of history.

"The sovereign nation" is, in Molinari's view, "a simple fiction"; the reality is parties that are organized with the aim of taking over and exploiting state power. Parties, and even their subdivisions, always correspond to the grouped interests from which they issue and among which they recruit their members. Everywhere in politics, Molinari sees ideology, in the sense of a rationalization of class interests, at work. Thus, Napoleon III's policy of having France defend the "oppressed nationalities" of Europe was an ideological cover for the expansionary demands of the Army, one of the Emperor's main pillars of support. In general, in the "political marketplace," each group requires a justification for its depredations: hence, the "economic sophisms and utopias" ground out for the use of the various parties. Molinari states, anticipating the "irrationalist" phase in the thinking of his follower, Pareto, that this charade

---

62 See Ceri Crossley, *French Historians and Romanticism*, 53, 65, where the author points out that Thierry, for instance, glorified the bourgeoisie per se, as the historical embodiment of the "eternal principles of reason, justice, and humanity," and considered the triumph of this class in 1830 as the culmination of French history. See the essay on "The Conflict of Classes: Liberal vs. Marxist Theories," in the present volume.
63 Molinari, *L'évolution politique et la Révolution*, 307, 311–12, 317.

never fails to mislead the masses, always more open to emotion and imagination than to logical reflection.[64]

In his ninety-second year, in what Molinari called his "last word," he displays much of the radicalism of his youth. Politics is still essentially the arena of class conflict, where "successive proprietors of the state" vie to gain the right to levy taxes. Taxes are a continuation, through various merely formal transformations, of slavery: the tribute exacted by whoever exercises power over others. There is more than a hint of his earlier anarcho-capitalism:

> What does a tax do? It takes either from the producer or the consumer a more or less sizeable portion of the product destined in part to consumption and in part to savings, in order to apply it to less productive or even destructive ends, and more rarely to savings.

It is impossible, he states, "to know if the price fixed by the government invested with a monopoly in furnishing its services [of protection] does not unjustly exceed what would have been established through competition."[65] But the State possesses an obligatory clientele, so that, "whether it raises the price or lowers the quality of its services, its client cannot refuse them. As ruinous as taxes may be, the State is amply provided with the powers necessary to force him to pay them."[66]

The tendencies of modern society are deeply disappointing to Molinari. In the middle of the nineteenth century it appeared that peace and free trade would "rule the civilized world." Now it is evident that "the parliamentary and constitutional regime has ended up in socialism." Molinari feared the coming of the "socialist Mardi Gras"—the confiscation of the wealth created by capitalism—to be followed by the depletion of that wealth, and then "a long Lent." He noted that, in order to disarm socialism, "certain states have had recourse to philanthropy," i.e., the welfare state. Freedom of labor has practically disappeared, as the

---

64 Ibid. 314–15, 319–20, 322, 327–29.
65 Gustave de Molinari, *Ultima Verba: Mon Dernier Ouvrage* (Paris: Giard and Brière, 1911) 39–44.
66 Ibid. 60.

workers, after winning the right to organize, went on—"such is the protectionist nature of man"—to employ violence against employers and non-unionized workers; in this way, "the unionized workers taught fraternity to the non-unionized." And on the eve of the First World War Molinari declared that "the interests of the most influential classes"—state functionaries, military and civilian, and armaments makers—"are pushing towards war."[67]

In this last work, Molinari continues to voice "conservative" and even "reactionary" views out of keeping with the customary profile of the nineteenth century laissez-faire liberal. Seeing rather further than many other French liberals, Molinari was no supporter of the Northern side in the American Civil War;[68] here, too, he perceived class interest at work. The war "ruined the conquered provinces," but permitted the industrialists of the North to impose the protectionist policy that led ultimately "to the regime of trusts and produced the billionaires."[69] It is noteworthy that while Molinari was an "absolutist" when it came to the natural right to liberty *in the abstract*, it appears that historical circumstances could temper his position, as in the question of the emancipation of the slaves in the United States:

> In truth, it was in masking their own practical and egoistic interests in domination and protectionism under the cover of humanitarian sentiments that the politicians of the Northern states emancipated the Negroes while ruining their proprietors. They won the admiration of naïve abolitionists throughout the world by bestowing on the freed slaves their total freedom overnight, with the responsibility and demands that the latter were incapable

---

67 Ibid. i, x, 61–62, 64, 175, 261.
68 See, for instance, Montalembert, "La victoire du Nord aux États-Unis," in idem, *Oeuvres polémiques et diverses*, (Paris: Jacques Lecoffre, 1868) 3: 297–367, especially 308–09, where Montalembert states, amazingly, that "the true miracle and the supreme victory" was that the North won without infringing freedom: "no liberty [was] suppressed, no law violated, no voice stifled, no guarantee abandoned . . ."—this, in the face of Lincoln's manifold violations of civil liberties, suppression of dissenting newspapers, imprisonment of dissenters, suspension of habeas corpus, and so on.
69 Molinari, *Ultima Verba*, iii-iv.

of meeting, and even adding the improbable bonus of political rights.[70]

Laissez-faire as Political Guideline

In distinguishing the good, British liberals from their negative images across the Channel, Hayek comments on the place of the laissez-faire idea in his typology. Of the British he writes:

> Their argument was never a complete laissez faire argument, which, as the very words show, is also part of the French rationalist tradition and in its literal sense was never defended by any of the English classical economists. . . . In fact, their argument was never antistate as such, or anarchistic, which is the logical outcome of the rationalistic laissez faire doctrine . . .[71]

Hayek gives two sources for his characterization of the British classical economists. One, Lionel Robbins, is so eager to acquit them of the charge of adhering to laissez-faire that he even adduces the following, from Nassau Senior, with evident approval:

> the only rational foundation of government, the only foundation of a right to govern and a correlative duty to obey, is expediency—the general benefit of the community. It is the duty of a government to do whatever is conducive to the welfare of the governed. The only limit to this duty is power . . .[72]

Hayek's second source, D.H. Macgregor, widened the defense to include virtually all British economists, in particular, Alfred Marshall.

---

70 Ibid. 37–38.
71 F.A. Hayek, *The Constitution of Liberty*, 60.
72 Lionel Robbins, *The Theory of Economic Policy in English Classical Political Economy* (London: Macmillan,1953), 45. The three representatives of the "extreme individualist," "night watchman state" position whom he cites are the Physiocrat Mercier de la Rivière (whom he parodies), Herbert Spencer, and Bastiat.

Marshall is quoted as pronouncing in 1907 that "every economist of the present generation is a Socialist,"[73] further declaring:

> a new emphasis is given to the watchword *laissez-faire*:—Let everyone work with all his might; and most of all let the government arouse itself to do that work which is vital and which none but the government can do efficiently. . . . So I cry, *Laissez-faire*: let the State be up and doing.[74]

Macgregor cites Keynes to the same effect, summarizing his position: "Thus the end of laissez-faire is '*Laissez-faire l'État*'; the principle is transferred to a higher sphere."[75]

Yet invoking these august authorities hardly settles the question of the desirability of the laissez-faire doctrine. One important point that Hayek, Robbins, and others neglect in their brusque dismissal was elucidated by the English legal historian, A.V. Dicey:

> The beneficial effect of State intervention, especially in the form of legislation, is direct, immediate, and, so to speak, visible, whilst its evil effects are gradual and indirect, and lie out of sight . . . these good results of State intervention are easily noticeable . . . [the] evils results . . . are indirect and escape notice . . . few are those who realize the undeniable truth that State help kills self-help. Hence the majority of mankind must almost of necessity look with undue favor upon governmental intervention. This natural bias can be counteracted only by the existence, in a given society as in England between 1830 and 1860, of a presumption or prejudice in favor of individual liberty, that is, of laissez-faire.[76]

---

73 D.H. Macgregor, *Economic Thought and Policy* (Oxford: Oxford University Press, 1949), 69.
74 Ibid.
75 Ibid.
76 A.V. Dicey, *Lectures on the Relation of Law and Public Opinion in England during the Nineteenth Century*, 2nd. ed. (London: Macmillan, 1963 [1914]) 257–58.

Milton Friedman, in *Capitalism and Freedom*, quotes this passage and expresses his agreement with Dicey.[77]

As for Hayek's claim that the laissez-faire doctrine was quintessentially French, that is certainly true. The French coined the slogan, and it is always used in the French form in other languages. The laissez-faire concept permeates French liberal thought from the mid-eighteenth century on. Even Benjamin Constant, whose name is not usually associated with economic questions, was a confirmed advocate of the principle, a fact that comes out most clearly in his only major work on economics, *Commentaire sur l'ouvrage de Filangieri*:

> Whenever there is no absolute necessity, whenever legislation may fail to intervene without society being overthrown, whenever, finally, it is a question merely of some hypothetical improvement, the law must abstain, leave things alone, and keep quiet.[78]

Constant ends the work with the words: "*Laissez-faire, laissez-passer.*"

French economists remained faithful to laissez-faire long after it had fallen out of fashion elsewhere. In histories of thought, this dogged attachment is often traced to the supposed backwardness, superficiality, and general inferiority of the French economists.

Yet Joseph Schumpeter tells a different story. When he comes to discuss the "the laissez-faire ultras," as he calls them, of the last decades of the nineteenth century and the first decades of the twentieth—Paul Leroy-Beaulieu, Émile Levasseur, the "indefatigable" Gustave de Molinari, Yves Guyot, Léon Say, and others—he notes that they

---

77 Milton Friedman, *Capitalism and Freedom* (Chicago: University of Chicago Press, 1962) 201. Typically, John Gray, *Limited Government: A Positive Agenda* (London: Institute for Economic Affairs, 1989) 20–21, makes no mention, much less attempts a rebuttal, of this argument in favor of laissez-faire, presented in well-known works by Dicey and Friedman, in his attack on that principle as a "mirage."

78 Benjamin Constant, *Commentaire sur l'ouvrage de Filangieri*, 70. Interestingly, Constant's rejection of state action is based largely on the inherent difficulties of correcting errors and eliminating failures in state activity. See Ralph Raico, "Benjamin Constant," *New Individualist Review*, 3, No. 2 (1964) (repr. Indianapolis: Liberty Press, 1981) 499–508.

are known as the Paris group because they controlled the *Journal des Économistes*, the new dictionary, the central professional organization in Paris, the Collège de France, and other institutions, as well as most of the publicity . . . they stood staunchly by the drooping flag of unconditional free trade and laissez-faire.[79]

They held out, in Schumpeter's words, "like Leonidas' Spartans at Thermopylae."[80] He admits that they were "unscientific" according to his Walrasian standards, but insists that "the frank contempt with which both higher-powered theorists and anti-liberals treated the group is . . . not justified."[81] For when these men wrote on practical questions, they

> *knew what they were writing about.* That is to say, they lived and thought in close proximity to business and political practice, which most of them knew from experience and not from newspapers. There is an atmosphere of realism and shrewdness about their works that partly compensates for lack of scientific inspiration. (Emphasis in original)[82]

This suggests the foundation of the French liberals' commitment to laissez-faire. For Dicey, and with him Friedman, the chief value of the rule lies in preventing an immediate and obvious but inferior good from replacing a longer-range, less obvious but superior one. For the French thinkers the central concern was *spoliation*, or state-mediated plunder. From at least the time of Dunoyer and Charles Comte, the French economists had been preoccupied with the problem of public policy employed for the wholesale usurpation of property rights. Protectionism, socialism, all varieties of state favoritism and restrictions on competition, and the growth of bureaucracy and jobbery were the means by which special interests sought to exploit the public, the great mass of consumers and taxpayers. The "Paris group's" knowledge of business and political practice to which Schumpeter refers—a knowledge

---

79 Joseph A. Schumpeter, *History of Economic Analysis*, Elizabeth Boody Schumpeter (ed.) (New York: Oxford University Press, 1954), 841.
80 Ibid. 843.
81 Ibid. 842, n.5.
82 Ibid.

not gained from "newspapers," i.e., not subverted by the ideological rationalizations of interested parties—confirmed them in their view that only a solid barrier such as the laissez-faire doctrine could protect the public against the incessant onslaught of the would-be exploiters.[83]

The same considerations dominated economic thinking in Italy, which was strongly influenced by the French liberal economists, and where for decades economists were nearly as dedicated to laissez-faire as in France.[84] The dean of nineteenth century Italian economists, the Sicilian Francesco Ferrara, wrote of a battle between "privilege, secret interest, political advantage, everything that is capable of coveting" and its "natural enemy," the science "whose emblem, from the time of its birth, has been: *laissez-faire, laissez-passer.*"[85] As this passage implies, Ferrara conceived of the laissez-faire principle above all as a necessary barrier to the attack of what today would be called rent-seekers. This was the position of mainstream of Italian economics, which included Vilfredo Pareto and Maffeo Pantaleoni, until around 1920.[86]

In the following generation, the laissez-faire tradition effectively died out in Italy. Luigi Einaudi, probably the most prominent economist of this period and later the first president of the Italian Republic, while oriented to the free market in policy questions, rejected strict laissez-faire and adopted a "pragmatic" approach. He correctly chided nineteenth

---

83 Such an understanding is missing from the discussion by J.E. Cairnes, "Political Economy and Laissez-Faire," in idem, *Essays in Political Economy. Theoretical and Applied* (London, Macmillan, 1873), 232–64. Cairnes states that "as a practical matter I hold *laissez-faire* to be incomparably the safer guide [compared to the principle of state control]. Only let us remember that it is a *practical rule*, and not a doctrine of science; a rule in the main sound, but like most other sound practical rules, liable to numerous exceptions; above all a rule which must never for a moment be allowed to stand in the way of the candid consideration of any promising proposal of social and industrial reform" (251, emphasis in original). With Cairnes's "rule" so readily defeasible, it is hard to see what protection it could afford against anti-social policies.
84 See Salerno, "The Neglect of the French Liberal School," and Rothbard, *Classical Economics*, 448–49 and 455–59.
85 Francesco Ferrara, "G. B. Say," in *Prefazioni alla Biblioteca dell'Economista*, Part 1 of idem, *Opere Complete*, Bruno Rozzi Ragazzi (ed.) (Rome: Associazione Bancaria Italiana/Banca d'Italia, 1955) 2, 567.
86 On the Italian liberal economists and the rent-seeking state, see the essay, "Mises on Fascism, Democracy, and Imperialism," in the present volume.

century economists for abolishing the distinction between normative and scientific propositions in their enthusiasm for laissez-faire. When he comes to analyze the various meanings of economic liberalism, Einaudi distinguishes among them the "religious": "From the frequency of the cases in which economists, for contingent reasons, are inclined to recommend free-market [liberistiche] solutions to individual concrete problems, there arises a third meaning of the free market maxim, which I will call 'religious.'" Einaudi clearly means this to deny any scientific status to this "religious" conception. Nonetheless, he adds:

> I will not say, however, that the religious conception of economic liberalism [liberismo] is devoid of practical value. On the contrary, its value can be very great. It is extremely useful that, in the face of the practice of asking everything from the state, of expecting everything from collective action, the economic liberal rises up to indict the sloth of the interventionist and the greed of the protectionist. Putting science aside, the moral figure of the first in practical and political life rises a thousand cubits above that of his opponents. Without him, the state would not only fulfill the tasks appropriate to it and complement individual action where convenient, but, intervening in economic affairs at the instigation of thieves and fools, would do harm to the whole society.[87]

---

[87] Luigi Einaudi, "Liberismo e liberalismo," in Benedetto Croce and Luigi Einaudi, *Liberismo e liberalismo*, Paolo Solari, ed. (Milan/Naples: Riccardo Ricciardi, 1957), 125–26. In his review of Keynes pamphlet, "The End of Laissez-Faire," Einaudi asks why Keynes, after "having once again placed the rule of laissez-faire *hors de combat* as a scientific principle, did not add some additional page examining the present importance of that rule as a practical norm of conduct?...has the practical importance of the laissez-faire rule for the conduct of men really diminished? That state intervention has become quantitatively more frequent may be a correct proposition, but its truth does not prove the decadence of the laissez-faire rule, since it may well be that, contemporaneous with the extension of public activity and interference in some branches of economic life, there has been a much greater increase of new kinds of activity where the old rule of laissez-faire retains its value intact." Luigi Einaudi, "La fine del 'laissez-aire'" *La Riforma Sociale*, 3rd series, 37, Nos. 11–12 (November-December, 1926) 572–73. Einaudi, incidentally, found nothing original or particularly significant in Keynes's pamphlet. Einaudi's continuing preoccupation with the question of *spogliazione* is indicated by his comments in "Epilogo," in *La condotta economica e gli effetti sociali della guerra italiana* (Bari: Laterza, 1933) 397–416, where he excoriates "the immoral state, the state that does not

James Buchanan, as is well known, was strongly influenced by the Italian liberal economists. Many years later he made a point similar to Einaudi's, when he spoke of the lack on the part of the democratic electorate of "a generalized willingness to leave things alone, to let the economy work in its own way, and outside of politicized interference." Despite loss of faith in socialism, "we are a long way from regaining any faith in the laissez-faire principle of the classical economists." Buchanan spells out the consequences of the absence of any commitment to laissez-faire for political economy:

> exploitation by those interest groups that have their own ready-made agenda for state action designed to yield these groups differentially high rents or profits. Building on the public's unwillingness to act on principle in support of market solutions to apparent problems, whether real or imagined, these interest groups secure arbitrary restrictions on voluntary exchanges and, in the process, secure rents for their members while reducing both the liberties and economic well being of other members of the economic nexus, both domestically and internationally.

Buchanan concludes that what is required to thwart the impending protectionist-mercantilist regime are "*principles* that can be incorporated in constitutional structure, principles that dictate the imposition of constraints that will prevent the intrusions of ordinary politics into market exchange" (emphasis in original).[88]

Today, in every Western country, the sphere of state action grows inexorably, if not year by year, then decade by decade. If, in 1852, the state was already what Karl Marx called it, a parasite which "enmeshes society in a net and chokes all its pores,"[89] what must we call it now? This leads us to the question: as between Bastiat and Alfred Marshall,

---

fulfill its primordial duties [the protection of personal liberty and property] but makes itself the center of intrigues, of favors, of transfers of wealth" (415).
88 James Buchanan, "The Potential and Limits of Socially Organized Humanity," in idem, *The Economics and Ethics of Constitutional Order* (Ann Arbor, Mich.: University of Michigan Press, 1991) 248–49.
89 Karl Marx, "The Eighteenth Brumaire of Louis Bonaparte," in Karl Marx and Friedrich Engels, *Selected Works in Three Volumes* (Moscow: Progress Publishers, 1983) 1, 477.

who was—not the better *economist* in a technical sense, a point that is widely assumed to be settled[90]—but who was the better *political economist*? Who better understood the dynamic of state expansion? Was it Bastiat and the other Frenchmen, who insisted on the rule of laissez-faire? Or was it Marshall and the British, whose sage advice was: "Let the state be up and doing!"?

---

90 But see the well-informed essay by Jörg Guido Hülsmann, "Bastiat's Legacy in Economics," *Quarterly Journal of Austrian Economics*, 4, No. 4, where Hülsmann calls him one of history's "greatest economists," as well as his briefer treatment in the *Mises Daily*, February 17, 2006.

7 Ludwig von Mises's *Liberalism* on Fascism, Democracy, and Imperialism

Mises's *Liberalism*

Ludwig von Mises's exposition of liberal economic and political philosophy, *Liberalism*,[1] is noteworthy for a number of reasons.

In the first place, there can be no doubt that Mises was among the foremost liberal thinkers of the twentieth century, if not the foremost.[2] Second, although F.A. Hayek (1992: 145) characterized it as "rather hastily written,"[3] *Liberalism* remains Mises's most systematic attempt "to present a concise statement of the essential meaning" of his social philosophy, and to restate liberalism for the contemporary world (Mises 1978a: 3). Moreover, as will be seen, Mises's presentation raises

---

1 First published as *Liberalismus* in 1927, in Jena by Gustav Fischer and republished in German in 1997, with an important introduction by Hans-Hermann Hoppe. The first edition in English, translated by myself, (Mises 1962) was titled, on Mises's suggestion, *The Free and Prosperous Commonwealth*. In its second edition (1978a), the English version was titled, *Liberalism: A Socio-Economic Exposition*, with a foreword by Louis M. Spadaro. The third edition (1985), with a preface by Bettina Bien Greaves, carried the title, *Liberalism. In the Classical Tradition*. Citations in the text will be from the 1978 edition.
2 F.A. Hayek 1992: 127, for instance, noted that already with the publication in 1922 of *Socialism*, Mises was marked as "the leading interpreter and defender of the free enterprise system." See also the tributes to Mises in Sennholz (ed.), 1956.
3 Hayek also states that it was "less successful" than *Socialism*, hardly a major criticism.

a number of highly important issues regarding his version of the liberal doctrine.

Mises's starting point is itself rather interesting:

> The program of liberalism, therefore, if condensed into a single word, would have to read: *property*, that is, private ownership in the means of production. . . . All the other demands of liberalism result from this fundamental demand. (19, emphasis in the original)

Whether deliberate or not, Mises's statement parallels Marx and Engels's dictum in the *Manifesto*, that the Communist program can be "summarized in a single expression: Abolition of private property" (1848: 22). Just as the two founders of Marxism held that socialism would benefit the great majority of the members of society, so Mises maintained that liberalism, founded on the right to property, was in the general interest. In this respect, his position stands in sharp contrast to two much more famous works on the subject published around the same time.

In his *History of European Liberalism* (1959), which first appeared two years earlier than *Liberalism*, the Italian philosopher Guido de Ruggiero chose to deal with liberalism in an "idealistic" fashion, limiting his treatment of its economic aspect to a few pedestrian and hostile remarks.[4] In 1936, in what was to become another standard work, *The Rise of Liberalism*, Harold Laski did indeed stress the economic dimension of his subject. But, as the book's subtitle—*The Philosophy of a Business Civilization*—suggests, Laski reflected the climate of opinion of his time. He simply assumed with no argument that, as the "product" of the middle or "bourgeois" classes, liberalism served the interests of those classes alone.

---

4 The original Italian edition dates from 1925. Ruggiero's consistently antagonistic attitude towards economic liberalism is reflected in his assault on Frédéric Bastiat. According to Ruggiero 1951: 187, the works of the great French liberal "very properly became a butt for the satire of Socialists," since in them "the hostility towards the State which marks the earlier Liberalism finds . . . a singularly crude and grotesque expression."

In English-speaking countries, Mises's approach goes against the grain of the venerable tradition traceable to John Stuart Mill's *On Liberty*. In that presumptuously titled work, Mill focuses on freedom of discussion and "experiments in living," while explicitly banning from the debate *economic* freedom—freedom of labor, exchange, and contract, property ownership, etc.—areas of much more urgent concern to the vast majority of mankind. More than anyone else, it was the "muddle-headed Mill," as Murray Rothbard (1995: 277–95) aptly termed him,[5] whose great influence has produced the present-day's conceptual morass, with the virtual obliteration of any distinction between liberalism and social democracy (see the essay on "Liberalism True and False," in the present volume).

Following in Mill's footsteps, many expositors of the liberal idea have deemed it possible to discuss the subject while virtually ignoring property rights. That they have viewed as the higher, more ethically elevated road, a choice which has the advantage of not miring the would-be liberal in any embarrassing defense of the rights of property owners. Such is the case, for example, with Isaiah Berlin, in his day celebrated as the premier liberal thinker in Britain. A critic of liberalism has shrewdly noted how, in his vindication of Benjamin Constant, Berlin focuses on Constant's championing of intellectual freedom and personal privacy, "discreetly overlooking, or underplaying, Constant's firm commitment to property power [sic] and a wholly unregulated market" (Arblaster 1984: 234 and 317 n. 29). Like countless other writers, Berlin preferred to carry on his discussion of liberalism in terms of "the value-neutrality of state policy" and "the needs of the human personality." On this side of the Atlantic, the currently most acclaimed liberal writer John Rawls in his major work (1971: 258) is able to state that, "Throughout the

---

5 Rothbard (277) singles out for scorn Mill's famous agility at intellectual "synthesis" for producing "a vast kitchen midden of diverse and contradictory positions." A good example of this trait in Mill is his assertion (1977: 308) of the desirability of "possess[ing] permanently a skillful and efficient body of functionaries—above all, a body able to originate and willing to adopt improvements"—this after pages of warning of the many dangers of state bureaucracy.

choice between a private-property economy and socialism is left open . . ."[6]

Mises and Italian Fascism.

In 1925, a Soviet writer had already labeled Mises "a theorist of fascism" (Kapelush 2002). The publication of *Liberalism* furnished his enemies with considerably more ammunition. Strangely enough, practically the only context in which this work has been mentioned in recent decades is in connection with the short chapter on "The Argument of Fascism" (47–51). Here Mises declares (51):

> It cannot be denied that [Italian] Fascism and similar movements aiming at the establishment of dictatorships are full of the best intentions and that their intervention has for the moment, saved European civilization. The merit that Fascism has thereby won for itself will live on eternally in history.[7]

That Fascism "saved European civilization" from Bolshevism was a commonly held view among anti-Communists of the period. In the same year that *Liberalism* first appeared, for instance, Winston Churchill, visited Italy, met with Mussolini, and publicly lauded "Fascismo's triumphant struggle against the bestial appetites and passions of Leninism," claiming that "it proved the necessary antidote to the Communist poison" (*New York Times* 1927; cf. Hughes 1955: 119–23).

Nonetheless, Mises's remarks in *Liberalism* and a few similar passages from his other writings have given rise to harsh criticism from some socialist writers. In a 1934 article, later republished, Herbert Marcuse (1968: 10) cited this passage in an attempt to show the

---

6 The appallingly anti-individualist implications of Rawls's system are convincingly demonstrated by Antony Flew 1989.

7 When I undertook to translate *Liberalismus* into English in the late 1950s, Mises at one point suggested that I include a translator's note explaining the historical context of these and similar remarks on Italian Fascism. My reply, in retrospect mistaken, was that such a note was superfluous, since the grounds for the views he expressed in 1927 were obvious. The English translation appeared, unfortunately, without any such explanation. I had vastly underestimated the prevelance of historical cluelessness among Mises's socialist critics.

fundamental congruence of liberalism and fascism. Perry Anderson (1992: 8) has alluded to Mises's early position on Fascism in a discussion of the "Intransigent Right" in twentieth century political thought:

> There was no more outspoken champion of classical liberalism in the German-speaking world of the Twenties [than Mises]. Yet the Austrian political scene, dominated as it was by the conflict between a social-democratic Left and a clerical Right, left little room for this outlook. Here Mises had no hesitation; in the struggle against the labor movement, authoritarian rule might well be required. Looking across the border, he could see the virtues of Mussolini. The blackshirts had for the moment saved European civilisation for the principle of private property: "the merit that Fascism has thereby won for itself will live on eternally in history." Advisor to Monsignor Seipel, the prelate who ran Austria in the late Twenties, Mises approved Dollfuss's crushing of labor and democracy[8] in the Thirties, blaming the repression of 1934 which installed a clerical dictatorship on the folly of the Social Democrats in contesting his alliance with Italy.[9]

The most aggressive critic of Mises on this score has been a German writer on twentieth century economic thought, Claus-Dieter Krohn. In a translated work, Krohn asserts that Mises's sympathy for Italian Fascism is attributable to his fear of "the masses' demands for

---

8 As is customary among writers on modern history, by "labor" and "the labor movement" Anderson means coercive labor unionism. By "democracy," he seems to have in mind the socialist-dominated regime in the Vienna of the times, which employed its coercive authority to plunder property owners; see the remarks by Richard M. Ebeling, note 403, below.

9 See also Anderson 1993: 17–18. This is a translated version of the English-language essay, with footnotes added. (I am grateful to Professor Anderson for this reference.) Anderson goes on to claim that Mises also attempted an "exculpation of Austria," by incriminating only Germany in the deeds of the Nazis. He cites Mises's claim that the Austrians were "'the only people on the European continent who—in the days of the Heimwehr—'seriously resisted Hitler.'" (Cf. Mises 1978c: 142.) On this fairly trivial point, Mises can perhaps be forgiven his Austrian patriotism. On his implicit support for the Austrian government in suppressing the Social Democrats, it should be noted that Mises held (1978c: 140–41), correctly, that Mussolini's "was the only government ready to support Austria in her fight against a Nazi take-over" in 1934, and that the Social Democrats' violent opposition to the alliance with Mussolini threatened to lead to a Nazi absorption of Austria, which eventually came to pass.

participation in a modern industrial society and the need for collective regulation of potential social conflicts." Citing the passage from *Liberalism* quoted above, Krohn (1993: 47) states that "as early as 1927 Mises detected in Italian Fascism a welcome bulwark against advancing collectivism," suggesting, deceptively, that Mises continued to support Fascism afterwards.[10]

Krohn presents a more detailed, and venomous, critique of Mises in an earlier work (Krohn 1981: 33–38, 111–17). Here he states that Mises attained the high point of his influence later in America, "in the phase of the Cold War," when he belonged to the group promoting "the so-called totalitarianism theory," which was "less an analytical theory than an irrational defensive-evasive ideology [*Abwehrideologie*]." Mises, in Krohn's view, was always not so much in the tradition of liberalism as in that of the German bourgeoisie, which, out of fear of the "'Red Republic' had often sought protection under the wide wings of the authoritarian state":

> His conceptions of the social order reduced to an apology for private property necessarily required for their realization an authoritarian complement. Just as the great [special] interest-groups from the end of the thirties revealed a growing interest in Italian corporatism, so Mises also demonstrated in this period not merely latent sympathies for Fascism. (Krohn 1981: 37)

Unlike Marcuse and Anderson, Krohn acknowledges that Mises's gratitude to the Fascists was based on their opposition to the perceived Communist threat of the time. He then goes on, however, to misrepresent Mises's position in a paraphrase. According to Mises:

> The fascist movements in Germany[11] and Italy are the progressive force of the future, because they alone have found the élan, in

---

10 In any case, Krohn's statement is characteristically misleading, since Mises's remarks pertain to the period 1919–22, before the establishment of the Fascist regime.

11 This is only one of many examples of Krohn's outright dishonesty. The common understanding of "German fascism" today, especially in Germany, is National Socialism, or Nazism. Mises, of course, always vehemently rejected Nazism in every respect. When he referred to the German movement that was similar to Italian Fascism in its aggressive opposition to

the extreme exigency of the situation, to do away with the traditional limits of justice and morality and to be prepared for "bloody counter-actions." Even if from the standpoint of the liberal some excesses must be condemned, these are in any case only momentary "reflex-actions," and committed in the heat of passion. As the initial anger blows away, Fascist policy would "take on a more moderate course and will probably become even more so with the passage of time," for it cannot be denied "that Fascism and similar movements aiming at the establishment of dictatorships are full of the best intentions and that their intervention has for the moment, saved European civilization. The merit that Fascism has thereby won for itself will live on eternally in history." (Krohn 1981: 37–38)

It should be pointed out at once that Mises's alleged reference to the German and Italian fascist movements as "the progressive force of the future" is pure invention on Krohn's part.

It should also be made clear that the excerpt from Mises occurs in the context of an *attack* on Italian Fascism. Mises criticized and rejected Fascism on a number of crucial grounds: for its illiberal and interventionist economic program, its foreign policy based on force, which "cannot fail to give rise to an endless series of wars," and, most fundamentally, its "complete faith in the decisive power of violence" instead of rational argument to gain ultimate victory (49–51).[12]

Communism, he had in mind (48) the "militarists and nationalists" of the first years following World War I, particularly the Freikorps. As he presents the situation in *Omnipotent Government* (1944: 198–200, 206–07), the danger of a Bolshevik conquest of Germany in January, 1919 was very real. The German Communists had risen in armed revolt and were in control of most of Berlin besides other centers. "But for the nationalist gangs and troops and for the remnants of the old army, they could have seized power throughout Germany. There was but one factor that could stop their assault and that really did stop it: the armed forces of the Right" (1944: 200–01). See also his praise as well as criticism of the Freikorps bands (1944: 206–07). Mises's interpretation of the role of the rightist forces in putting down the Communist uprising of 1919 is supported by the historian of Weimar, Hagen Schulze 1982: 180–82.

12 See also Murray N. Rothbard 1981: 251, n. 3, for a defense of Mises against Marcuse on this issue. A much more balanced critic of Mises, Gerald Mozetic (1992: 33–34 and 36 n. 22 and 33) refers to Mises's assertion that Fascism and similar movements in Germany could never become as brutal as Bolshevism, since they developed in countries with a thousand years

While Krohn does at least allude to Mises's reasoning, by referring to his belief in the Communist menace of the early 1920s, he does not, of course, do justice to Mises's argument. This is in keeping with the prevalent contemporary habit of ignoring the role of international Communism in engendering a violent radical-right backlash.

A half-century ago, the great English historian Herbert Butterfield (1952: 50) complained that ideological bias was leading to a serious distortion of the history of the interwar years:

> It is unfortunate that the partisanship of so much of our historical writing has led to the burying of many significant facts which were well known to the world a few decades ago. Amongst them is the fact that the repeated attempts of the communists to call the mob out into the streets created a desperate problem for the early Weimar republic; indeed they help explain the development of those counter-revolutionary armed bands which at the next stage in the story so assisted the purposes of Hitler. Similarly, the extravagances and outrages of communism in Italy in the years after the First World War helped to provoke a counter-movement so serious that it almost blotted out the memory of them—there emerged the violent bands that followed the leadership of Mussolini.

Butterfield is surely correct here. As the events of the decades preceding the Second World War—and of the war itself—are more and more reduced to set of Hollywood stereotypes, any sense of a *dialectical* process at work fades away. Thus, the circumstances that occasioned—and justified—Mises's approval of the Fascists at an early historical juncture are today virtually forgotten. For this reason, and because it raises questions of fundamental importance for liberal theory, the issue merits extended discussion.

---

of civilization behind them. As Mozetic states, this was "unfortunately, a prognostic disaster," but he notes that "Mises shared this opinion with Karl Renner [the Austrian Social Democratic leader], who also considered the advanced culture of the Germans an insuperable obstacle to fascism, and with many other contemporaries."

Mises begins by pointing out that Italian Fascism (and to an extent similar movements in other countries, such as the Freikorps in Germany) gained prominence in response to what many millions in Europe perceived as a mortal challenge. In 1919, Lenin formed the Third, or Communist, International (Comintern), constituted of the Communist parties throughout the world and openly aiming at world revolution by any means necessary. As Mises states (47), the Comintern parties did not shrink from "the frank espousal of a policy of annihilating opponents."[13]

Already "in December 1917, Lenin had launched a campaign of incitement to terror, encouraging the masses to take the law into their own hands, "to 'rob the robbers' [i.e., despoil the landowners and the bourgeoisie], to perpetrate 'street justice' [practice lynch law], against 'speculators' [i.e., black marketeers], and in general to engage in fratricidal class carnage in town and village" (Leggett: 1981: 54). Grigory Zinoviev, first head of the Comintern, declared, in 1918, that, if necessary, the Bolsheviks would exterminate 10,000,000 people in Russia (Nolte 1987: 558–59 n. 41). In the end, the total was considerably higher. The creation in 1918 of the Cheka—the first incarnation of the Soviet secret police—began the conversion of the Red Terror into a system. This, and economic transformations that wrecked the economy and produced mass famine, was what the Comintern promised to bring to the nations of Europe, and then the world.[14]

---

[13] Mises's analysis of the character of Leninism and the Comintern is confirmed by Stanley G. Payne (1995: 77–78), who writes that among the many oppressive policies introduced by Lenin into the European political equation were "systematic mass terror and mass murder, with institutionalized permanent concentration camps for political prisoners, featuring large-scale forced labor combined with liquidationist policies," and "the liquidation or elimination of entire classes and categories of people ... the [Communist] International created a persistent challenge and menace from the extreme revolutionary left that had never existed before. . . . The response was not simply more rigorous and repressive policies by many governments, but the formation of new rightist anti-Communist groups ready to practice violence in turn . . ."
[14] In the summer of 1919, Zinoviev (later murdered by Stalin) stated (quoted in Pipes 1993: 174–75): "The movement advances with such a dizzying speed that one can confidently say: in a year . . . all Europe shall be Communist. And the struggle for Communism shall be transferred to America, and perhaps to Asia and other parts of the world."

Communist uprisings broke out in various parts of Germany, and Soviet Republics were established, briefly, in Bavaria and Hungary. In 1920, Lenin turned the Polish-Soviet war into a campaign for the conquest and Communization of Poland, as a prelude to further expansion westwards (Pipes 1993: 177–83, 187–93). He called for the "merciless liquidation of landlords and kulaks [successful farmers]," and proposed paying bounties to murderers of "class enemies" (Pipes 1993: 188). The Poles, however, stood firm and stopped the Red Army at the gates of Warsaw.

The Threat of Communist Revolution in Italy

Lenin and the other Bolshevik leaders looked on Italy as a particularly promising area for revolution. The Italian Socialist Party (PSI) fell under the control of the "maximalists," who considered themselves Leninists and looked to the Comintern for ideological direction.

In the program adopted at the Sixteenth Party Congress, in Bologna, in October, 1919, the PSI proclaimed the start of "a period of revolutionary struggle, to bring about the forcible suppression of the bourgeoisie within a short time," and called for the "armed insurrection of the proletarian masses and proletarian soldiers," to institute the dictatorship of the proletariat (cited in Peterson 1982: 279).[15] The Socialists declared that "the proletariat must have recourse to the use of violence for the conquest of power over the bourgeoisie…we must use new and proletarian organizations such as workers' soviets, and we must adhere to the Third International" (cited in Smith 1959: 327–28).

With the general elections of 1919, the PSI became the largest party in parliament, as well as the best organized.[16] Its spokesmen and agitators heralded the coming socialist revolution, as the PSI worked to destabilize state institutions, including parliament as a prelude (Morgan

---

15 Petersen emphasizes, however, that "de facto nothing had happened to give this rhetoric of revolution and violence a firm base on which to plan and act." See also Salvatorelli and Mira 1964: 103–04.

16 It is worth noting that the Bolsheviks had obtained only about 25% of the votes for the Constituent Assembly that met in Petrograd in January, 1918.

1995: 11).[17] The party newspaper, *Avanti!*, went so far as to state that "soon all the parties will be eliminated" (Settembrini 1978: 125–26 and 125 n. 5). When the left-leaning Francesco Nitti was made prime minister, the party's leading intellectual, Antonio Gramsci, hailed him as the Kerensky of the impending Italian Communist revolution (Smith 1959: 330).

Socialist violence had long been a feature of public life in Italy. Directed against employers' property and especially against non-striking workers, it had been systematically practiced by labor unions during industrial disputes. In 1906, the premier Italian social scientist, Vilfredo Pareto (1974: 97–98), complained that the right to strike had turned into "the freedom, for the strikers, to bash in the brains of workers who wish to continue to work and to set fire to the factories with impunity." A decade and a half later, the situation had not improved. In one of his last essays, Pareto again protested that the right to strike had come to be understood as including "the ability to constrain others to do so and to punish strikebreakers." All manner of pressure and violence was permitted the strikers and justified as necessary "to promote the strike, to set conditions advantageous to labor, to facilitate 'the ascent of the proletariat,' the transformations demanded by 'modernity'" (Pareto 1981: 141). In his day, the only ones left to defend the freedom to work were, Pareto ironically wrote, "those abominable Manchesterians" (i.e., the supporters of laissez-faire) (Pareto 1992: 328).

This endemic labor union violence—not limited to Italy, of course—has vanished from the commonly held picture of the rise of Fascism, as well as of the history of the twentieth century in general. The cause of such an Orwellian gap in historical consciousness is to be sought in the mediating intellectual class which has produced the benign picture of "labor" violence (mainly against *other* workers), and which has always been deeply committed to the same pro-union prejudices that Pareto condemned.

---

17 On the leftwing of the Catholic Party (PPI), there were those who joined the Leninist struggle on behalf of the "Christian proletariat" (Morgan 1995: 19).

Union violence in Italy was not confined to the industrial centers. Systematic coercion had already been introduced into large parts of the countryside by the Socialist agricultural unions. A writer sympathetic to these unions has written, of the lands of the Po valley, subject to a chronic labor surplus:

> By a remarkable *tour de force*, the Socialist peasant leagues had overcome this difficulty in the first two decades of the century. But their achievement had a price. The need to maintain cohesion in the face of the constant threat of blacklegging [sic] by unemployed or migrant workers made necessary extremely harsh methods of discipline. Boycotting and violent intimidation were frequent in the "red" provinces. (Lyttelton 1982: 258)

The period 1919–1920 is known as the *biennio rosso*, "the two Red years." Strikes and demonstrations were conducted in an atmosphere of wild rhetoric and "messianic revolutionary expectations" (Morgan 1995: 21–34; Lyttelton 1982: 258). Italy was pounded by a veritable "strikeomania" (*scioperomania*), an incessant series of politically-motivated strikes that, besides creating an economic shambles, claimed many victims killed and wounded (Salvatorelli and Mira 1964: 127–35, 148–49). Socialist excesses in the northern and central countryside and cities, and the lack of any adequate government response, led many to fear an imminent revolutionary takeover.

Membership in the Socialist agricultural union, the *Federterra*, surged; by 1920 it had recruited close to a million members. Its ultimate aim was to collectivize all the farm land, which would be worked by co-operatives of laborers. One strike in July 1920, involving most of the farm workers of Tuscany, ended with a contract which the landowners felt "destroyed the very viability of the commercialized sharecropping system." What the employers especially resented was the *Federterra*'s demand to control the labor supply and employment opportunities. In the end, the employers were forced "to recognise the employment offices run by the *Federterra* as the exclusive source of the supply of labor, and

... year-round employment quotas [were imposed] on all farmers, large and small ..." (Morgan 25–26; see also De Grand 1982: 28–29). As one historian has written:

> An absolute labor monopoly was so crucial yet so precarious in the overpopulated countryside, that it could only be maintained by the discipline and control of the whole agricultural sector, including small peasants who had to be prevented from exchanging labor and thereby avoiding the quota. The system had to be watertight to function at all. This accounted for the coercive aspects of the [Socialist] leagues' attempts to secure and retain the labor monopoly, through fining, boycotting, and sabotaging the crops, livestock, and property of those farmers employing non-union labor and those "blackleg" workers who agreed to work for them. (Morgan 1995: 26)[18]

Another historian observes that violence against employers and non-strikers "often extended to an intolerance of political or religious dissent. . . . Even where the local [Socialist] leadership professed reformist principles, their methods of control were scarcely compatible with the bourgeois liberal order" (Lyttelton 1982: 258–59; see also Joes 1982: 168–70).

In July 1920, representatives of the Italian General Confederation of Labor (CGL) signed a pact in Moscow, adhering to the social revolution and the universal republic of soviets. In September, union workers in Milan, Turin, and Genoa hoisted the Red Flag, seized control of factories, and proceeded to try to run them. "In order to protect the experiment, the works were put in a state of defense, with Red Guards and, in some cases, barbed wire and machine guns" (Salvatorelli and

---

18 Cf. another historian sympathetic to the Socialist unions, Lyttelton 1973: 62–63: "The discipline of the [Socialist] leagues, in order to avoid blacklegging [sic], had been extremely harsh; and many individual workers had suffered." Cf. Settembrini 1978: 154: "The Socialist leagues in fact based their power on the monopoly of manual labor, exercised through harassment whether of the landed proprietors, large and small, and even the share-croppers and tenant farmers, or of the laborers themselves."

Mira 1964: 152). The Socialist unions demanded control of employment and challenged the owners' direction of production. In Turin, workers' councils were formed, which Gramsci and other Communist intellectuals welcomed as the Italian version of the Russian soviets (Morgan 1995: 27).

The local elections of November, 1920 put control of nearly one-third of communal and half of all the provincial councils in the hands of the PSI. Since Socialist influence in the South was minimal, this amounted to Red domination of many of the northern and central districts, especially in Tuscany, Lombardy, Emilia, and the Romagna. Sometimes declaring their towns revolutionary "republics," the local Socialists "announced their intention to use the communes as a springboard for revolution" (Lyttelton 1982: 259). "Socialist councils used their powers to raise taxes on wealth and property, increased spending on public services, favored workers' co-operatives in municipal contracts, and subsidized consumer co-operatives to undercut the private retail and distribution trades" (Morgan 1995: 27).[19]

Millions in the middle classes became convinced that Bolshevism was on the point of overwhelming the country. Nowadays, it has become customary to maintain that the Communist threat was all bluff and posturing, mere "verbal revolutionism" (Knox 2000: 34),[20] "all bark and

---

[19] Maffeo Pantaleoni (1922: xxxvi) noted that the Socialist administration in Milan went so far as to raise a loan in the United States, "in order to eat up even the future revenue of the taxpayers." Interestingly, as Richard M. Ebeling points out (2002: xxix–xxxi), the Social Democrats who controlled post-World War I Vienna pursued a similar program, massively subsidizing their clienteles through an array of welfare programs and rent control and other regulations. The heavy burden of new taxes and other measures amounted to the large scale plundering of those considered relatively affluent. Naturally, Mises was a close observer of these events and strenuously fought against the socialists, but, as he finally admitted, to little avail. See also Hoppe 1993: 21.

[20] Cf. Vivarelli 1991: 40: "a vast number of monographs on local situations as well as on general aspects of socialist policy during the years 1918–22 have proved beyond any doubt how fatally damaging revolutionary socialism was in upsetting the Italian parliamentary regime and in spreading all over the country the fear of civil war. It is well known how well this fear played into the hands of the fascists."

no bite" (Smith 1959: 328).[21] This was not, however, the view of contemporaries.[22] As Philip Morgan (1995: 27) writes, of the real prospect of a Bolshevik Italy: "in late 1920, after the propertied classes had suffered disastrous economic and political defeats in north and central Italy, this was exactly the perception of recent events. At a local and provincial level, the Socialist revolution was being inaugurated; it was already under way."[23]

Meanwhile, the government vacillated. A decree of 1919 permitted "temporary occupation of uncultivated land," which had the predictable effect of inciting more occupations. The government officially assumed a posture of "neutrality" in labor disputes, which meant scant protection for the rights of property or of non-striking workers. In the seizure of the factories, it refused to use force to evict the workers, and in fact supported their right to share in running the factories (Lyttelton 1973: 38; Salvatorelli and Mira 1964: 40–41).

The Fascist Reaction as Middle-Class Self-Help

The events of the *biennio rosso* provided the occasion for the spectacular rise of the Fascist movement, which until then had lacked focus and support. It is astonishing but symptomatic that the torrent of

---

21 In a later work (1982: 41), Smith continues to maintain that it should have been obvious that "Italy's trade unionists and socialists were not of Lenin's ilk and would never seize control of the state: they were revolutionaries only in name and would be defenseless if the fascist armed squads went into action against them." He adds (55), concerning widespread public support for Mussolini's seizure of power in 1922: "Fear of communism can have been only a minor motive as there was no communist threat." This is an astonishing non sequitur for such a famous historian to have committed. Leaving aside the question of the reality of a Communist threat, what is more obvious than that people's actions are conditioned by their perceptions and subjective estimations and not merely by the "objective" situation?
22 Settembrini (1978: 125–29) states that the only contemporary who understood the real position of the Socialists in Italy was—Mussolini, the ex-Socialist, who composed a sophisticated analysis of the political realities confronting his former comrades.
23 Philip Morgan writes (1995: 34): "Socialism provided the platform for the counter-reaction of Fascism. It created the fears on which Fascism grew, and almost literally set the stage for Fascism." Cf. Carsten 1967: 55: "It is thus somewhat superficial to consider the fears of the middle classes unjustified and exaggerated. In retrospect they certainly were, but at the time the middle classes' existence seemed at stake, and the Bolshevist danger appeared very real." See also the arguments of an early liberal Fascist, Leandro Arpinati, that Fascism prevented a Communist takeover, in Iraci 1970: 41–45.

Socialist violence goes unmentioned in a standard work on Mussolini by Denis Mack Smith, of All Souls College, Oxford, the *doyen* of Anglophone historians of modern Italy.[24]

The great increase in Fascist membership and influence came initially in the rural areas, where Fascist squads (*squadre*) were formed. (This element of the overall Fascist movement is referred to as *squadrismo*, and the members of the *squadre* as *squadristi*.)

> The squads were gangs of mainly middle-class young men, many of whom had served as lower-rank officers during the war. They were university and secondary school students, sons of the professional people, local traders, officials, businessmen and farmers who supported or sympathized with Fascism's drive against socialism. (Morgan 1995: 50)

The Socialist program had alienated even many sharecroppers and tenant farmers, who, together with other agrarians and local businessmen, financed and equipped the Fascist *squadre*. Especially in the Po valley, the *squadre* were often supported and joined by small proprietors, leaseholders, and sharecroppers, as a defensive measure against the Socialists' mobilization of the day laborers and their long-range goal of collectivizing the land.[25]

---

24 See his *Mussolini* 1982: 35–56, including his extraordinary statement (36) that the Socialists were "essentially pacifists." In an earlier work 1959: 348, Smith asserted: "Socialist counterviolence [sic] in the countryside was equally horrible and inexcusable . . . whoever started the reign of terror, the fascists were certainly better organized, better armed, and had more money . . ." Somehow or other, two decades later, Smith had lost sight of the "horrible and inexcusable" "counterviolence" of the Socialist "pacifists." Jan Petersen's conclusion 1982: 278 seems very much to the point: "the fact that the violence of Left and Right existed both successively and simultaneously, that its causes and justifications are inextricably tangled, constitutes a very singular feature which so far has not been adequately studied . . ." In a remarkably uninformed piece, Oxford don John Gray (1996: 14) is able to treat European fascism with no mention at all of any Communist threat anywhere in the 1920s and 30s, and no mention whatever of the Comintern. Instead, he finds room in his review to castigate the followers of Herbert Spencer and Albert Jay Nock as dangers to present-day democracy.

25 Cf. Lyttelton 1982: 267: "Here it is impossible to overlook the contribution of socialist violence to the genesis of agrarian squadrismo. In Ferrara at least it was the small [anti-Socialist] leaseholders who were most in danger of their lives . . ." The Socialists often attacked even members of the Catholic peasant organizations. Salvatorelli and Mira (1964: 171) point out that in the Po valley many older landowners, fearing the Socialists, had sold out to tenants

Farmers and local businessmen complained bitterly of the failure of the government to protect their property. For them, supporting the *squadre* was "a kind of middle-class self-help" (Morgan 1995: 56; see also Lyttelton 1973: 37, 60–61). In Carrara, where the local Socialist authorities threatened outright expropriation of the marble quarries, the *squadristi* very forcefully disrupted their plans. In Genoa, the squads, largely composed of non-union workers, broke the union monopoly over the docks, winning the acclaim of the workers who had until then been excluded (Lyttelton 1973: 70–71).

The counter-actions of the *squadre* were by no means merely defensive in any narrow sense. Instead, they undertook a successful campaign of violence to root out the Socialist "infrastructure." Applying physical force that their opponents could not match, the Fascists destroyed Socialist-run town halls, union headquarters, newspapers, and "cultural centers."

It goes without saying that the Fascists can be sharply and legitimately criticized on a number of counts, including their violent excesses and their ultimate statist program. It is odd, however, to read in a standard history of the Fascist coming to power of "the sordid facts behind *squadrismo*," namely, its "dependence on official police connivance and funds from industrialists or agrarians" (Lyttelton 1973: 54). One wonders what exactly was "sordid" about property owners resorting to the only means open to them to safeguard their rights. Such rebukes—and they are routine—bring to mind the French saying:

> *Cet animal est très méchant;*
> *Quand on l'attaque il se défend.*
> This animal is quite vicious;
> When attacked it defends itself.[26]

---

and share-croppers: "in defending the possessions they had finally acquired, with the rights and interests attached to them, the new proprietors displayed a combativeness unknown to their predecessors."

26 Cf. Salvatorelli and Mira 1964: 177: "Many of the bourgeoisie, especially the young and war veterans" came to believe that "the neutrality of the government in the class conflict [was] ... by now incapable of guaranteeing respect for the law and the constituted order, and turned to fascism." By 1921, Pantaleoni 1922: 108 was exulting that the fascist counter-attack had

The Italian Economists and "the Insurrection against Bolshevism"

How to maintain liberal constitutional principles in the face of a radical-socialist movement menacing the foundations of the social order—above all, private property—had deeply troubled liberals in central and eastern Europe in the later nineteenth century. Confronted with a rising socialist party in a German Empire, where the Reichstag was elected by universal manhood suffrage, John Prince Smith, the founder of the German free-trade movement and its leader for over three decades, ended as an advocate of the military-authoritarian state (Raico 1999: 77–86).[27] In Russia, Boris Chicherin, eminent legal historian and social philosopher and the leading Russian liberal of his time, declared: "At the sight of this communist movement nothing remains for the sincere liberal but to support [Tsarist] absolutism . . ." (Leontovitsch 1957: 142). In the crisis produced by radical socialism in Italy, liberals—including notables like Benedetto Croce and Luigi Albertini—reacted similarly, welcoming Fascism to one degree or another (Benedetti 1967; Cannistraro (ed.) 1982; Lyttelton 1973: 38).[28] Among the more enthusiastic supporters of the Fascist movement were the Italian liberal economists.

In his *History of Economic Analysis*, Joseph Schumpeter (1954: 855) wrote:

> The most benevolent observer could not have paid any compliments to Italian economics in the early 1870s; the most malevolent

---

demonstrated how "discredited is by now the theory that the [Italian] bourgeoisie, like the French aristocracy of 1789, would of its own climb into the wagon carrying it to the guillotine."

27 The first important liberal thinker to have evolved into a supporter of an authoritarian state under the perceived threat of socialism may well have been Charles Dunoyer; see Edgard Allix 1911 and the essay on "The Conflict of Classes: Liberal vs. Marxist Theories," in the present work.

28 Denis Mack Smith 1959: 360–61 professes to be baffled by this general support for the early fascist movement by Italian liberals; it shows, he claims, that they "put riches and comfort before liberty." Given that the liberals believed that Italy might very well be on the verge of a Leninist revolution—with all the terror, persecution, mass murder, and famine that implied—it is amazing how little historical *Verstehen* for the motives of the Italian liberals Smith displays in his naïve "analysis."

observer could not have denied that it was second to none by 1914.

Most of the noted Italian economists Schumpeter had in mind were politically speaking classical economic liberals, or, in the Italian terminology, *liberisti*.[29]

A small but prestigious economic-liberal movement had existed in Italy throughout the nineteenth century. In the later decades of the century, the writers in this camp were harsh critics both of the interventionist Italian state, with its corrupt support of capitalist special interests at the expense of taxpayers and consumers, and of the incipient socialist movement.

With the Leninist turn of the PSI after the First World War and the emergence of the Fascist movement, the liberal economists began openly to side with the latter. A particularly distinguished member of the group was Maffeo Pantaleoni, whom Hayek referred to (1991: 360) as the author of "one of the most brilliant summaries of economic theory that has ever appeared."[30] Pantaleoni, the longtime friend of Vilfredo Pareto, to whom he introduced the writings of Walras, was among Fascism's earliest and most fervent supporters. "If it had not been for the intervention of Fascism," he wrote (1922: vii), "Italy would have suffered not merely an economic and political catastrophe, but rather a catastrophe of its very civilization, equal in its kind to that of Russia and Hungary."[31]

---

29 Italian appears to be the only language in which a distinction is drawn between *liberale*, *liberalismo* (liberal, liberalism), on the one hand, and *liberista*, *liberismo* (economic liberal, economic liberalism), on the other.

30 Hayek had in mind Pantaleoni's *Principii di economia pura* (1889). Schumpeter, too, (1954: 857 and n. 4) had a high opinion of this work, as of Pantaleoni's scientific contributions in general. He endorsed Edgeworth's judgment that the *Principi* was a "gem," and wrote that Pantaleoni "understood 'pure theory' as few people ever did." It should be noted, however, that Pantaleoni's methodology was essentially Walrasian and by no means in the tradition of the Austrian school.

31 Pantaleoni adds (1922: viii, xxxi emphasis in original): "I say: a catastrophe of the Russian or Hungarian *kind*, because with us it would have been even graver, by reason of the *enormous density of our population*." Italy was saved from the "destructive hurricane" of Bolshevism "only by fascism and by the heroism of the fascists who died *pro libertate Patriae* in the struggle of civil war." On Pantaleoni's politics, see the *Enciclopedia Italiana* and Ricci 1939: 15–16,

The most famous (or notorious) liberal supporter of Fascism, Pareto himself, was by no means the most committed. Yet in the end he endorsed the Fascist takeover, and, a year before his death, permitted Mussolini to appoint him to the Senate.

At the beginning of his career as an economist, Pareto was, ideologically, a crusading liberal doctrinaire, an Italian version of the *Journal des Économistes* writers like Gustave de Molinari, with whom he was in close contact and whom he addressed as *cher maître*. Pareto contributed frequently to that Parisian journal, the flagship of the laissez-faire idea in Europe, and even occasionally to *Liberty*, the organ of the American individualist-anarchist movement headed by Benjamin Tucker. He revealed his idealistic motives to his friend Pantaleoni (Pareto 1962, 1: 103): "What is the use even if we advance economic science, if then we are alone, the few of us, to know the truth? Isn't it our duty to have others know it as well? To strive so that justice vanquishes the corruption and injustice that oppresses us?" His chief animus was reserved for the thieving interventionist, "pro-business" establishment, while he expressed admiration for the courage and sincerity of the young Italians who were becoming converts to socialism. During the persecution of the left by the Italian government in the late 1890s, he personally assisted socialist refugees in his home in Lausanne, as Pantaleoni did in Geneva. (Pareto 1962, 1: 500; 2: 197).[32]

But Pareto soon began to grow skeptical of the good faith of the socialists. Even while the Italian government was oppressing socialists, in Geneva socialist-led workers, including many Italians, were physically assaulting workers who refused to join a strike of masons: "The socialist

---

25, where Pantaleoni is referred to as a "friend of Mussolini and of Fascism." Pantaleoni's position was similar to that of Mises, e.g., when the Italian economist states 1922: 131–32: "As regards socialism in action, there is no other remedy than to oppose force to force. And it is here that, in the present state of affairs, the work of fascism is the most useful work of all for the salvation of the civilization of our country. When the Bolshevik assault—whose preparation over many years we tolerated—shall have been stopped, then our work of education, of propaganda, and of vigilance can be effective in forming sentiments different from the present ones and in enlarging the sphere of influence of logical actions."

32 See also Pareto 1980: 108. This work is an excellent compilation of the essentially liberal Pareto in the various phases of his career.

gentlemen in Italy ask only for liberty; here [in Switzerland] they have it, and look at them becoming the tyrants. They cease being victims only to become persecutors . . . the violent acts of the socialists in Geneva, in France, etc., will finish with justifying the Italian and German governments" in their suppression of socialism. By 1898 he had already concluded that: "Against force there remains nothing to oppose but force" (Pareto 1962, 2: 224–25).[33]

In the years that followed, Pareto became embittered and thoroughly disillusioned. The astonishing popularity of Marxism in Italy led him to recast his sociological views to emphasize the priority of the irrational in human affairs (Finer 1966: 11, Finer 1968: 447–48; and Rothbard 1995: 455–59). Social and economic theories are deployed in political struggles not in virtue of their "objective value," but "rather principally for the quality they may have of evoking emotions" (Pareto 1974: 98).

Pareto was particularly disgusted by the growing "humanitarianism" of the bourgeoisie, which expressed itself in sympathy for the excesses of unionized labor and even in a "sentimental mania" for the criminal element. The bourgeoisie manifested its decadence through its support of educators who taught that capitalism was founded on theft and of writers who besmirched every decent social value and undermined the very foundations of society (Pareto 1981: 90–95). Instead of fighting manfully for its rights, the bourgeoisie was basely surrendering to its socialist enemies. Pareto was fond of quoting the Genoese proverb: "He who plays the sheep will find the butcher."[34]

The decay of the Italian bourgeoisie could be traced in the transformation of its political expression, the Liberal party, according

---

[33] Another inkling of Pareto's later pro-Fascist position is his suggestion that the author of an article in the socialist paper *Avanti!* endorsing the strikers' violence should be taken care of by General Bava Beccaris, who had just supervised a massacre of violently protesting socialists in Milan.

[34] Cf. Pareto's statement 1991: 93: "To lack the courage needed to defend oneself, to abandon any resistance, to submit to the generosity of the victor, even more, to carry cowardice to the point of assisting him and facilitating his victory, is the characteristic of the feeble and degenerate man. Such an individual merits nothing but scorn, and for the good of society it is useful that he should disappear as quickly as possible."

to Pareto. "In the time of Cavour, the party that called itself liberal aimed at respecting the liberty to dispose of one's own goods, then it limited it more and more, finally permitting the occupation of the lands and factories and the infinite acts of demagogic insolence of the *biennio* 1919–20" (Pareto 1981: 157). In fact, he came to see liberalism as having paved the way for "the demagogic oppression" of his own time. The liberals who demanded equality of taxation on behalf of the poor, for instance, "did not imagine that they would obtain progressive taxation to the disadvantage of the well-off, and that they would end up with an arrangement in which taxes are voted by those who do not pay them" (Pareto 1974: 97–98).

Witnessing the birth of the Fascist movement (he died in 1923), Pareto looked on it as a healthy reaction to the crisis of the Italian body politic:

> One of the principal ends of every government is the protection of persons and property; if it neglects this, then from the bosom of the people there arise forces capable of making good the deficiency. . . . [Fascism arose] as a spontaneous and somewhat anarchical reaction of a part of the population to the "Red tyranny," which the government permitted to run rampant, leaving it to private individuals alone to defend themselves. (Pareto 1981: 148)[35]

Fascism was a welcome sign that at least a certain physical courage was not lacking in the Italian bourgeoisie. But, essentially a classical liberal to the end, in one of his last articles Pareto warned the Fascist leaders against the dangers of abuses of power and of entanglement in foreign military adventures. To avoid such mistakes, he urged provision of "an ample freedom of the press" (Pareto 1981: 160).

Another leading free-trade economist was Antonio de Viti de Marco. Looking back after a decade, de Viti de Marco described the

---

35 Cf. Femia 1998: 160, who writes that it was small wonder that Pareto "welcomed fascism as the only possible savior of values he held dear—sound money, public probity, market discipline, personal responsibility. Pareto thus became a fascist by default. . . . The totalitarian nature of fascism was not self-evident in those embryonic stages."

"fearful period of complete anarchy" of the *biennio rosso*, when the authority of the law had given way "to the arbitrary will of private groups, even to the destructive instinct of the slums and the violent men of every private group." Railroad and telegraph workers considered themselves the bosses of the public services, strikes were called to intimidate the public, the homeless occupied the homes of private citizens, shops were ransacked under the eyes of the police, the workers took over the factories, and the agricultural laborers took over the land (de Viti de Marco 1929: viii–ix).

> Against the chaos there rose up Fascism, the private organization of resistance, without doubt a sign of vitality in the nation. With *squadrismo* one had the phenomena typical of a civil war. The victorious party re-established public order and took the place of the state that had practically disappeared; then it shaped it little by little in its image. (de Viti de Marco 1929: ix)

Of all the Italian free-trade economists, Luigi Einaudi was to become the most prominent and achieve the greatest political influence. After the Second World War, Einaudi became the first president of the Italian Republic and probably the best known liberal in Europe. Though he was no "dogmatic" liberal, he shared the views of the *liberisti* school both on the basic malignancy of the Italian political and economic order and the dangers of socialism for his country. The sinister alliance of the parasitism of the industrialists and the privileged unionized workers was a special target of his attacks. Together with the other economists, Einaudi hailed the emergence of the Fascist movement and Mussolini's ascent to power. Revolted by the Socialists, who were preoccupied with "obtaining funds and loans and works and favors for their co-operatives, influence over economic affairs for their organizers, even at the cost of ruining industry with their controls," Einaudi extolled the Black Shirts as "those ardent youths who summoned the Italians to insurrection against Bolshevism." The struggle between the Fascists and Socialists he characterized as a conflict between "the spirit of liberty and the spirit of oppression" (Decleva 1965: 218; Vivarelli 1981: 309–10).[36]

Thus, Mises was hardly alone among liberal thinkers in praising Fascism at an early stage of the movement. In fact, he was simply reiterating the views of those in Italy in the best position to know. His critics, however, whether out of pure ignorance or bad faith, have neglected to acquaint themselves with that fact.

The Impasse of the Italian Rent-Seeking State

The condemnation of the Italian "liberal" state by the liberal economists stemmed from their fundamental social philosophy. Drawing on the rich nineteenth century liberal tradition of social analysis, including the thought of Herbert Spencer, the *liberisti* stressed that society prospers and progresses through creative human production and exchange. Yet historically, much of this advance has been rendered nugatory by the process of *spogliazione*, or plunder—by wandering bands of barbarians, by criminals, or by those who make use of the state power for their own rapacious ends. The decades following unification, they believed, had seen the creation of a multifaceted system of plunder, organized by the governing class for the benefit of various parasitic categories of the populace (Vivarelli 1981: 241–53 and passim).[37]

---

[36] Most of the liberals, including Einaudi and the other economists, broke with the Fascist regime, in most cases rather quickly. They were disillusioned by the dictatorial methods, and, in the case of the economists, by the continuation and even intensification of parasitism under the new regime. De Viti de Marco 1929: ix clearly distinguished the two aspects of the *liberisti* relationship to Fascism: "These are two distinct phases: in the first, fascism confronted socialism that had degenerated into Bolshevism; in the second, it opposes those who place the liberties of the individual at the foundation of the state. We had in common with fascism a point of departure: the critique and the struggle against the old regime."

[37] It was no accident, of course, that a number of these liberal economists were among the pioneers of the "Scienza delle finanze," which James Buchanan 1960: 24–74 credits with influencing his public choice orientation. However, in discussing "the theory of the ruling class" of the Italian economists (32–33), Buchanan, in this early essay, neglects the real derivation of that approach, which is from Dunoyer and Charles Comte, via Bastiat, Molinari, and Francesco Ferrara; here the key concept was *spoliation*. Buchanan also confuses the issue by suggesting that democratic decision-making would, in the Italian theory, provide a solution for the problems of ruling-class government. Pantaleoni, for one, was a bitter opponent of universal suffrage precisely because of the immense vista it opens up for lower-class plunder of the economically successful.

The domination of Italian politics by special interests was evident virtually from the beginnings of the Italian constitutional monarchy. Later, under the "liberal" regime of Giovanni Giolitti, the Chamber of Deputies was turned into a permanent carnival of shameless rent-seekers and their agents. As de Viti de Marco (1929: vii) sketched it:

> The advance of the liberal and democratic idea [in Italy] has consisted in the gradual extension of legislative favors, passing from the major to the minor groups, from the older established groups to the newly established ones, from the landed proprietors to the industrialists, to the state functionaries, to the laborers' co-operatives, to the proletarian organizations. There was the hierarchy of the great, the medium, and the little privileges. Parliament became, logically, the marketplace where state favors, great and small, were bargained for, the costs of which were paid for by the great mass of consumers and taxpayers. The defense of the latter was banished from the parliamentary arena.

Typical of the Italian economists, Pareto was a fierce, even fanatical opponent of the "plutocracy," or "pluto-democracy" that reigned in Italy (Femia 1998). Tariffs, government contracts, naval and military spending, nationalized industries, tax policy, social welfare, the legal privileging of labor unions were among the means at the disposal of the governing class to exploit the public at large for the benefit of its various clienteles. As one scholar noted, in Pareto's view:

> Parliament is a necessary part of this arrangement, for it acts as a forum in which these transactions and arrangements between the various clienteles . . . are "aggregated" and it also acts as a platform by which the masses are persuaded to assent to them. (Finer 1968: 447–48)

Thus, from the outset liberals like Pareto had no great love for "parliamentary democracy."

For a time, Mussolini gave the impression that he intended to cleanse the Augean stables of the Italian rent-seeking state. He spoke of privatizing public services, including secondary education, of slashing spending, taxes, and bureaucracy, even of reducing the state to, in his phrase, the "Manchesterian conception." There were suggestions of a "Paretian" revolution in the offing, with Mussolini calling for a new front of "producers" to combat the "parasites" of the political class and the Socialist communal bureaucracy (Smith 1959: 350–51; Morgan 1995: 48, 51).[38]

The Fascist economic program of July, 1922, elaborated by Ottavio Corgini and Massimo Rocca, two economic liberals, seemed to herald such a revolution (Papa 1970: 66). Einaudi endorsed the program enthusiastically, describing it as a return "to the old-fashioned liberal traditions ... to the pristine sources of the modern state" (Decleva 1965: 228). Mussolini's appointment of the *liberista* Alberto de Stefani as Minister of Finance was seen in the same welcome light.[39] Looked on by his admirers as a modern-day Turgot, de Stefani was, unfortunately, doomed to suffer the same fate as Turgot had in the France of the 1770s, when his program of liberalization collided with the hard realities of entrenched special interest politics.

Edoardo Giretti was probably came closer than anyone else to being an Italian version of Richard Cobden, although it is deeply disappointing that Giretti, like the other liberal economists, supported his country's disastrous entry into the European War, a position that Cobden would not have countenanced for a minute.[40] For decades a tireless crusader for free trade, Giretti was a leading participant in the Italian peace movement, a bitter opponent of military expenditures and colonial adventures, particularly the Libyan war of 1911 (Cooper 1986: 210–11).

---

38 Mussolini's major pronouncement in this direction was his speech of June 21, 1921 in the Chamber, which Pantaleoni 1922: 211–13, unsurprisingly, praised profusely. Interestingly, he endorsed (212) Mussolini's demand that the state cease acting as "the monopolizer and censor of thought with [its control of] the post and the school." Pantaleoni was also happy to report (249) that in a speech of November 8, 1921, Mussolini stated: "In economic matters, we are liberals in the more classical sense of the word."
39 Industrial interests forced De Stefani out of office in 1925, on account of his opposition to tariffs and subsidies. See Cannistraro (ed.) 1982, s.v. "De Stefani, Alberto."
40 In taking a pro-war position, the Italian liberals were tragically misled by their equation of Germany with statism and Britain and France with "liberalism." In this case, they were oblivious not only to the dynamics of the mobilization of the state for war, but also to the "law of unintended consequences" that rules in politics.

He was fond of the "sublime motto" of William the Silent: "There is no need of hope in order to endeavor, nor of success in order to persevere." In an obituary notice, his friend Luigi Einaudi said that the motto applied perfectly to Giretti's life (Einaudi 1941: 67. See also Josephson [ed.] [1985] s.v. "Giretti, Edoardo").

Giretti's initial support of the Fascist movement is highly illuminating:

> I am more than ever convinced that without economic liberty, liberalism is an abstraction devoid of any real content, when it is not a mere electoral hypocrisy and imposture. If Mussolini with his political dictatorship will give us a regime of greater economic freedom than that which we have had from the dominant parliamentary mafias in the last one hundred years, the sum of good which the country could derive from his government would surpass by far that of evil. (Papa 1970: 67)[41]

Thus, at this early point, Giretti, like the other *liberisti*, shared the interpretation of Fascism which one scholar has attributed to Luigi Albertini, editor of Italy's most influential newspaper *Corriere della Sera*, that it was "a movement at once anti-Bolshevik (in the name of the authority of the state) and economically liberal, capable, that is, of giving a new vigor" to the liberal idea in Italy (Decleva 1965: 233).

A major early Fascist figure who was also an economic liberal was Leandro Arpinati, leader of the *squadristi* of Bologna. Arpinati later broke with Mussolini over the latter's increasingly interventionist economic policies and was placed under close Fascist surveillance. He was murdered in 1945, during the liberation, by Communist partisans (Iraci 1970).

---

41 The term used by Giretti that is here translated as "mafias" is *camorre*, and refers to the Neapolitan version of the Sicilian mafia.

Democratic Quandaries

The episode of Fascism and the support it garnered from the liberal economists suggests certain problems for democratic theory, particularly as set forth by Mises in *Liberalism*.

According to Mises (1978a: 39), a liberal state "must not only be able to protect private property; it must also be so constituted that the smooth and peaceful course of its development is never interrupted by civil wars, revolutions, or insurrections." Mises was no adherent of the "classical republican," or "civic humanist" ideal. Unlike Benjamin Constant and particularly Alexis de Tocqueville, for instance, he makes no mention of the value of democratic participation in elevating and helping perfect the character of the citizens. In Mises's analysis (41–42), the fundamental justification of democracy is that, when it comes down to it, "the majority will have the power to carry out its wishes by force. . . . Democracy is that form of political constitution which makes possible the adaptation of the government to the wishes of the governed without violent struggles . . . no civil war is necessary to put into office those who are willing to work to suit the majority."[42]

While it is true that in Italy during the *biennio rosso* the Socialists never enjoyed a parliamentary majority,[43] they nevertheless did obtain majorities in numerous city and district elections. Pareto (1981: 150) describes how the victorious Socialists conducted themselves:

> The conquest of the municipalities was for [the Socialists] merely the occasion for plunder, for dividing among themselves the

---

[42] Hans-Hermann Hoppe (2001: 79–80) states, on the basis of some of Mises's earlier writings and of the section in *Liberalism* on "The Right of Self-Determination" (108–10) that Mises's proclamation of a virtually unlimited right of secession (down to "a single village, a whole district, or a series of adjacent districts") would obviate the dangers to liberty and property posed by democratic rule in the conventional sense. But Mises also asserts that self-determination in his sense would lead to "the formation of states composed of a single nationality" (110). Moreover, he writes that realization of self-determination "is the only feasible and effective way of preventing revolutions and civil and international wars" (109). How might this apply to post-World War I Italy? Could a liberal order have been preserved by, say, the secession of the wealthier districts in Milan and Bologna from the socialist municipal jurisdictions? Would their secession have prevented civil war in those areas?

[43] In Germany in 1919, it is certain that the Communists did not have the support of the majority of the population.

product of taxes, increasing them beyond any measure, and squandering the endowments of the charitable institutions and hospitals. There was a moment when Milan and Bologna became little states independent of the central power.[44]

Some questions suggest themselves. On what basis is a liberal required to submit to the "majority will" in cases such as this? Is it possible that the course adopted by the Fascist *squadre*, of disrupting the democratically elected Socialist administrations, was preferable to permitting them to plunder property at will? Suppose that the Italian Socialists *had* acquired a majority in the country at large and proceeded to implement a Leninist economic program through parliamentary means: would their opponents have been obliged to accede to this?

The question had already been raised and answer by Pareto's mentor, Gustave de Molinari, in this famous essay "On the Production of Security," the first exposition of the anarcho-capitalist argument. Molinari strenuously rejects the notion that property owners were in any way obliged to accede passively to the confiscatory measures of a socialist democratic majority. This point is discussed in the essay on "The Centrality of French Liberalism," in the present volume.

Today the question of the legitimacy of the democratic regime—of the moral right of the democratic state to the obedience of its subjects—becomes more pressing as that state lays claim to ever greater portions of its subjects' property and ever deeper levels of their freedom. At what point are citizens morally justified in replying with force to the state's expropriation of their wealth for redistributionist purposes—or of its assumption of ever greater control over the minds and character of themselves and of their children? What recourse legitimately remains to citizens if the democratic state should, for example, decide to confiscate all firearms in private hands?

Mises admits (45) that "if judicious men see their nation . . . on the road to destruction" they may well be tempted to use forcible means to avert general disaster. But this enlightened minority will not, he holds,

---

44 Pareto held that, instead of proceeding to seize power in Italy, the Socialists busied themselves with immediately dividing the spoils of their victories.

be able to maintain itself in power unless it convinces the majority. Yet, is this necessarily so? Doesn't everything here depend on the particular circumstances of the case, the relative passivity of the majority and the unflinching resolve of the minority threatened in its rights?[45]

Similar questions arise in regard to the second consideration on the minds of the Italian economists: the possibility of using Fascism to break the impasse of the rent-seeking state. In reality, that did not come about; instead, under Mussolini the state became even more interventionist and burdensome than before, besides embroiling Italy in absurd and catastrophic military adventures. However, such an outcome would not appear to be inevitable, given different historical conditions.

It would seem, then, that a liberal of Mises's way of thinking owes an answer to Pareto's proposition (1981: 154), set forth after Mussolini's assumption of power: "A coup d'état can be useful or damaging to the country, depending on the use that is made of power obtained by it. For now, it seems that in Italy, one is on the right road."

But How Is a Liberal Order to be Maintained?

In his memoirs, Mises wrote (1978c: 68), of the great questions of politics:

> The people must decide. It is true, economists have the duty to inform their fellow men. But what happens if these economists do not measure up to the dialectic task and are pushed aside by demagogues? Or if the masses lack the intelligence to understand the teachings of the economists? Is the attempt to guide the people on the right road not hopeless, especially when we recognize that men like John Maynard Keynes, Bertrand Russell, Harold Laski and Albert Einstein could not comprehend economic problems?

---

45 Mises (1978a: 45–46) cites the Bolsheviks as an example of the futility of attempts at minority rule: they were forced against their will to concede private ownership of land because of the irresistible demands of the peasants. But Mises wrote this in 1927; a very few years later the Soviets totally reversed their policy on the land question, carried out unprecedented terrorism and mass murder of the peasantry, and ruled for another sixty years.

This was an expression of the despair that assailed Mises at the time of the First World War. By what means could the masses in democratic societies be won for the principles of private property and the free market? It was a problem that had claimed the attention of liberals from at least the time of the Idéologues around 1800, in France. Richard Cobden and the German liberal leader Eugen Richter were among those who followed these French writers in proposing the use of the public education system to instill the principles of sound economics in the masses.[46] More generally, it was supposed to be the task of all true liberals to foster "public enlightenment" in order to forestall popular acceptance of disastrous economic and social policies. Mises (1978c: 69, emphasis added) considers this option:

> It has been said that the problem lies with public education and information. But we are badly deceived to believe that more schools and lectures, or a popularization of books and journals could promote the right doctrine to victory. In fact, false doctrines can recruit their followers the same way. *The evil consists precisely in the people's intellectual disqualifications to choose the means that lead to the desired objectives.* The fact that facile decisions can be foisted onto the people demonstrates that they are incapable of independent judgment. This is precisely the great danger.

Mises candidly concedes the logical implication of this view, as far as he was personally concerned: "I thus had arrived at this hopeless pessimism that for a long time had burdened the best minds of Europe." What escape could there be from this pessimism? He tells us that in his *Gymnasium* days he had chosen as his personal motto a verse from Virgil: *Tu ne cede malis sed contra audentior ito* ("Do not yield to the bad, but

---

[46] This course foundered, among other reasons, because the direction of public education in western countries was eventually assumed by forces hostile to liberal ideals. Benjamin Constant, in the early nineteenth century, had already warned against the use of state power—including the educational system—to promote a desirable ideology for the very reason that it was in this sense a two-edged sword. Montalembert, leader of the French Liberal Catholics in the mid-nineteenth century, understood why state education and state teachers undermined both religion and property rights. See the essay "The Centrality of French Liberalism," in the present book.

always oppose it with courage"). He resolved to "do everything an economist could do. I would not tire in professing what I knew to be right." He proceeded with his plan to write a major work on socialism (Mises 1978c: 69–70), which in fact accomplished much good (see Hayek's foreword to Mises 1981: xix).

Still, the question remains: in the long run what guarantees for liberty and property can exist in a democratic regime?

Mises ends *Liberalism* (193) by speaking of the future of the ideology, and what it must do in order to prevail. Liberalism, he holds, is in a radically different position from its rivals:

> No sect and no political party has believed that it could afford to forgo advancing its cause by appealing to men's senses. Rhetorical bombast, music and song resound, banners wave, flowers and colors serve as symbols, and the leaders seek to attach their followers to their own person. Liberalism has nothing to do with all this. It has no party flower and no party color, no party song and no party idols, no symbols and no slogans. It has the substance and the arguments. These must lead it to victory.

Thus, having overcome his personal pessimism with a kind of existential leap of faith in the value of rational argument in the ideological struggle, Mises imputes this austere position to liberalism as a whole. Unfortunately, this does not appear to be satisfactory.

In *Capitalism, Socialism and Democracy,* Joseph Schumpeter (1950: 144) addressed the very question at issue here:

> Why should the capitalist order need any protection by extra-capitalist powers or extra-rational loyalties? Can it not come out of the trial with flying colors? Does not our own previous argument sufficiently show that it has plenty of utilitarian credentials to present? Cannot a perfectly good case be made out for it?

His Schumpeterian answer to these questions is: "Yes—certainly, only all that is quite irrelevant."

He provides a number of reasons for this negative response. With virtually no knowledge of or interest in history, the masses simply take their unprecedented high living standards under capitalism for granted. Moreover, the inevitable petty resentments arising from every day life are often directed against the capitalist system because "*emotional* attachment to the social order" is something capitalism is "constitutionally unable to produce" (1950: 145, emphasis in original).

Two of Schumpeter's further reasons are ones that Mises could have endorsed. First, the attack on capitalism often arises from "extra-rational" grounds, and "utilitarian reason" is no match for such extra-rational grounds of action. Mises himself conceded as much in the section of *Liberalism* on "The Psychological Roots of Antiliberalism" (13–17), where he expatiates on the "Fourier complex." Psychoanalysis is unhelpful here, because "the number of those afflicted with [this complex] is far too great." Again, the solution Mises proposes (17) is a purely rationalistic one: "Through self-knowledge [the afflicted individual] must learn to endure his lot in life without looking for a scapegoat on which he can lay all the blame, and he must endeavor to grasp the fundamental laws of social cooperation." Since such an understanding appears to be beyond the ken of average, non-"neurotic" individuals, not to mention the likes of Bertrand Russell and Albert Einstein, it is a mystery what hope this could hold out for the liberal order.

Schumpeter, perhaps more realistically, sees no solution at all. It is in this context that he pronounces (1950: 144) his famous judgment that "capitalism stands its trial before judges who have the sentence of death in their pockets." Furthermore, the ethos promoted by the market economy exacerbates the problem, because it causes the anti-rational, anti-capitalist impulses to gain the upper hand by subverting traditional and religious restraints.

Schumpeter's goes on to observe that the case for capitalism "could never be made simple." Here (1950: 144) he echoes Mises at his gloomiest:

> People at large would have to be possessed of an insight and a power of analysis which are altogether beyond them. Why, practically every nonsense that has ever been said about capitalism has been championed by some professed economist.

Connected to this is the fact that "any pro-capitalist argument must rest on long-run considerations . . . the unemployed of today would have completely to forget his personal fate and the politician of today his personal ambition . . . for the masses, it is the short-run view that counts . . . from the standpoint of individualist utilitarianism they are of course being perfectly rational if they feel like that" (1950: 144–45).[47]

Walter Sulzbach's Critique

The same point had already been made in the most extensive review of Mises's *Liberalism*, by the sympathetic Austrian economist, Walter Sulzbach (1928). Sulzbach expresses his agreement with Mises on a wide array of important issues, such as private property as the basic demand of liberalism, liberalism's class-neutral character, and the nature of the state. "The fact is that the most important of the fundamental theses of liberalism remain unrefuted." Despite its evident successes, however, it has fallen on hard times: "liberalism once ruled and was voluntarily abandoned." There are various reasons for this, according to Sulzbach, but one that he presents impugns the Misesian system most seriously. He asks: "Are the interests of all individuals really identical in the last analysis? That is the central question of liberalism" (383, 385, 389).

The affirmative answer to this question is the motif running through *Liberalism*. Mises even asserts (1962: 22) that: "We [liberals] attack involuntary servitude, not in spite of the fact that it is advantageous to the 'masters,' but because we are convinced that, in the last analysis, it hurts the interests of all members of human society, including the 'masters.'" The same holds for all those who enjoy special privileges: unionized workers, workers shielded from the competition of immigrants, "protected" industrialists, and so on.

Yet it is impossible to deny that these groups are in an important sense benefited by their various privileges. Mises's claim is that the renunciation of these advantages is only "provisional," that it is "very

---

47 Schumpeter makes the ancillary but highly significant point: "The long-run interests of society are so entirely lodged with the upper strata of bourgeois society that it is perfectly natural for people to look upon them as the interests of that class only."

quickly compensated for by higher and lasting gains." But this will not work, according to Sulzbach (390):

> For a particular group to behave in a way that is useful to the "whole," what is required is an appeal to their conscience, not enlightenment, as rationalistically-oriented liberalism in the end always believed . . . the problem is less that of a present sacrifice in favor of the future than that of a personal sacrifice in favor of the greater social grouping, and thus it is less a question of an enlightened understanding than of the readiness for personal renunciation. . . . At best liberalism could show in a logically compelling way that, if the interests of mankind are to be safeguarded, free competition is the correct path to this goal. But where does the postulate come from that the individual or the small group should sacrifice itself for mankind—if its justification is not to be found in the religious sphere or in metaphysics?

Thus, Sulzbach persuasivly argues (391), Mises's alleged grounding of liberalism on the bedrock of science is a mirage. In reality, "it is the old Christian-theological doctrine of the special election of the human soul that lives in all liberal and democratic enlightenment, and which, because it has forgotten its origin, considers itself the result of 'science.'"

The Question of Unlimited Immigration

Serious problems, again involving the democratic state, arise for Mises on the question of unlimited immigration. His position in *Liberalism* (130–34) is that free trade, with the international division of labor, was only a starting point for liberalism. The ultimate liberal ideal is a world where not only goods but also capital and particularly labor are free to move to the areas of their highest productivity. The liberal demand is "that every person have the right to live wherever he wants" (137).[48]

---

[48] In asserting this, Mises doubtless did not have in mind the current situation in every Western country, where a panoply of "civil rights" laws have abolished the right to personal

Mises considers the counter-argument of "national interests": that with open borders immigrants would "inundate," for example, Australia and the United States, that "they would come in such great numbers that it would not longer be possible to count on their assimilation."

As regards America, he states that such fear are "perhaps exaggerated" (presumably because of its much larger population).[49] But with Australia, which had about as many people as Austria when Mises was writing, the case is quite different: "If Australia were thrown open to immigration, it can be assumed with great probability that its population would in a few years consist mostly of Japanese, Chinese, and Malayans" (139–40). It is not just the labor unions that oppose this prospect: "the entire nation . . . is unanimous in fearing inundation by foreigners." There is an obvious "aversion" to members of other nations and especially other races (140–41).

Yet Mises seems to place sole blame for the existence of a problem on the interventionist state (142):[50]

> It cannot be denied that these fears are justified. Because of the enormous power that today stands at the command of the state, a national minority must expect the worst from a majority of a different nationality. As long as the state is granted the vast powers which it has today and which public opinion considers to be its right, the thought of having to live in a state whose government

---

racial, ethnic, and other discrimination and where a munificent welfare state attracts hordes of immigrants seeking to live without participating in the social division of labor.

49 Mises appears to base this statement on the very large population of the United States at that time (over 100 million, according to the 1920 census), and the relatively limited number of potential immigrants. It is an open question how Mises would have dealt with the present-day situation, including the low-birth rate of native Americans relative to immigrants, and the eagerness of tens of millions south of the Rio Grande to emigrate to America (see Brimelow 1996).

50 Cf. the remark by Milton Friedman (*Forbes* 1997), objecting to the "open borders" stand of *The Wall Street Journal* as "an *idée fixe*": "It's just obvious that you can't have free immigration and a welfare state." The notion that supporters of the free market must necessarily also support free immigration is rife in both pro- and anti-immigration camps but is nonetheless fallacious; see, for instance, Hoppe 1998 and other contributors to that issue of *The Journal of Libertarian Studies*.

is in the hands of members of a foreign nationality is positively terrifying.

Mises's solution (142) is the adoption of laissez-faire in economic and social life—the reduction of governmental functions to the protection of life and property—whereupon any problems connected with free immigration would "completely disappear." "In an Australia governed according to liberal principles, what difficulties could arise from the fact that in some parts of the continent Japanese and in other parts Englishmen were in the majority?"

This rhetorical question appears peculiarly constructed. Since Mises has no theory of what forces tend to create and maintain a liberal society—aside from incessant rational economic argumentation—he has no reason to suppose that an Australia governed at a certain point according to liberal principles would continue to be so governed. But if Australia should, by some off chance, slip back into interventionism, then the "national minority [now Australians of European descent] must expect the worst" from the majority of Japanese, Malayans, and others. Yet Mises does not consider what, dynamically, might go into the creation of a political majority in a country with free immigration. Many years later he conceded (1944: 244) that "the maintenance of migration barriers against totalitarian nations aiming at world conquest is indispensable to political and military defense." But what then of cases in which the liberal social order is threatened by the influx of immigrants who are unlikely, because of history and culture, to support that order?

Free immigration would seem to be in a different category from other policy decisions in that its consequences permanently and radically alter the very composition of the democratic political body that assumes the authority to make those decisions. The liberal order, wherever and to whatever degree it exists, is the product of a highly complex cultural development. That Mises implied the need to assimilate new immigrants to the culture of host countries like Australia and the United States suggests that he was well aware of this fact.

Yet today proponents of free immigration seem heedless of its potential for damaging structural change in the recipient country. One wonders, for instance, what would become of the relatively liberal society of Switzerland under a regime of "open borders."

Was Mises an Imperialist?

In *Liberalism* Mises (125) has harsh words for the practices of the European colonial powers ("No chapter of history is steeped further in blood than the history of colonialism," etc.). At the time he was writing, western colonialism, though destined to crumble in a few decades, was still at its height. The British Empire alone covered a quarter of the globe, while the French Empire included vast territories in Africa and holdings elsewhere, and the Dutch, Portuguese, and others ruled over smaller colonial areas.

Despite imperialism's atrocious record, Mises contends (127–28) that the withdrawal of the western powers from their overseas territories is out of the question: "The economy of Europe today is based, to a great extent, on the inclusion of Africa and large parts of Asia in the world economy as suppliers of raw materials of all kinds. . . . European officials, troops, and police must remain in these areas, as far as their presence is necessary in order to maintain the legal and political conditions required to insure the participation of the colonial territories in international trade."

Mises had expressed himself even more forcefully in favor of imperialist rule at an earlier point. In Socialism (1981: 207), he heaps extravagant praise on British imperialism: "The wars waged by England during the era of Liberalism to extend her colonial empire and to open up territories which refused to admit foreign trade laid the foundations of the modern world economy. To measure the true significance of these wars, one has only to imagine what would have happened if India and China and their hinterland had remained closed to world commerce." He insists (1981: 208) that

> Liberalism aims to open all doors closed to trade. . . . Its antagonism is confined to those governments which, by imposing prohibition and other limitations on trade, exclude their subjects from the advantages of taking part in world commerce.

Indeed, British imperialism could not even rightly be called by that name: "The Liberal policy has nothing in common with Imperialism. On the contrary, it is designed to overthrow Imperialism and expel it from the sphere of international trade." This implies that, in Mises's personal usage, "imperialism" does not retain its customary significance, but instead means something like protectionism applied to colonial territories.

Mises claims that this was, historically, the position of classical liberalism. Yet the most famous nineteenth century free-traders—Richard Cobden and John Bright, the leaders of the Manchester school, or Bastiat in France—were staunch opponents of *any* use of state power to extend commerce. It is ironic that Mises (1981: 207 n. 2) defends the English Opium Wars against China, which were bitterly assailed by Cobden as examples of the rankest imperialism.

Overall, it must be said that Mises's views on these questions are in sharp contrast to the traditional liberal perspective represented by Cobden and his school, which held that any government involvement in international trade was illegitimate (Hobson 1968 and Dawson 1927). Furthermore, Mises is open to a standard objection to the "free-trade" imperialists: would Britain have been justified in the later nineteenth century in applying diplomatic or even military pressure on the United States to abandon protectionism and open up its market to foreign goods? Is the only objection to such a hypothetical British policy the fact that the United States was too powerful for such a stratagem to succeed, while Imperial China was satisfactorily weak?

A great part of Mises's problem here, as occasionally elsewhere, lies in his antiseptic conception of the state. For him, the state is simply "the apparatus of compulsion and coercion." He contemptuously rejects (57) Nietzsche's dictum that "the state is the coldest of all cold monsters": "The state is neither cold nor warm. . . . All state activity is human activity," and its goal is "the preservation of society."

But what if the state apparatus has a dynamism of its own? What if imperialism and the military and civilian bureaucracies it brings into being lead to state activism far beyond merely assuring free trade? As Schumpeter wrote of the evolution of imperialism (1951: 25, emphasis in original): "*Created by wars that required it, the machine now created the wars it required.*" Yet none of this appears to have entered into Mises's economic calculations.

Nor does he consider the historical effect of British imperialism as a model and spur to expansionist strivings in other nations, the United States and others, above all Germany, with all of the baleful consequences that followed.

References

Allix, Edgard (1911) "La déformation de l'économie politique libérale après J.-B. Say: Charles Dunoyer," *Revue d'histoire des doctrines économiques et sociales* 4 (2): 115–47.

Anderson, Perry (1992) "The Intransigeant Right at the End of the Century," *London Review of Books* 14 (18) (September 24).

Anderson, Perry (1993) "Die eiserne Rechte am Ende des Jahrhunderts: Über Michael Oakeshott, Carl Schmitt, Leo Strauss, und Friedrich von Hayek," *Freibeuter*, No. 55.

Arblaster, Anthony (1984) *The Rise and Decline of Western Liberalism*, Oxford: Basil Blackwood.

Benedetti, Ulisse (1967) *Benedetto Croce e il fascismo*, Rome: Volpe.

Brimelow, Peter (1996) *Alien Nation: Commonsense about America's Immigration Disaster*, New York: Harper Perennial.

Buchanan, James M. (1960) "'La Scienza delle Finanze': The Italian Tradition in Fiscal Theory," in *idem*, *Fiscal Theory and Political Economy: Selected Essays*, Chapel Hill, N.C.: University of North Carolina Press.

Butterfield, Herbert (1952) *Liberty in the Modern World*, Toronto: Ryerson.

Cannistraro, Philp V. (ed.) (1982) s.v. Croce, Benedetto and Albertini, Luigi, in *Historical Dictionary of Fascist Italy*, Westport, Conn.: Greenwood.

Carsten, F.L. (1967) *The Rise of Fascism*, Berkeley: University of California Press.

Cooper, Sandy E. (1986) "Patriotic Pacifism: The Political Vision of Italian Peace Movements, 1867–1915," in Frank J. Coppa (ed.) *Studies in Modern Italian History from the* Risorgimento *to the Republic*, NewYork: Peter Lang.

Dawson, W.H. (1927) *Richard Cobden and Foreign Policy*, New York: Frank-Maurice.

Decleva, Enrico (1965) "Il Corriere della Sera," in Brunello Vigezzi (ed.) *Politica e Stampa in Italia: Dopoguerra e Fascismo, 1919–1925*, Bari: Laterza.

De Grand, Alexander (1982) *Italian Fascism: Its Origins and Development*, Lincoln, Neb.: University of Nebraska Press.

de Viti de Marco, Antonio (1929) *Un trentennio di lotte politiche, 1894–1922*, Rome: Meridionale.

Ebeling, Richard (2002) Introduction to Mises.

Einaudi, Luigi (1941) "Edoardo Giretti," *Rivista di Storia Economica* 6 (1) (March).

Femia, Joseph V. (1998) *The Machiavellian Legacy: Essays in Italian Political Thought*, New York: St. Martin's.

Finer, S.E. (1966) Introduction to Pareto.

Finer, S.E. (1968) "Pareto and Pluto-Democracy: The Retreat to Galapagos," *American Political Science Review* 62 (2) (June).

Flew, Antony (1989) "Annihilating the Individual," in idem, *Equality in Liberty and Justice*, London: Routledge.

Friedman, Milton, (1997) *Forbes*, Interview, December 29.

Gallagher, John and Ronald Robinson (1953) "The Imperalism of Free Trade," *Economic History Review,* 2nd series, 6 (1): 1–15.

Gray, John (1996) "Defining Evil," *The New York Times Book Review*, February 25.

Hayek, F.A. (1991) "Hermann Heinrich Gossen," in *Collected Works*, 3, *The Trend of Economic Thinking: Essays on Political Economists and Economic History*, W.W. Bartley and Stephen Kresge (eds.), Chicago: University of Chicago Press.

Hayek, F.A. (1992) *Collected Works*, 4 , *The Fortunes of Liberalism: Essays on Austrian Economics and the Ideal of Freedom*, Peter G. Klein (ed.), Chicago: University of Chicago Press.

Hobson, J.A. (1968 [1919]) *Richard Cobden: The International Man*, New York: Barnes and Noble.

Hoppe, Hans-Hermann (1993) Introduction to Mises.

Hoppe, Hans-Hermann (1998) "The Case for Free Trade and Restricted Immigration," *Journal of Libertarian Studies* 13 (2) (Summer): 221–33.

Hoppe, Hans-Hermann (2001) *Democracy: The God that Failed: The Economics of Politics, Monarchy, Democracy, and Natural Order*, New Brunswick, N.J.: Transaction.

Hughes, Emrys (1955) *Winston Churchill, British Bulldog: His Career in War and Peace*, New York: Exposition.

Iraci, Agostino (1970) *Arpinati: l'oppositore di Mussolini*, Rome: Mario Bulzoni.

Joes, Anthony James (1982) *Mussolini*, New York: Franklin Watts.

Josephson, Harold (ed.) (1985) *Biographical Dictionary of Modern Peace Leaders*, Westport, Conn.: Greenwood Press.

Kapelush, F. (2002 [1925]) "'Anti-Marxism': Professor Mises as a Theorist of Fascism," in Mises.

Knox, MacGregor (2000) *Common Destiny: Dictatorship, Foreign Policy, and War in Fascist Italy and Nazi Germany*, Cambridge, Eng.: Cambridge University Press.

Krohn, Claus-Dieter (1981) *Wirtschaftstheorien als politische Interessen: Die akademische Nationalökonomie in Deutschland 1918–1933*, Frankfurt a.M.: Campus Verlag.

Krohn, Claus-Dieter (1993) *Intellectuals in Exile: Refugee Scholars and the New School for Social Research*, Rita and Robert Kimber (trs.), Amherst, Mass.: University of Massachusetts Press.

Laski, Harold (1936) *The Rise of Liberalism: The Philosophy of a Business Civilization*, New York: Harper and Bros.

Leggett, George (1981) *The Cheka: Lenin's Political Police*, Oxford: Clarendon Press.

Leontovitsch, Victor (1957) *Geschichte des Liberalismus in Russland*, Frankfurt a.M.: Klostermann.

Lyttelton, Adrian (1973) *The Seizure of Power: Fascism in Italy, 1919–1929*, NewYork: Scribner's.

Lyttelton, Adrian (1982) "Fascism and Violence in Post-War Italy: Political Strategy and Social Conflict," in Mommsen and Hirschfeld (eds.)

MacDonagh, Oliver (1962) "The Anti-Imperialism of Free Trade," *Economic History Review*, 2nd series, 14 (4): 489–501.

Marcuse, Herbert (1968) *Negations: Essays in Critical Theory*, Jeremy J. Shapiro (tr.), Boston: Beacon Press.

Marx, Karl and Friedrich Engels, (2006 [1848]) *The Communist Manifesto*, Penguin: New York.

Mill, John Stuart (1977) *Collected Works*, 17, *Essays on Politics and Society*, J.M. Robson (ed.), Toronto: University of Toronto Press.

Mises, Ludwig von (1927) *Liberalismus*, Jena: Gustav Fischer.

Mises, Ludwig von (1944) *Omnipotent Government*, New Haven, Conn.: Yale University Press.

Mises, Ludwig von (1962) *The Free and Prosperous Commonwealth*, Ralph Raico (tr.), Princeton, N.J.: Van Nostrand.

Mises, Ludwig von (1978a) *Liberalism: A Socio-Economic Exposition*, Ralph Raico (tr.), Kansas City, Mo.: Sheed, Andrews, and McMeel.

Mises, Ludwig von (1978b) *Erinnerungen*, Stuttgart: Gustav Fischer.

Mises, Ludwig von (1978c) *Notes and Recollections*, Hans F. Sennholz (tr.) South Holland, Ill.: Libertarian Press.

Mises, Ludwig von (1981 [1922]) *Socialism: An Economic and Sociological Analysis*, Indianapolis, Ind.: Liberty Classics.

Mises, Ludwig von (1985) *Liberalism: In the Classical Tradition*, Ralph Raico (tr.), Irvington, N.Y., Foundation for Economic Education and San Francisco: Cobden Press.

Mises, Ludwig von (1993 [1927]) *Liberalismus*, Sankt Augustin: Academia Verlag.

Mises, Ludwig von (2002) *Selected Writings: Between the Two World Wars: Monetary Disorder, Interventionism, Socialism, and the Great Depression*, Richard M. Ebeling (ed.), Indianapolis, Ind.: Liberty Press.

Molinari, Gustave de (1849) "De la production de la securité," *Journal des Économistes* 22 (95) (February 15): 277–90.

Mommsen, Wolfgang J. and Gerhard Hirschfeld (1982) (eds.) *Social Protest, Violence, and Terror in Nineteenth- and Twentieth-Century Europe*, New York: St. Martin's Press.

Morgan, Philip (1995) *Italian Fascism, 1919–1945*, New York: St. Martin's Press.

Mozetic, Gerard (1992) "Outsiders and True Believers: Austrian Sociologists Respond to Fascism," in Stephen P. Turner and Dirk Käsler (eds.) *Sociology Responds to Fascism*, London: Routledge.

New York Times (1927) "Churchill Lauds Fascismo for Italy," January 21.

Nolte, Ernst (1987) *Der europäische Bürgerkrieg, 1917–1945: Nationalsozialismus und Bolschewismus*, Frankfurt a.M.: Propyläen.

Pantaleoni, Maffeo (1922) *Bolcevismo italiano*, Bari: Laterza.

Papa, Antonio (1970) "Edoardo Giretti," *Belfagor* 15 (1) (January).

Pareto, Vilfredo (1962) *Lettere a Maffeo Pantaleoni, 1890–1923*, 2 vols., Gabriele de Rosa (ed.), Rome: Edizioni di Storia e Letteratura.

Pareto, Vilfredo (1966) *Sociological Writings*, Derick Martin (tr.), Totowa, N.J.: Rowman and Littlefield.

Pareto, Vilfredo (1974 [1906]) *Manuale di economia*, Padua: Antonio Milani.

Pareto, Vilfredo (1980) *The Other Pareto*, Placido Bucolo (ed.), Placido and Gillian Bucolo (trs.), London: Scholar Press.

Pareto, Vilfredo (1981) *Borghesia, Elites, Fascismo*, Marcello Veneziani (ed.), Rome: Volpe.

Pareto, Vilfredo (1992) "Le péril socialiste," in *idem, Libre-échangisme, protectionnisme et socialisme*, Giovanni Busino (ed.), Geneva: Droz.

Payne, Stanley G. (1995) *A History of Fascism 1919–1945*, Madison, Wisc.: University of Wisconsin Press.

Petersen, Jan (1982) "Violence in Italian Fascism, 1919–25," in Mommsen and Hirschfeld (eds.).

Pipes, Richard (1993) *Russia under the Bolshevik Regime*, New York: Knopf.

Raico, Ralph (1999) *Die Partei der Freiheit: Studien zur Geschichte des deutschen Liberalismus*, Jörg Guido Hülsmann (tr.) Stuttgart: Lucius & Lucius.

Rawls, John (1971) *A Theory of Justice*, Cambridge, Mass.: Harvard University Press.

Ricci, Umberto (1939) *Tre economisti italiani: Pantaleoni, Pareto, Loria*, Bari: Laterza.

Roberts, Kate Louise (1940) *Hoyt's New Cyclopedia of Practical Quotations*, New York: Funk and Wagnalls.

Rothbard, Murray N. (1981) "The Laissez-Faire Radical: A Quest for the Historical Mises," *Journal of Libertarian Studies* 5 (3) (Summer).

Rothbard, Murray N. (1995) *An Austrian Perspective on the History of Economic Thought*, 2, *Classical Economics*, Aldershot, Eng.: Edward Elgar.

Ruggiero, Guido de (1959 [1927]) *The History of European Liberalism*, R.G. Collingwood (tr.), Boston: Beacon Press.

Salvatorelli, Luigi and Giovanni Mira (1964) *Storia d'Italia nel periodo fascista*, Rome: Guilio Einaudi.

Schulze, Hagen (1982) *Weimar: Deutschland 1917–1933*, Berlin: Siedler.

Schumpeter, Joseph (1950) *Capitalism, Socialism, and Democracy*, 3rd ed., New York: Harper and Bros.

Schumpeter, Joseph (1951) *Imperialism and Social Classes: Two Essays*, New York: Meridian.

Schumpeter, Joseph (1954) *History of Economic Analysis*, Elizabeth Boody Schumpeter (ed.), New York: Oxford University Press.

Sennholz, Mary (1956) (ed.) *On Freedom and Free Enterprise: Essays in Honor of Ludwig von Mises*, Princeton, N. J.: Van Nostrand.

Settembrini, Domenico (1978) *Fascismo: controrivoluzione imperfetta*, Florence: Sansoni.

Smith, Denis Mack (1959) *Italy: A Modern History*, Ann Arbor, Mich.: University of Michigan Press.

Smith, Denis Mack (1982) *Mussolini*, New York: Knopf.

Sulzbach, Walter (1928) "Liberalismus," *Archiv für Sozialwissenschaft und Sozialpolitik* 59 (2): 382–95.

Vivarelli, Roberto (1981) *Il fallimento del liberalismo: studi sulle origini del fascismo*, Bologna: Il Mulino.

Vivarelli, Roberto (1991) "Interpretations of the Origins of Fascism," *Journal of Modern History* 63 (March).

8 Eugen Richter and the End of German Liberalism

Introduction

For several generations now there has existed an interpretation of modern history conditioning and shaping the views held by nearly all educated people on the great issue of socialism vs. the market economy.

This interpretation goes roughly as follows: once there was a "class"—"the" bourgeoisie—that rose to prominence with the colossal economic and social changes of early modern history, and strove for domination. Liberalism, which admittedly helped to achieve a limited degree of human liberation, was the ideological expression of the bourgeoisie's self-interested struggle.[1]

Meanwhile, however, another, much larger class came into being, "the" working class, victims of the triumphant bourgeoisie. This class strove in its turn for recognition and domination, and, accordingly, developed its own ideology, socialism. Socialism aimed at the transition to a higher, broader level of human liberation. The natural and inevitable

---

This is a modified version of an essay that first appeared in *The Review of Austrian Economics*, 4, 1990, 3–25.

1 See, for instance, Theo Schiller, *Liberalismus in Europa* (Baden-Baden: Nomos, 1979), 19: "Our starting-point is the universally accepted [sic] conclusion that the social interest-situation of the bourgeoisie was the foundation of classical liberalism."

conflict of interests of these two classes—basically, of the exploiters and the exploited—fills modern history, and has led in the end, in the welfare state of our own time, to a kind of accommodation and compromise.

With this historical paradigm I think we are all quite familiar.

Recently, however, a different interpretation has begun to gain ground. The outstanding historian Ernst Nolte, of the Free University of Berlin, has expressed its central point:

> The real and modernising revolution is that of liberal capitalism or of economic freedom, which began 200 years ago in England and which was first completed in the USA. This revolution of individualism was challenged at an early date by the so-called revolutionary socialism, whose guideline was the archaic community, with its transparency of social conditions, as the most comprehensive counterrevolution, namely as the tendency for totalitarian collectivism.[2]

Although capitalism "radically chang[ed] the living conditions of all those affected in a relatively short time and improv[ed] them to an extraordinary degree, at least materially," "it did not understand how to awaken love."[3] The great capitalist revolution called forth a socialist movement, which "in a certain sense [was] thoroughly reactionary, indeed, radical-reactionary."[4]

The Place of Liberalism

This more recent conception suggests a new interpretation of liberalism. Liberalism is, in fact, the ideology of the capitalist revolution that prodigiously raised the living standards of the mass of people; a doctrine gradually elaborated over several centuries, which offered a new concept of social order, encompassing freedom in the only form suited

---

2 Ernst Nolte, "Between Myth and Revisionism, The Third Reich in the Perspective of the 1980s," in H.W. Koch (ed.) *Aspects of the Third Reich* (London: Macmillan, 1985) 24. Nolte notes that the view he presents is that of Domenico Settembrini, of the University of Pisa.
3 Ernst Nolte, *Marxism, Fascism, Cold War*, Lawrence Krader (tr.) (Atlantic Highlands, N.J.: Humanities Press, 1982) 79.
4 Ibid. viii. In fact, the similarities and historical connections between the conservative and socialist indictments of liberal capitalism are remarkable; see, for instance, ibid. 23–30.

to the modern world. Step by step, in practice and theory, the various sectors of human activity were withdrawn from the jurisdiction of coercive authority and given over to the voluntary action of self-regulating society.

Practically all the peoples of western and central Europe (as well as the Americans) contributed to the working out of the liberal idea and the liberal movement. Not just the Dutch, French, Scots, English, and Swiss, but, for instance, in Spain, the Late Scholastics of the School of Salamanca and at other academic centers,[5] and a number of Italians, especially at the beginnings of political economy. In this evolution, the Germans also played an often overlooked part.[6]

Particularly striking for foreigners who have concerned themselves with German liberalism has been the bitter hostility that it met with in its own time and at the hands of historians, and which is linked to the first, conventional interpretation of modern history described above. Paul Kennedy has quite accurately referred to "the sheer venom and blind hatred behind so many of the assaults in Germany upon *Manchestertum* [Manchesterism, i.e., laissez-faire]."[7]

This hostility was directed especially against the man who was for two generations in Germany *the* representative of the liberal movement that embraced all civilized nations: Eugen Richter. Malice has now been replaced by oblivion. Last year, in July, was the 150th anniversary of Richter's birth, and if any notice was taken of the occasion in the Federal Republic, aside from my own very modest contribution,[8] it has not come to my attention.

That should not be surprising, however. Since both the conservatives and the socialists—the two camps that have by and large written the history of Germany—found Richter insufferable, he has usually

---

[5] Alejandro A. Chaufen, *Christians for Freedom: Late Scholastic Economics* (San Francisco: Ignatius Press, 1986).
[6] See Ralph Raico, "Der deutsche Liberalismus und die deutsche Freihandelsbewegung: Eine Rückschau," *Zeitschrift fur Wirtschaftspolitik* 36, no. 3 (1987) 263–81.
[7] Paul M. Kennedy, *The Rise of the Anglo-German Antagonism, 1860–1914* (London: Allen and Unwin, 1980) 152.
[8] Ralph Raico, "Eugen Richter: Ein unerbittlicher Liberaler," *Orientierungen zur Wirtschafts- und Gesellschaftspolitik* 37 (September 1988) 77–80.

been treated with disparagement or else totally disregarded. Thus, he remains unknown to the vast majority of educated people, even in his homeland. Given the older historical interpretation, this circumstance might possibly make a certain sense; it by no means corresponds to the newer one. Thus, an attempt to evaluate Richter's significance for German liberalism and German history is called for and, indeed, overdue.

Differences of Opinion on Richter

Eugen Richter[9] was the brilliant, if occasionally too masterful, leader of the Progressive Party (*Fortschrittspartei*) and later of the Liberals (*Freisinn*), the political expressions of German "Left Liberalism,"[10] or "determined" (*entschieden*) liberalism, through thirty years, in the Imperial German Reichstag and in the Prussian House of Delegates; he was, moreover, an untiring journalist and publisher.[11] Outside of a narrow group of friends and political associates, the attitudes and opinions on Richter, in his own time and afterwards, have been mostly very negative.[12]

This is naturally the case on the authoritarian-conservative side. Crown Prince Wilhelm, later Kaiser Wilhelm II, even hatched a plan

---

9 The literature on Richter is very meager. See principally Felix Rachfahl, Eugen Richter und der Linksliberalismus im Neuen Reich," *Zeitschrift für Politik* 5, Nos. 2–3 (1912) 261–374. Also, Eugen Richter, *Jugenderinnerungen* (Berlin: Verlag "Fortschritt," 1893); idem., *Im alten Reichstag: Erinnerungen*, 2 vols. (Berlin: Verlag Fortschritt," (1894–1896); Oskar Klein-Hattingen, *Geschichte des deutschen Liberalismus*, 2: *Von 1871 bis zur Gegenwart* (Berlin-Schoneberg: Fortschritt-Buchverlag der "Hilfe," 1912); Leopold Ullstein, *Eugen Richter als Publizist und Herausgeber: Ein Beitrag zum Thema "Parteipresse"* (Leipzig: Reinicke, 1930); and Jesse Rohfleisch, *Eugen Richter: Opponent of Bismarck*, unpubl. diss., history, University of California, Berkeley, 1946. The most recent work on Richter, Ina Suzanne Lorenz, *Eugen Richter: Der entschiedene Liberalismus in wilhelminischer Zeit 1871 bis 1906* (Husum: Matthiesen, 1980), is noteworthy above all owing to the author's inexhaustible aversion to her subject and her total lack of understanding for classical liberalism in Germany and altogether.
10 "Left Liberalism" is a direct translation of *Linksliberalismus* and refers to the middle- to late-nineteenth century German political movement in opposition to the regime-oriented National Liberals. It has no connection with what is often called "left-liberalism" in the present day.
11 Kurt Koszyk and Karl H. Pruys, *Wörterbuch zur Publizistik* (Munich-Pullach/Berlin: Verlag Dokumentation, 1970), 223–25.
12 See also Ralph Raico, "Der deutsche Liberalismus," 275.

(never realized) to have Richter "beaten up" by six junior officers,[13] and Richter's old adversary, Prince Bismarck, confided to the old Kaiser, Wilhelm I, that it was among men like Richter that "the material for deputies to the [French Revolutionary] Convention" was to be found.[14] Hans Delbrück, whose portrayal of Richter influenced later writers, compared him to the Athenian demagogue Cleon and branded him the leader of a party whose highest passion was reserved for pieces of silver,[15] while for the Marxist Franz Mehring, Richter was merely "a servant and helper of Big Capital."[16] Richter's "rigidity," "dogmatism," and "carping doctrinairism" have been repeatedly attacked,[17] and a present-day German historian simply reflected the nearly unanimous view of his colleagues when he summarily characterized Richter as "the eternal nay-sayer."[18]

Yet even Bismarck was compelled to concede, "Richter was certainly the best speaker we had. Very well informed and conscientious; with disobliging manners, but a man of character. Even now he does

---

13 According to the report of the Austro-Hungarian Crown Prince Rudolf; Brigette Hamann, *Rudolf: Kronprinz und Rebell* (Munich/Zurich: Piper, 1978), 333.
14 Otto von Bismarck, *Werke in Auswahl*, 8, A, *Erinnerungen und Gedanken*, Rudolf Buchner (ed.), with Georg Engel (Stuttgart: W. Kohlhammer, 1975) 732.
15 Hans Delbrück, *Vor und nach dem Weltkrieg. Politische und historische Aufsätze 1902–1925* (Berlin: Stollberg, 1926) 136–48; Annelise Thimme, *Hans Delbrück als Kritiker der wilhelminischen Epoche* (Düsseldorf: Droste, 1955) 31–32
16 Franz Mehring, *Gesammelte Schriften,* Thomas Höhle, Hans Koch, and Josef Schleifstein, (eds.), 14, *Politische Publizistik, 1891 bis 1914* ([East] Berlin: Dietz, 1964) 35. Why precisely of "Big Capital" is baffling, except that it fits Mehring's radical Marxist viewpoint. Richter fiercely opposed, for instance, the big banks and exporters who promoted German colonialism.
17 See, among innumerable others, Thomas Nipperdey, Über einige Grundzüge der deutschen Parteigeschichte," in *Moderne deutsche Verfassungsgeschichte (1815–1918),* Ernst-Wolfgang Böckenforde (ed.), with Rainer Wahl (Cologne: Kiepenheuer and Witsch, 1972), 238, where the author writes of Richter's accentuation of the theoretical orientation of liberalism "to the very extreme of rigid dogmatism." Typical of many non-German historians is Kenneth D. Barkin, *The Controversy over German Industrialization, 1890–1902* (Chicago: University of Chicago Press, 1970), 239, who complains that Richter "had not shed the dogmatic liberal principle of non-intervention."
18 Winfried Baumgart, *Deutschland im Zeitalter des Imperialismus, 1890–1914. Grundkräfte, Thesen, und Strukturen*, 5th ed. (Stuttgart: W. Kohlhammer, 1986) 135. Curiously, Baumgart passes this verdict in connection with Left Liberalism's turn towards support for the aggressive armaments policy of Wilhelm II, made possible by Richter's death.

not turn with the wind . . ."[19] Another opponent, this time from the liberal camp, the first President of the Federal Republic, Theodor Heuss, admitted that Richter was "the most influential leader of 'determined' liberalism," and "certainly in detail work [sic] the most knowledgeable deputy in the German parliaments . . ."[20] An observer closer in spirit to his subject expressed it more simply: Richter "was the liberal doctrine incarnate."[21]

Richter's Career

Eugen Richter was born on July 30,1838, in Düsseldorf, the son of a regimental doctor. The atmosphere in the parental home was "oppositional," e.g., the family read the *Kölnische Zeitung* "eagerly"—evidently rather bold behavior for the time. Richter's "predominantly critical-rational disposition" developed from his early youth.[22] He studied political science with Friedrich Christoph Dahlmann at Bonn and with Robert von Mohl at Heidelberg, where he also studied public finance with Karl Heinrich Rau, then the most celebrated expert in the field. While still a student he went to Berlin, where the proceedings of the Prussian House of Delegates interested him much more than his university lectures. He began attending the meetings of the *Kongress deutscher Volkswirte* (Congress of German Economists, a liberal reformist organization) and, through newspapers and journal articles, avidly took part in the growing movement for economic liberalism; he was also active in the consumer cooperative movement.

By 1884 Richter headed a united Left Liberal party, the *Deutschfreisinnige Partei* that boasted of more than 100 seats in the Reichstag. Liberalism's hour in Germany seemed to have come: the

---

19 Rachfahl, "Eugen Richter," 371. Theodor Barth, one of Richter's many liberal opponents, declared: "Bismarck was no match for Richter dialectically, and the frequent eruptions of the Bismarckian temper against the implacable man of the opposition often sprang from the feeling that the omnipotent Chancellor would come up short in dialectical argumentation with Richter." In *Politische Porträts*, new ed. (Berlin: Schneider, 1923) 84.
20 Theodor Heuss, *Friedrich Naumann: Der Mann, das Werk, die Zeit*, 2nd ed. (Stuttgart/Tübingen: Rainer Wunderlich, 1949) 180.
21 Rachfahl, "Eugen Richter," 372.
22 Ibid. 262–63.

Kaiser, Wilhelm I, was very old, the Crown Prince, Friedrich, the most liberal of all the Hohenzollerns.

It turned out otherwise than might have been desirable for the Germans. Bismarck's political skill saw to it that the *Freisinnige Partei* was smashed in the next two elections, and when Friedrich finally ascended the throne, in 1888, he was already mortally ill.

These vicissitudes could make no difference in Richter's political convictions, however. For another two decades he held fast to the same principles, which appeared increasingly obsolete and irrelevant. He was the last authentic liberal leader in the parliament of any European power.

Social Philosophy and the Two-Front Strategy

Already in his earliest journalistic activity, Richter emphasized not only the economic disadvantages of the antiquated mercantilist system, but at the same time the infringement of civil and political freedom bound up with it. Thus, in his brochure, *On the Freedom of the Tavern Trade*, he attacked the concessions system, which invested the political authorities with wide-ranging licensing and regulatory authority for all trades and professions:

> As long as the police administration in our state unites in itself such legislative, judicial, and executive powers, Prussia does not yet deserve the name of a *Rechtsstaat* [state founded on the rule of law].[23]

Thus from the start, the cornerstone of Richter's social philosophy was the connection between political and economic freedom, a conception that distinguished him, and Left Liberalism in general, from the mass of "National Liberals." Two decades later, Richter closed, his great speech against Bismarck's protective tariff with the words:

> Economic freedom has no security without political freedom, and political freedom can find its security only in economic freedom.[24]

---

23 Ibid. 266.
24 Richter, *Im alten Reichstag*, 2, 114.

This tenet determined Richter's continuing political strategy. All his life, he conducted a "two-front war," against Bismarckian "pseudo-constitutionalism" and a recrudescent mercantilism on the one hand, and the rising socialist movement on the other.[25]

Richter and the other *entschieden* liberals have often been reproached for this policy. Critics maintain that the Left Liberals should have allied with the Social Democrats, in a common resistance to the militarist-authoritarian Second Reich, and Richter's famous "rigidity" and "dogmatism" are supposed to be largely responsible for the fact that such a united front never came into being. Some historians even give the impression that liberal opposition to Social Democracy in Imperial Germany is only comprehensible as the product of "fear" of the "lower orders."[26]

But it can scarcely be surprising that Richter rejected such an alliance. He saw himself faced with a socialist party that did not trouble to conceal its ultimate aim, abolition of the system of private property and the market economy, and that viewed "the class struggle between bourgeoisie and proletariat as the 'pivot of all revolutionary socialism.'"[27] After 1875, the Social Democratic Party of Germany (SPD) was officially a Marxist party, and, despite later revisionist tendencies, its acknowledged leaders, like Bebel, Liebknecht, and Kautsky, were confirmed orthodox Marxists. Of course, the SPD presented various democratic demands "to start with"; its ultimate goal remained, however, the social elimination of all non-proletarians.

---

25 August Bebel, leader of the German socialists, described an early encounter with Richter, "whose chilly, reserved nature struck me even then. Richter gave the impression that he viewed all of us with sovereign disdain." August Bebel, *Aus Meinem Leben* (1910; reprint, Frankfurt a. M., Europäische Verlaganstalt, n.d.), 92. One wonders why, given Richter's character and well-known principles, the socialist leader was in the least surprised.

26 See, e.g., Konstanze Wegner, *Theodor Barth und die Freisinnige Vereinigung. Studien zur Geschichte des Linksliberalismus im wilhelminischen Deutschland (1893–1910)* (Tübingen: J.C.B. Mohr [Paul Siebeck] 1968) 138.

27 Ernst Engelberg, "Das Verhältnis zwischen kleinbürglicher Dernokratie und Sozialdemokratie in den 80er Jahren des 19. Jahrhunderts," in Otto Pflange (ed.), with Elisabeth Müller-Luckner, *Innenpolitische Probleme des Bismarck-Reiches* (Munich/Vienna: Oldenberg, 1983) 26. The East German historian adds: "This conception was accepted not only by the most influential leaders around August Bebel, but also by the mass of members and sympathizers."

The Social Democratic standpoint confronting Richter may be illustrated by Franz Mehring, a major theoretician and the biographer of Marx. In 1903, Mehring wrote, in the socialist *Neue Zeit*, of the German "bourgeoisie" (and its defenders): "It had to be aware, and basically it was aware, that, without the help of the working class, it could not defeat absolutism and feudalism. It had further to be aware, and basically it was also aware, that, in the moment of victory, its previous alliance-partner would face it as an adversary," at which point the bourgeoisie would fall victim to the proletariat in the final, decisive conflict.

Nonetheless, Mehring insisted that in this putative state of affairs the bourgeoisie must draw the conclusion "that a pact with the working class on tolerable [sic] conditions offers it the only possibility it has."[28] But for liberals like Richter, the Marxist scenario was by no means all that "tolerable." It is understandable, therefore, that Richter held that the "Social Democratic state of the future," because it was hypothetical, was for the time being less dangerous than the existing military-authoritarian state, yet essentially "much worse."[29]

Even aside from the fact that "from 1869, meetings of the Progressive Party in Berlin were violently disrupted by the Social Democrats,"[30] how would an alliance with them have been at all conceivable? As liberals, men like Richter viewed socialism as the great modern counter-revolution, and believed that the achievement of the socialist goal would lead both to appalling poverty and state absolutism. There was nothing in the socialist doctrine of the time that would suggest otherwise. Historians would do well to recognize that the blame

---

28 Franz Mehring, *Gesammelte Schriften*, 14, 553.
29 Quoted in Peter Gilg, *Die Erneuerung des demokratischen Denkens im wilhelminischen Deutschland. Eine ideengeschichtliche Studie zur Wende vom 19. zum 20. Jahrhundert* (Wiesbaden: Franz Steiner, 1965) 135–36. Gilg adds, reasonably enough: "To this opposition [of Richter's] the theory of revolution of the Social Democratic program, which permitted collaboration solely as a means to winning autocratic rule, naturally contributed, as well as the successful competition of Social Democracy in the struggle for the urban voting masses." Ibid. 135.
30 Richter, *Im alten Reichstag*, 2, 63, 178. "This occurred," according to Richter, "with the permission of the Minister of the Interior." In Britain, the Chartists had earlier used similar strong-arm methods against meetings of the Anti-Corn Law movement; see Wendy Hinde, *Richard Cobden. A Victorian Outsider* (New Haven, Conn.: Yale University Press, 1987) 65.

for the non-occurrence of a common front against militarism in Germany must be borne by the Social Democrats themselves.

Pictures of a Social Democratic Future

The socialists engaged in a relentless, scathing critique of the liberal economic order. But, as Richter pointed out:

> The Social Democrats are very garrulous in criticizing the present social order, but they are careful not to clarify in detail the goal that is supposed to be achieved through the latter's destruction.[31]

This omission Richter attempted to make good in his *Pictures of a Social Democratic Future*.[32] In its time, this little book, with its ironic subtitle, "Freely drawn from Bebel," was a sensation. It was translated into a dozen languages, with more than a quarter-million copies printed in Germany alone.

It must be conceded that in some respects Richter's narrative is dubious. It leans too heavily on the pathos of family problems under the new socialist regime, although that was to be expected, since it was directed at a popular audience. Sometimes the work even verges on what at first seems absurd, especially in connection with the relations of social equality that will supposedly obtain under socialism, e.g., the new socialist Reich Chancellor must shine his own boots and clean his own clothes, in Richter's account.

The explanation for this, however, is that Richter took the egalitarian promises of the socialists too literally, too *seriously*. He lacked any inkling of Marxism's drive to bring to power a *new class* of privileged higher-echelon state functionaries and their supporters.

Still, Richter was able to anticipate many of the characteristics later displayed by Marxist states. Emigration is prohibited in Marxist Germany, since "persons who owe their education and training to the

---

31 Richter, *Politisches ABC-Buch: Ein Lexikon parlamentarischer Zeit- und Streitfragen*, 9th ed. (Berlin: Fortschritt Verlag, 1898), 307.
32 Richter, *Sozialdemokratische Zukunftsbilder Frei nach Bebel* Berlin: Verlagsanstalt Deutsche Presse, 1907 [1891]). In 1922, in his *Socialism*, Ludwig von Mises undertook the same task, but on a strictly scientific level.

State cannot be accorded the right to emigrate, so long as they are of an age when they are obliged to work."[33] Bribery and corruption are to be found everywhere,[34] and the products of the nationalized economy are unable to meet the standards of competition of the world market.[35]

But above all, Richter again emphasized the connection between economic and political freedom:

> What is the use of freedom of the press if the government is in possession of all the printing presses, what does freedom of assembly avail if all the meeting places belong to the government? ... in a society in which there is no more personal and economic freedom, even the freest form of the state cannot make political independence possible.[36]

When the worst imaginable happens and the socialist state proves incapable of provisioning the German Army as the Fatherland is invaded by France and Russia, a counter-revolution breaks out, restoring a free society.

Marxists and Conservatives: Mutual Aid

Richter presents his two-sided campaign as part of one and the same war, by arguing that it was a question merely of two forms of state paternalism. Interestingly, this interpretation was supported from an unexpected quarter, although without Richter's normative charge. Accused of political offenses, the founder of German socialism, Ferdinand Lassalle, addressed his judges as follows:

> As wide as are the differences that divide you and me from one another, Sirs, against this dissolution of all morality [threatening from the liberal camp] we stand shoulder to shoulder! I defend with

---

33 Richter, *Zukunftsbilder*, 32.
34 Ibid. 42–43.
35 Ibid. 48.
36 Ibid. 50, 52.

you, the primeval Vestal flame of all civilization, the State, against those modern barbarians [the laissez-faire liberals].[37]

Richter reiterated that the right-wing parties—the Conservatives and the Anti-Semites—aided socialism "especially [by] the agitation against mobile capital, against 'the exploitation' it allegedly perpetrates, and, moreover, by the limitless promises handed out to all occupational classes of special state help and provision."[38] In turn, socialism helped the Conservatives and Anti-Semites through its revolutionary threats, intimidating the middle classes and driving them into the arms of a strong State power.[39]

State Socialism and *Sozialpolitik*

Richter fought Bismarck's state-socialist program, including the nationalization of the Prussian railroads and the establishment of state monopolies for tobacco and brandy, and, naturally, Bismarck's turn towards protectionism, towards rendering dearer the cost of life's necessities, by which the great Chancellor, landowner, and hater of the "Manchester money-bags" manifested his compassion for the poor. Richter considered the planned tariff wall "the ideal nurturing ground for the formation of new cartels," which in fact occurred.[40] While Richter, together with other liberal leaders, like Ludwig Bamberger, supported the introduction of the gold standard in the newly formed empire, unlike

---

37 Quoted in Werner Sombart, *Händler und Helden: Patriotische Besinnungen* (Munich/Leipzig: Duncker und Humblot, 1915) 77.
38 Richter, *Politisches ABC-Buch*, 306. Bismarck's hostility to Richter and the Left Liberals on account of their economic liberalism was intense, e.g., his demagogic reference to "the Progressive Party and clique of Manchester politicians, the representative of the pitiless moneybags, have always been unfair to the poor, they have always worked to the limit of their abilities, to prevent the state from helping them. Laissez-faire, the greatest possible self-government, no restraints, opportunity for the small business to be absorbed by Big Capital, for exploitation of the ignorant and inexperienced by the clever and crafty. The State is supposed to act only as police, especially for the exploiters." Willy Andreas and K.F. Reinking, *Bismarcks Gespräche: Von der Reichsgründung bis zur Entlassung* (Bremen: Carl Schünemann, 1965), 339.
39 Richter, *Politisches ABC-Buch*, 322.
40 Fritz Blaich, *Kartell- und Monopolpolitik im kaiserlichen Deutschland. Das Problem der Marktmacht im deutschen Reichstag zwischen 1870 und 1914* (Düsseldorf: Droste, 1973) 230, 259.

them he opposed the centralization of the banking system through the creation of a Reichsbank; such a central bank, he felt, would tend to privilege "big capital and big industry."[41]

Probably Richter's most famous attack in this field was directed against Bismarck's *Sozialpolitik* [social reform], with which the modern welfare state was born. Richter, together with Bamberger, was the chief speaker in opposition to the program, which began with the accident insurance bill of 1881, and over the years he persevered in his point of view when other liberal critics were converted to the new approach. One remark of his was, and is, deemed particularly notorious: "A special social question does not exist for us [the Progressives]. *The social question is the sum of all cultural questions*"[42]—by which he meant that, in the last analysis, the standard of living of working people can only be raised through higher productivity, a viewpoint perhaps not totally devoid of sense.

It is above all this opposition to *Sozialpolitik* with which Richter is reproached.[43] If one judges from the standpoint of world history as the tribunal of the world, Richter was certainly in the wrong. The welfare state is today conquering the whole globe; even the grandiose socialist idea is on the point of being reduced to a mere set of comprehensive

---

41 Richter, *Im alten Reichstag*, 1, 112.
42 Ibid. 2, 86. (Emphasis in original)
43 See, among many others, Dieter Langewiesche, *Liberalismus in Deutschland* (Frankfurt a.M Suhrkamp, 1981 195–96, where Left Liberal opposition on this question is ascribed in part to "Manchesterite blindness." Oskar Stillich, *Die politischen Parteien in Deutschland*. 2, *Der Liberalismus* (Leipzig: Klinkhardt, 1911) 125, referred to "ice-cold laissez-faire in the area of the workers' question," and even maintained that "Liberalism was indifferent and without feeling towards the interest of the broad masses." Erich Eyck, *Bismarck*, (Erlenbach-Zurich: Rentsch, 1941) 3, 372, demonstrated a rare if limited understanding for the Left Liberal position: "In spite of all that, that opposition was not without an internal justification. For it rests on the idea that the feeling of personal responsibility, of the individual citizen for his own destiny is indispensable for the sound development of a people, and that the omnipotence of the state is, in the long run, incompatible with the freedom of the individual." Eyck, too, favored the Bismarckian policy, however, as do all present-day German historians I have consulted. But it should be obvious that even the question of the economic effects of the program is not as simple as is usually supposed, and cannot be resolved by pure assumption: Bismarck's *Sozialpolitik* was based, in the last analysis, on *deductions* (either direct or indirect) from the wages of labor. Cf. W.H. Hutt, *The Strike-Threat System: The Economic Effects of Collective Bargaining* (New Rochelle, N.Y.: Arlington House, 1973), 206–15.

welfare programs. Still, at least one of the reasons Richter advanced against the beginnings of the welfare state has a certain cogency.

> By hindering or restricting the development of independent funds, one pressed along the road of state-help and here awoke *growing claims on the State that, in the long run, no political system can satisfy*.[44]

Richter's words give pause, when one considers the complex of problems gathered under the heading, "The Over-Straining of the Weimar Social State" (the "most progressive social state in the world" in its day), the collapse of the Weimar Republic, and the accompanying seizure of power of the National Socialists.[45] One might also reflect on a circumstance that today appears entirely possible: that, after so many fatal "contradictions" of capitalism have failed to materialize, in the end a genuine contradiction has emerged, one that may well destroy the system, namely the incompatibility of capitalism and the limitless state welfarism yielded by the functioning of a democratic order.

Civil Liberties and the *Rechtsstaat*

While the majority of the Progressives supported the *Kulturkampf*—it was the celebrated liberal and friend of Richter's, Rudolf Virchow, who gave the crusade against the German Catholic Church the label, "struggle of cultures"—Richter generally opposed this fateful conflict, which contributed so much to hardening the Catholic Church's hostility to liberalism.[46] Although he did not challenge his own close political collaborators as much as he might have—he claimed the *Kulturkampf* did "not particularly excite" him[47]—his own position was basically that of authentic liberalism, of the French Catholic liberals and the Jeffersonians: a clear separation of State and Church, including

---

44 Richter, *Politisches ABC-Buch*, 173 (empahsis in original).
45 Cf. Jurgen von Kruedener, "Die Überforderung der Weimarer Republik als Sozialstaat," *Geschichte und Gesellschaft* 11, No. 3 (1985) *Kontroversen uber die Wirtschaflspolitik in der Weimarer Republik*, Heinrich August Winkler (ed.) 358–76.
46 Richter, *Im alten Reichslag*, 1, 54–55.
47 Ibid.78.

complete freedom for private education, and in the case of the Americans a principled rejection of state subsidizing of any religion.[48]

Particularly interesting in this connection is that, for Richter, "the private school was the last possible refuge."[49] In contrast to the majority of German (and of French and other) liberals of his time, Richter was not inclined to place obstacles in the way of the private school system in order to promote his own secular *Weltanschauung*. As he expressed it:

> Even if it were true that by using the free private system of instruction schools would come into being less agreeable to my point of view than the public schools, I would still not let myself be led astray, or desist, out of a fear of Catholics or a fear of socialists.[50]

Similarly, Richter took to the field against the emerging anti-Semitic movement,[51] with which Bismarck coquetted in another of his efforts to subvert the liberals. Richter branded the anti-Semites "unnational," referring to them as "this movement damaging to our national honor." In turn, the anti-Semites labeled the Left Liberals around Richter "Jew guard-troops,"[52] and attempted, as had the Social Democrats, to disrupt liberal meetings in Berlin through violence.[53] Until the end of Richter's career, the German-Jewish middle classes formed an important

---

48 Rohfleisch, *Eugen Richter: Opponent of Bismarck*, 37–40, and Rachfahl, "Eugen Richter," 278.
49 Urs Müller-Plantenberg, *Der Freisinn nach Bismarcks Sturz: Ein Versuch über die Schwierigkeiten des liberalen Bürgertums, im wilhelminischen Deutschland um zu Macht und politischem Einfluss zu gelangen* (unpubl.diss.; Free University of Berlin, 1971) 201.
50 Ibid.
51 See Richter, *Im alten Reichstag*, 2, 176–83, 200–03, and the articles, "Anti-Semiten" and "Juden," in *ABC-Buch*, 17–23 and 174–79; also Alfred D. Low, *Jews in the Eyes of the Germans: From the Enlightenment to Imperial Germany* (Philadelphia: Institute for the Study of Human Issues, 1979) 392–94.
52 Fritz Stern, *Gold and Iron: Bismarck, Bleichröder, and the Building of the German Empire* (New York: Viking/Penguin, 1987), 524.
53 To protect their meetings against anti-Semitic assaults, the liberals had recourse to a sort of private police agency; Richter, *Im alten Reichstag* 2, 203.

part of the liberal following, in part on account of the liberal principle of separation of Church and State.[54]

In general, Richter had learned very well from the great theoreticians of the *Rechtsstaat*, Dahlmann and Mohl. He fought a bill to criminalize the slander and mockery of state institutions, marriage, and private property.[55] In the case of the Social Democrats themselves, he opposed the notorious and futile Socialist Laws, with which Bismarck attempted to suppress the SPD.[56] (In this matter, however, Richter appears on one occasion to have played, in the midst of Reichstag machinations, the politician rather than the principled liberal.[57]) Similarly with measures for the suppression of the Poles in Germany's eastern territories. Ideas and competing cultural values, in Richter's view, were not to be combated by force.[58]

Richter's familiarity with the financial affairs of Prussia and of Germany was unequaled.[59] From the beginning of his parliamentary service, his attention was focused most particularly on the military budget, and this old question, which had produced the great constitutional conflict of the 1860s and split German liberalism on several occasions, accompanied him throughout his whole political life. A proponent of low taxes, especially for the poorer classes,[60] Richter was concerned with moderating the enormous financial demands of the military; in this effort he did not shy away even from wrangling with the venerable Count von Moltke. Above all, he was concerned that the authority of the people's representatives, the Reichstag, should prevail over the Army, that the citizen should not be submerged in the soldier. Thus, his insistence on the two-year, rather than three-year, military

---

54 Low, *Jews in the Eyes of the Germans* 389–90.
55 Richter, *Im alten Reichstag* 2, 128–29.
56 Ibid. 81–84; Wolfgang Pack, *Das Parlamentarische Ringen um das Sozialistengesetz Bismarcks 1878–1890* (Düsseldorf: Droste, 1961) 81–82.
57 Ibid. 153–60.
58 Richter's lifelong fight for the *Rechtsstaat* and the predominance of parliament is so well known in the literature that Leonard Krieger's assertion, "Radical liberalism in him tended to be wholly absorbed in the dogma of economic freedom," *The German Idea of Freedom* (Boston: Beacon Press, 1957) 397, can only be explained by simple-minded political bias.
59 Rachfahl, "Eugen Richter," 274–75.
60 See, e.g., Richter, *Im alten Reichstag*, 1, 103, 127; 2, 58, 68–69.

service, which led to a further split in the liberal party, in 1893.[61] His tireless probing into every single expenditure once caused Bismarck to cry out that in this fashion one would never come to the end of a budget.[62] Regarding his interrogation of a minister on a financial matter, Richter wrote, with proud underscoring: *"But I didn't let go."*[63] In the field of the spending of public money, that could well have been his lifelong motto.

The great social scientist Max Weber, who was a National rather than a Left Liberal, nevertheless declared:

> Despite Eugen Richter's pronounced unpopularity within his own party, he enjoyed an unshakable power position, which rested on his unequalled knowledge of the budget. He was surely the last representative who could check over every penny spent, to the very last canteen, with the War Minister; at least, this is what, despite any annoyance they felt, has often been admitted to me by gentlemen of this department.[64]

In this continuing feature of Richter's, activity it is possible to see the most significant example in the whole history of parliamentary liberalism of the standpoint expressed by Frédéric Bastiat, when he wrote of peace and freedom and their connection with the "icy numbers" of a "vulgar state budget":

> The connection is as close as possible. A war, a threat of war, a negotiation that could lead to war—none of these is capable of coming to pass except by virtue of a small clause inscribed in this great volume [the budget], the terror of taxpayers. . . . Let us seek

---

61 Müller-Plantenberg, *Der Freisinn nach Blsmarcks Sturz.*
62 Rohfleisch, *Eugen Richter: Opponent of Bismarck*, 103.
63 Richter, *Im allen Reichstag*, 1, 68.
64 Max Weber, *Gesammelte Politische Schriften*, Johannes Wickelmann (ed.) (Tübingen J.C.B. Mohr [Paul Siebeck], 1958) 333. Weber's allusion to Richter's unpopularity refers to others in the liberal leadership, not to the ordinary liberal voters.

first of all frugality in government—peace and freedom we will have as a bonus.[65]

War, Peace, and Imperialism

On questions of war and peace, Richter shared the views of the radical-liberals, or "Manchester men," of the nineteenth century, who were hostile to war and highly skeptical of the arguments for large military establishments and colonial adventures.[66] In Britain this was the position of Richard Cobden and John Bright, and later of Herbert Spencer; in France, of Benjamin Constant, J.-B. Say, Bastiat, and many others. The German liberals, too, placed a high value on peace (although their attitude was somewhat skewed by the problem of national unification). John Prince Smith and his followers were spokesmen for the ideal of "peace through free trade."[67]

Richter criticized increases in the strength of German military forces, pointedly remarking that they have "substantially contributed to a subsequent reciprocal increase in relation to France and Russia."[68] Admiral von Tirpitz's Naval Bills, from 1898 on, which, by setting Germany on a collision course with England, proved to be so fateful, were rejected and denounced by Richter.[69] For Wilhelm II's "*Weltpolitik*" [world politics], he simply had no understanding. To the question, "What is '*Weltpolitik*'?" Richter replied: "Wanting to be there wherever some-

---

[65] Frédéric Bastiat, "Paix et liberte, ou le budget républicain," *Oeuvres complètes*, 5 (Paris: Guillaumin, 1854) 410–11. Even Lorenz, in her disparaging work on Richter, *Eugen Richter*, 235, is forced to admit that, with all of Richter's haggling over military expenditures, at many points one can sense "the spirit of unconditional opposition, that, beyond the saving of money, wanted to spare the people militarism," as well.

[66] Cf. E.K. Bramsted and K.J. Melhuish, *Western Liberalism. A History in Documents from Locke to Croce* (London/New York: Longman, 1978) 278–84. Richter always kept his distance from the organized German peace movement, however, although his cousin, Adolf Richter, and a close political collaborator, Max Hirsch, were among its leaders. Roger Chickering, *Imperial Germany and a World Without War. The Peace Movement and German Society, 1892–1914* (Princeton: Princeton University Press, 1975) 252, 254.

[67] Julius Paul Kohler, *Staat und Gesellschaft in der deutschen Theorie der auswärtigen Wirtschaftspolitik und des internationalen Handels von Schlettwein bis auf Fr. List und Prince-Smith* (Stuttgart: Kohlhammer, 1926) 22–42.

[68] Richter, *Im alten Reichstag*, 1, 93.

[69] Richter, *ABC-Buch*, "Die deutsche Flotte," 416–90.

thing is going wrong."[70] Under his leadership, the *Freisinnige Volkspartei* continued to spurn it. The growing hostility between England and Germany and the war it presaged nearly drove him to despair.[71]

Richter experienced the Age of Imperialism, which began for Germany with Bismarck's initiatives in 1884–85 in Africa and the South Seas. Although he repudiated these early initiatives, his attitude eventually was somewhat ambivalent, and requires examination.

Richter's initial position, which he expressed in June, 1884, was that "colonial policy is extraordinarily expensive," and

> the responsibility for the material development of the colony, as well as for its formation, [is] to be left to the activity and entrepreneurial spirit of our seafaring and trading fellow citizens; the procedure followed should be less of the form of annexation of overseas provinces to the German Reich, than of the form of the granting of charters, on the model of the English royal charters... at the same time, to the parties interested in the colony should essentially be left its governing, and they should be accorded only the possibility of European jurisdiction and its protection that we could furnish without having standing garrisons there. For the rest, we hope that the tree will generally thrive through the activity of the gardeners who planted it, and if it does not, then the plant is an abortive one, and the damages affect less the Reich, since the costs we require are not significant, than the entrepreneurs, who were mistaken in their undertakings.[72]

---

70 Quoted by Müller-Plantenberg, *Der Freisinn nach Bismarcks Sturz*, 284. In the author's opinion, "no bourgeois politician fought against the military, naval, and colonial policy of Wilhelmine Germany as sharply, energetically, and consistently as Eugen Richter."
71 Paul Kennedy, *The Rise of the Anglo-German Antagonism, 1860–1914*, 150–51.
72 Quoted in Hans Spellmayer, *Deutsche Kolonialpolitik im Reichstag* (Stuttgart: Kohlhammer, 1931) 15–16.

Not Total "Dogmatism," but Occasional Pragmatism was Richter's Failing

A critic of Richter's, the influential Weimar radical-democratic historian Eckart Kehr, maintained that Richter rejected the Naval Bills and *Weltpolitik* merely from "capitalist motives," simply because they were not profitable.[73] The truth is that, as always, Richter supported his position with statistics and "pragmatic" reasons of all kinds. But even Kehr had to concede that, for Richter, there were also certain principles involved. As he put it, Richter's standpoint was

> that the State should leave exports to the exporters, to industry, and to the merchants, and should not identify itself with the interests of the exporting class. . . . If industry . . . values the protection afforded by warships, let them go and shell out a part of the surplus profit they have captured in this way and build the cruisers for themselves.[74]

In other words, in this question Richter defended the same principle as on the questions of *Sozialpolitik* and the protective tariff: the State exists for the common good and it ought not to be debased to an instrument of special interests. As naive as this attitude may be, it demonstrates that Richter manifested traits of what can be called the civic humanism or classical republicanism of the Stein-Hardenberg variety.[75]

The genuine failing in Richter's approach to imperialism is that he never systematically posed the question, "Profitable for *whom*?" It is true that Richter opposed Bismarck's colonial plans in the conviction that their core was "the burdening of the relatively unpropertied to the advantage of the relatively propertied."[76] Yet, in the next decade, when

---

73 Eckart Kehr, *Schlachtflottenbau und Parteipolitik, 1894–1901* (Berlin: Ebering, 1930) 293.
74 Ibid. 297–98.
75 A civic humanist, rather than liberal slant is evident also in Richter's advocacy of a "citizen-army," recruited by conscription. This was aimed at placing the army under the control of the people at large, rather than the rulers, the central issue in the constitutional struggles of the 1860s.
76 Hans-Ulrich Wehler, *Bismarck und der Imperialismus* (Cologne/Berlin: Kiepenheuer und Witsch, 1969) 444.

Germany occupied Kiaochow, in China, and undertook the construction of a railroad in Shantung, Richter showed himself more amenable than before.[77] He declared:

> we [the *Freisinn*] view the acquisition of the [Kiaochow] Bay otherwise and more favorably than all the previous flag-raisings in Africa and Australia [i.e., New Guinea and the South Seas]. The difference for us is that ... China is an old civilized country ... and that transformations that have been introduced into China, especially by the last Sino-Japanese War, could cause it to appear desirable to possess a base there for safeguarding our interests.[78]

Yet, Richter's last parliamentary speeches, in 1904, both in the Reichstag and in the Prussian House of Delegates, dealt with colonial questions in a sharply negative manner. Again, he put himself forward as, above all, "the representative of the whole community, the representative of the taxpayers," and complained of "the neglect of urgent needs in domestic policy on account of the demands of a misconceived colonial policy."[79]

In explaining Richter's inconsistency in this area, the comment of Lothar Albertin is pertinent: Richter "remained, in regard to imperialism, without a theory [*theorielos*]."[80] He was never able to advance to the interpretation of imperialism of a Richard Cobden, for example, according to which economic expansion supported by means of the state *always* redounds to the advantage of certain interests and to the disadvantage of the taxpayers and the majority. Thus, on this issue Richter belonged, in Wolfgang Mommsen's suggestive typology, to the

---

77 Spellmayer, *Deutsche Kolonialpolitik im Reichstag*, 81, 89.
78 Quoted in Ludwig Elm, "Freisinnige Volkspartei," in *Die bürgerlichen Partien in Deutschland*, Dieter Fricke, et al. (eds.), ([East]Berlin: Das europäische Buch, 1970) 2, 84.
79 Rachfahl, "Eugen Richter," 369–70.
80 Lothar Albertin, "Das Friedensthema bei den Linksliberalen vor 1914: Die Schwäche Ihrer Argumente und Aktivitaten," in Karl Holl und Günther List (eds.), *Liberalismus und Imperialistischer Staat. Der Imperialismus als Problem liberaler Parteien in Deutschland, 1890–1914* (Gottingen: Vandenhoeck and Ruprecht, 1975) 92–93.

"pragmatic" *entschieden* liberals, rather than to the "principled" radical-liberals.[81]

The Liberal Surrender

The final capitulation of German liberalism was inaugurated by Friedrich Naumann,[82] today viewed in what pass for liberal circles in the Federal Republic as a kind of secular saint. Ambitious and endowed with enormous drive, Naumann was politically insightful, as well. He recognized how the rules of the political game had changed:

> What fundamentally destroyed liberalism was the entry of the class-movement into modern politics, the entry of the agrarian and industrial-proletarian movements. . . . The old liberalism was no representative of a class-movement, but a world-view that balanced all differences among classes and social orders . . .[83]

In some respects, Naumann anticipated the central insight of the school of Public Choice when he described the development of modern democracy:

> The economic classes contemplated to what end they might make use of the new means of parliamentarianism . . . gradually, they learned that politics is fundamentally a great business, a struggling and a haggling [Markten] for advantages, over whose lap collects the most rewards cast by the legislation-machine.[84]

Richter, too, understood this.[85] The small difference, however, was that the opportunist Naumann *endorsed* the new rules of the game

---

81 Wolfgang Mommsen, 'Wandlungen der liberalen Idee im Zeitalter des Imperialismus," in ibid. 122.

82 See Peter Theiner, *Sozialer Liberalismus und deutsche Weltpolitik: Friedrich Naumann im Wilhelminischen Deutschland (1860–1919)*, (Baden-Baden: Nomos, 1983), and William O. Shanahan, "Liberalism and Foreign Affairs: Naumann and the Prewar German View," *The Review of Politics*, 21, No. 1 (January 1959).

83 Friedrich Naumann, "Der Niedergang des Liberalismus," *Werke*, 4 (Opladen: Westdeutscher Verlag, 1964), 218.

84 Ibid. 220.

85 See, for instance, his remarks regarding Bismarck's legislation ("the foyer of the Reichstag resembled a marketplace."), cited in Raico, "Der deutsche Liberalismus," 279.

and wished to see a revived liberal movement adopt them wholeheartedly.[86] Together with his close friend, Max Weber, Naumann tried to fashion a liberalism more "adapted" to the circumstances of the twentieth century, and to win liberal leaders like Theodor Barth to his strategy. In contrast to the hopelessly prosaic Richter, Naumann knew how to shape a political vision and offer it to a new generation alienated from classical liberal ideas.[87]

In Naumann's conception, liberalism had to make its peace with Social Democracy, by taking up the cause of *Sozialpolitik* and other "claims" of labor. At the same time, it had to snatch the national cause from the conservatives, by becoming the most zealous advocate of *Weltpolitik* and imperialism and learning to appreciate the German drive to authority and prestige in the world (*Weltgeltung*). It must both "absorb state-socialist elements"[88] and develop "an understanding for the power-struggle among the nations."[89] In short, liberalism must become "national-social." Naturally, Naumann was wild about the naval build up. Already in 1900, he was blissfully convinced that war with England was a "certainty."[90]

For the sake of liberalism's future in Germany, Eugen Richter had to be "definitely fought."[91] Towards Richter, now the grand old man of Left Liberalism, Naumann had a kind of good-natured contempt. To one of his National Social audiences, he declared:

---

86 Friedrich Naumann, "Klassenpolitik des Liberalismus," *Werke*, 4, 257–58.
87 Of Richter, Urs Müller-Plantenberg, *Der Freisinn nach Bismarcks Sturz*, 89, very correctly writes: "In his *ABC-Books* for liberal voters, Richter processed a plethora of statistics, dates, facts, and legislative paragraphs into rational arguments, which, absent a whole that might have come to light behind it all, could never have their full effect."
88 Friedrich Naumann, "Liberalismus als Prinzip," *Werke*, 4, 252.
89 Friedrich Naumann, "Niedergang des Liberalismus," ibid. 224.
90 Paul M. Kennedy, *The Rise of the Anglo-German Antagonism, 1860–1914*, 340. Typical of the historical treatment of the Richter-Naumann dichotomy, Winfried Baumgart, *Deutschland im Zeitalter des Imperialismus, 1890–1914*, 160, writes of "the mitigation of the earlier [liberal] dogmatism" in foreign as in domestic policy that is "to be ascribed to the work of Friedrich Naumann." When all is said and done, however, one may well be of the opinion that even more important than whether a given foreign policy position was or was not "dogmatic" is whether it promoted peace or war. One may also question whether the concept of "dogmatism" itself has much heuristic, in contrast to polemical, value.
91 Friedrich Naumann, "Niedergang des Liberalismus," *Werke*, 4, 234.

Eugen Richter is unchangeable, and that is his greatness [Laughter]. But under this man, with his unique tenacity in work and will—which must be admired even by those who consider him a peculiar fossil—there are a whole series of people who say, in assemblies and in private: Of course we are for the fleet, but as long as Richter is alive—the man surely has his greatness [Laughter] . . .[92]

Evolution or Dissolution of Liberalism?

Even from the ranks of the younger leaders of Richter's own party there was growing criticism of his position on the colonies and the naval buildup. In 1902, on the floor of the Reichstag one of Richter's own protégés, Richard Eickhoff, thanked the War Minister on behalf of his constituents for a new armaments contract, taking the opportunity to request still more contracts, and joking that "*l'appétit vient en mangeant* ["appetite comes in the eating]."[93] With Richter's death in 1906, the old liberal negativity and carping criticism in military matters—and the history of German Manchesterism—came to an end. German Left Liberalism had no further objections to the Imperial military budget. Eight years later would come that summer of 1914 and the confrontation with the powerful and hostile coalition including England that Richter had feared and warned against, and which proved a monumental disaster for Germany.

A few years after Richter's death, the then well-known nationalist historian, Erich Marcks, spoke of the "supersession of the older liberalism." This liberalism had, to be sure, saturated and impregnated the whole life of the modern nations; its effects continued to be felt everywhere. It was indestructible. But, added the biographer and adulator of Bismarck:

---

92 Ibid. 232. Theodor Heuss faithfully follows his mentor Naumann, when he writes of Richter: he saw "the objective of the power-state only in the distortion of militarism," *Friedrich Naumann: Der Mann, das Werk, die Zeit*, 242.
93 Roger Chickering, *Imperial Germany and a World Without War. The Peace Movement and German Society, 1892–1914*, 255.

Together with its own most distinctive political principle it has now been eclipsed. The idea of increased state force, the idea of power, has displaced it. And it is this idea that everywhere fills the leading men mightily and decisively dominates them: we have met with this same drive, quite apart from Russia, where it never disappeared, in [Theodore] Roosevelt and [Joseph] Chamberlain, and recognize it in Bismarck and Kaiser Wilhelm II.[94]

German Liberalism as "English Trader-Spirit"

Ultimately, the enmity between England and Germany, which Richter had so bitterly fought, contributed greatly to the outbreak of the Great War—the enmity, it should be noted, not the *economic competition*, since England and America were also in that sense competitors (and, of course, also customers), a circumstance that did not result in contention. German hatred of England[95] found its culmination, and its *reductio ad absurdum*, in a work by the scholar who was then probably the most famous economic historian in the world, Werner Sombart, a leader of the interventionist *Verein für Sozialpolitik*. To understand what the German anti-liberalism of the early twentieth century meant, the best work to consult is Sombart's *Traders and Heroes*,[96] which appeared in the war year 1915.

The underlying thesis is that there exist two "spirits" whose eternal strife comprises world history, the trader-spirit and the hero-spirit, and two peoples who today incarnate each of these. Naturally, the English are the traders, the Germans the heroes. Sombart's work, to the extent that it is not a hymn of praise to war and death, is often even comical, e.g., when the author asserts: "The foundation of everything English is

---

94 Erich Marcks, *Männer und Zeiten: Aufsätze und Reden zur neueren Geschichte* 4th rev. ed. (Leipzig: Quelle und Meyer, 1916) 260.
95 Concerning the equally fateful English hatred of Germany, see my contribution, "The Politics of Hunger: A Review," *The Review of Austrian Economics* (1988), 253–59, reprinted in my collection, *Great Wars and Great Leaders: A Libertarian Rebuttal*.
96 Werner Sombart, *Händler und Helden: Patriotische Besinnnngen* (Munich/Leipzig: Duncker und Humblot, 1915).

certainly the unfathomable spiritual limitedness of this people"[97]; or when he devotes a chapter to English science without mentioning even Isaac Newton[98]; or when he maintains that the English since the time of Shakespeare have produced no cultural value.[99]

Much more serious than this claptrap and characteristic for the time is Sombart's seconding of Ferdinand Lassalle in dismissing the liberal ideal as merely that of "the nightwatchman state."[100] Many in the next two generations would echo Sombart's judgment on German liberalism, when he described its golden age and decline:

> But then there came another bleak time for Germany, when in the 1860s and 1870s the representatives of the so-called Manchester School quite shamelessly hawked imported English goods on the streets of Germany as German products. . . . And it is well-known how today this "Manchester theory" has been contemptuously shoved aside by theoreticians and practitioners in Germany as totally mistaken and useless.

The two sentences that conclude this passage end, however, in question marks:

> So that perhaps we may say that in the conception of the state, it is the German spirit that in Germany itself has achieved sole sway? Or does the English trader-spirit still haunt some heads?[101]

As regards Richter, it would be pointless to deny that a certain air of "trader-spirit," or, rather, of a middle-class mentality, always surrounded him. There is certainly some truth in Theodor Heuss's accusation of a "monumental petty-bourgeois quality" about Richter.[102] He knew no foreign languages, and the few times he traveled abroad it was to vacation in Switzerland. Richter seems to have had little interest in

---

97 Ibid. 9.
98 Ibid. 17–34.
99 Ibid. 48.
100 Ibid. 25.
101 Ibid. 75.
102 Heuss, *Friedrich Naumann: Der Mann, das Werk, die Zeit*, 180.

the affairs of other countries, even in the fortunes of the liberal movement there. Theodor Barth, spokesman for a Left Liberalism associated with the big banks and exporting merchant houses, jokingly replied to the question, what distinguished his own party from Richter's: if a man can tell Mosel from Rhine wine, he was a member of Barth's party, if not, then of Richter's.[103]

But Richter's "petty-bourgeois quality" was something that his followers in the German middle-classes, in the liberal professions and small business, particularly in the great cities and above all in Berlin, felt, understood, and responded to.[104] A dwindling remnant as the years went by, they represented a German version of William Graham Sumner's "Forgotten Man."[105] Six years after Sumner's classic description was published in the United States, the journalist Alexander Meyer wrote in Richter's *Freisinnige Zeitung* that the liberals were

> the party of the small man, who depends on himself and his own powers, who demands no gifts from the state, but only wants not to be hindered in improving his position to the best of his abilities and to strive to leave his children a better lot in life than came to him.[106]

A rare glimpse of such a German "forgotten man" is given in the moving portrayal by the eminent conductor Bruno Walter of his father, a Berlin Jew,

> accountant in a larger silk firm, for which he worked, in gradually rising positions and with a growing income, for over fifty years. He was a quiet man, with a strict sense of duty and total dependability, and outside of his profession he knew only his family . . .

---

103 Konstanze Wegner, *Theodor Barth und die Freisinnige Vereinigung. Studien zur Geschichte des Linksliberalismus im wilhelminischen Deutschland (1893–1910)* 100.
104 Ibid. 99–101.
105 William Graham Sumner, "On the case of a Certain Man Who is Never Thought Of" and "The Case of the Forgotten Man Further Considered" (1884), in idem, *War and Other Essays*, Albert Galloway Keller (ed.), (New Haven, Conn.: Yale University Press, 1911) 247–68.
106 Quoted in Müller-Plantenberg, *Der Freisinn nach Bismarcks Sturz*, 146.

he voted liberal and venerated Rudolf von Virchow and Eugen Richter.[107]

Undeniably "petty-bourgeois" through and through, such men had little love for *Weltpolitik* and invigorating wars or for the overthrow of all existing social conditions in the name of a Marxist dream, and they stood by Richter to the end.[108]

"What Richter Can Still Mean for Us"

In 1931, the 25th anniversary of Richter's death, the social-liberal historian Erich Eyck posed the question whether Eugen Richter could "still mean something for us."[109]

After all that the Germans have gone through since Richter's time, it is easier to ascertain where his significance lies. He was, as regards Germany, *the* principal advocate of the liberal world-revolution that constitutes the meaning of modern history. Through four decades he fought, as politician and publicist, for what Werner Sombart scorned as the "English trader-spirit": for peace; a decent life for all classes through the market economy and free trade; pluralism and the peaceable rather than violent clash of world-views and cultural values; and citizenly self-respect instead of servility. As against all conservative reproaches, he was always a proud patriot. But he could never understand why it was the Germans—of all people—who should not enjoy their individual rights.

Florin Afthalion has remarked, in the case of Frédéric Bastiat:

> How are we to explain that a man who fought for free trade a century before the majority of the industrialized nations made it their official doctrine, who condemned colonialism also a century

---

107 Bruno Walter, *Thema und Variationen; Erinnerungen und Gedanken* (Stockholm Bermann-Fischer, 1947) 16 and 21.
108 Cf. Franz Mehring's view, admittedly sardonic, "that [Richter] did not create the *Freisinnige Partei* in his own image, but that they chose him as their leader, because they saw in him their most fitting image." *Gesammelte Schriften*, Thomas Höhle, Hans Kock, and Josef Schleifstein (eds.), 15, *Politische Publizistik 1905 bis 1918* ([East]Berlin: Dietz, 1966) 165.
109 Erich Eyck, "Eugen Richter," in *Auf Deutschlands Politischem Forum* (Erlenbach-Zurich: Rentsch, 1963) 47.

before decolonization . . . who, above all, proclaimed an era of economic progress and the enrichment of all classes of society, should be forgotten, while the majority of his intellectual adversaries, prophets of stagnation and pauperization, who were wrong, still have freedom of the city?[110]

The case of Eugen Richter is similar and perhaps even more egregious. Certainly, in his own time Richter "failed." But if this is proposed as the grounds for neglecting the most important of the political leaders of authentic liberalism in Germany, then the ready reply would be: which politician in modern German history before Adenauer and Erhard did not sooner or later fail?

For what he was and what he represented—if one may say so: from the mere fact that this great man "never trusted any government"[111]—the gruff old Rhineland liberal deserves to be better treated by the historians and, by the Germans, not to be completely forgotten.

---

110 Florin Afthalion, "Introduction," in Frédéric Bastiat, *Oeuvres économiques* (Paris: Presses Universitaires de France, 1983) 8.
111 Müller-Plantenberg, *Der Freisinn nach Bismarcks Sturz*, 200.

9 Arthur Ekirch on American Militarism

In 1783 the treaty ending hostilities between Great Britain and its rebellious colonies along the eastern seaboard of North America was signed in Paris. For their part the English proclaimed that, "His Britannic Majesty acknowledges the said United States, viz., New Hampshire, Massachusetts Bay, Rhode Island and Providence Plantations . . ."—there followed the rest of the thirteen colonies—"to be free sovereign and independent states," with the British Crown relinquishing all claims to "the same and every part thereof."

Amazingly, a collection of artisans, merchants, and mostly farmers had defied one of the great military machines of Europe, and the greatest empire, and won. It was a triumph that gladdened the hearts of lovers of liberty and republican government the world over.

Today, this United States, now definitively in the singular, is itself the world's greatest military machine and sole imperial power. How did this happen? In *The Civilian and the Military*, Arthur Ekirch traces this portentous transformation, at least to 1972 (counting his preface.)

Murray Rothbard called Ekirch's work "brilliant," and praised it as "an example of a revisionist outlook on all three great wars of the twentieth century." Robert Higgs, in his foreword to the Independent

Institute's new edition of Ekirch's *The Decline of American Liberalism*, provides a summary of the life and highly productive academic career of Arthur Ekirch. He notes that Ekirch registered as a conscientious objector in the Second World War but was nonetheless sentenced to work without pay as a logger and later in a school for the mentally retarded, experiences that did not endear the American state to the feisty scholar.

Militarism can be defined as the permeation of civil society by military institutions, influences, and values.
The Anglo-American heritage of explicit anti-militarism began to be formed in seventeenth century England, especially with the Levellers and resistance to a standing army.

This tradition continued among the British settlers of what became the United States. It is evident in the attitudes of the leaders of the American Revolution. James Madison, for instance, stated:

> Of all the enemies to public liberty war is, perhaps, the most to be dreaded, because it comprises and develops the germ of every other. War is the parent of armies; from these proceed debts and taxes; and armies, and debts, and taxes are the known instruments for bringing the many under the domination of the few.

The connection between antimilitarism and non-intervention in the affairs of foreign nations—what its crafty opponents have succeeded in labeling "isolationism"—was often marked among the rebellious colonials. Ekirch points out that "An important argument for independence had been that it would free the American people from involvement in the wars of Europe and from the necessity of helping to support a British army." The radical republican position was put boldly by Jefferson: "I am for free commerce with all nations; political connection with none; and little or no diplomatic establishment."

But during their presidencies, Jefferson and especially Madison reneged on their non-interventionist and antiwar position. The War Hawks in their party clamored for confrontation with England, hoping to acquire Canada. Though this proved impossible, Madison's War of 1812 was considered a success. A military spirit was awakened, shown in the popular adulation of war heroes and military displays at Fourth of July parades.

As war with Mexico drew near, Daniel Webster criticized the maneuvers of President James Polk. His words were to be the key to America's future wars, from the provisioning of Fort Sumter on. "What is the value of this constitutional provision [granting Congress the sole power to declare war] if the President on his own authority may make such military movements as must bring on war?" Easy victory over Mexico, however, further fueled the military spirit.

If the Jeffersonians can be accused of surrendering their principles, what are we to say of some of the celebrated anti-statists of the nineteenth and early twentieth centuries? Henry David Thoreau, whose conscience rebelled at the U.S. war against Mexico, became an enthusiast for the "just war" against the slave states. He revered John Brown, referring to him as a Christ upon the Cross when Brown tried to raise a servile rebellion among the millions of slaves of the South, a move "credited" with helping start the Civil War. That awful bloodletting cost some 620,000 lives.

Charles Sumner, famous classical liberal and free trader, wrote in his 1845 work, *The True Grandeur of Nations*, "Can there be in our age any peace that is not honorable, any war that is not dishonorable?" But he also found an honorable war in the attack on the South.

Later, Benjamin Tucker, individualist anarchist, was a cheerleader for the Entente's war with Germany. For his part, the anarchist Peter Kropotkin urged Russia on to war with Germany and Austria-Hungary, the Central Powers, in 1914. Poor Kropotkin was bewildered by how it turned out, a Bolshevik tyranny worse than anything ever experienced before. The war itself cost many millions of lives, the worst bloodbath in European history to that time.

The point is that these individualists were no Frédéric Bastiats or Herbert Spencers. None could resist the pull of a *just* war. None understood the insight of Randolph Bourne, whom Ekirch calls one of the few who "stood firm," that "war is the health of the state."

During the Civil War the United States "was placed under what amounted to a military dictatorship." Lincoln suspended the writ of habeas corpus, shut down newspapers critical of his policies, and held thousands as political prisoners. Conscription led to draft riots, particularly in New York City, but a militarist precedent had been set.

Union veterans formed the Grand Army of the Republic, demanding pensions and preference in government jobs. The Army continued to justify their jobs by their taxpayer-funded backing of the railroad barons in the West in their campaigns to exterminate the Plains Indians. Military training and "education" proliferated in schools and colleges. In the 1880s and 90s, navalism surged ahead, with U.S. industry, steel above all, promoting their own vested interest. The tradition of a navy solely for the coastal defense of the country—as old as the Republic—was abandoned.

There were critics of the new militarism, prominent among them E.L. Godkin of *The Nation* and William Graham Sumner, whose essay on *The Conquest of the United States by Spain* (1898), against the war on the Philippines, has inspired anti-imperialists ever since.
But they could not prevail against the powerful cabal of Alfred Thayer Mahan, Henry Cabot Lodge, and Theodore Roosevelt, who represented a turning point on the road to empire.

Mahan was not much of a naval commander (his ships tended to collide), but he was a superb propagandist for navalism. His work *The Influence of Sea Power Upon History, 1660–1783* was seized upon by navalists in Germany, Japan, France, and elsewhere. It fueled the arms race that led to the First World War, and was no great blessing to mankind.

In the Senate, Lodge pushed for war with Spain, the takeover of the Philippines, later for war with Germany, and following the war, for a vindictive peace treaty that would keep the Germans down for the foreseeable future. Throughout, Lodge pressed for a navy second to none, demanded by America's new empire. The Navy League, funded by big business, helped the cause.

Heaven only knows what Theodore Roosevelt is doing on that endlessly reproduced iconic monument on Mount Rushmore, right alongside Jefferson. He despised Jefferson as a weakling, and Jefferson would have despised him as a warmonger. The great Charles Beard truly wrote of Roosevelt that he was probably the only major figure in American history "who thought that war in itself was a good thing."

Included in the cabal was Elihu Root, secretary of war and then of state under TR, who advocated "the creation of a military spirit among the youth of the country."

The acquisition of the Philippines cast the United States into the arena of contending imperialisms in the Far East, including especially Japan's. Anti-war congressmen exposed the links between the drive for a great ocean-going navy and the munitions industry, to no avail.

Ekirch is perhaps too lenient on Woodrow Wilson. Already, Wilson's note to Germany following the sinking of the *Lusitania*, in which he reiterated the U.S. position, that Germany would be held to a "strict accountability" for the deaths of any Americans at sea from U-boats, even when traveling on armed British merchant ships carrying munitions through war zones, set the United States on a collision course for war.

Here Walter Karp's *The Politics of War* presents a more reliable account. During the war, the Espionage and Sedition Acts were used to curb dissent. The Creel Committee on Public Information propagandized for war to a hitherto unprecedented extent. The mass media incited public opinion against the demonized enemy as would become standard to our own day.

Historical revisionism flourished as the archives of major powers were opened up, forced by the Bolsheviks' unlocking of the Russian archives. True accounts of the machinations by which the European powers and then the United States entered the war led to the brief flourishing of anti-war sentiment after 1918.

In 1933 Franklin Roosevelt was sworn in as president. This genial master of deception was not only a fanatic for naval expansion but also harbored grandiose plans for reordering the world. The geopolitical situation of the 1930s in Europe and the Far East gave Roosevelt ample opportunity for overseas meddling. In 1940 the formally opposition party nominated for president Wendell Willkie, as much of an interventionist as FDR. The greatest antiwar movement in history, the

America First Committee, boasted 800,000 members, but quickly folded when Roosevelt got the war he needed and wanted, at Pearl Harbor. In the Second World War America embraced militarism wholeheartedly. It has never looked back.

The worst violation of civil liberties was the rounding up and imprisonment of some 80,000 American citizens of Japanese descent and 40,000 resident Japanese aliens (not eligible for citizenship because foreign born). Emblematic of the hysteria generated by this most just of just wars, the U.S. Supreme Court upheld their incarceration. Renowned liberals Hugo Black, Felix Frankfurter, and William Douglas joined the majority. California Attorney-General Earl Warren was a passionate advocate.

Following the war, "the atmosphere of perpetual crisis and war hysteria" engendered by Washington never let up. Harry Truman initiated what Ekirch rightly calls "the aggressive American foreign policy of the Cold War." Scores of entangling alliances were formed, committing the nation to defending the existing international order against anyone who would challenge it. A new enemy intent on world-conquest was conjured up in the form of the Soviet Union and international communism. This conflict included two "hot wars" and entailed vast continuing military budgets, now including nuclear weapons. It lasted over 40 years and cost civil society trillions of dollars.

As Ekirch presciently foresaw, even a peaceful resolution of the Cold War was not "sufficient to release the American people from the power of the Pentagon and its corporate allies." Incursions of the armed forces occurred in Yugoslavia, the Philippines, Somalia, and elsewhere.

Now the United States is involved in wars in Iraq, Afghanistan, Pakistan, and Yemen, soon perhaps also in Iran.

Today there is no conscription, which caused too many problems for the militarists in the Vietnam years. But the American empire bestrides the globe. The United States has over 700 military bases overseas, plus some dozen naval task forces patrolling the oceans, with a multitude of space satellites feeding information to the forces below. Every year its "defense" (i.e., military) budget is nearly equal to those of all other countries combined. Does anyone doubt that for America there are more wars, many more wars, in the offing?

As the great social scientist Joseph Schumpeter wrote of the military in imperialist states:

> *Created by the wars that required it, the machine now created the wars it required.*

Index

absolutism, 93
Acton, H. B., 120
Afthalion, Florin, 328–329
Albertin, Lothar, 321
Alter, Max, 4
American militarism, xxii
Ancient Liberty, 222–223
Anderson, Gary M., 132
Anderson, Perry, xxi, 259
Angel, Pierre, 83
Annals of the American Academy of Political and Social Science, 112
Anti-Capitalistic Mentality, The, xvii
Appleby, Joyce, 95
apriorism, 13–18
Aquinas, St. Thomas, 92
Arblaster, Anthony, 74–75
Aron, Raymond, 120
Arpinati, Leandro, 281
Ashton, T. S., 112
Augustine, St., 93
Austrian Economic Theory, 19–23
   business cycle theory, 20
   cause of economic action, 22
   ideology behind, 27–32
   prices as information, 21
   social philosophy, 32–39
   ties to liberalism, 19–23, 32–29
Austrian School of economics, ix, xiv, 1
   and classical liberalism, 1–51
   criticism of methodology, 7
   economic policy, 32–35
   vs. neoclassical economics, 8–11
   and subjectivism, 7–12
   see also, subjectivism
   on welfare economics, 10–11

Balogh, Thomas, 158
Barry, Norman, 80, 95, 99, 130
Bastiat, Frédéric, 221, 240
Bellamy, Edward, 84
Berger, Suzanne, 213
Berlin, Isaiah, 18, 222, 257
Berman, Harold J., 91
Bernstein, Eduard, 83
Birdzell, L. E., 18
Birken, Lawrence, 12
Bismarck, Otto von, 88
Blanqui, Adolphe, 185–186
Böhm, Stephan, 35
Böhm-Bawerk, Eugen, 5, 32
   on Austrian economic policy, 35–38
Bolsheviks, 134–136
Boos, Margarete, 51
Boudon, Raymond, 123
bourgeois economics, 7
Brandt, Karl, 31
Brentano, Lujo, 35
Briefs, Goetz, 87
Bright, John, 69
Bringing the State Back In (Skocpol), 213

Bronfenbrenner, Martin, 116
Brunner, Karl, 71, 150, 154, 175
Buchanan, James, 153, 252
Bukharin, Nikolai, 30
Burke, Edmund, 24, 80

Cairncross, Alec, 157
Cairnes, J. E., 250
Calhoun, John C., 212
Cantor, Norman F., 92
Capital (Marx), 17, 184
Capital and Interest (Böhm-Bawerk), 10
Capitalism and Freedom (Friedman), 248
Capitalism and the Historians (Hayek), 18, 112, 113–115
Capitalism, Socialism and Democracy (Schumpeter), 286
Carlyle, A. J., 91
Catholic Church
 role in liberalism, 90–93
Censeur Européen, Le, 189–204, 220, 231
centralized power, 226–228
Chadwick, Owen, 79
Chicherin, Boris, 272
Choi, Young Back, 128
Churchill, Winston, 151, 258
Cicero, 127
Civil War in France, The (Marx), 200
Civilian and the Military, The (Ekirch), 332
class conflict, xix, 183–214
classical economics, 7
classical liberalism, xiii, xvi, xviii, 1, 222, 259
 see also liberalism
Coase, Ronald, 111
Cobden, Richard, 69, 77, 133
Colbert, 208
Colburn, Forrest D., 133
Cole, Margaret, 169, 171

Collectivist Economic Planning (ed. Hayek), 174
Commentaire sur l'Esprit des Lois de Montesquieu (Destutt de Tracy), 201
Commentaire sur l'ouvrage de Filangieri (Constant), 248
commerce, 190
Communist Manifesto see *Manifesto of the Communist Party*
Comte, Charles, 79, 193, 200, 201, 204, 206
Constant, Benjamin, xx, 9, 100, 121, 194, 222–226, 231, 248, 257
Constantin, C., 234
Constitution on Liberty, The (Hayek), 220
Counter-Revolution of Science, The, xvii, 6
Cours d'économie politique (Pareto), 185
Cowling, Maurice, xv, 78–79
Cranston, Maurice, 85, 150
credit expansion, 20
Crisis and Leviathan (Higgs), 137
Cubeddu, Raimondo, 68

Dahrendorf, Ralf, 99
Dasgupta, A. K., 23
Davis, R. W., 83
de la Mare, Nicolas, 87
de Stefani, Alberto, 280
de Viti de Marco, Antonio, 276–279
De officiis (Cicero), 127
De l'esprit de conquête et de l'usurpation (Constant), 190
Decline of American Liberalism, The (Ekirch), 333
Democracy in America (Tocqueville), 227
Den Uyl, Douglas J., 71
desacralization of the state, 93
Descartes, René, 13
Destutt de Tracy, Antoine, 189–190, 201

Dewey, John, 84
Dicey, A. V., 247
Diggers, 94
Disquisition on Government (Calhoun), 212
Doctrinaires, 205
Döhn, Lothar, 70
Dolan, Edward G., 10
Döllinger, Ignaz von, 233
Droll, 133
Dunn, John, 80
Dunoyer, Charles, xix, 189–190, 193, 195–196, 201, 240

Eccleshall, Robert, 102
economic growth
  savings vs. credit expansion, 20
Economists and the Public (Hutt), 150
education system, 138–139
Eighteenth Brumaire of Louis Bonaparte, The (Marx), 199
Einaudi, Luigi, 250–251, 277–278
Ekelund, Robert B., Jr., 32
Ekirch, Arthur, xxii, 332–338
Elster, Jon, xiv, 4, 141
Employment Act of 1946 (US), 155
Engelhardt, H. Tristram, 237–238
Engels, Friedrich, xix, 121, 183–188
Envy (Schoeck), 128
envy and envy-avoidance, 128–129
Erhard, Ludwig, 155
Esai sur l'Histoire de la Formation et des Progrès du Tiers État (Thierry), 206–209

Faguet, Émile, 222
fascism, 153, 258–264
  Mises's rejection of, 261
  rise of, 269–271
Federal Reserve, 130, 151
Ferguson, Adam, 27
Ferrara, Francesco, 250

Fetter, Frank A., 28
Figgis, John Neville, xvi
Fourier, Charles, 126
Fourier complex, 126, 287
Freeden, Michael, 73–74
French liberalism, 219–253
  Molinari, 238–246
  Montalembert, 230–238
  political centralization, 226–228
Freud, Sigmund, 172
Friedman, Milton, xiv, 72, 248
  attack on Mises, 14–15
  response to attack, 15

Garrison, Roger W., 10, 159
Gaxotte, Pierre, 241
General Theory of Employment, Interest, and Money, The (Keynes), 150, 151, 161, 163
George, David Lloyd, 69
German Liberalism, 303
Gesell, Silvio, 152
Giretti, Edoardo, 280–281
goods of higher order, 23
Gorbachev, Mikhail, 136
Gottfried, Paul, 75, 88
government action, *see* state intervention role of, 239
government jobs, 197–198
Gramsci, Antonio, 265
Gray, John, 71
Great Wars and Great Leaders: A Libertarian Rebuttal, xxiii
Green, T. H., 81
Gruner, Shirley M., 205
Guizot, François, 187, 205–207, 233

Hacker, L. M., 112
Hall, John A., 72
Hamburger, Joseph, xv, 79
Hardin, Russell, 94
Harrod, Roy, 162

Hartwell, R. M., 114–115, 130, 140
Hayek, Friedrich, xv, xvii, xx, 112, 117, 136, 157, 220, 239
  apriorism, 13–18
  on British liberals, 246
  on individualism, 13
  on intellectuals and socialism, 117–121
  on macroeconomics, 10
  political attitudes, 40–44
Heilperin, Michael, 155, 162, 163
Hekman, Susan J., 98
Herbert, Auberon, xxi
Higgs, Robert, 120, 128, 137–138
Himmelfarb, Gertrude, 72
Hirschman, Albert O., xix, 185, 188
"History and Politics" (Hayek), 139
History of Economic Analysis (Schumpeter), 272–273
History of European Liberalism (Ruggiero), 256
Hobhouse, L. T., 74, 81
Hobson, J. A., 152
Holmes, Stephen, 81, 85–86, 228
Hoppe, Hans-Hermann, 40, 44, 96, 282
Hufeland, 31
Hülsmann, Jörg Guido, 10
Human Action (Mises), 2, 10
human action, 8–9, 14
Humboldt, Wilhelm von, 9, 44, 87
  on government intervention, 11
Hume, David, 94
Hutchison, T. W., 30, 31
  attack on Mises, 13–16
  response to attack, 15–16
Hutt, W. H., 23, 150, 152

ideology, 137–138
Illusion of the Epoch, The (Acton), 120
immigration, 289–292
imperialism, 292–293

In Coena Domini, 92
individual human beings, 7–12
  human actors, 8–9
  see also, human action
individual rights, xiii
individualism, 13, 95
individuality
  as effects inequality, 12
Industrialism, 189, 193–204
  critique of, 204
inequality of humans, 12
Influence of Sea Power Upon History, The 1660–1783, xxii, 334
intellectuals, anti-capitalism, 111–141
  bias, 140
  envy, 128–129
  historical myths, 139–141
Investigations (Menger), 3, 5

Jaguaribe, Helio, 72
Jasay, Anthony de, 43–44
John Stuart Mill and the Religion of Humanity (Raeder), 79
Johnson, Harry, 151–152
Jouvenel, Bertrand de, 112–114
July Monarchy, 210

Kautsky, Karl, 29
Kauder, Emil, 22, 26, 33, 34
Kehr, Eckart, 320
Kennedy, Paul, 303
Keynes, John Maynard, xvii, xviii, 69
  and the arts, 160–161
  on eugenics, 159–160
  hatred of money, 171–175
  and liberalism, 149–175
  Keynesian System, 151–156
  on Soviet Communism, 166–171
  and totalitarian "experiments," 161–166
  and utopia, 158–161

Khrushchev, Nikita, 135
Kirzner, Israel, 4, 8, 9, 11, 18, 22, 116
   on freedom in market processes, 21–23
   on welfare economics, 11
Kitch, Edmund, 111
Klinger, Friedrich, 93
Krieger, Leonard, 86
Krohn, Claus-Dieter, 259–262

labor theory of value, 28–32
Lachmann, Ludwig, 7, 8, 97
   on inequality, 12
Lacordaire, Henri-Dominique, 228
laissez-faire, 81–82, 156, 162, 201
   as a political guideline, 246–253
Lange, Oskar, 20
Langton, Stephen, 92
Laski, Harold, 256
Lassalle, Ferdinand, 34, 311–312
Law and Revolution (Berman), 91
Law of Force, The (Wieser), 33
Leggett, William, 211–212
Lenin, Vladimir, 264
Levellers, 93–94, 333
Levy, Carl, 124
liberalism, ix, x, xiii, xiv, xv, 1, 23
   American liberalism, 73
   attack on the modern state
      liberal response, 93–96
   Christian roots, xvi
   conceptual misuse, 68–75, 84
   differing definitions of, 70–71, 81
   "means" of liberalism, 83
   and the medieval Church, 90–93
   "Old" vs. "New," 81–85
   religious freedom, 94
   roots of authentic liberalism, 89–90
   utilizing the "ideal" type of, 97–102
   and the welfare state, 85–89
Liberalism (Mises), xxi, 255–293
libertarianism, 73–74, 75

liberty, 77
Lilburne, John, 93
Limits of State Action, The (Humboldt), 12, 87
List, Friedrich, 47
Locke, John, 15, 150–151
Lomansky, Loren, 78
Looking Backward (Bellamy), 84
Lord Acton, xx, 85, 90
Loria, Achille, 29
Lukes, Steven, 80–81
Lycurgus Myth, 26–27
Lyon, Eugene, 171

Mably, 27
Macedo, Stephen, 229
Macgregor, D. H., 246
Machlup, Fritz, 3
macroeconomics, 9–10
Madison, James, 333
Magna Carta, 92
Mahan, Alfred Thayer, xxii
Malia, Martin, 134
Manent, Pierre, 67, 89
Manifesto of the Communist Party, xix, 121, 183, 256
Mann, Golo, 121
Manning, David, 77
Mao Zedong, xvii
Marcks, Erich, 324–325
Marcuse, Herbert, 258
marginal utility theory, 32, 37, 41, 138
marginalism, 12, 27, 29
   as an answer to socialism, 27–28
market economy, 22–23
market processes, 10
Marshall, Alfred, 246–247
Marx, Karl, xv, xix, 4, 121, 183–188, 199–201, 209, 252
Marxism, xiv, 7, 199–201
   Marxism-Leninism, 134
Meek, Ronald L., 7, 30

Mehring, Franz, 187, 309
Mencken, H. L., 173
Menger, Karl, 3, 5, 9, 32, 33
   order in society, 23–27
   political positions, 33–34
   social development, 24
   social philosophy, 46–51
   view of the capitalist system, 23
mercantilism, 150–151, 153, 195
Merquior, José, 72–73
methodological individualism, xiv, 3–7
Meyer, Alexander, 327
Mignet, François, 206–207
militarism, 332–338
Mill, John Stuart, xv, xvi, 12, 28, 47, 49, 82, 86, 165, 225, 257
   distortions of liberalism, 76–81
Mirabeau, 87
Mises, Ludwig von, ix, x, xi, xiv, xvii, xxi, 2, 35, 38, 39, 75, 114, 125, 141
   apriorism, 13–18
   attacks on, 13–15
   against interventionism, 21
   critique of socialist planning, 19
   on Fascism, democracy, and imperialism, 255–293
   on immigration, 289–292
   on inequality of humans, 12, 21
   on intellectuals and anti-market attitudes, 126–128
   praxeology, 14
   on reason and history, 44–45
Mises seminar, x
Molinari, Gustave de, xxi, 234–235, 238–246, 283
Montalembert, Charles, Comte de, xix, xx, 230–238, 245
Montesquieu, 201
Montlosier, 190
morality in economics, 2, 3
Morgan, Philip, 269
Morgenstern, Oscar, 32

Muggeridge, Malcolm, 171
Myers, A. R., 92

National Liberals of Imperial Germany, 69
Naumann, Friedrich, 69–70, 322–324
neoclassical economic theory, 8
   minimizing the individual, 8–9
Niebuhr, Reinhold, 24
Nitti, Francesco, 265
Nolte, Ernst, 302
North, Douglass C., 136–137
Nozick, Robert, 116
Nyiri, J. C., 44

O'Donnell, 159
On Liberty (Mill), xvi, 12, 79, 257
Open Society and Its Enemies, The (Popper), xv, 16
Opium of the Intellectuals, The (Aron), 120
order
   in society, 23–27
   spontaneous, 24–27
Oriental Despotism, xxi–xxii

Paine, Thomas, 99
Pantaleoni, Maffeo, 273
Pareto, Vilfredo, 8, 12, 185, 279–284
   and fascism, 265, 274–276
Partei der Freiheit, Die (*The Party of Freedom*), ix, x, xxii
Patterson, Annabel, 94
Paul, Ellen, 86
Peacock, Alan, 162
Pictures of a Social Democratic Future (Richter), 310
Pipes, Richard, 135
"police science," 87
Pollard, Arthur, 140
Popper, Karl, xiv, xv
   mislabeled a liberal, 16–18

Positive Theory of Capital, 34
positivism, 124
praxeology, 2, 14
Principles, (Mill), 49
Principles of Economics (Menger), 1, 28
private property, xiii, xv, 71, 73, 153, 256
progressive taxation, 32, 35, 37, 41
public schools *see* education system

Radnitzky, Gerard, 17
Raeder, Linda, xv, 79
Raico, Ralph, ix–xi, xiii–xxiii
Rauschning, Hermann, 135
Rawls, John, 257
rhetoric, 138 *see also* ideology
Ricardo, David, 28
 labor theory of value, 28
Richelieu, 208
Richter, Eugen, x, xxii, 303–329
 career, 306–307
 opposition to *Sozialpolitik*, 312–314
 social philosophy, 307–310
 on war and imperialism, 318–319
Riehl, Wilhelm Heinrich, 123–124
Rise and Decline of Western Liberalism, The (Arblaster), 74
Rise of Liberalism (Laski), 256
Road to Serfdom, The (Hayek), 42, 119, 157
Robbins, Lionel, 246
Robinson, Joan, 37
Roosevelt, Franklin, 164
Roosevelt, Theodore, xxiii, 334
Röpke, Wilhelm, 155
Roscher, Wilhelm, 31
Rosen, Sherwin, 20
Rosenberg, Nathan, 18
Rothbard, Murray, x, xi, 7, 30, 34, 45, 94, 129–130, 153, 156, 219, 260–261
 on the free market and social order, 23–24

Rousseau, Jean-Jacques, 26
Rowley, 150, 157
Ruggiero, Guido de, 68, 256
Ruyer, Raymond, 122–123, 130
Ryan, Alan, 75, 76

Saint-Simon, Henri de, 6, 79, 189
Salerno, Joseph, 158
Sartori, Giovanni, 137
Savigny, 24
Say, J. B., 31, 47, 185
Schacht, Hjalmar, 164
Schäffle, Albert, 26
Schatz, Albert, 100
Schlesinger, Arthur Jr., 112–113
Schmoller, Gustav, 5, 6, 24, 48
Schoeck, Helmut, 128–129
Schumpeter, Joseph, 81, 115, 119, 132, 138, 248–249, 287, 293, 338
 on the intellectual proletariat, 121–126
scientism, 6
self-image, 138
Sen, Amartya, 138
Shaw, George Bernard, xiv
Shearmur, Jeremy, 17–18
Short View of Russia, A, 166
Silverman, Paul, 35
Skidelsky, Robert, xvii, 98, 120, 154, 157, 162, 166
Skocpol, Theda, 213
Smith, Adam, 33, 34, 50, 99, 112, 132, 240
 social philosophy, 46–47
Smith, David, 82
Smith, Dennis Mack, 270
Social Contract (Rousseau), 26
socialism, 82–83
 as a negative label, 84
socialization of investment, 153
Sombart, Werner, 325

Sonnenfels, Joseph von, 87
Sorokin, Pitirim, 183–184
Soviet Communism: A New Civilization (Webb), xviii, 168–171
Soviet Communism, 134–136, 166–171
Spartan Man, 26
Spencer, Herbert, 9, 69, 72, 89
Spitz, David, 72
spoliation, 188, 194, 249, 278
Stalin, Joseph, xvi, 164–165
state intervention in the economy, 11, 247
　collective economy, 41–43
　credit expansion, 20
　instability of, 21
Stigler, George, 116, 120, 128, 130–133, 136
Streissler, Erich, 15, 21, 29–31, 38
　analysis of Menger's social policy, 46–51
　on Austrian theory and Menger, 32–34
strikes, 265–266
subjective theory of value, xiv, 29
　scientific usefulness of, 36
subjectivism, 7–12
　effects on policy, 9–10
Sulzbach, Walter, 288–289
Sumner, Charles, 334
Szasz, Thomas, 81

taxation, 92
Taylor, Harriet, 78
Taylor, John, 211
Theory and History (Mises), 45
Thierry, Augustin, xiii, xix, 187–189, 193, 205
　and Industrialism, 201–204
　rejection of Industrialism, 207–209
Thiers, Adolphe, 207
Third Estate, 195, 205–209, 255

Tocqueville, Alexis de, xx, 226–228
Tollison, Robert D., 132
Traders and Heroes (Sombart), 325
Traité de l'économie politique (Say), 190
Traité de police (De la Mare), 87
Treatise on Money (Keynes), 172
Treatise on Political Economy (Destutt de Tracy), 189
Trilling, Lionel, 70
Trotsky, Leon, 160
True Grandeur of Nations, The (Sumner), 334
Turner, Henry Ashby, Jr., 140–141

union violence, 265–266
universalized conscription, 241
utility, 37, 132, 191, 193, 196
　see also marginal utility theory

Vaughn, Karen, 20, 151
Verein für Sozialpolitik (Association for Social Policy), 38, 42, 125
Viner, Jacob, 92
Vleugels, Wilhelm, 36–37
voluntary exchange, xv

Wagener, Otto, 163
Walter, Bruno, 327
Warner, Stuart D., 71
Webb, Sidney and Beatrice, 158, 169–172, 175
Weber, Max, xv, 2, 72, 97, 99, 317
Webster, Daniel, 334
Weiss, Franz X., 22, 38
welfare economics, 10–11
welfare state, xv, xxii, 41–43, 74, 124–125, 323–324
　and liberalism, 85–89
　stages of, 87–88
Werner, Karl Ferdinand, 93
Weydemeyer, Joseph, 186
White, Lawrence H., 4, 8

Why the Intellectuals do not Like Liberalism (Boudon), 123
Wicksteed, Philip, xiv
Wieser, Friedrich von, 5, 6, 21, 32, 41
   on socialism, 27–28

Winch, Donald, 157
Winter in Moscow (Muggeridge), 171
Wittfogel, Karl, xxi

Yeager, Leland, 9